Bartholomew's

Touring Atlas and Gazetteer

of the

British Isles

BY

John Bartholomew F.R.G.S.

John Bartholomew & Son, L^{td}

The Geographical Institute, Park Road, Edinburgh.

PUBLISHER'S NOTE

This Bartholomew Touring Atlas and Gazetteer of the British Isles has been recreated from the Practical Motorist's Touring Maps and Gazetteer published by John Bartholomew and Sons Ltd. Edinburgh.

These maps were produced between 1897-1903 from reduced Ordnance Surveys at a scale of 4 miles to 1 inch. The original map series was hand-drawn, hand-lettered and printed from copper-engraved plates at the Bartholomew premises in Park Road, Edinburgh.

Subsequent additions and corrections to the maps were made directly onto the copper plates, consequently some of the pages may carry later additions to the original cartography. The atlas does however, accurately, represent the first ever Bartholomew Motorist's Atlas and shows in detail the roads, railways, canals and settlements as they existed at that time.

The Gazetteer, originally compiled in 1900, lists many of the important settlements and physical features shown on the map pages. This Gazetteer may also contain some later corrections.

In order to make the original documents easier to interpret this edition has been published at a slightly enlarged scale.

The Atlas and Gazetteer is introduced by text extracted from The Highways and Byways of England by T. W. Wilkinson and published by Iliff and Sons Ltd. London and Coventry in 1900. This introduction charts the history and development of our road system and predicts, with uncanny accuracy, the future of both road and rail transport within Britain.

Mike Cottingham.

Published by Collins
An Imprint of HarperCollins*Publishers*
77-85 Fulham Palace Road, Hammersmith, London W6 8JB

Copyright © HarperCollins*Publishers* Ltd 1998
Mapping © Bartholomew Ltd

First published 1897-1903

Printed in Italy

ISBN 0 0044 8835 0   LC9949

INTRODUCTION

Within living memory the King's highway has undergone changes to which it is difficult to find a parallel. First it was thronged with traffic, then deserted, and now it is thronged with traffic again. This expansion and growth, its decline, and its revivification with the advent of cycling, and still more of motoring, have all taken place in a span of about seventy years.

As a result of the return of traffic to the old roads, the faults of these roads are no longer, as they were during the great development of railways in the Victorian era, matters of merely academic or antiquarian interest; they are matters of practical importance, and, as such, are steadily forcing themselves upon public notice. The condition of our roads is already a serious impediment to cheap, rapid, and safe communication. Upon whether they can be remedied, and our roads thereby made suitable for modern methods of transport, may depend the solution to many great problems that confront the nation.

One of those problems may be the retention of our place in the domain of trade. Nearly a century before the opening of railways, when our roads were the principal channels of communication, much of our prosperity and commercial eminence was attributed to the circumstances that our highways, bad though they were judged by the engineering standard, were superior to those of other countries. Adam Smith's contention, that the increasing wealth of England was mainly due to improvements in her roads, was endorsed by other political economists; and about 1840 the French Minister of Commerce eulogised our highways, declaring that it was principally owing to them that England had an advantage over France in the markets of the world. But while we neglected our roads, allowing the existing system to fall into decay and making very few additions to it, both France and Germany displayed great activity in highway construction, and are today intersected by routes which are to our own what the Holyhead Road (in many respects the best of our trunk lines) is to a meandering byway. As long as railways were the controlling agencies in our internal transport this circumstance was practically negligible; but now that motor traffic is rapidly increasing in England and on the Continent it is of great importance, and may have to be taken seriously into account in connection with our competition with our countries.

The history of our highways not only shows how the faults which handicap us originated and have come down to us, but also indicates how the needed improvements may be effected. It tells us that our roads, with their erratic lines and severe gradients, their narrowness and sinuosity, their breakneck hills and dangerous corners, were made so nearly as often from choice as from necessity and that opportunities for improving them were not always taken.

Though our highway system is made up of bits of all the ages, it still curiously reflects, as a whole, the physical state of England in the earliest days of our history. About one-third of the country was then covered with dense wood, thicket, or scrub, and over much of the rest stretched dismal swamps. In general, therefore, animals and carriers travelled over the high lands, and thus, in a large measure, our roads acquired their principal characteristic.

Centuries later, when regular communication had been established between different parts of the country, the same conditions were still factors in road-making. Clearings and drainage had greatly extended the open areas; but numerous forests remained, and there were many tracts of clay impassable for half the year, as well as series of bogs as perilous to travellers as those of Dartmoor are to the incautious tourist of our own times.

Owing to the danger of becoming engulfed in clay or of sinking into a bog, carriers, like the early road-makers, kept to the high lands. Their packhorse trains wore tracks over the hill ranges, and these became recognised trade routes, and were ultimately, in many cases, turned into roads. The conversion began towards the end of the seventeenth century, when carts and wagons had come into general use. As ways suitable for wheeled traffic were then called for, and as the contemporary road-makers could not throw such ways over soft ground, or, at all events, could not make a hard way except on a naturally good and stable foundation, such as rock or stone, the packhorse lines were followed in all their climbing and twisting and abrupt turnings.

Instances of this are many. The Wells-Shepton Mallet road, the Whitby-Ruswarp road, and scores of the emphatic highways linking Lancashire and Yorkshire are unquestionably on packhorse routes, running as they do over steep hills instead of through valleys along the line of least resistance. But it is enough to note that the unscientific race of road-makers never crossed low-lying ground if they could possibly avoid it, and that in consequence they intensified the circuitous and hilly nature of our highways in general.

The turnpike system, introduced as a solution of the 'road problem' as it existed in Stuart times, and peculiar to this country, no other having ever adopted it, was the next factor in moulding our roads, to which it gave many of the bad qualities they now possess. To it we owe many of the extremely erratic lines that vex the engineer and cause so vast a waste of energy. These were brought about in many ways. A prolific cause of the resultant expense and loss of time to generations of travellers was squabbling between two highway authorities. One opposed a turnpike Bill promoted by the other, and in consequence a scheme was held up for years or abandoned altogether. The effect can be seen to this day even in connection with so important a highway as the Great North Road, the remarkable line of which is, in some parts of its course, due to fights over obtaining power to turnpike.

Besides hampering communication in this manner, the trusts added largely to the number of hilly roads. As one of the necessary results of making a highway was a material increase in the value of the adjoining lands, the line was frequently taken precisely where it would best suit the pockets of the promoters, sometimes over hills that might easily have been avoided. It is for this reason that certain of the roads extending from Manchester into Cheshire, Derbyshire, and Staffordshire across the summits of hills. A number of similar highways, in the construction of which public requirements were subordinated to private interests, have now practically disappeared; for so little did they return in tolls that they brought nothing but sorrow to their bondholders, and, being neglected in consequence, are represented at the present time by a few parallel ruts. The construction of some of such roads, however, was beneficial to the districts through which they pass, because otherwise those districts would have lacked roads practicable for wheeled vehicles, and of great service, therefore, to agriculturists, till many years later.

In numerous cases, again, turnpike trusts made their roads so narrow that on them two coaches could not run abreast. They considered that it was enough to provide semi-circular refuges, into which a coach could draw and wait while another, travelling in the opposite direction, passed it. Some of these makeshifts are still in existence, and curiously exemplify the haphazard and un-systematic manner in which our highway system was formed.

There was, in truth, insufficient Parliamentary supervision over turnpike trusts, which, bound and restricted though they were in many particulars, were allowed far too much liberty in the making of roads. Had they been placed under the control of a central authority, investors would have been spared some bitter pangs, and our highway system would have been extended with more regard to national requirements and less to purely local needs.

Public attention was first sharply focused on the many faults and shortcomings in the products of the early road-makers and of the turnpike trusts by the Rebellion of 1745. General Wade's failure to relieve Carlisle owing to the vileness of the highway between that city and his headquarters at Newcastle, and the ease with which the Highlanders, unencumbered by baggage or wagon, outstripped the royal army, and left the cavalry and artillery far in the rear, compelled Parliament to direct its attention to the highways in the northern part of the kingdom, with the result that it passed an Act for the formation of a road for wheeled traffic between Newcastle and Carlisle, which were then connected by nothing but a bridle-way. This was carried into effect in 1756, General Wade employing his army on the undertaking. The line of the Roman Wall was followed for thirty miles, and a long stretch of that structure was pulled down to furnish materials for the work, which has ever since been known as the 'Military Road'. Subsequently other highways were made for military and civil purposes, and the impulse thus given to the construction of roads resulted in a vast improvement in communication, particularly in Cumberland.

A new era then dawned, an era of road-making and mending. Side by side with the construction of new highways was carried on the improvement of the principal old roads, all of which were modernised to a greater or lesser degree. Every trunk road in the kingdom was added to in some parts and taken from in others, straightened out, and generally made less trying to horse and man alike. Long hollows were filled up by embankments; hills were cut through, crossed at a lower level, or altogether removed; widenings were effected to facilitate the flow of traffic; and loops and dangerous corners were cut off.

While, however, our highway system was revolutionised by the numerous works carried out in this coaching age, it could not be freed from all of its old faults. Ineffaceable were the marks of the packhorse and of the early road-maker. The accumulated defects of centuries could not be remedied without a combined effort and an outlay impossible to the trusts, which, besides being heavily in debt, were neither responsible for nor specially interested in roads other than those under their own management. Nothing short of State action would have sufficed to accomplish so stupendous a task.

The principal faults of our highways are, therefore, relics of far-off days, and they have patently descended to us, through many generations, mainly because of insufficient public care for internal communication. For this neglect the blame must be laid at the door of the State, which, since the departure of the Romans, has not taken upon itself the provision of roads for general use. Parliament has probably devoted more care and time to the subject of highways than to any other. It has debated every phase of it at great length, called in to its aid eminent engineers and other experts, held costly inquiries, and by legislative enactments dealt with the most minute details respecting traffic, down to the shape of the heads of nails for affixing the tyres to wheels and the precise form of axles to be used in given circumstances. But the making of roads it has nearly always left to philanthropic effort and municipal and private enterprise; and, as a natural corollary, system and co-ordination have been conspicuously lacking, and no large, well-conceived scheme of road construction has ever been carried out.

It is probable that, had not traffic temporarily left the roads, England would have followed the example of France, which solved her 'road problem' by constituting a Minister of Roads and Bridges, in whose hands was placed the supervision of her highway system. Under his directions the roads were divided into several classes, the most important of which are *Routes Nationales* (constructed and maintained by the various departments at the expense of the Government). By this means the whole of the French highway system was re-made and brought up to its present high standard. The scheme, on its inauguration, attracted much notice in this country, and many times it was proposed that we should adopt it or a modification of it. Weary of the turnpike system, which had always been costly and irksome, and was then plainly moribund, as well as disgusted with the chicanery and negligence in connection with parochial highways, reformers saw in the bold measures taken in France a means of disposing once for all of controversies and nuisances which had lasted for centuries. But railways were monopolising the attention of the public at large, and partly for this reason, and partly because the general opinion was that there would be little further use for roads, the Legislature continued on its old course.

By 1840 the traffic which had ebbed and flowed for centuries ceased, apparently for ever, on some main roads, and soon afterwards there were many miles of highway deserted save for idle toll-collectors, whose time was profitlessly spent in mourning the life which had surged past them and in cursing the railways. The Brighton Road did not retain its old-time glories much later than September, 1840, when the railway was opened. In 1846 coaches stopped running on the Norwich Road, the last mail through Bury St. Edmunds covering the familiar ground on January 6th of that year. Four months later ended the Southampton and Oxford service. In the same year, too, railways extended along the whole course of the Great North Road. With the opening of the Edinburgh and Berwick Railway the last stretch of the ancient way to the north was superseded, and coaches disappeared from every part of it. Before 1845, in fact, coaching was patently moribund all over the country, though it survived here and there for years afterwards, nowhere, perhaps, more strangely than at Manchester, the last four-horse coach out of that city, the "Derby Dilly," not finishing its course before October, 1858.

One of the earliest results of the growth of the railways was the abandonment of any highway improvements. A few years before railways were initiated there had been contemplated some road works which, had they been completed, would have been the most important carried out in this country since the Roman era, including as they did nothing less than a road to replace, or, at least, supplement, the ancient way to Scotland. The course of this undertaking, of which Telford was appointed engineer, was to be as straight as possible. About 1824 the section from Edinburgh to Morpeth was actually completed, and some years later the other and larger portion was begun; but the coming of the railways stopped further work for many years to come. All that was finished of the proposed new Great North Road was the highway from Morpeth to Wooler, Coldstream, and Edinburgh. This road, though hilly, is much shorter and better than that by the coast, and indicates that the planned road has been a great improvement.

Other schemes of a similar nature were also abandoned. Relics of one of these ill-starred enterprises remain for years at Ferrybridge, near Doncaster. When the coaching age was rapidly nearing its end, some speculators proposed to cut off a part of the Great North Road, and substitute for it a straight and level road across the valley. The work was started, and pushed forward rapidly, the promoters calculating on a satisfactory return from the tolls for which Parliamentary powers had been obtained. When, however, the enterprise was nearing completion, traffic deserted the North Road for the railway, and consequently it was left unfinished. For years a lofty embankment was the most prominent feature of the derelict work, in connection with which a large sum was lost.

On wayside inns also the diversion of traffic was disastrous, practically all their trade going away at once. Even large houses gladly welcomed customers whom they had aforetime openly despised. These were foot travellers, the scorned of all the coaching inns in pre-railway days.

Little imagination is needed to visualise the King's highway itself undergoing, in these circumstances, rapid decay and becoming again cut up into longitudinal strips by infantile ruts; but the actual degeneration was far greater than the conditions warrant us in picturing. As early as 1846, the year when the Norfolk Railway was opened, roads in that county were stated to be "half-a-yard deep in mud" and almost impassable. "Heavy goods in large quantities," it is said, were "sent from Norwich to London and from thence to Ipswich by rail, 196 miles, instead of [by] the direct route of 40 miles by road, the rail conveyance being cheaper and quicker." If the deterioration was not so rapid in other parts of the country, it was, at all events, marked and continuous. In many places the old coaching highways became like sheep tracks; and before 1870 parts of even the Great North Road were covered with grass. The public apathy was such, too, that once more greedy landowners were allowed to practise that filching which Harrison had denounced in the reign of Elizabeth, and to add to their estates by annexing the grassy strips which the trusts had used as summer roads, and which they had had to purchase from those same landowners at grossly extortionate rates. There was, moreover, a recrudescence of road diverting, the effect of which was to make our highway system still more tortuous.

A great change for the worse, in fact, took place in the condition of the King's highway. As turnpike trusts expired the roads again became wholly under the jurisdiction of parishes, which had always been responsible for them, and also partly liable, except for a short period, for their maintenance. "The obligation to maintain all public roads, with the exception of those which are to be repaired *ratione tenurÉ* or *clausurÉ*, is," a royal commission reported in 1840, "a public obligation and in the nature of a public tax." It then proceeded to point out that "when a highway has been converted into a turnpike road and placed under the management of trustees, with power to collect tolls to be applied to the repairs, if the way be out of repair, the parish (or township, as the case may be) are the only parties who are liable to be indicted, and must seek their remedies against the trustees, which they have, after conviction, by motion for relief against the trustees under the Turnpike Act 3 George IV., c. 126, sec. 10." During most of the time that the turnpike system was in operation, moreover, trustees were empowered to, and frequently did, call upon parishes to assist in the maintenance of their roads either by statute labour or by a payment in lieu. The only alteration brought about by the abolition of the turnpike system, therefore, was that parishes had to repair all their roads without any help from tolls. For this reason the position of those bodies after the discontinuance of trusts was not very different from what it had been before. Since, however, parishes had for so many years been relieved of part, at least, of the cost of their highways, they sustained by the abolition of turnpikes a shock which paralysed them, and, there being nobody sufficiently interested in road communication to galvanise them into activity the old lines of traffic suffered greatly.

While roads in rural districts were rapidly deteriorating, those in towns and their environs steadily improved. A reform which gave rise to much bitterness was the sweeping away of obstructions. London rid itself of many relics, including Temple Bar, for centuries its western gate. Pulled down in 1879, the fabric lay dismembered for some time, and then the stones were given to Sir H.B. Meux, who re-erected them at the principal entrance to Theobald's Park, near Cheshunt, Herts. The removal of so famous a landmark had some influence in sealing the fate of impediments to traffic in other parts of the country, though it was not a precedent recognised when the Bar, at Southampton, was threatened with demolition or when iconoclasts wished to remove Hotspur's Gate, Alnwick. In some towns, most of them in manufacturing districts where the growth of industries and the consequent increase of traffic had brought on numbers of old structures the scorn of the utilitarian, a middle course was taken, and relics which obstructed the way were transplanted on fresh sites belonging to the public. A sweeping removal of this kind took place at Bingley, in the West Riding, where a market, a cross, and a set of stocks were transferred to the public park, and the main street, which had been nearly blocked, was cleared from side to side. This kind of improvement, however, was not confined to the industrial parts of England, several villages clearing the way in the comparatively simple method adopted by Nether Stowey, near Bridgwater.

Here a clock tower and a lock-up which stood in the middle of the road were moved to the side, and are now as much out of the way as is the local gazebo, a summerhouse from which many a party witnessed the passing of the Minehead coach.

About 1870 the King's highway reached its low-water mark. For twenty years scarcely a new road had then been made except in urban districts, and the repairs to the old highways, even those which formed arteries of communication, had been of the most contemptible character. Roads in general were in consequence in a worse condition than they had been for a generation. In summer multitudinous weeds luxuriated in their depths, and in winter they bore a thick coat of rutty mud, through which the pedestrian struggled with difficulty and the horseman at no little risk. Our whole highway system, outside of towns, was well-nigh derelict, and a traveller might have journeyed over it for many leagues without encountering any traffic other than local.

Then begun that remarkable revival which still continues and gathers force yearly. It was with the advent of the cycle that the renaissance set in. The "ordinary" had a vogue, and before its novelty had time to pall the tricycle was introduced and taken up with enthusiasm by the middle-aged. Next came the "safety," with the aid of which the open road may be said to have been "discovered" by the present generation. Just as cycling began to wane the automobile was brought forward, or, rather, brought forward again, and, though for a time its progress was checked by reactionary legislation similar to that which had killed self-propelled traffic in the early part of the century, its course was ultimately cleared by the "Emancipation"

Act of 1896, which relieved the driver of such a vehicle from the necessity of being proceeded by a man bearing a red flag, such as it had been obligatory to carry in front of a traction engine. Finally, from the automobile for personal conveyance sprang motor vans for the delivery of goods, merchandise, etc.

As a result of this unparalleled series of improvements in transport, there has been a remarkable drift back to the open road. If the adventurous youths who bestrode the high wheel did not make much impression on the countryside, the tricyclists, and still more the riders of the "safety," roused the King's highway from its somnolence and brought a measure of prosperity to wayside inns. Greater far are the results which the automobile has since achieved; for it has not only resuscitated the whole of our highway system, but strangled the railway monopoly, which can never again dominate the country as it did less than twenty years ago.

In the service of the Royal Mail alone the automobile is now doing work of great interest and value. The Post Office, with which the history of road communication is very closely connected, never wholly deserted the King's highway, but clung to it, and retained much of the nomenclature of stage-coach days. When the parcels post was introduced, and the railway companies claimed about one-half of the postage paid on the parcels, it strengthened its old ties by introducing a service of road vans, which are now being displaced by big and fast motor vans, with "guards," as of old, only the present race carry a truncheon and whistle, instead of loaded firearms. The Post Office, by thus acting in accordance with its traditions, has materially helped in the return to the road.

It cannot be said that the improvements in highways have kept pace with those in transport; but our roads are certainly better now than they ever were. Twenty years' steady effort has not been wasted; it has borne some fruit, though not so much as was expected. The general improvement was started by cyclists, who, while everywhere preventing the King's highway from deteriorating further, actually stimulated some local authorities to bring their share of it into passable condition. Besides taking individual action to this end, they moved through their organisation, the Cyclists' Touring Club, which was formed in 1878, when touring awheel became popular. The club became known to the general public by the danger-boards which it placed on hills. It had been preceded in this useful work by the Bicycle Union (now the National Cyclists' Union), which set up a number of similar warnings, the first on the top of Muswell Hill, in the north of London. The "C.T.C." boards, indeed, probably attracted attention more by their number than by their novelty, though they were the first seen in many parts of the country. However this may be, the club missed no opportunity of stirring up highway authorities, and doubtless paved the way for many reforms. It was most successful in its efforts after the establishment of county councils. Before those bodies were formed the number of highway authorities was so great, and the views they took of their responsibilities were so divergent, that it was impossible to rouse them to effective action. When, however, main roads came under the control of county councils, some of the absurdities of highway administration were abolished, and real progress was made. That progress, thanks to the persistent agitation carried on by automobilists, has continued, and the institution of the Road Board marks an important stage in it. Already the dreams of old cyclists have thereby been realised, and that still greater improvements will be carried out in the near future, some of them of incalculable value to the country, cannot for a moment be doubted.

A pleasing vista thus opens out - a vista of a transformed countryside, of the decline of railways, of their relegation to very fast and very heavy traffic, of the road as the dominating feature in internal communication and as the greatest factor in the affairs of the nation.

It has been said that the coming question is, "first, roads; second, roads; and third and last, roads"; and it cannot be doubted that time will speedily justify the proposition.

T.W. WILKINSON. 1899

MAP 1

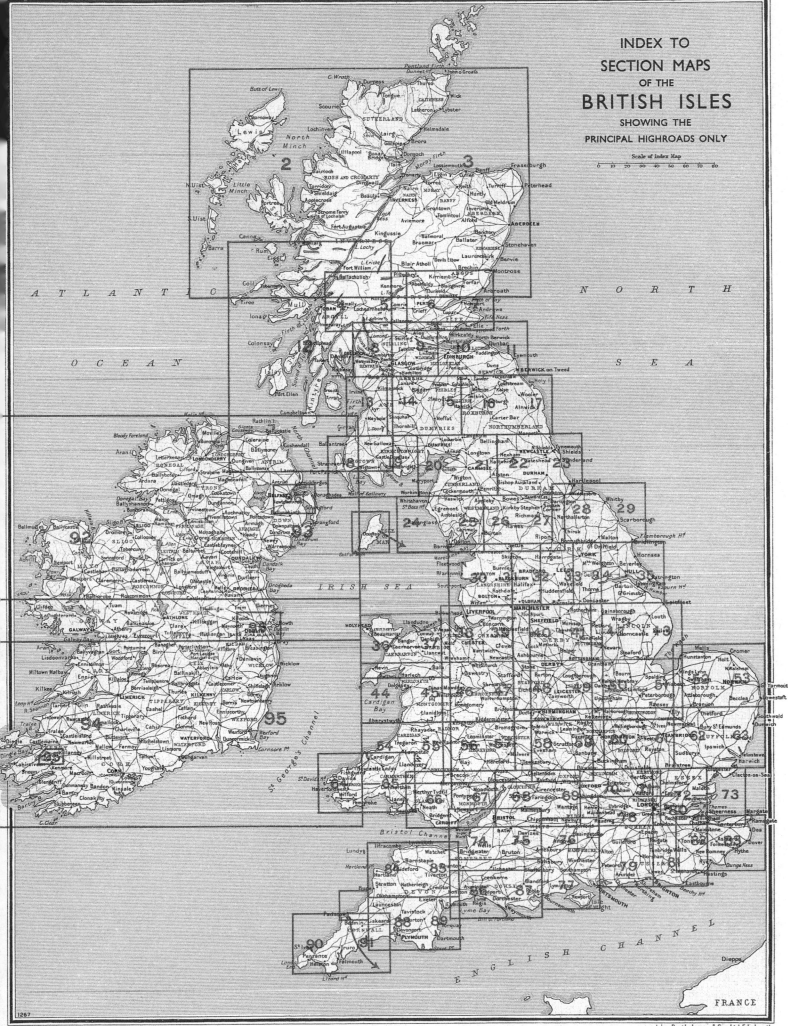

INDEX TO
SECTION MAPS
OF THE
BRITISH ISLES
SHOWING THE
PRINCIPAL HIGHROADS ONLY

Scale of Index Map

John Bartholomew & Son.Ltd.Edinburgh

MAP 2

Continued on

Main Roads ――20――   Other Roads ―――――   Railways ―――――
Red Figures indicate distances between places with Black Dots

MAP 3

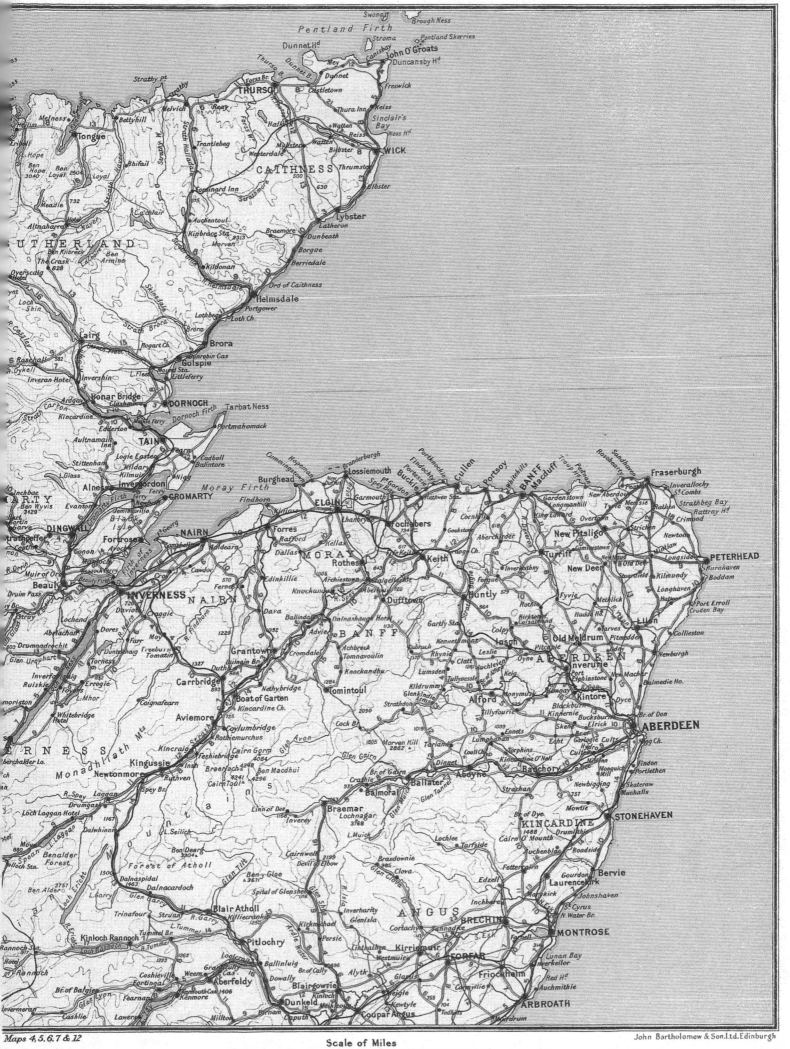

Scale of Miles

0 4 8 12 16 20 24 28 32 36 40

John Bartholomew & Son.Ltd.Edinburgh

MAP 4

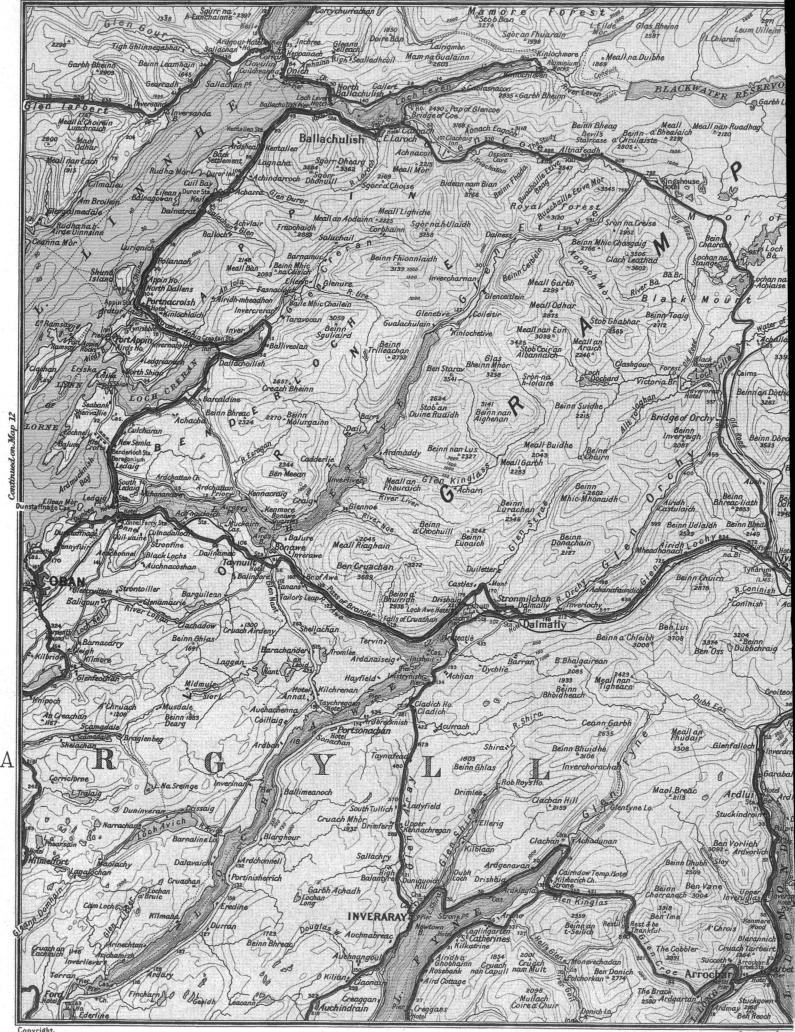

Scale of Miles

0 1 2 3 4 5 6 7 8 9 10

MAP 5

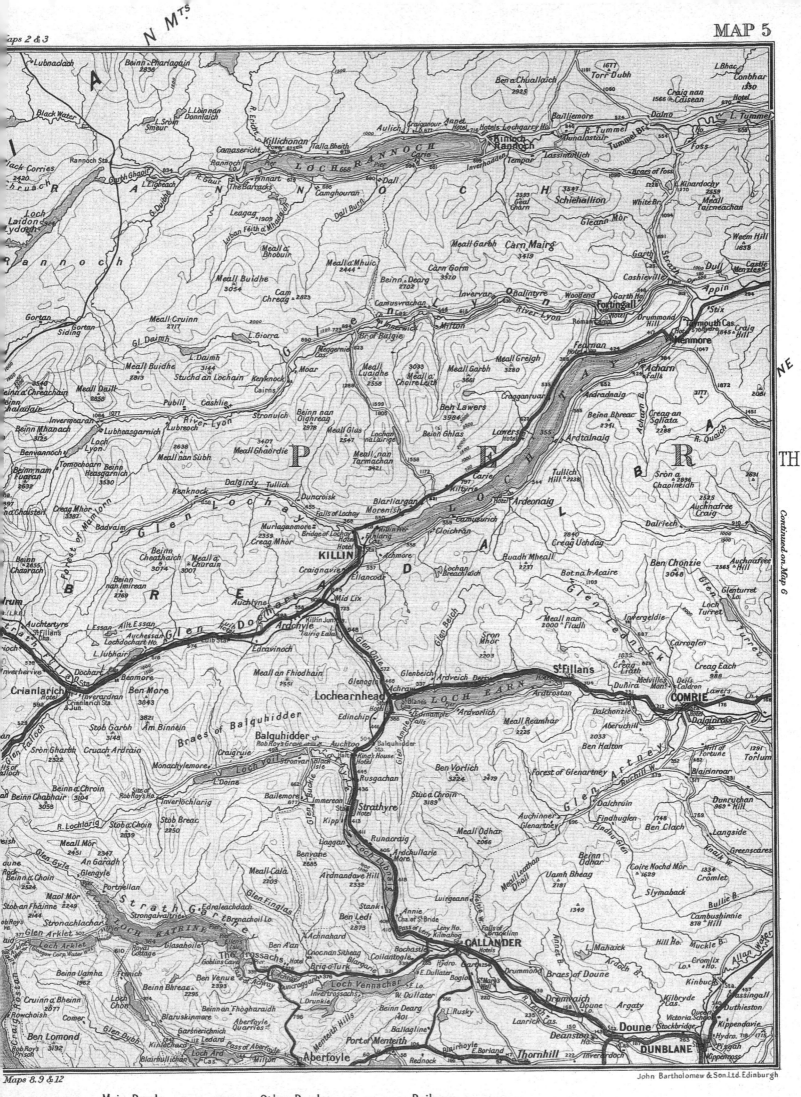

Continued on Map 6

John Bartholomew & Son Ltd. Edinburgh

Main Roads ———   Other Roads ═══   Railways ┅┅┅

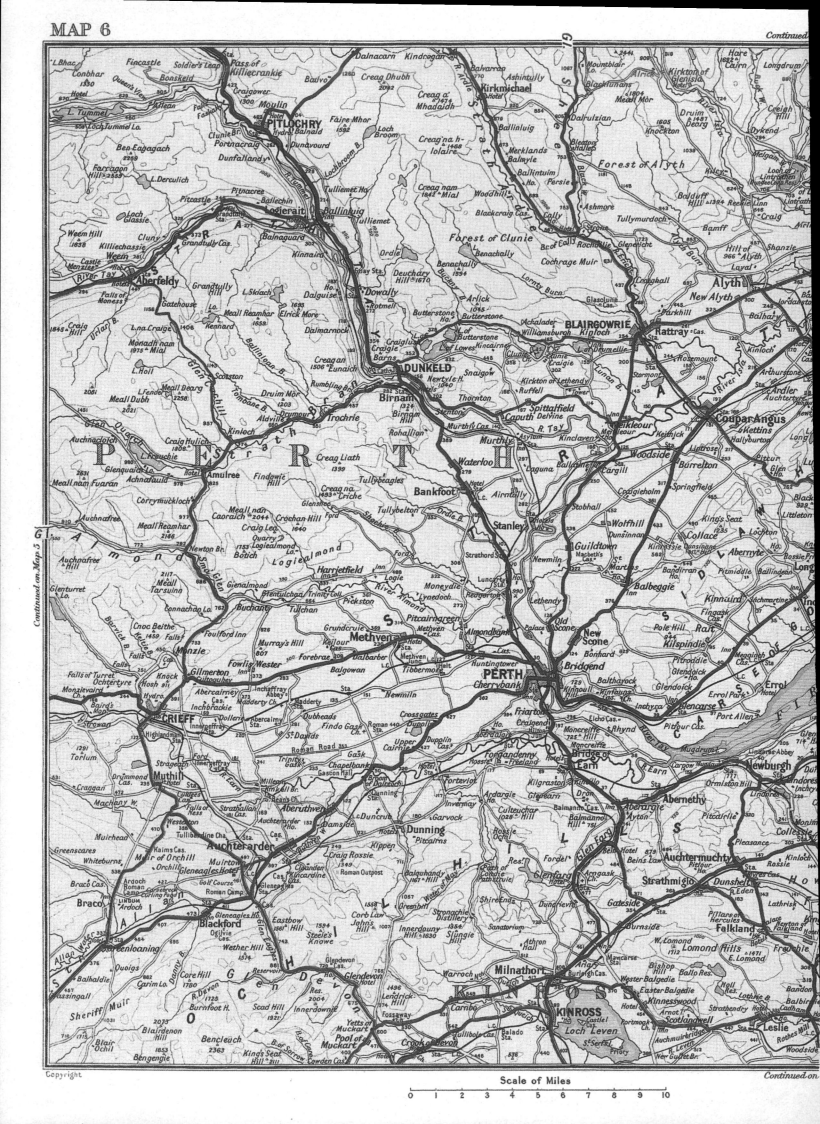

MAP 6

Scale of Miles

0 1 2 3 4 5 6 7 8 9 10

Copyright

MAP 7

Maps 2 & 3

R. North Esk

Cat Law 2196

ANGUS

BRECHIN

MONTROSE
Montrose Basin
Scurdy Ness
Ferryden

Kirriemuir

Southmuir

FORFAR

Inverkeilor
Lunan Bay
Red Head

Glamis

Letham

ARBROATH
Whiting Ness
Carlingheugh Bay

Newtyle

CARNOUSTIE
Buddon Links

Barry

Monifieth
Broughty Ferry
Buddon Ness

DUNDEE

Tayport
Newport
Wormit
Balmerino

FIRTH OF TAY

Tents Moor

Bell Rock Lighthouse

Leuchars

St Andrews Bay

CUPAR

ST ANDREWS
Kinkell Ness

Kingsbarns

Ceres

Crail
Fife Ness
Kilminning

Springfield
Ladybank

Anstruther
Pittenweem
St Monans

LEVEN
Methil
Largo Bay
Elie
Chapel Ness

Isle of May
South Ness

FIFE

Maps 9, 10 & 11

John Bartholomew & Son Ltd. Edinburgh

Main Roads ————   Other Roads ═══════   Railways ————

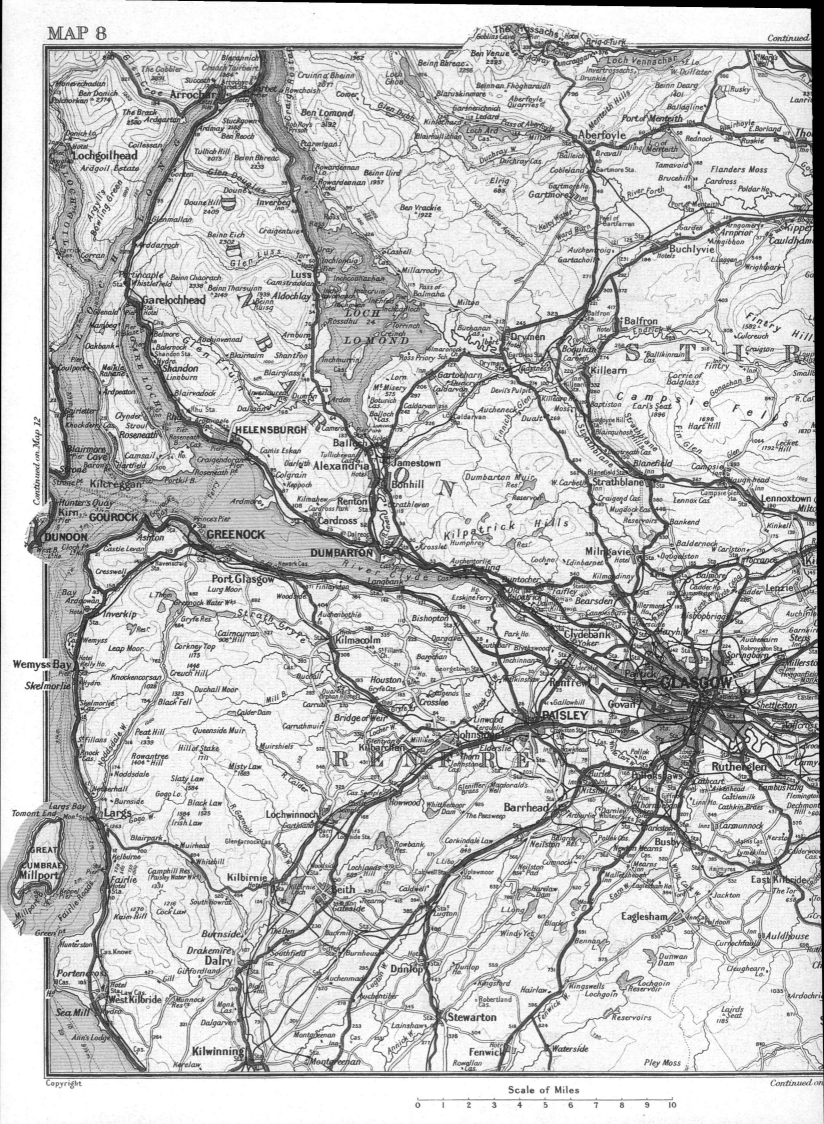

MAP 8

Continued

Continued on

Scale of Miles

0 1 2 3 4 5 6 7 8 9 10

MAP 9

Maps 4, 5 & 6

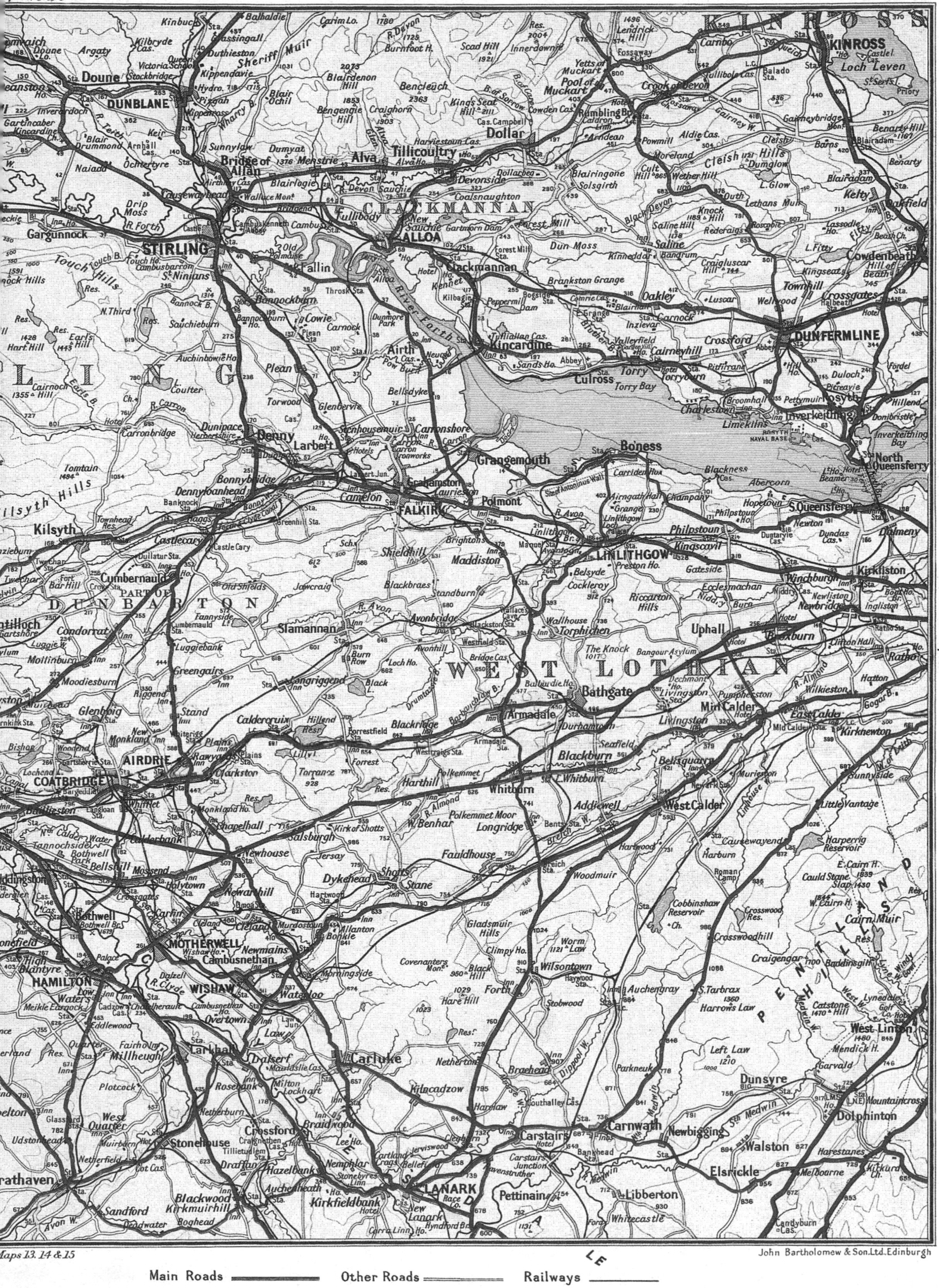

Continued on Map 10

Maps 13, 14 & 15

KINROSS
KINROSS
Loch Leven
St. Serf's I.
Priory

Lendrick Hill
Fossaway
Carnbo
Crook of Devon
Pool of Muckart
Yetts of Muckart
Cowden Cas.
Rumbling Br.
Powmill
Moreland
Aldie Cas.
Cleish Hills
Dumglow
Blairadam
Benarty
Kelty
Cowdenbeath
Hill of Beath
Crossgates
Townhill
Dunfermline
Crossford
Cairneyhill
Torryburn
Torry
Culross
Charlestown
Limekilns
Inverkeithing
North Queensferry
Rosyth Naval Base
S. Queensferry
Dalmeny
Kirkliston
Winchburgh
Newbridge
Ratho
Uphall
Broxburn
Linlithgow
Philpstoun
Kingscavil
Bo'ness
Blackness
Abercorn
Hopetoun
Queensferry

Doune
Dunblane
Sheriff Muir
Dollar
Tillicoultry
Alva
Bridge of Allan
Menstrie
Blairlogie
Stirling
St. Ninians
Bannockburn
Sauchieburn
Cowie
Plean
Airth
Kincardine
Alloa
Clackmannan
Sauchie
Fishcross
Saline
Oakley
Carnock
Valleyfield

CLACKMANNAN
River Forth

Gargunnock
Torwood
Larbert
Denny
Dunipace
Bonnybridge
Dennyloanhead
Camelon
Falkirk
Grahamston
Laurieston
Polmont
Grangemouth

Kilsyth
Castlecary
Cumbernauld
Condorrat
Kilsyth Hills

DUNBARTON

Slamannan
Avonbridge
Standburn
Maddiston
Shieldhill
Blackbraes
Brightons

WEST LOTHIAN

Bathgate
Armadale
Blackridge
Forrestfield
Whitburn
Blackburn
Seafield
Livingston
Mid Calder
East Calder
Kirknewton
West Calder
Addiewell
Pumpherston

Bangour Asylum
The Knock
Torphichen
Wallhouse
Riccarton Hills
Ecclesmachan
Dechmont
Livingstone

Airdrie
Coatbridge
Glenboig
Moodiesburn
Gartsherrie
Plains
Clarkston
Chapelhall
Calderbank
Holytown
Newhouse
Salsburgh
Harthill
Polkemmet
Longridge
Fauldhouse
Shotts
Kirk of Shotts
Stane
Dykehead
Hartwood
Woodmuir

Bellshill
Mossend
Uddingston
Bothwell
Bellshill
Motherwell
Wishaw
Newmains
Cambusnethan
Overtown
Hamilton
Larkhall
Stonehouse
Strathaven
Blackwood
Kirkmuirhill
Sandford

Carluke
Crossford
Braidwood
Kilncadzow
Carstairs
Carstairs Junction
Lanark
New Lanark
Kirkfieldbank
Pettinain
Libberton
Carnwath
Newbigging
Walston
Elsrickle
Dunsyre
West Linton
Dolphinton
Mountaincross
Melbourne
Candyburn

PENTLAND HILLS
Cairn Muir
Cobbinshaw Reservoir
Crosswood Res.
Harperrig Reservoir
Harburn
Causewayend
Little Vantage
Sunnyside

Covenanters Mon.
Black Hill
Climpy Ho.
Wilsontown
Haywood
Auchengray
Tarbrax
Harrows Law
Catstone Hill

Main Roads ————— Other Roads ========= Railways ———————

John Bartholomew & Son.Ltd.Edinburgh

MAP 10

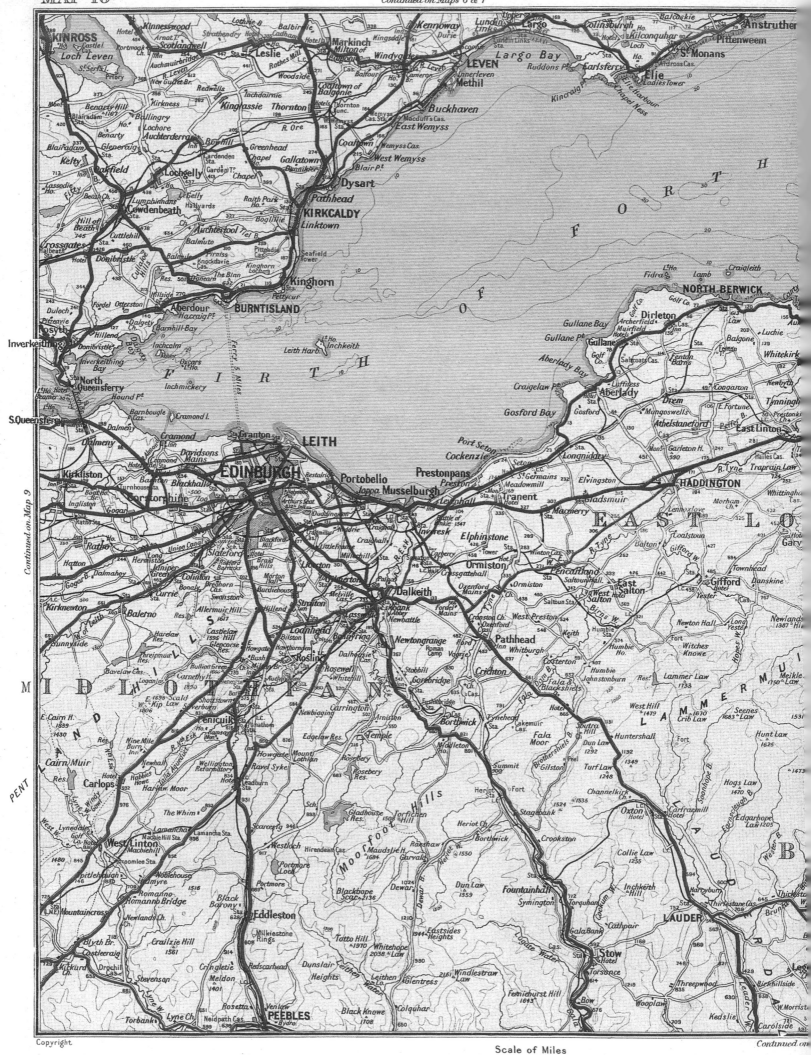

Continued on Map 9

Copyright

Scale of Miles

0 1 2 3 4 5 6 7 8 9 10

MAP 11

John Bartholomew & Son.Ltd.Edinburgh

Main Roads ———— Other Roads ═══════ Railways ————

MAP 12

Continued on Maps 2 & 3

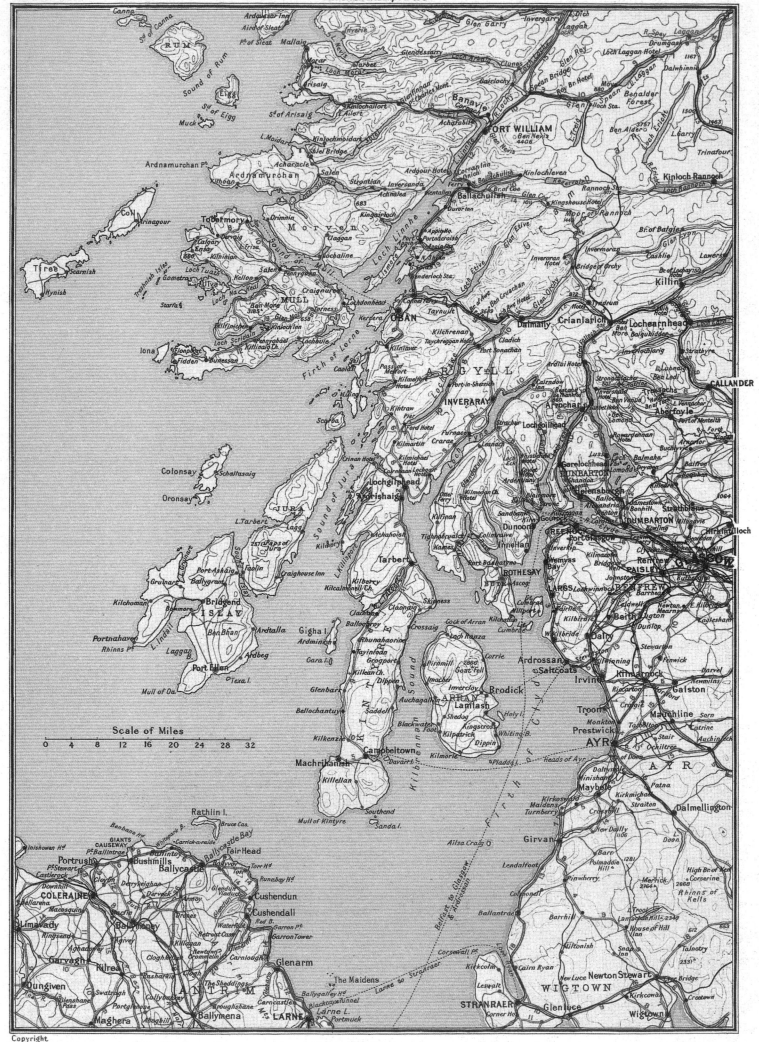

CALLANDER

Scale of Miles

0   4   8   12   16   20   24   28   32

Copyright

Main Roads ___20___   Other Roads _____   Railways _____

Red Figures indicate distances between places with Black Dots

MAP 13
Continued on Map 8
Continued on Map 14

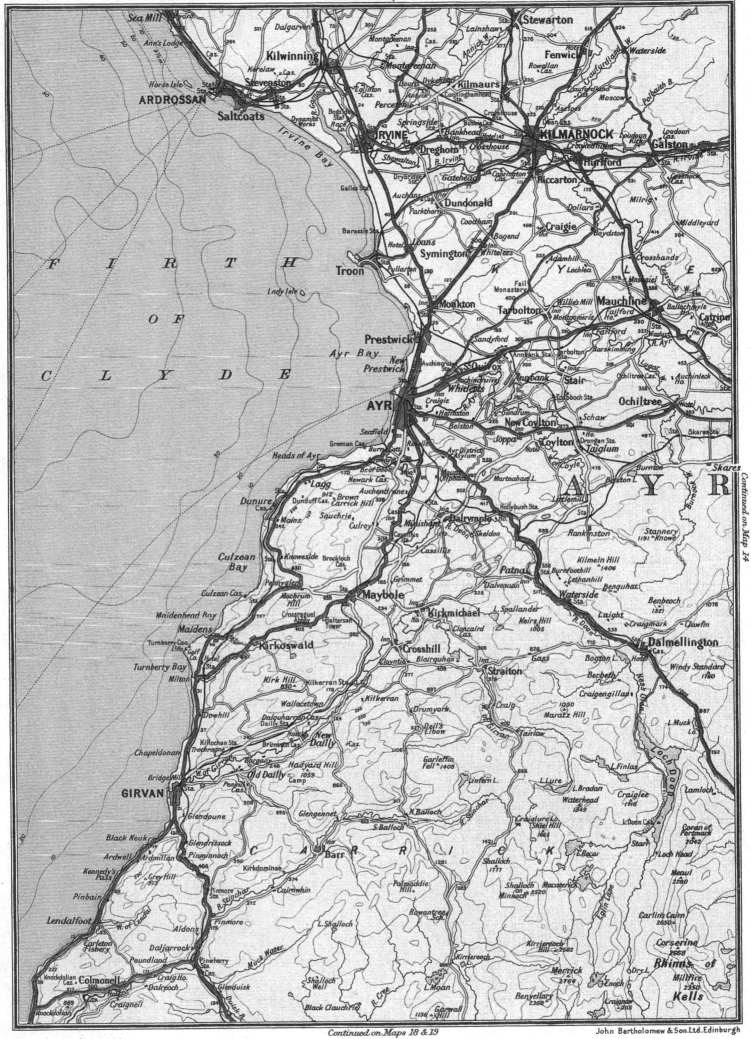

John Bartholomew & Son.Ltd.Edinburgh

Scale of Miles
0 1 2 3 4 5 6

Main Roads ——— Other Roads === Railways

MAP 14

Continued

LANARK

AYR

Strathaven · Lanark · Pettinain · Carmichael · Lesmahagow · Blackwood · Kirkmuirhill · Kirkfieldbank · New Lanark · Sandford · Boghead · Coalburn · Douglas · Douglas Cas. · Douglas Mill · Robert Law · Roberton · Crawfordjohn · Abington · Crawford

Galston · Newmilns Sta. · Darvel · Priestland · Loudoun · Moscow · Waterside · Mauchline · Catrine · Sorn · Muirkirk · Glenbuck · Parishholm · Cairn Table · Lit. Cairn Table

Ochiltree · Auchinleck · Cumnock · Cronberry · Lugar · Airds Moss · Darnconner · Leadhills · Wanlockhead · Crawick mill · Sanquhar

Pathhead · New Cumnock · Connel park · Bankglen · Dalleagles · Kirkconnel · Mennock · Eliock · Durisdeer · Enterkinfoot · Carronbridge · Thornhill

Dalmellington · Carsphairn · Cairnsmore of Carsphairn 2612 · Moniaive · Tynron · Penpont · Closeburn

Rhinns of Kells · Corserine 2668 · Loch Doon

Continued on Map 13

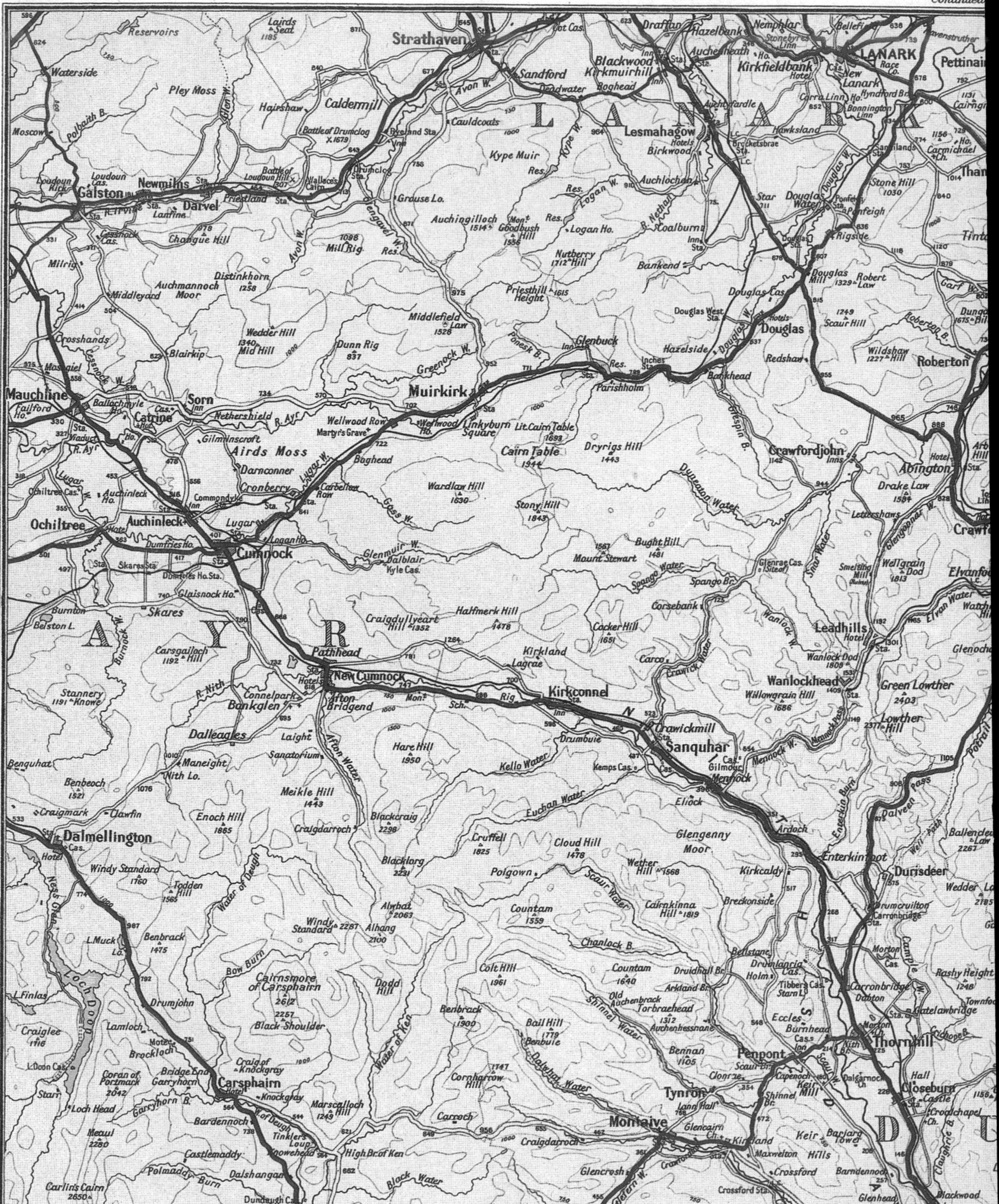

Scale of Miles
0 1 2 3 4 5 6 7 8 9 10

Copyright.

Continued on

MAP 15

Maps 8, 9 & 10

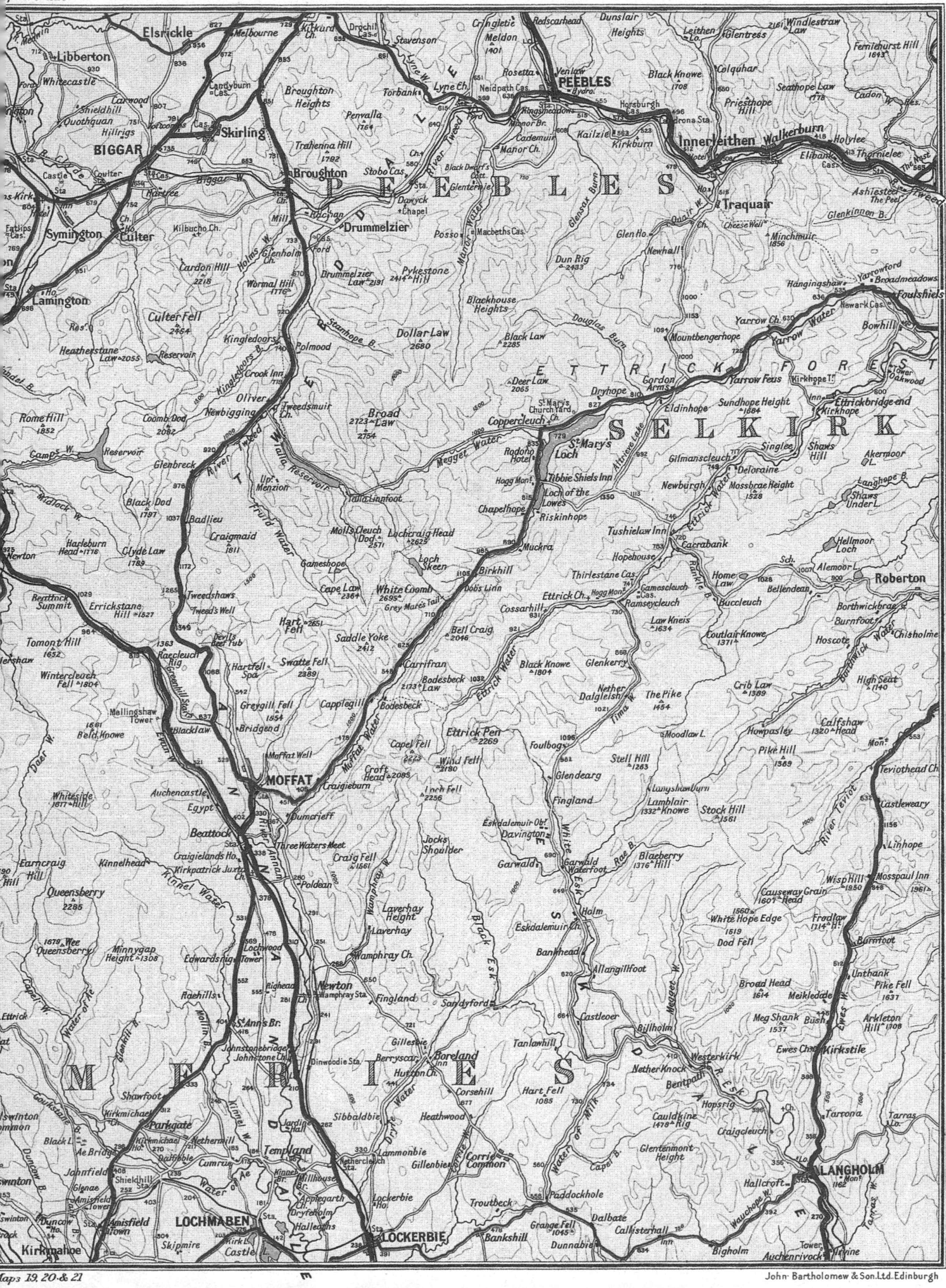

Continued on Map 16

Maps 19, 20 & 21

PEEBLES

SELKIRK

ETTRICK FOREST

Main Roads ——— **Other Roads** ——— **Railways** ———

John Bartholomew & Son Ltd. Edinburgh

MAP 16

Continued on Map 15

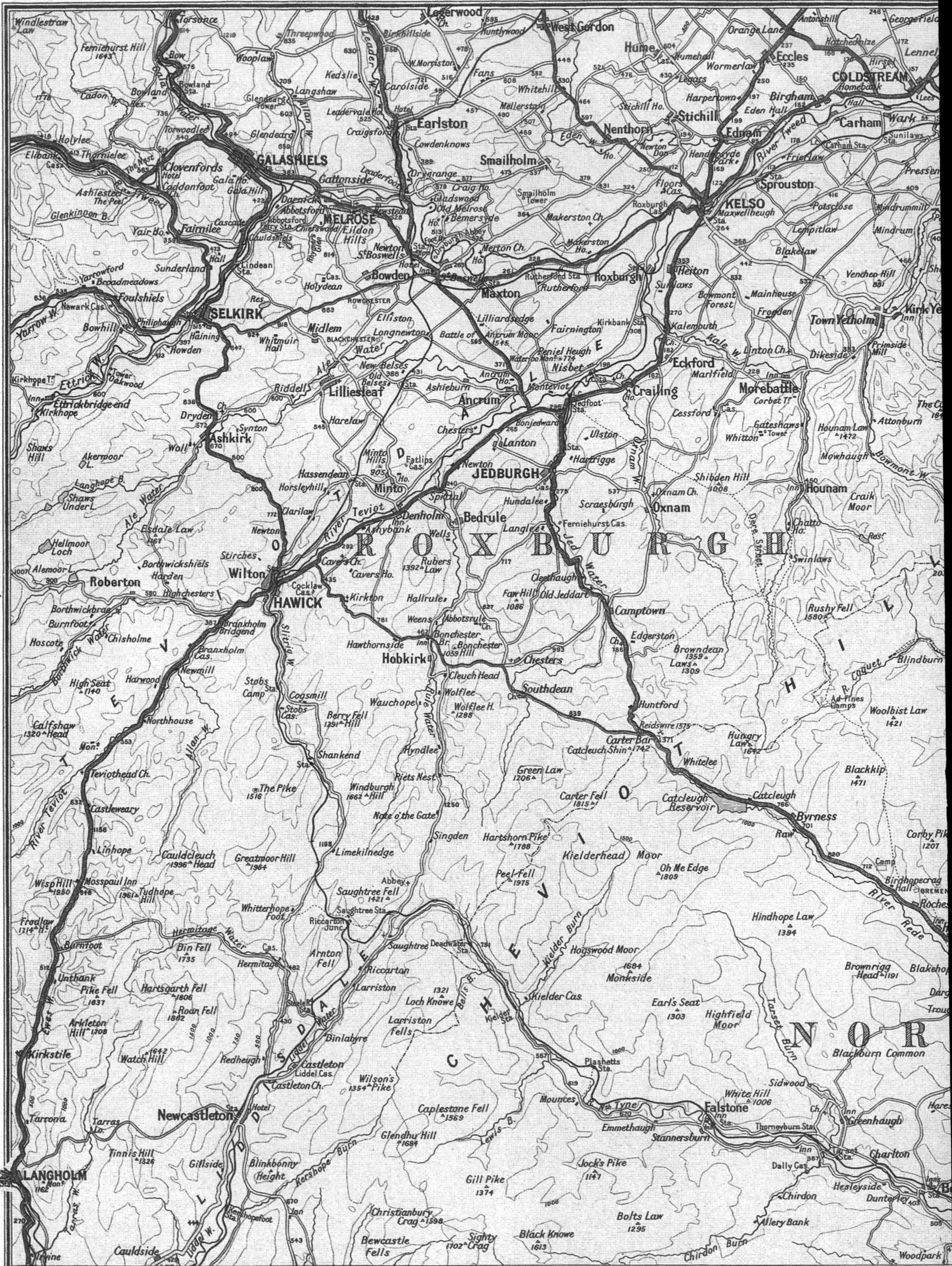

Windlestraw Law
Femiehirst Hill 1643
Torsonce
Threepwood 835
Legerwood Ch.
Huntlywood
West Gordon
Orange Lane
Antonshill
George Field
Bow
Wooplaw
Bickhillside
Hume
Humehall
Wormerlaw
Eccles
Hirsel
Lennel
COLDSTREAM
Bowland Sta.
W. Morriston
Cas.
Legars
Harpertown
Birgham
Homebank
Cadon
709
Kedslie
Carolside
Fans
Whitehill
Mellerstain
Nenthorn
Stichill Ho.
Eden Hall
Hall
Carham
Wark
Glendearg Tower
Leadervale Ho.
Hotel
Craigsford
Earlston
Cowdenknows
Smailholm
Newton Don
Floors Cas.
Stichill
Ednam
River Tweed
Carham Sta.
GALASHIELS
Gattonside
Dr.grange
Craig Ho.
Gladswood
Smailholm Tower
Roxburgh Cas.
KELSO
Maxwellheugh
Sprouston
Clovenfords
Gala Ho.
Caddonfoot
Darnick
Old Melrose
Bemersyde
Makerston Ch.
Heiton
Potsclose
Mindrummill
Ashlestiel
The Peel
MELROSE
Abbotsford
Chiefswood
Eildon Hills
Newstead
Merton Ch.
Makerston Ho.
Roxburgh
Sunlaws
Blakelaw
Venchen Hill
Fairnilee
Cauldshields
Newton
St. Boswells
Dryburgh Abbey
Rutherford Sta.
Bowmont Forest
Mainhouse
Sunderland Hall
Lindean
Bowden
Maxton
Rutherford
Kalemouth
Frogden
Town Yetholm
Kirk Ye
SELKIRK
Holydean
Rowchester
Elliston
Lilliardsedge
Kirkbank Sta.
Fairnington
Eckford
Morebattle
Midlem
Longnewton
Battle of 565
Ancrum Moor 1545
Peniel Heugh 774
Nisbet
Marlfield
Corbet Tr.
Whitmuir Hall
Blackchester
New Belses
Old Belses
Ashieburn
Ancrum Ho.
Monteviot
Crailing
Cessford Cas.
Gateshaws
Hounam Law 1472
Attonburn
Ettrick
Oakwood
Riddell
Lilliesleaf
Ancrum
Chesters
Bonjedward
Ulston
Hartrigge
Whitton
Ettrickbridge-end
Kirkhope
Dryden
Synton
Harelaw
Lanton
Newton
JEDBURGH
Screesburgh
Oxnam
Shibden Hill 1008
Hounam
Shaws Hill
Akermoor L.
Woll
Ashkirk
Minto Hills 905
Fatlips Cas.
Spittal
Hundalee
Oxnam Ch.
Mowhaugh
Langhope B.
Shaws Under L.
Hassendean
Horsleyhill
Minto
Bedrule
Langlee
Ferniehurst Cas.
Craik Moor
Esdale Law
Clarilaw
Teviot
Denholm
Wells
Chatto
Helmoor Loch
Stirches
Ashybank
ROXBURGH
Rubers Law 1392
Cleethaugh
Browndean Laws 1359
Swinlaws
Roberton
Borthwickshiels
Harden
Wilton
Cocklaw Cas.
Cavers Ch.
Cavers Ho.
Faw Hill 1086
Old Jeddart
Rushy Fell 1580
Borthwickbrae
Burnfoot
Highchesters
HAWICK
Kirkton
Hallrule
Camptown
Edgerston
Blindburn
Hoscote
Chisholme
Branxholm Bridgend
Branxholm Cas.
Weens
Abbotsrule Ch.
Bonchester Br.
Bonchester Hill 1059
Chesters
High Seat 1140
Harwood
Newmill
Hawthornside
Hobkirk
Southdean
Huntford
Reidswire 1575
Carter Bar 1371
Hungry Law 1642
Calfshaw Head 1320
Northhouse
Stobs Camp
Cogsmill
Stobs Cas.
Cleuch Head
Wolflee
Wolflee H. 1288
Catcleuch Shin 1742
Whitelee
Blackhip 1471
Mon
Teviothead Ch.
Berry Fell 1291
Shankend
Wauchope
Rule Water
Green Law 1206
Carter Fell 1815
Catcleugh Reservoir
Catcleugh
Byrness
Castleweary
Linhope
Cauldcleuch Head 1996
Greatmoor Hill 1964
Hyndlee
Riets Nest
Windburgh Hill 1662
Singden
Hartshorn Pike 1788
Kielderhead Moor
Oh Me Edge 1809
Raw
Corby Pi
Wisp Hill 1950
Mosspaul Inn
Tudhope Hill 1561
Whitterhope Foot
Note o' the Gate
Limekilnedge
Peel Fell 1975
River Rede
Froswick 1214
Burnfoot
Hermitage Water
Riccarton Junc.
Saughtree Fell 1421
Saughtree Sta.
Deadwater Sta.
Kielder Burn
Hogswood Moor
Hindhope Law 1394
Unthank
Pike Fell 1637
Hartsgarth Fell 1806
Roan Fell 1882
Hermitage
Hermitage Cas.
Arnton Fell
Riccarton
Larriston
Loch Knowe 1321
Kielder Cas.
Earl's Seat 1303
Highfield Moor
Brownrigg Head 1191
Blakehop
Arkleton Hill 1708
Watch Hill
Redheugh
Castleton
Liddel Cas.
Binlabyre
Larriston Fells
Kielder
Monkside 1684
Kirkstile
Tarras
Newcastleton
Hotel
Castleton Ch.
Wilson's Pike 1354
Mounces
Plashetts Sta.
White Hill 1006
Sidwood
Falstone
LANGHOLM
Tinnis Hill 1326
Gillside
Blinkbonny Height
Caplestone Fell 1569
Glendhu Hill 1684
North Tyne
Emmethaugh
Stannersburn
Thorneyburn Sta.
Greenhaugh
Charlton
Cauldside
Christianbury Crag 1598
Bewcastle Fells
Sighty Crag 1702
Black Knowe 1613
Jock's Pike 1147
Gill Pike 1374
Bolts Law 1295
Chirdon Burn
Hesleyside
Dunterley

NOR

Scale of Miles

0 1 2 3 4 5 6 7 8 9 10

Continued on

MAP 17

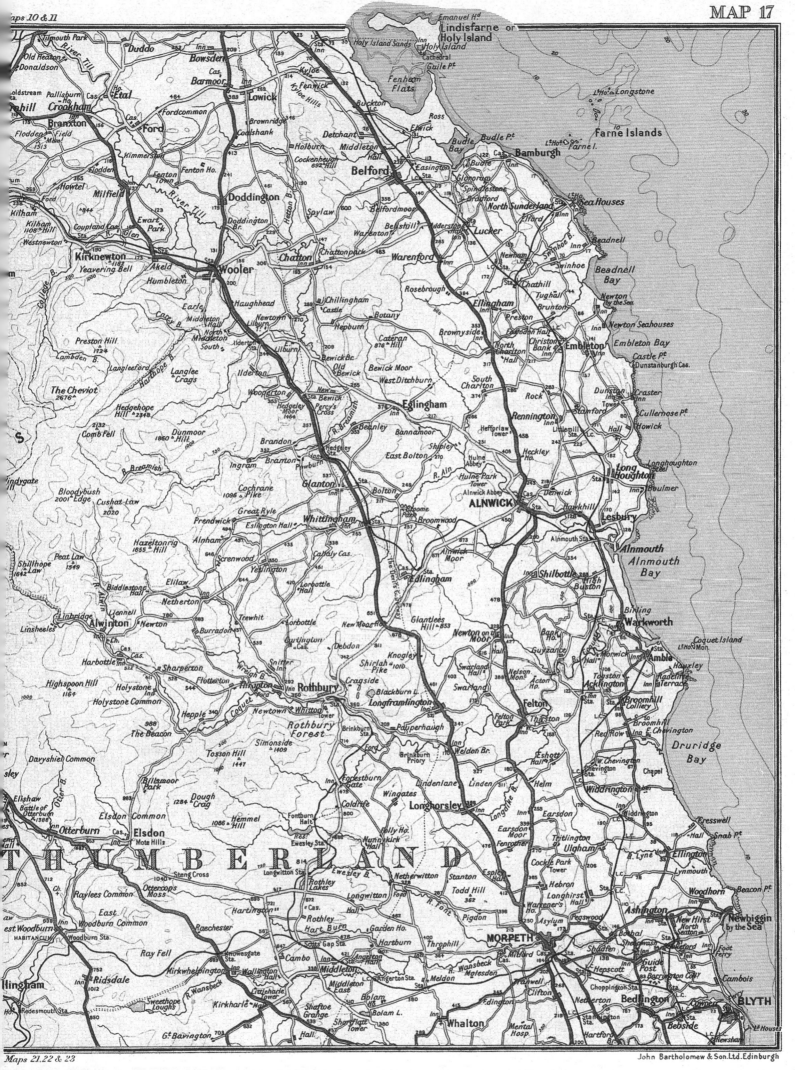

Maps 10 & 11

Maps 21, 22 & 23

John Bartholomew & Son Ltd. Edinburgh

Main Roads ———— Other Roads ———— Railways ————

MAP 18

Continued on Map

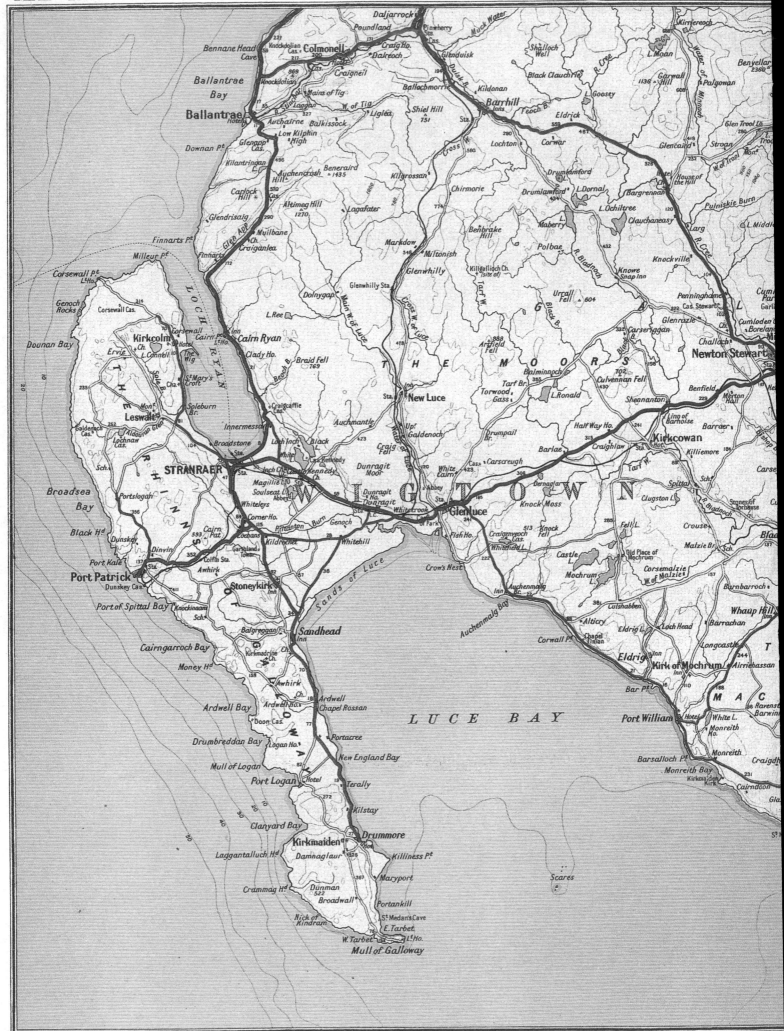

Scale of Miles

0 1 2 3 4 5 6 7 8 9 10

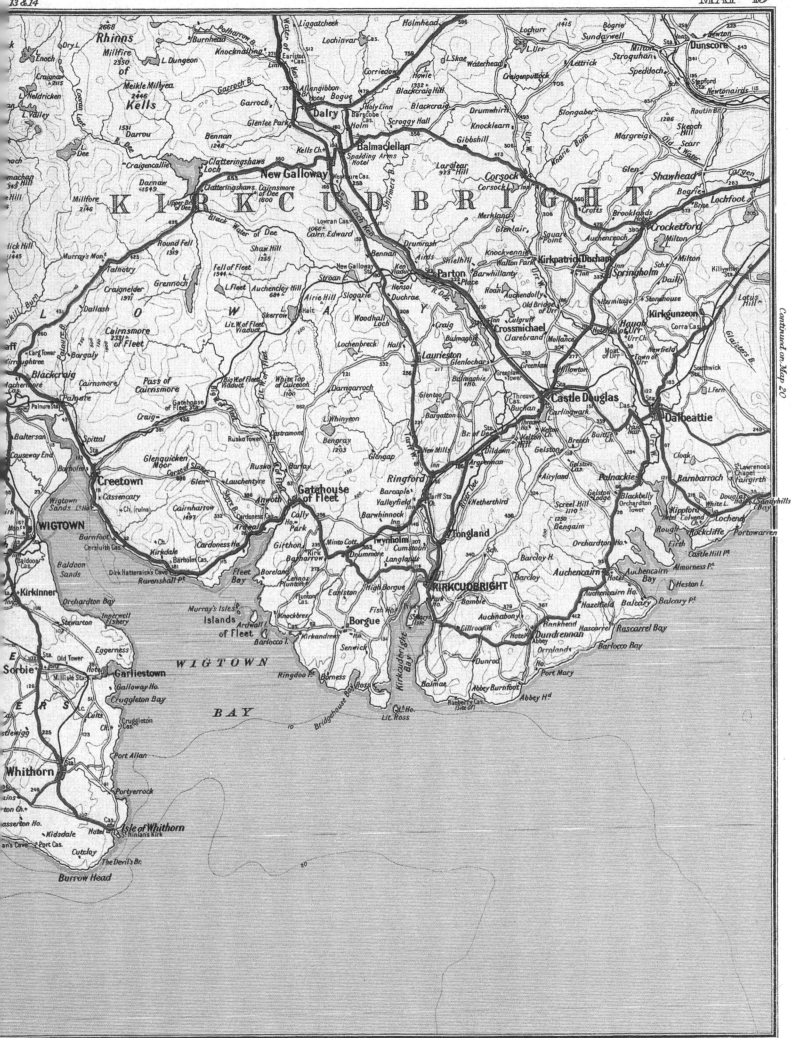

Continued on Map 20

Main Roads ━━━━━━   Other Roads ════════   Railways ━━━━━━

MAP 20

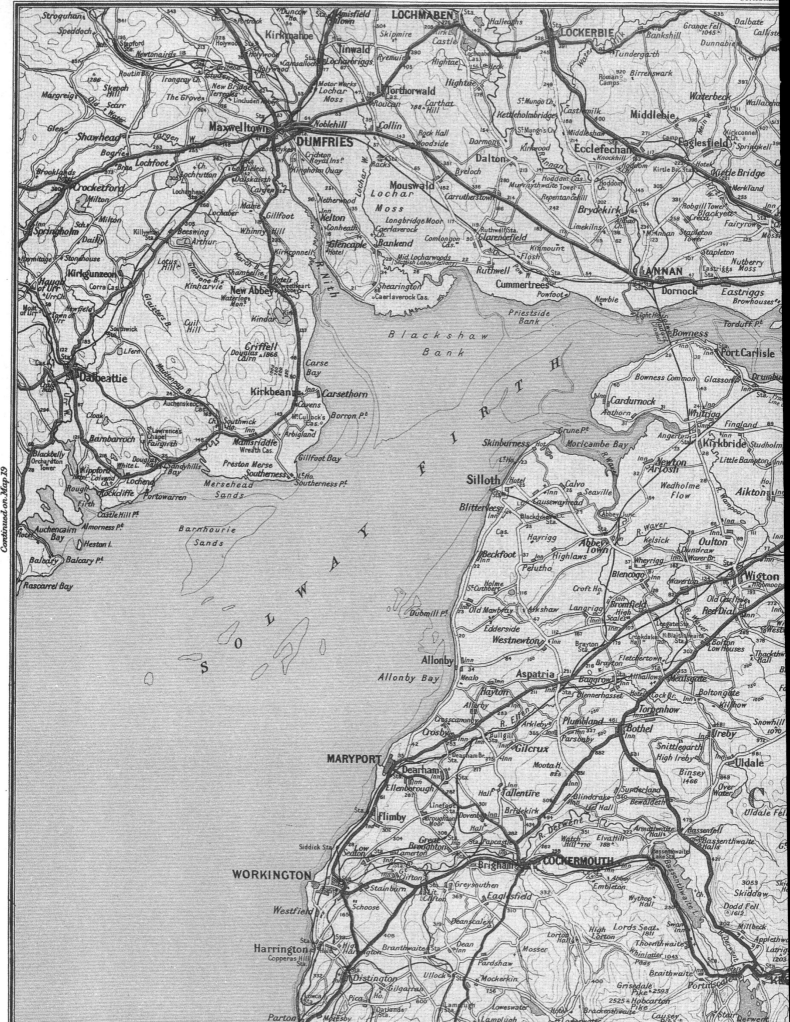

Continued on Map 19

Continued on

Scale of Miles

0 1 2 3 4 5 6 7 8 9 10

MAP 21

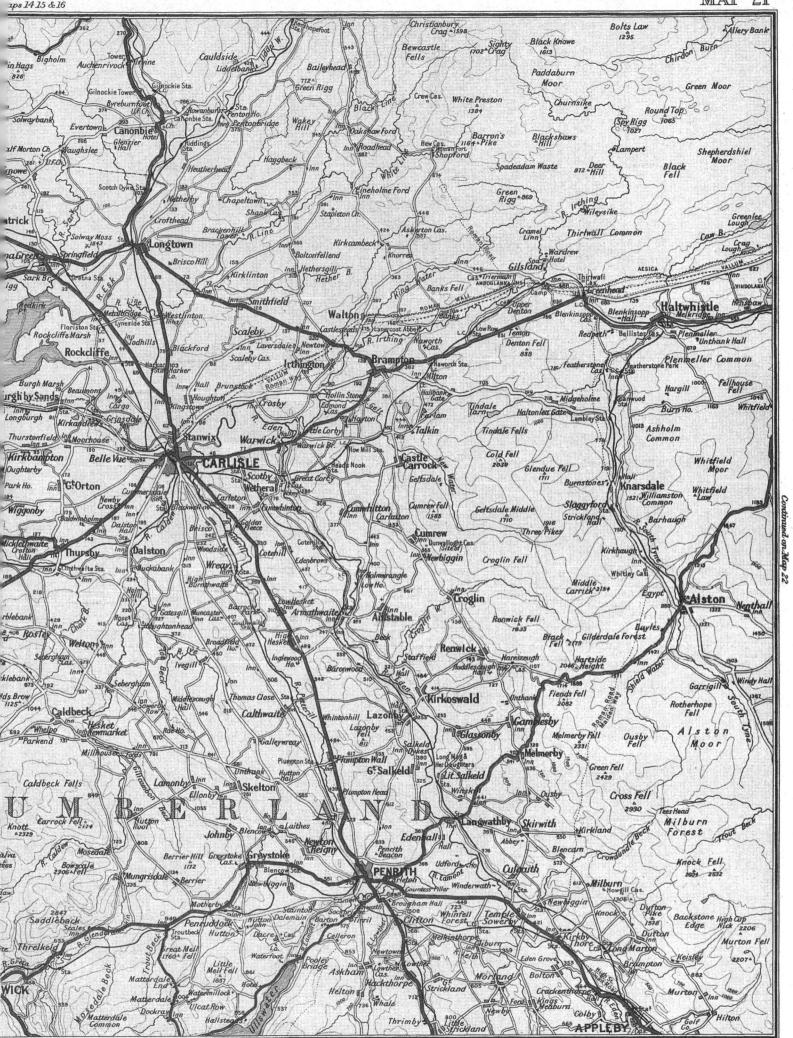

Continued on Map 22

John Bartholomew & Son.Ltd.Edinburgh

Main Roads ━━━━━   Other Roads ═════   Railways ━━━━━

MAP 22

Continued on Maps 16 & 17.

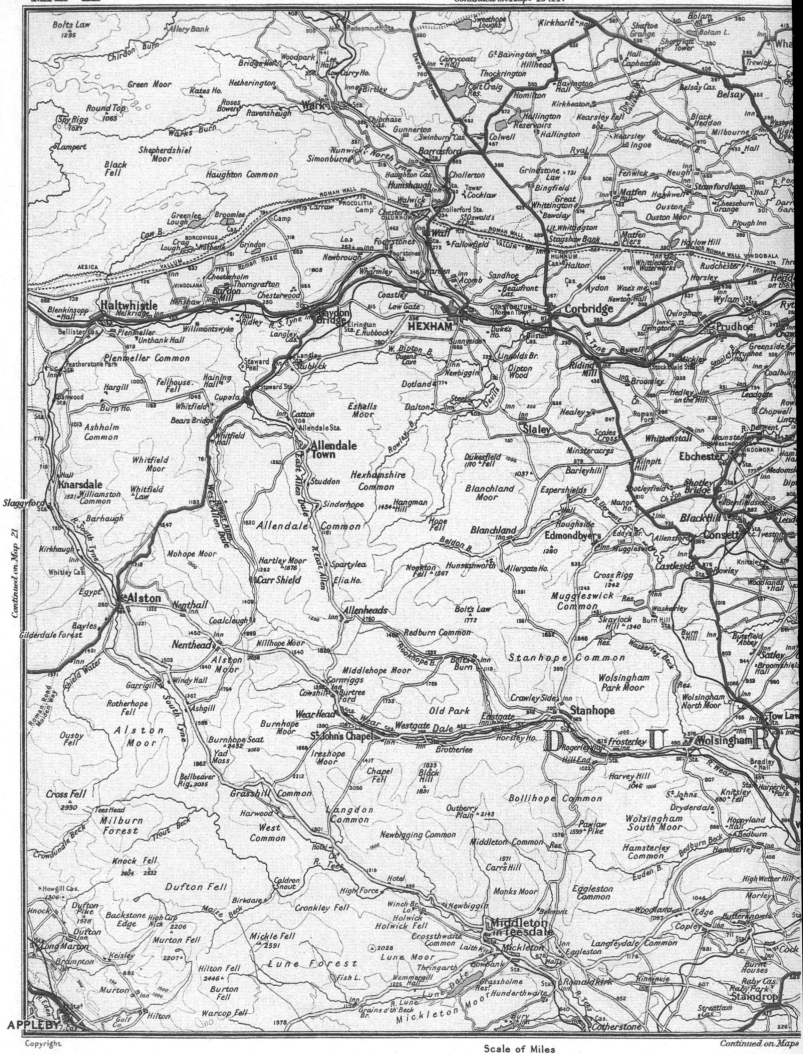

Continued on Map 21

Continued on Maps

APPLEBY

Scale of Miles

0 1 2 3 4 5 6 7 8 9 10

MAP 23

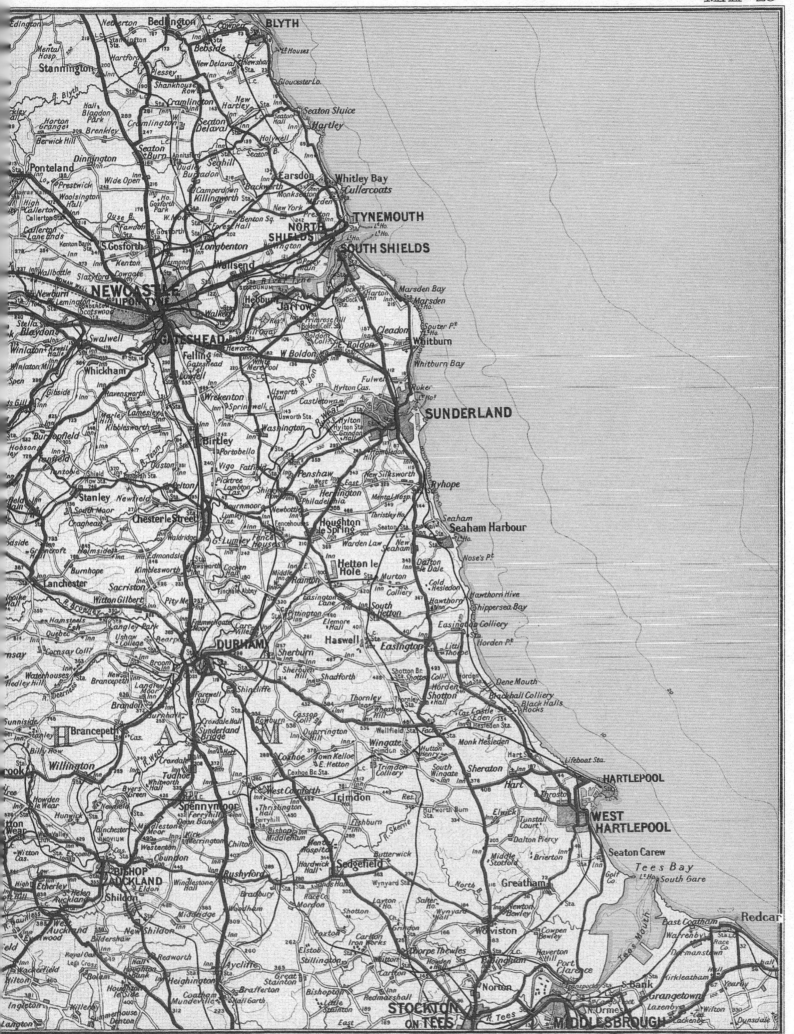

John Bartholomew & Son.Ltd.Edinburgh

Main Roads ————— Other Roads ————— Railways —————

MAP 24

On the same Scale

ISLE OF MAN

Scale of Miles

0 1 2 3 4 5 6 7 8 9 10

Copyright

MAP 25

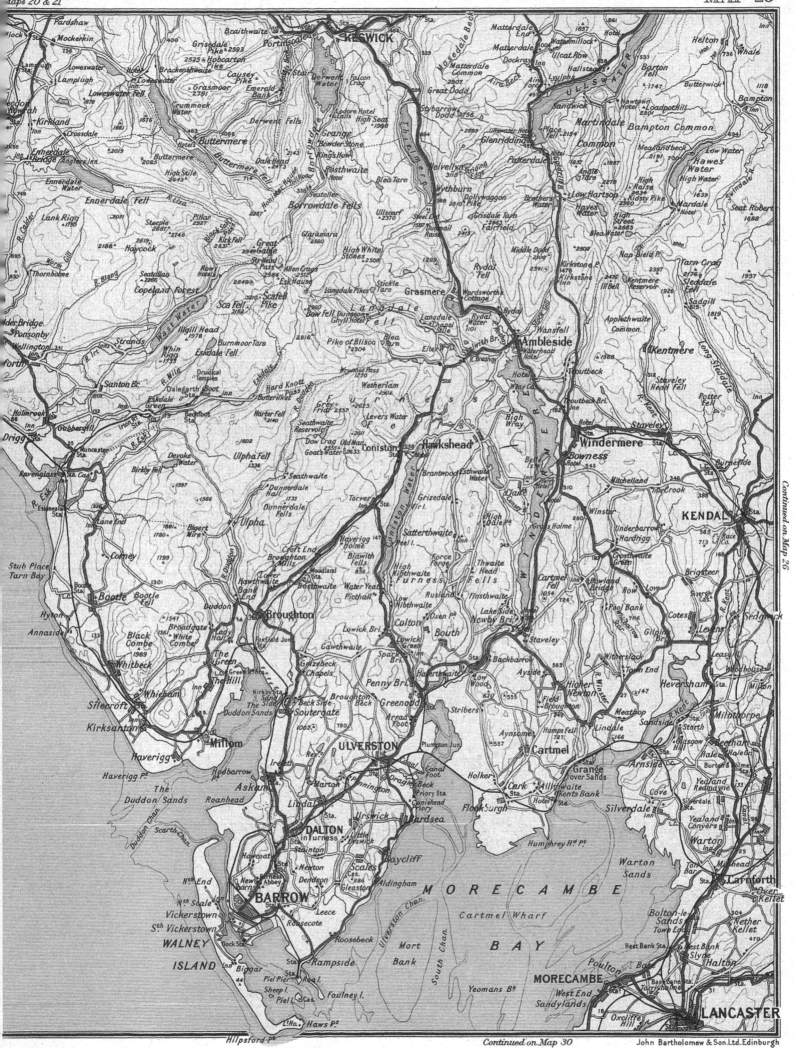

Continued on Map 26

Continued on Map 30

John Bartholomew & Son.Ltd.Edinburgh

Main Roads ——— Other Roads ═══ Railways ┄┄┄

MAP 26

Continued on Map

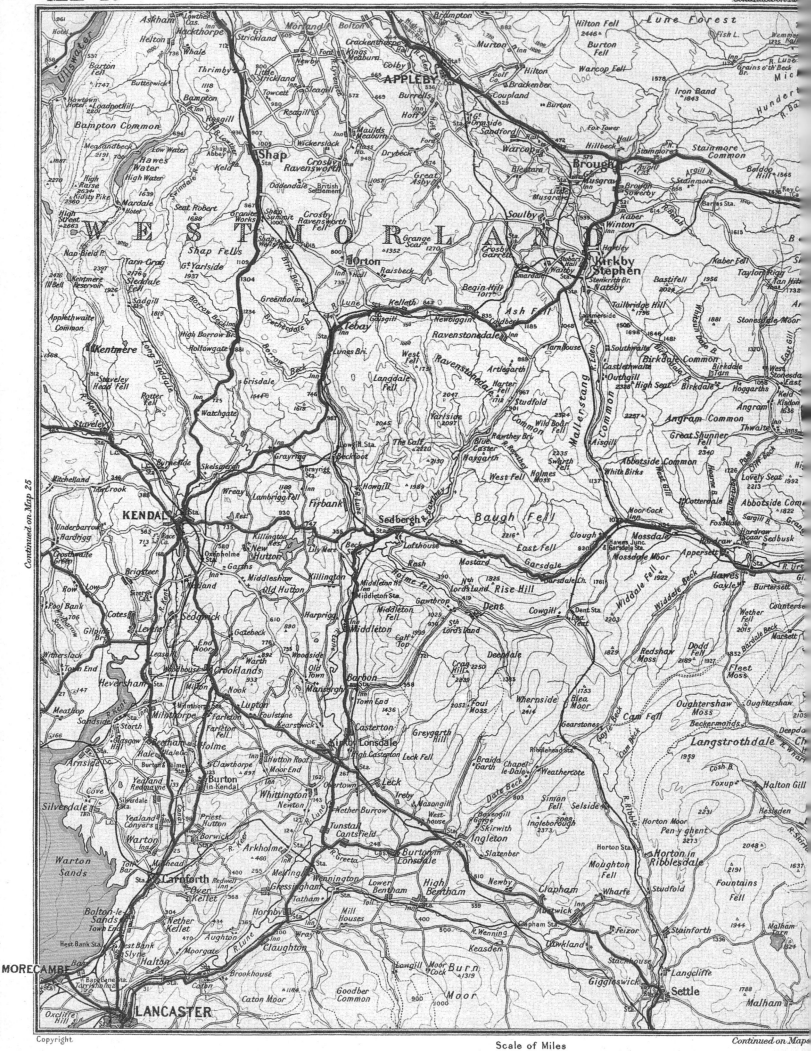

Continued on Map 25

Continued on Maps

Scale of Miles

0 1 2 3 4 5 6 7 8 9 10

MAP 27

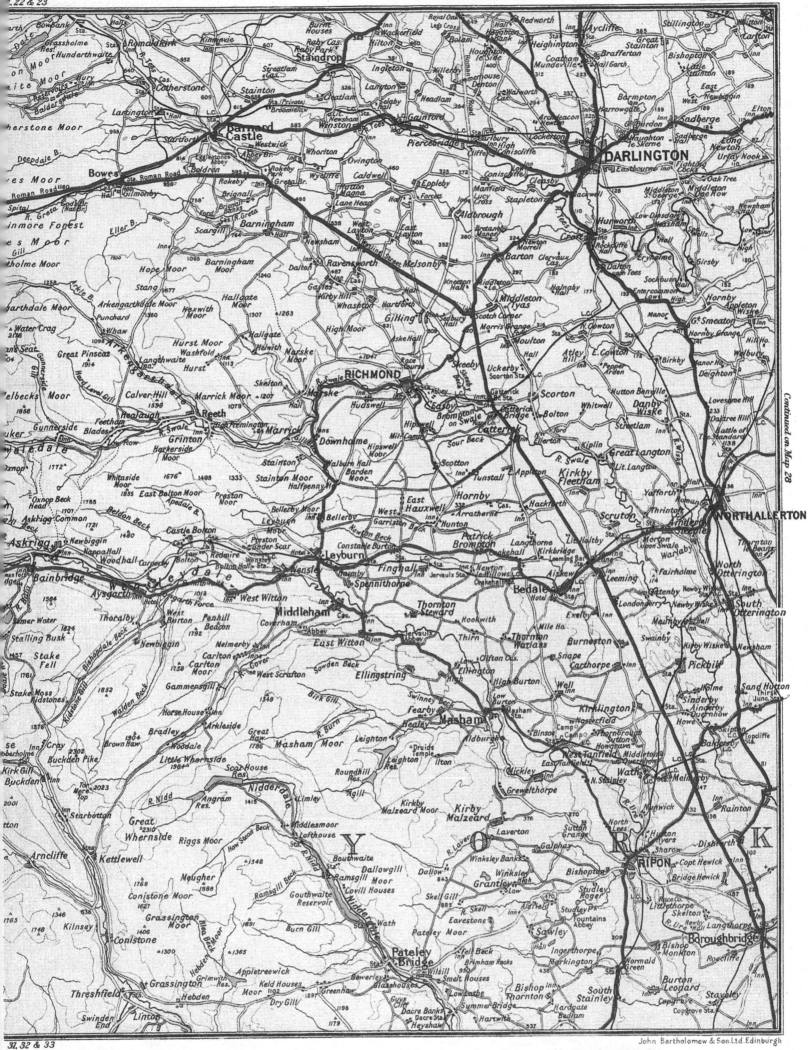

Continued on Map 28

John Bartholomew & Son, Ltd. Edinburgh

Main Roads ━━━━━   Other Roads ══════   Railways ─────

MAP 28
Continued on Map 23

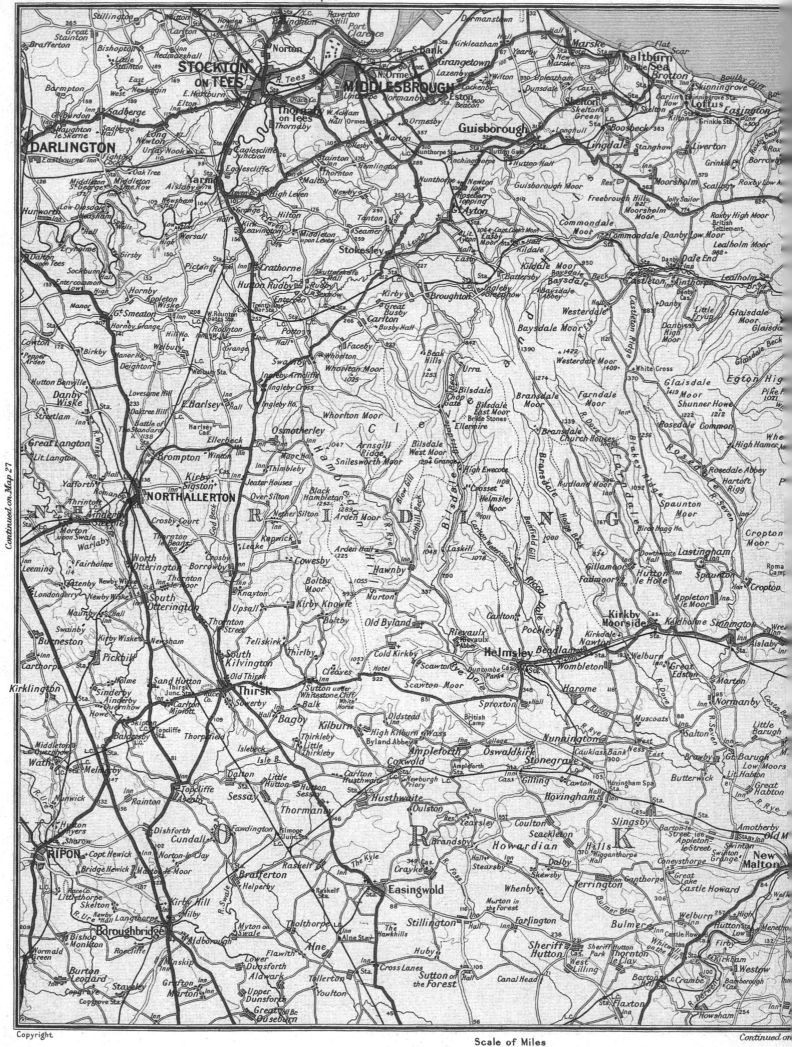

Continued on Map 27

Scale of Miles

0 1 2 3 4 5 6 7 8 9 10

Continued on

MAP 29

Main Roads ━━━━━━━ Other Roads ═══════ Railways ━━━━━━━

John Bartholomew & Son Ltd. Edinburgh

Maps 33, 34 & 35

MAP 30

Continued on Map

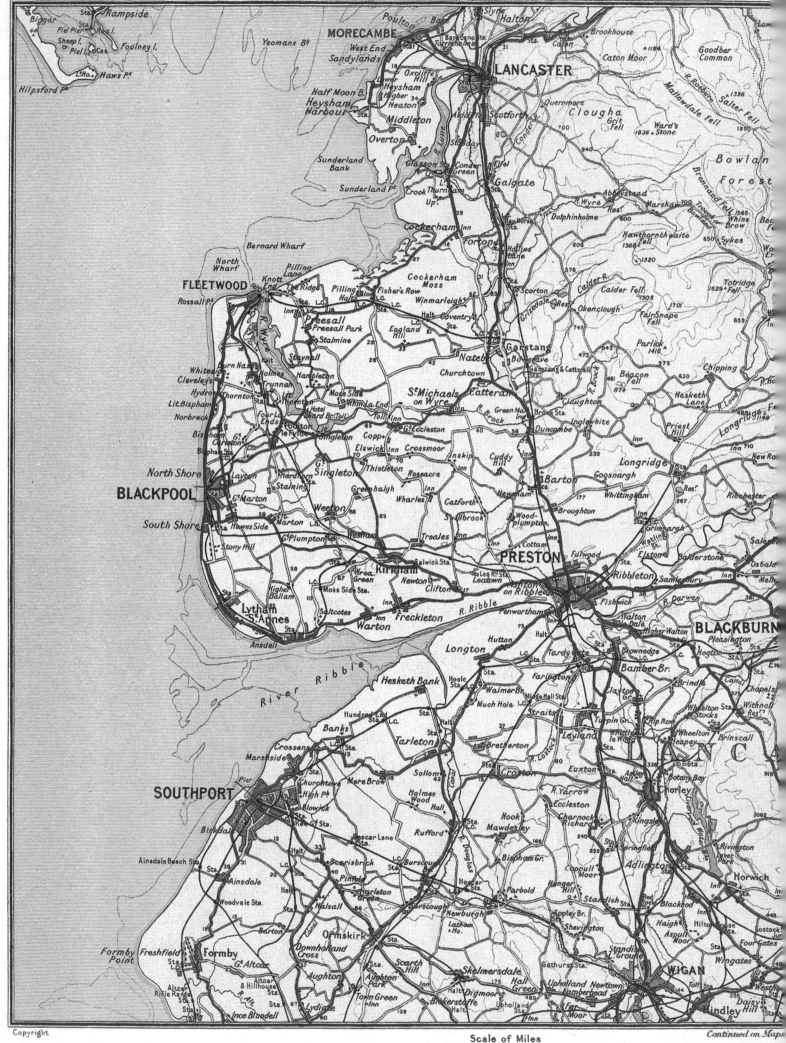

Scale of Miles

0 1 2 3 4 5 6 7 8 9 10

Continued on Maps

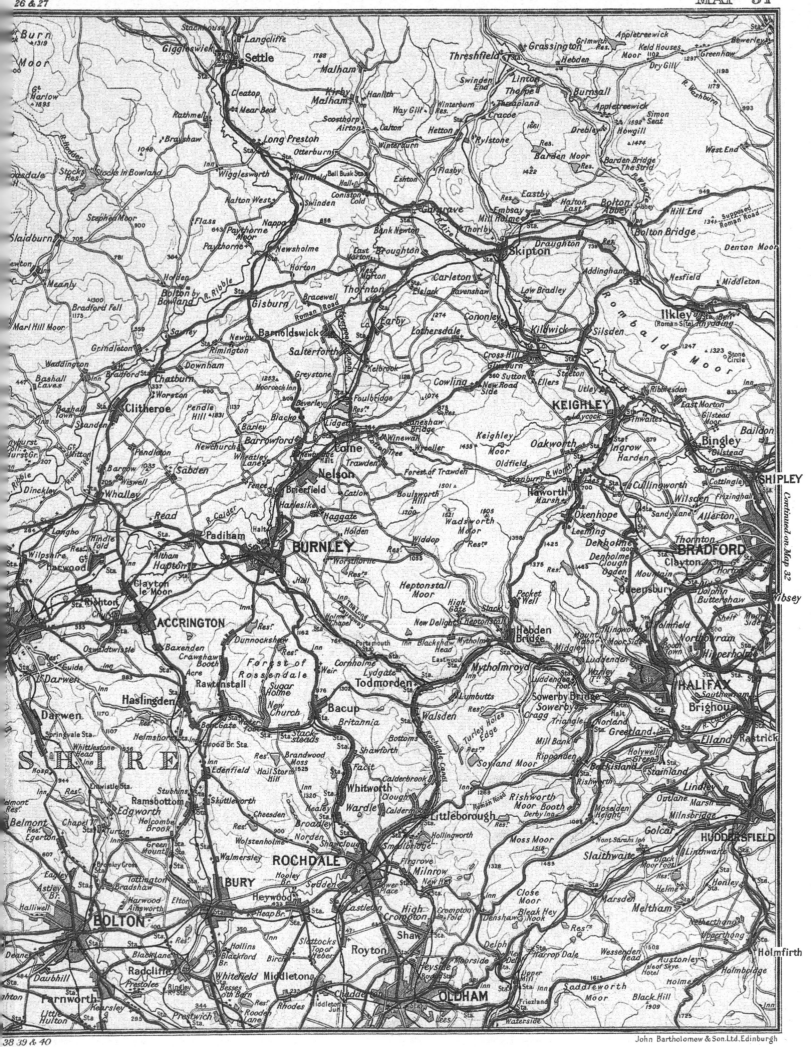

Main Roads ———— Other Roads ———— Railways ————

MAP 32

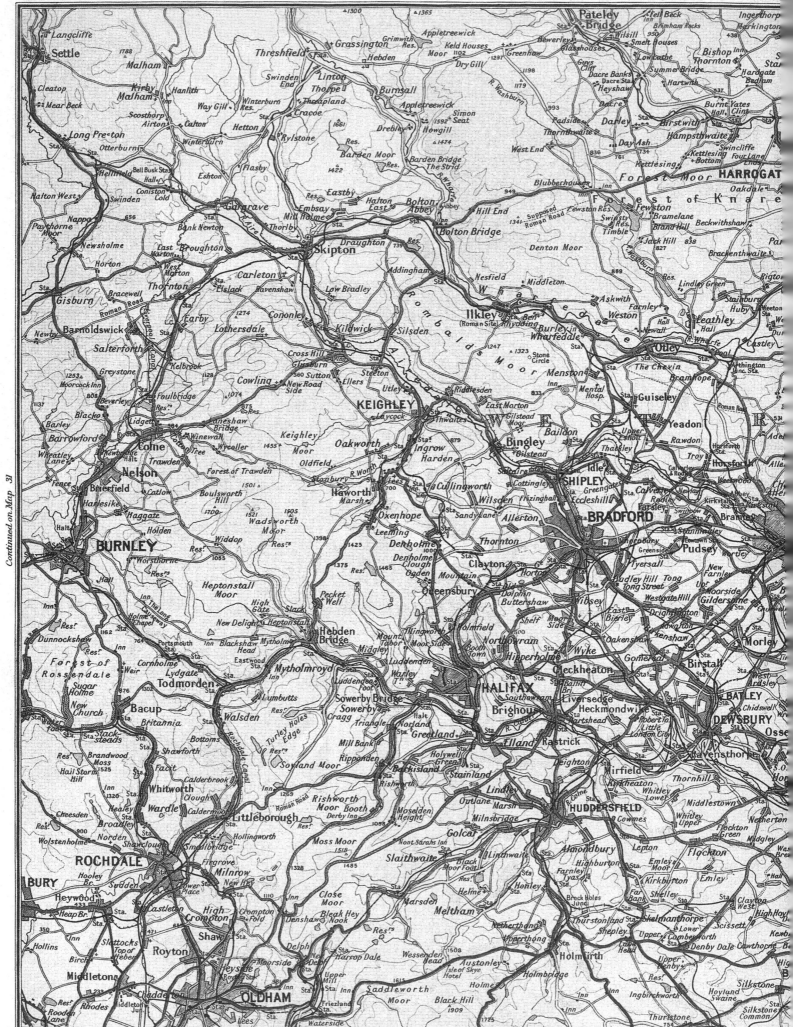

Scale of Miles

0 1 2 3 4 5 6 7 8 9 10

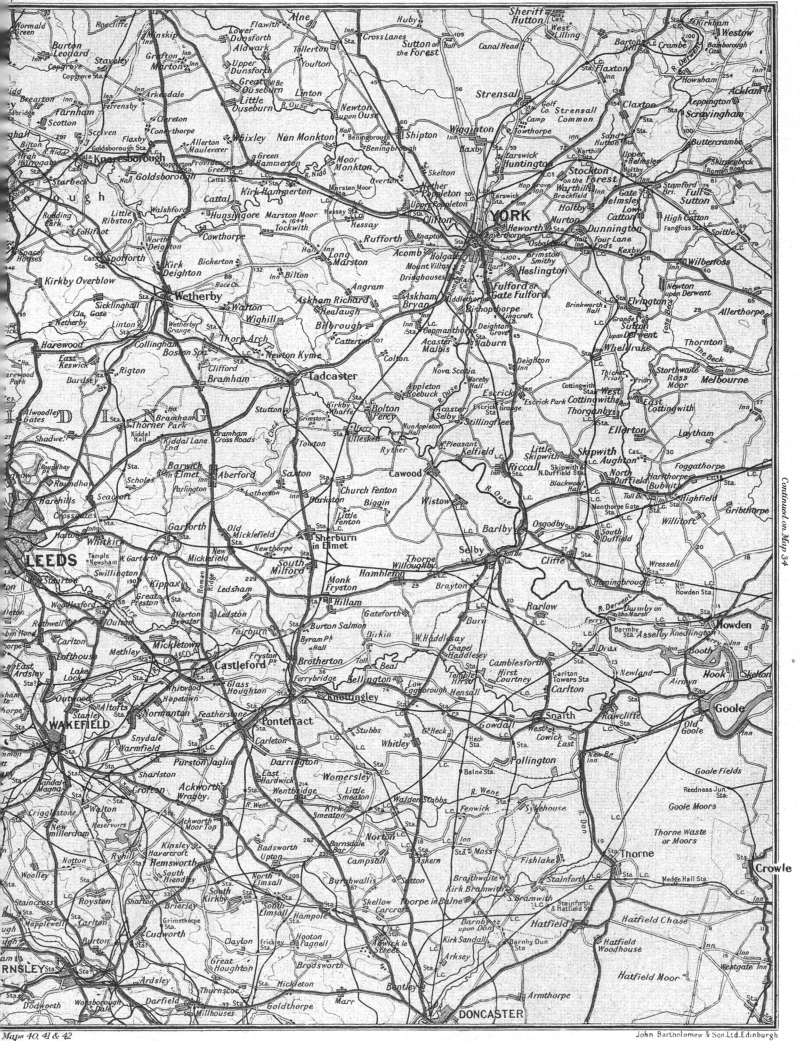

Continued on Map 34

Main Roads ———— Other Roads ═══════ Railways ╌╌╌╌

MAP 34

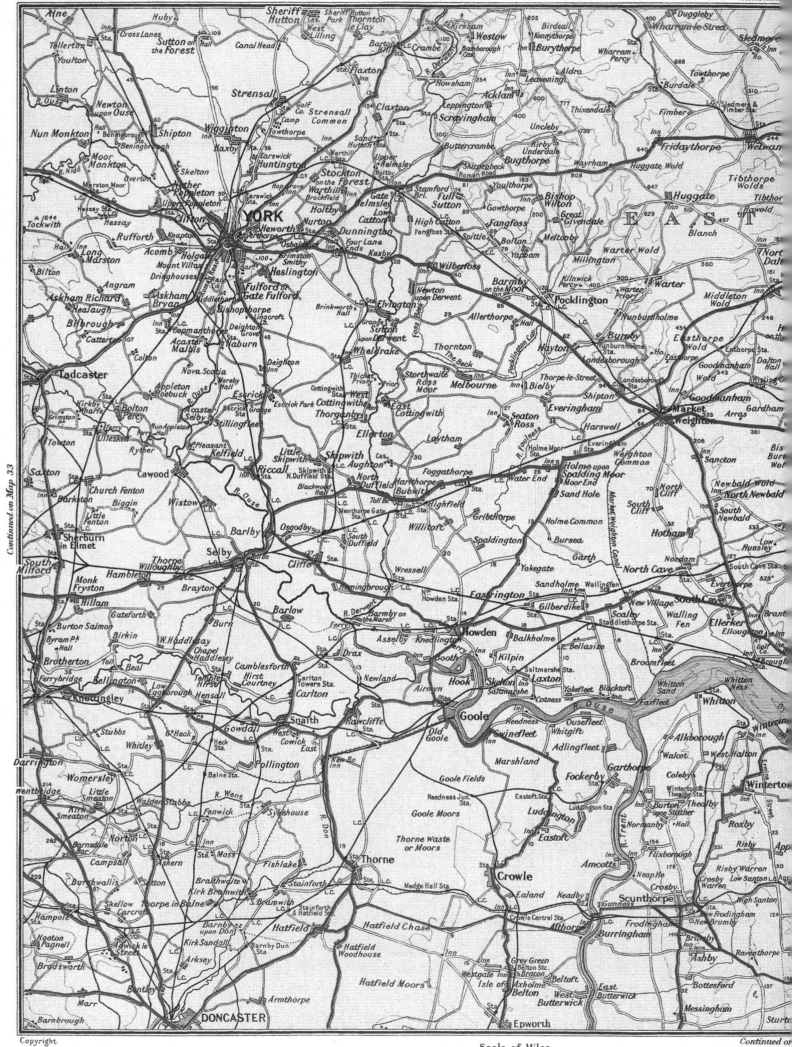

Continued on Map 33

Copyright.

Scale of Miles

0 1 2 3 4 5 6 7 8 9 10

Continued on

YORK

DONCASTER

Pocklington

Market Weighton

Selby

Goole

Howden

Thorne

Crowle

Scunthorpe

Tadcaster

Knottingley

MAP 35

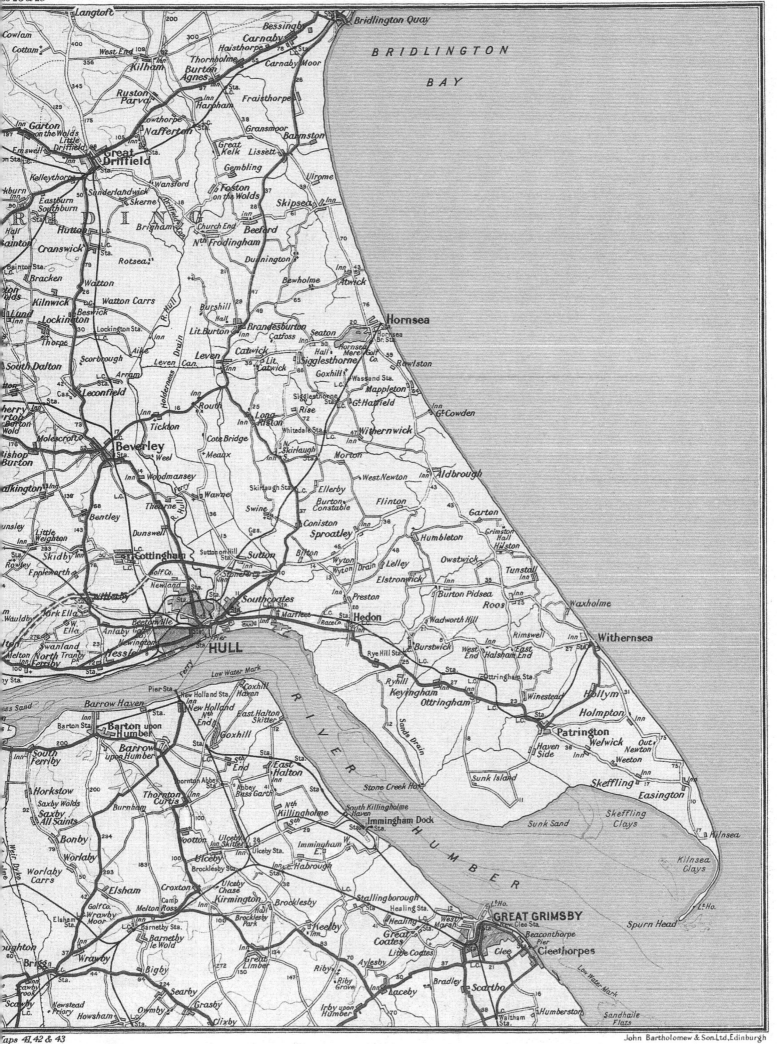

John Bartholomew & Son.Ltd,Edinburgh

Main Roads ━━━━━   Other Roads ═════   Railways ━━━━━

MAP 36

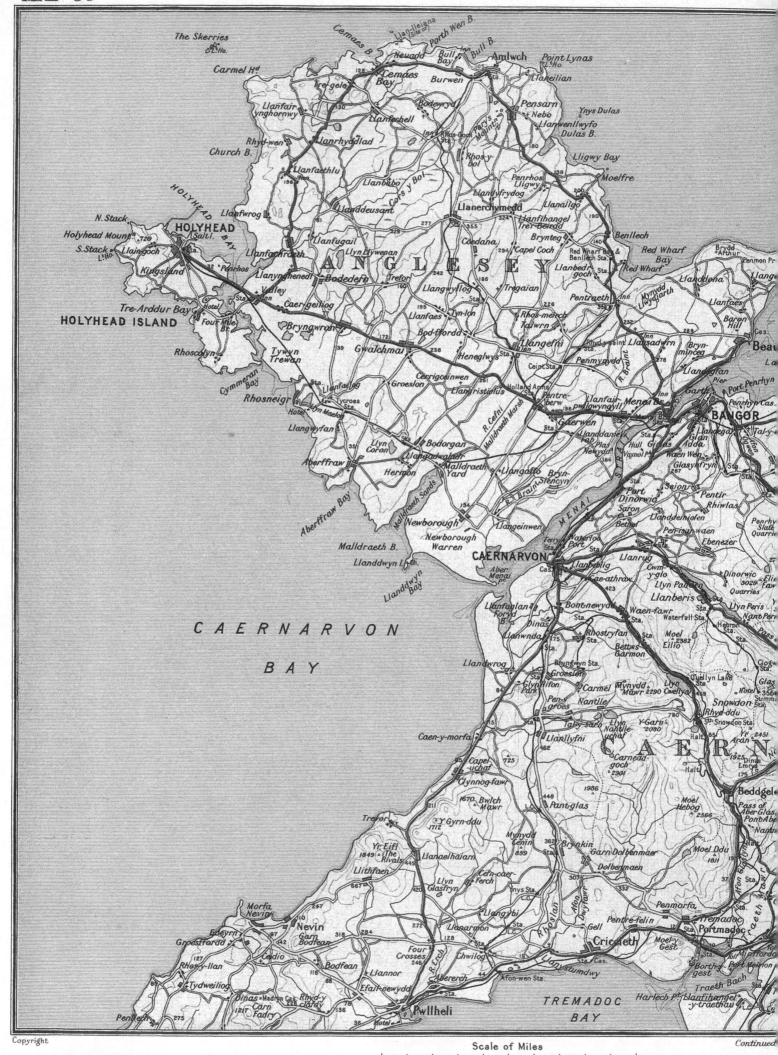

The Skerries
○L⋅Ho.

Cemaes B.
Llan-lleiana (Sta.)
Porth Wen B.

Carmel Hd.
Neuadd
Bull Bay
Bull B.

Amlwch
Point Lynas
L⋅Ho.

Tregele
Cemaes Bay
Burwen
Sta.
Llaneilian

Llanfair ynghornwy
128
Llanfechell
Bodewyrd
Pensarn
Nebo
Ynys Dulas

Rhyd-wen
130
Inn
Parys Mountn.
Rhos-goch Sta.
180
Llanwenllwyfo
Dulas B.

Church B.
Llanrhyddlad
Rhos-y-bol
Penrhos Lligwy
Lligwy Bay

Llanfaethlu
Inn
196
Llanbabo
Cors y Bol
Llandyfrydog
Llanallgo
206
Moelfre

Llanfwrog
81
Llanddeusant
Llanerchymedd
139

N. Stack
HOLYHEAD
Sta.
277
355
Llanfihangel Tre'r Beirdd
Brynteg
190
Benllech

Holyhead Mount
720
Salt
Ho.
324
140
Bryn Arthur

S. Stack L⋅Ho.
Llaingoch
Llanfugail
Coedana
Capel Coch
Red Wharf Bay & Benllech Sta.
Penmon

Kingsland
Penrhos
Llanfachraeth
Llyn Llywenan
242
294
Llanbedr goch
Red Wharf
Red Wharf Bay
Llanddona

32
Llanynghenedl
Bodedern
Trefor
Tregaian
Sta.
252
Llanfaes

Tre-Arddur Bay
Hotel
Valley
186
ANGLESEY
Pentraeth
Inn
Mynydd Llwydiarth
Baron Hill
Beau

Four Mile Br.
Caer-geiliog
Llangwyllog
195
Llyn-lon
Rhos-meirch
Talwrn
289

HOLYHEAD ISLAND
Bryngwran
226
Llanfaes
Sta.
278
Llandegfan
Pier
Port Penrhyn

Rhoscolyn
Tywyn Trewan
172
Bod-ffordd
Llangefni
Rhyd-y-saint Sta.
Llansadwrn
Garth
BANGOR

Cymmeran Bay
39
Gwalchmai
238
Heneglwys
Ceint Sta.
Penmynydd
Penrhyn Cas.
Tal-y

Rhosneigr
Llanfaelog
Cerrigceinwen
261
Holland Arms
Pentre-berw
Llanfair Menai Br.
Llandegai
Glan Adda
Waen Wen

Tycroes Sta.
Groeslon
Llangristiolus
198
Llanfair pwllgwyngyll
Inn
Hirael
Glasynfryn
287

Hotel
Llyn Maelog
Bodorgan
R. Cefni
Malldraeth Marsh
Gaerwen
Llanddaniel Fab
Plas Newydd
164
Vaynol Park
Saion
Pentir Rhiwlas

Llangwyfan
35
Llangadwaladr
Malldraeth Yard
Llangaffo
Bryn Siencyn
Llanedwen
Port Dinorwic
Saron
Bethel
Llanddeiniolen
Penrhyn Slate Quarries

Aberffraw
154
R. Braint
MENAI
Terry Port
Waterloo Port
Perisan-waen
Ebenezer

Aberffraw Bay
Hermon
Newborough
Llangeinwen
Aber Menai
Ferry Sta.
Sta.
Cwm-y-glo
Dinorwic
Quarries

Malldraeth Sands
Newborough Warren
CAERNARVON
Cas.
Llanrug
Llyn Padarn
3029
Elidir Fawr

Malldraeth B.
Llanddwyn I. Lth.
Aber Menai pt.
Llanbeblig
Cae-athraw
423
Llanberis
Sta.
Llyn Peris
Nant Per

Llanddwyn Bay
Llanfaglan Foryd
Bont-newydd
Sta.
Waen-fawr
Sta.
Waterfall Sta.
Hebron Sta.
Pass

C A E R N A R V O N
Dinas
Llanwnda
175
Rhostryfan
Sta.
Bryngwyn Sta.
Moel Eilio
2382
Clogwyn Sta.

B A Y
Llandwrog
L.C.
Groeslon
84
Carmel
Mynydd Mawr 2290
Llyn Nantlle
Llyn Cwellyn
Snowdon
3560
Glas
Summit

Glynllifon Park
Pen-y-groes
Nantlle
Y-Garn
2080
Sth. Snowdon Sta.
Rhyd-ddu
Hotel

Caen-y-morfa
15
Taly sarn
Llyn Nantlle-uchaf
780
Y-Garn
Ye. Aran
2451
C A E R N

Capel-uchaf
725
Llanllyfni
462
Carnedd goch
2301
1325
Dinas Emrys
175

Clynnog-fawr
95
Halt
651
Halt

1670
Bwlch Mawr
449
Pant-glas
1986
Moel Hebog
2566
Beddgel

Trevor
211
Y Gyrn-ddu
1712
L.C.
Pass of Aber Glas
Pont-Abe
Nant

Yr Eifl
1849
The Rivals
445
Llanaelhaiarn
Mynydd Cenin
659
Brynkin
362
Sta.
Garn Dolbenmaer
Moel Ddu
1811

Llithfaen
Cefn-caer-ferch
307
Dolbenmaen
37
Sta.

557
Llyn Glasfryn
420
Ynys Sta.
L.C.
332
Penmorfa
Sta.

Morfa Nevin
257
Llangybi
Tremadoc
Portmadoc

Nevin
Garn Bodfean
318
284
272
Llanarmon
128
Pentre-felin
Gell
Criccieth
Moely Gest

Edeyrn
87
142
Four Crosses
246
Chwilog
19
Llanystumdwy
Borth-y-gest
Port Meirion

Groesffordd
Celdio
116
88
Llannor
Abererch
44
Afon-wen Sta.
Traeth Bach

Rhos-y-llan
127
Bodfean
Efail-newydd
R. Erch
TREMADOC
Harlech Pt.
Llanfihangel-y-traethau

Tydweiliog
85
Dinas
Madryn Cas.
Rhyd-y-clafdy
136
Pwllheli
BAY

Penllech
Carn Fadryn
1217
275
Hotel

CAERNARVON
BAY

Scale of Miles
0 1 2 3 4 5 6 7 8 9 10

Continued

MAP 37

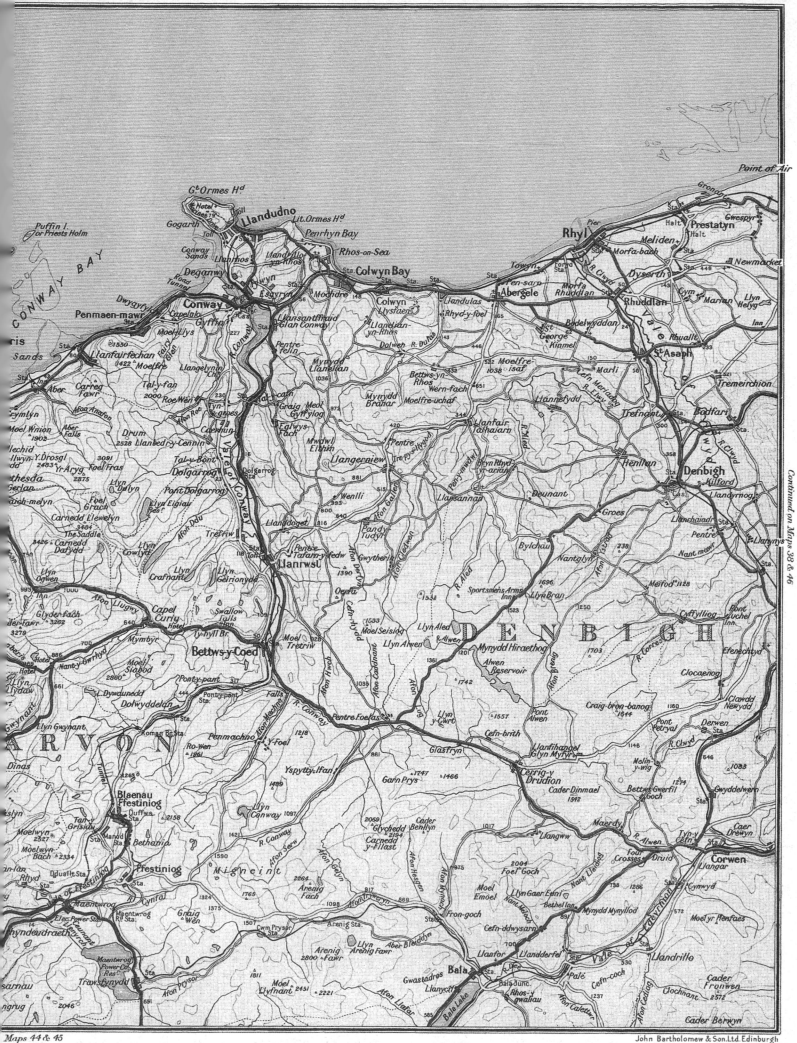

Continued on Maps 38 & 46

Main Roads ———— Other Roads ════ Railways ————

John Bartholomew & Son. Ltd. Edinburgh

Maps 44 & 45

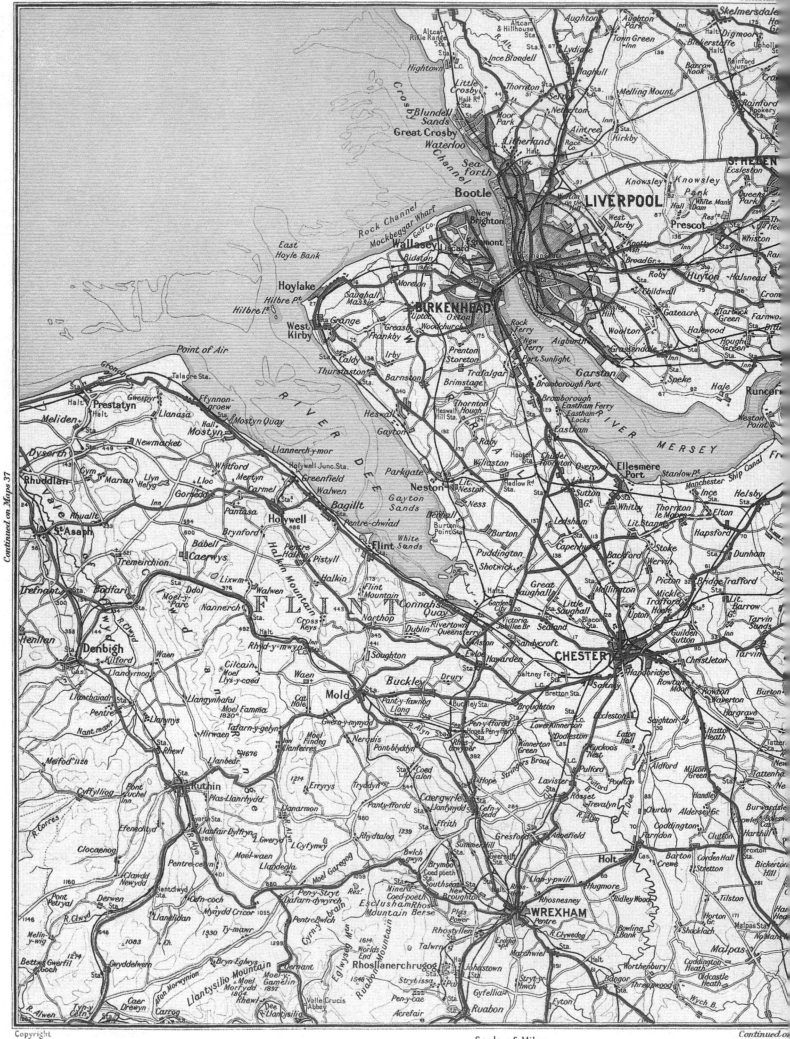

MAP 38

Continued

Skelmersdale

Continued on Maps 37

Copyright

Continued on

Scale of Miles

0 1 2 3 4 5 6 7 8 9 10

MAP 39

Maps 30 & 31

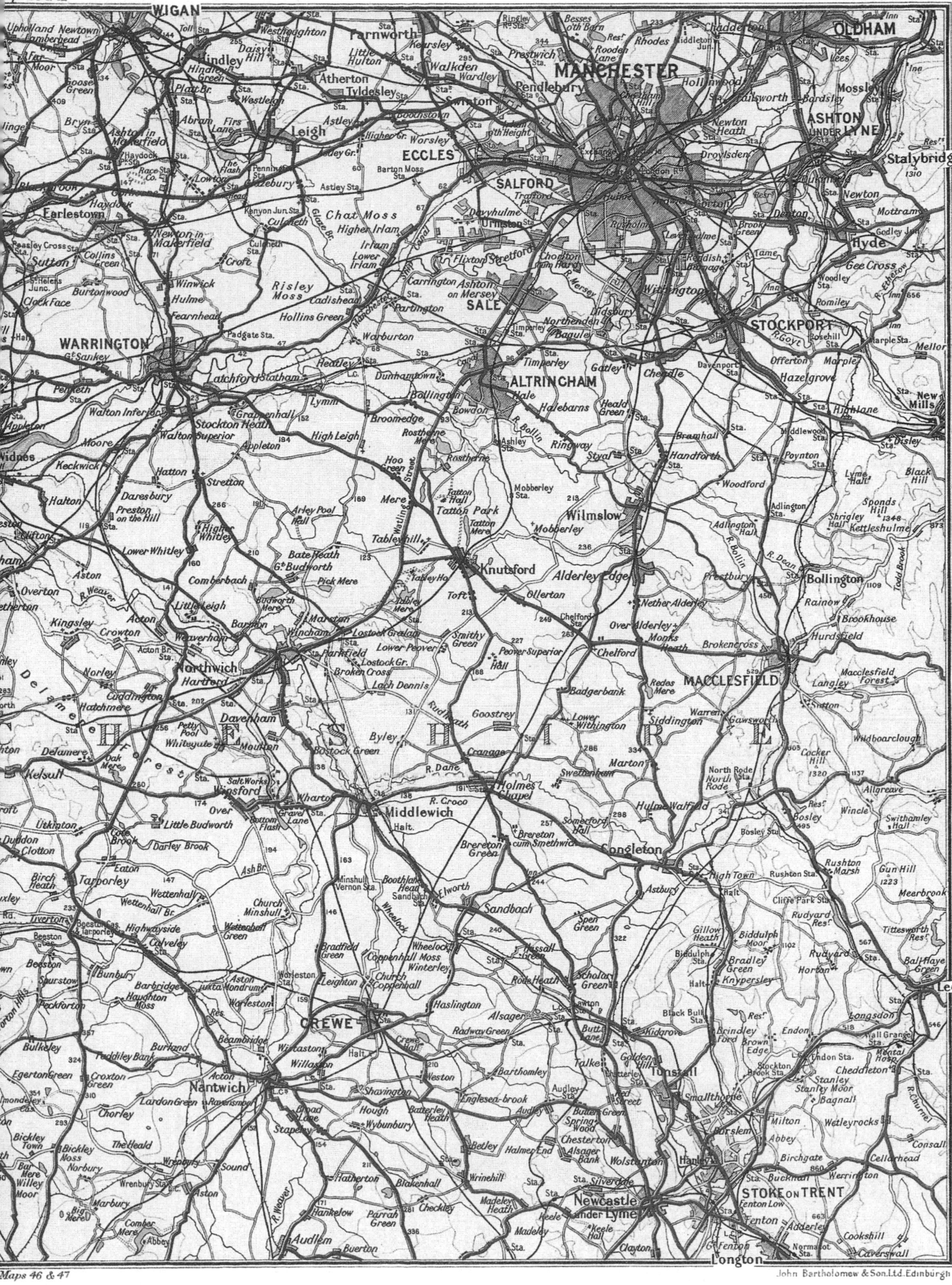

WIGAN · OLDHAM · MANCHESTER · SALFORD · ECCLES · ASHTON UNDER LYNE · Stalybridge · Hyde · STOCKPORT · SALE · ALTRINCHAM · WARRINGTON · Knutsford · Wilmslow · Alderley Edge · MACCLESSFIELD · Bollington · Congleton · Northwich · Winsford · Middlewich · Sandbach · CREWE · Nantwich · Newcastle under Lyme · STOKE ON TRENT · Leek

Continued on Map 40

John Bartholomew & Son Ltd. Edinburgh

Main Roads ——— Other Roads ——— Railways ———

MAP 40

Continued on Map 39

Continued on

Scale of Miles

0 1 2 3 4 5 6 7 8 9 10

MAP 41

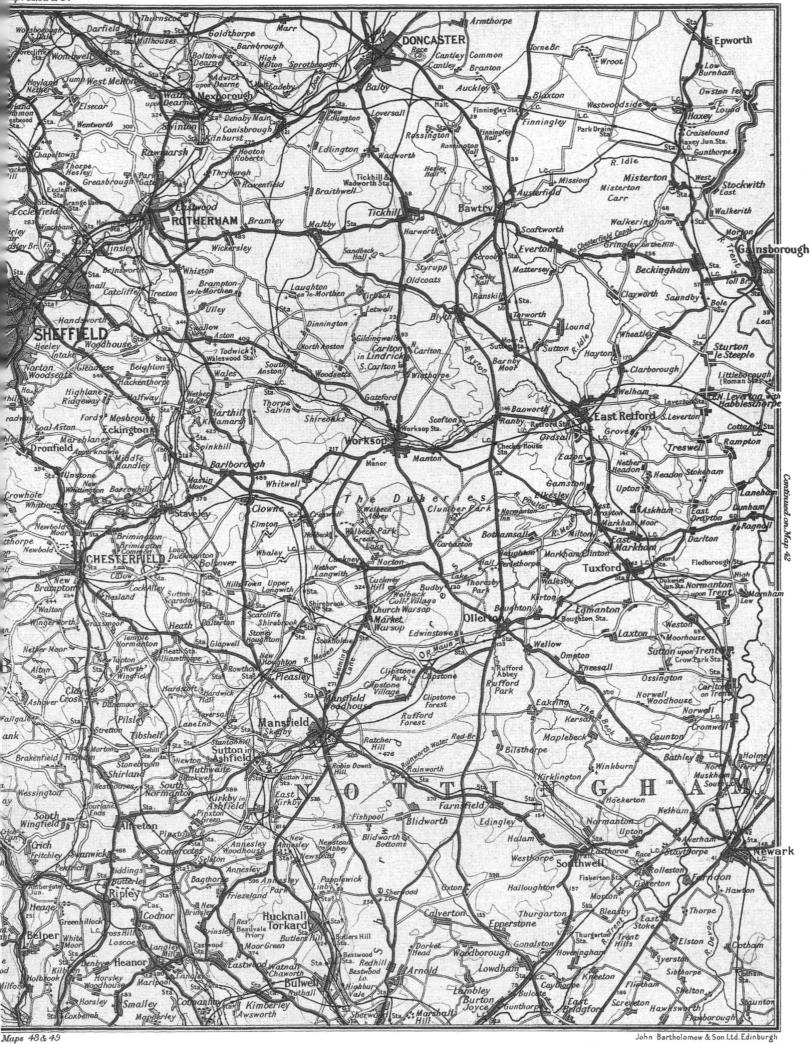

Maps 32,33 & 34

Continued on Map 42

Maps 48 & 49

John Bartholomew & Son Ltd. Edinburgh

Main Roads ━━━━━ Other Roads ═════ Railways ━━━━━

MAP 42

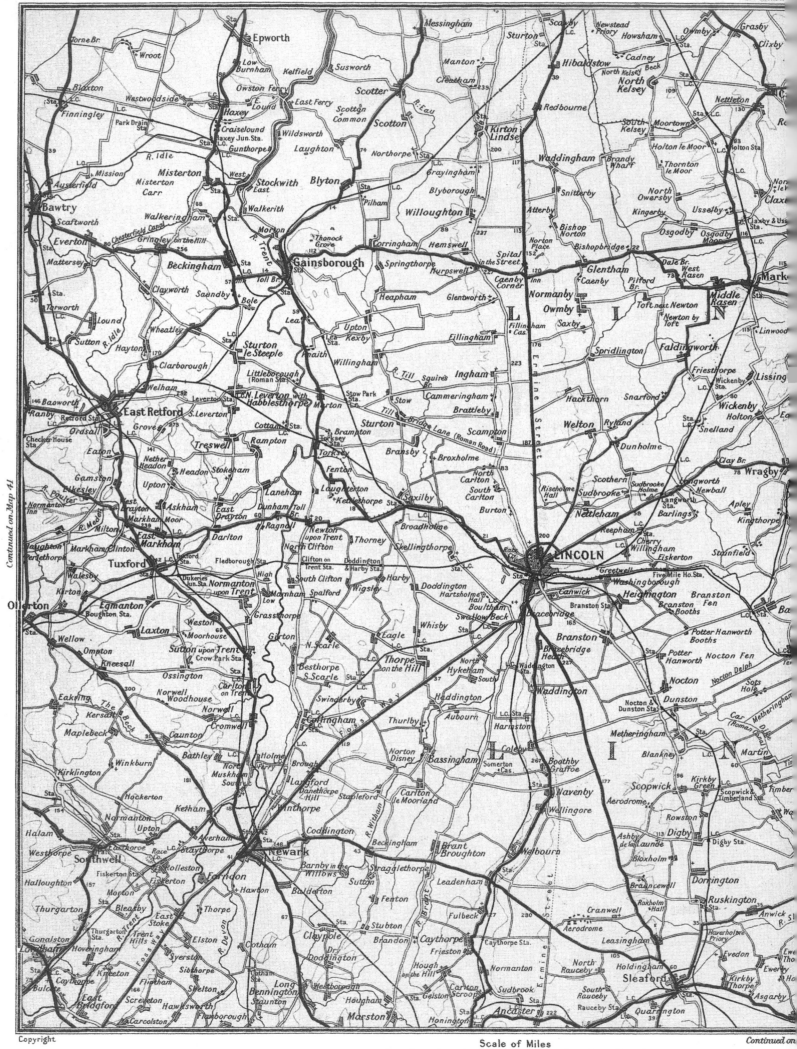

Continued on Map 41

Scale of Miles

0 1 2 3 4 5 6 7 8 9 10

Continued on

MAP 43

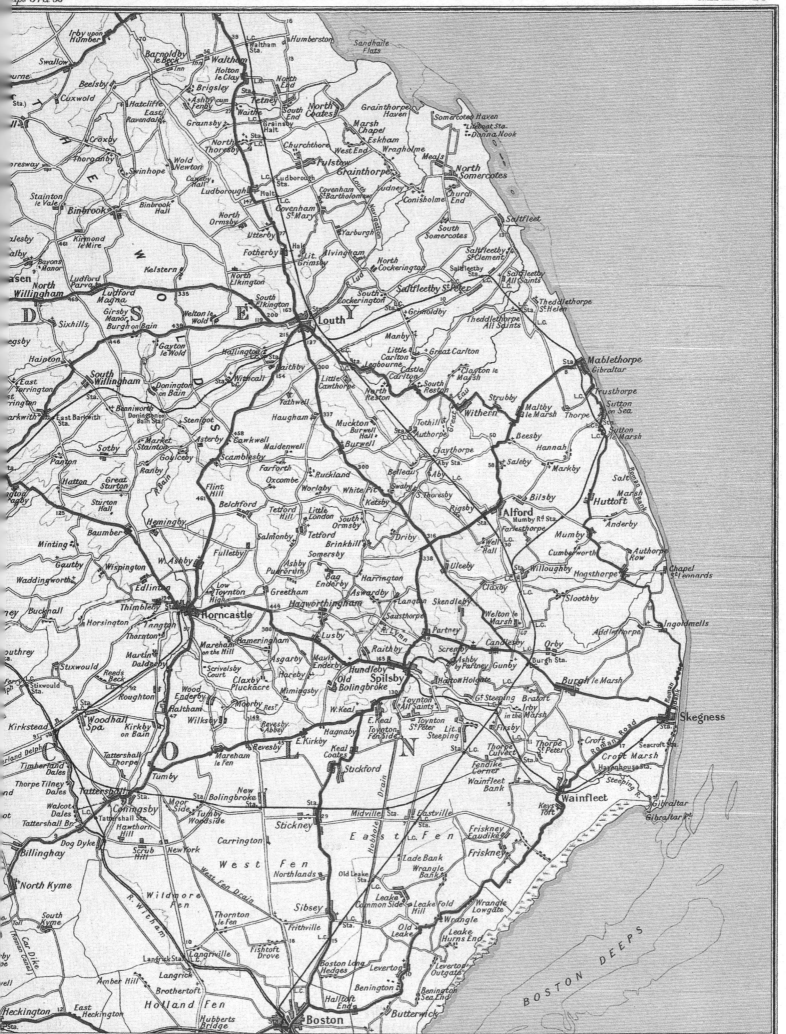

John Bartholomew & Son.Ltd.Edinburgh

Main Roads ━━━ **Other Roads** ═══ **Railways** ━━━

MAP 44

Continued

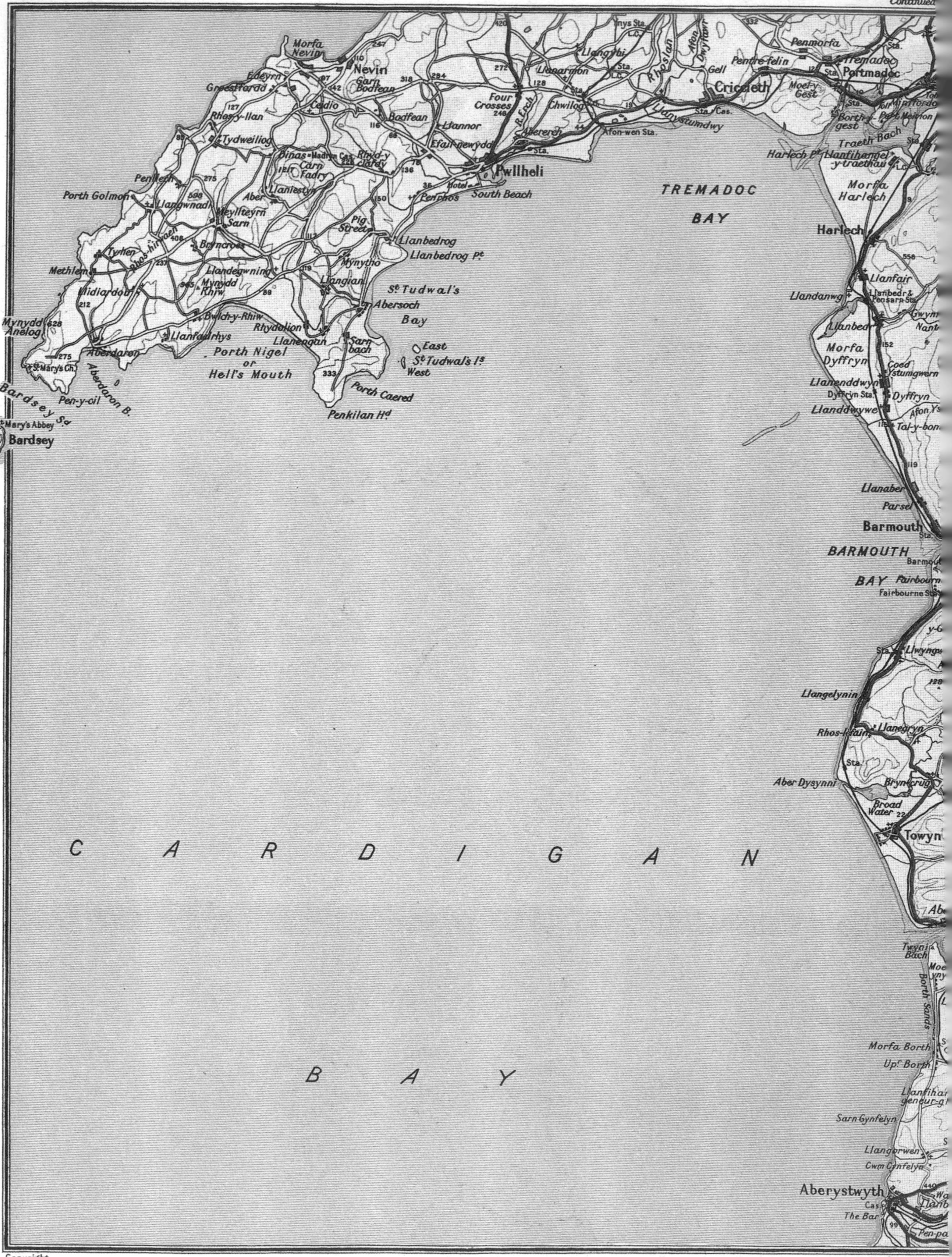

Morfa Nevin
Nevin
Edeyrn
Greestardd
Rhos-y-llan
Tydweiliog
Penllech
Porth Golmon
Llangwnadl
Methlem
Tyllen
Uidiardou
Mynydd Anelog
St Mary's Ch.
Bardsey S.d
St Mary's Abbey
Bardsey
Pen-y-cil
Aberdaron B.
Aberdaron
Porth Nigel
or
Hell's Mouth

Garn Bodfean
Ceidio
Bodfean
Dinas
Carn Fadry
Rhiw-y-clafdy
Aber
Llaniestyn
Meyllteyrn
Sarn
Bryncroes
Llandegwning
Mynydd Rhiw
Bwlch-y-Rhiw
Llanfaelrhys
Rhydolion
Llanengan
Llangian
Mynytho
Pig Street
Efail newydd
Llannor
Efail-newydd
Four Crosses
Llenarmon
Chwilog
Afon-wen Sta.
Aberereh
Pwllheli
Penrhos
Hotel
South Beach
Llanbedrog
Llanbedrog P.t
Abersoch
St Tudwal's Bay
Sarn bach
East
West
St Tudwal's I.s
Porth Caered
Penkilan H.d

Llangybi
Sta.
Rhoslan
Afon Dwyfar
Gell
Pentre-felin
Penmorfa
Tremadoc
Portmadoc
Moel-y-Gest
Borth-y-gest
Traeth Bach
Harlech P.t
Llanfihangel-y-traethau
Cricieth
Llanystumdwy

TREMADOC
BAY

Morfa Harlech
Harlech
Llanfair
Llandanwg
Llanbedr & Pensarn Sta.
Llanbedr
Morfa Dyffryn
Coed Ystumgwern
Llanenddwyn
Dyffryn Sta.
Dyffryn
Llanddwywe
Tal-y-bont
Llanaber
Parsel
Barmouth
BARMOUTH
BAY
Fairbourn
Fairbourne Sta.
Llwyngw
Llangelynin
Rhos-Ifain
Llanegryn
Aber Dysynni
Bryncrug
Broad Water
Towyn
Twyni Bach
Morfa Borth
Up.r Borth
Llanfihangel gendur-g
Sarn Gynfelyn
Llangorwen
Cwm Cynfelyn
Aberystwyth
The Bar

C A R D I G A N

B A Y

Scale of Miles
0 1 2 3 4 5 6 7 8 9 10

Continued on

MAP 45

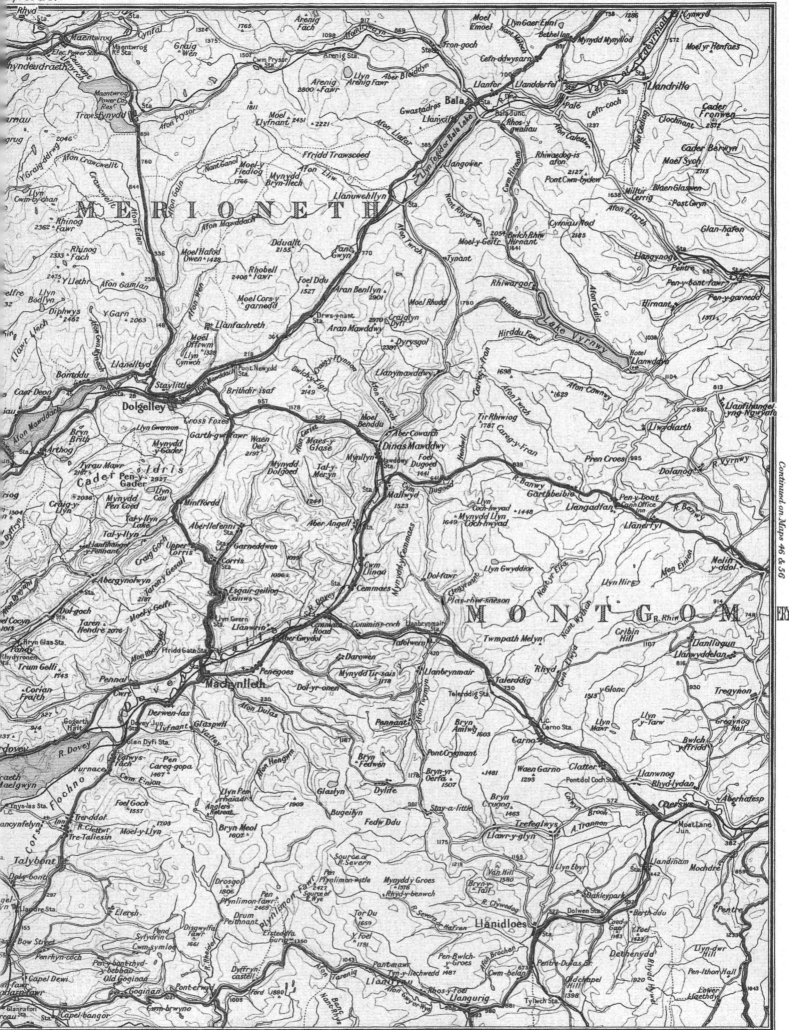

Continued on Maps 46 & 56

John Bartholomew & Son.Ltd.,Edinburgh

Main Roads ━━━━━ Other Roads ══════ Railways ━━━━━

MAP 46

PART OF FLINT

MONTGOMERY

SHRO...

Corwen
Druid
Llangar
Llangollen
Rhosllanerchrugos
Ruabon
Chirk
Oswestry
Ellesmere
Welshpool
Llanfair
Caereinion
Montgomery
Newtown
Bishops Castle
Church Stretton
Hope Bowdler
Little Stretton
All Stretton

Llantysilio Mountain
Valle Crucis Abbey
Castell Dinas Bran
Vale of Llangollen
Llandrillo
Cader Fronwen
Cader Berwyn
Moel Sych
Llanrhaiadr yn-Mochnant
Llanfyllin
Meifod
Berriew
Garthmyl
Tregynon
Llandinam
Mochdre

Shropshire Union Canal
Long Mountain
The Long Mynd
Clun Forest
Offa's Dyke

Scale of Miles
0 1 2 3 4 5 6 7 8 9 10

Continued on Maps 37 & 45

Maps 38 & 39

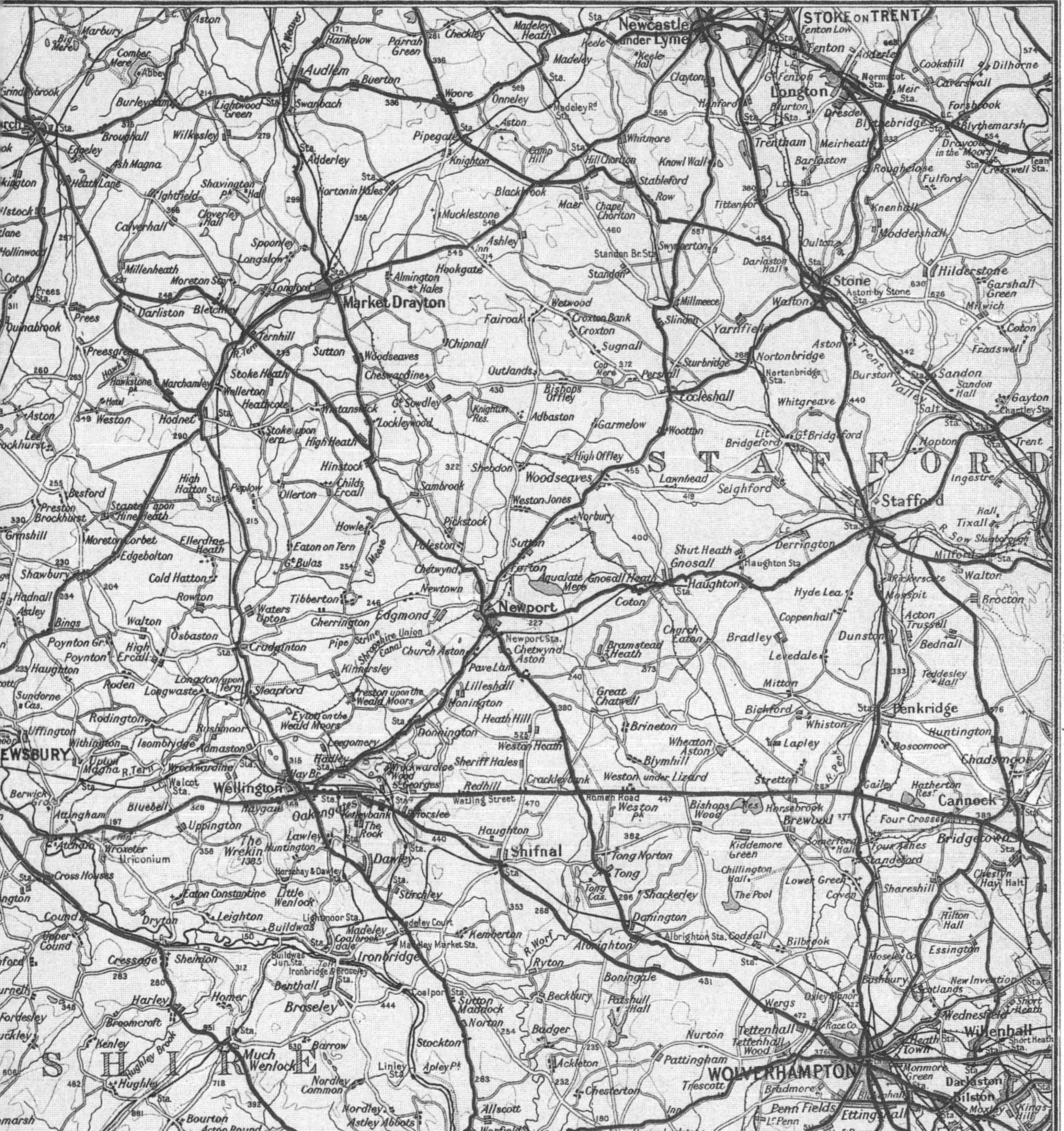
STAFFORD
SHIRE
Stoke on Trent
Newcastle under Lyme
Longton
Fenton
Audlem
Market Drayton
Newport
Wellington
Shifnal
Stafford
Stone
Eccleshall
Penkridge
Cannock
Brewood
Wolverhampton
Bridgnorth
Much Wenlock
Ironbridge
Broseley
Dawley
Oakengates
Hodnet
Sedgley
Tipton
Dudley
Bilston
Willenhall
Wednesfield
Stourbridge
Brierley Hill
Halesowen
Ettingshall
Coseley
Madeley
Woodseaves
Whitmore
Trentham
Cheswardine
Gnosall
Haughton
Tong
Albrighton
Codsall
Pattingham
Claverley
Quatt
Enville
Kinver
The Wrekin
Uriconium
Watling Street
Shropshire Union Canal
Aqualate Mere
R. Severn
R. Tern
R. Penk
R. Sow
R. Trent
Trent Valley

Continued on Map 48

Maps 56 & 57

John Bartholomew & Son. Ltd. Edinburgh

Main Roads ——— Other Roads ——— Railways ———

MAP 48

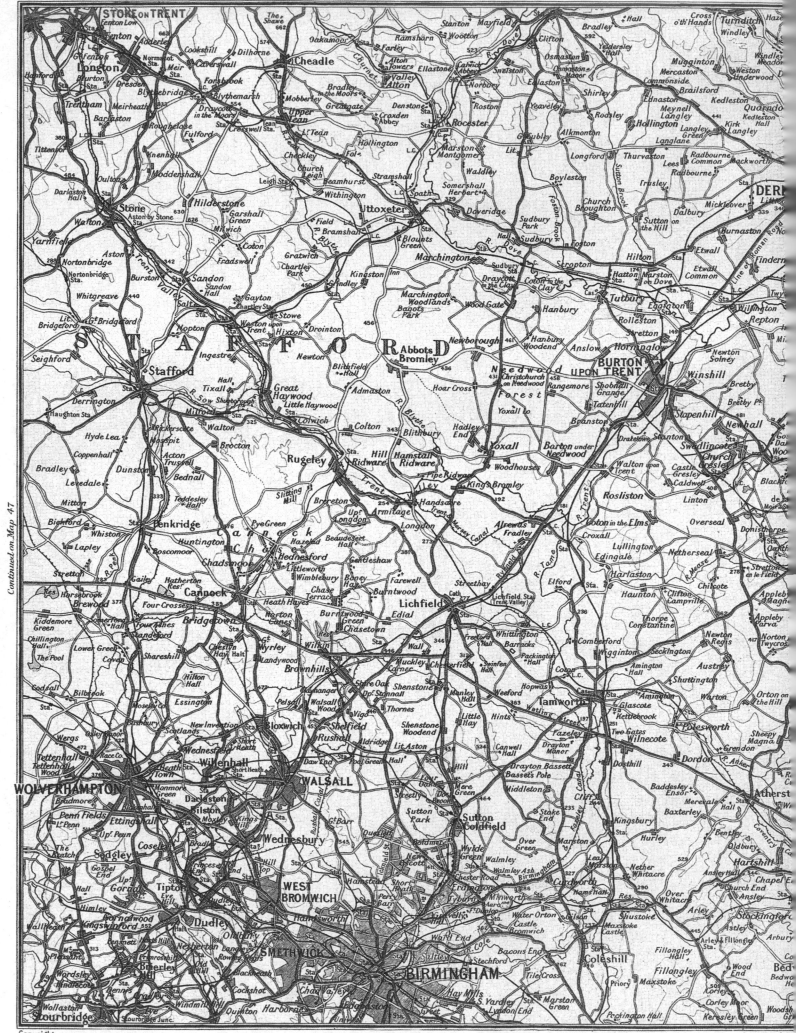

Scale of Miles

0 1 2 3 4 5 6 7 8 9 10

Continued on Map 47

MAP 49

Maps 40, & 41

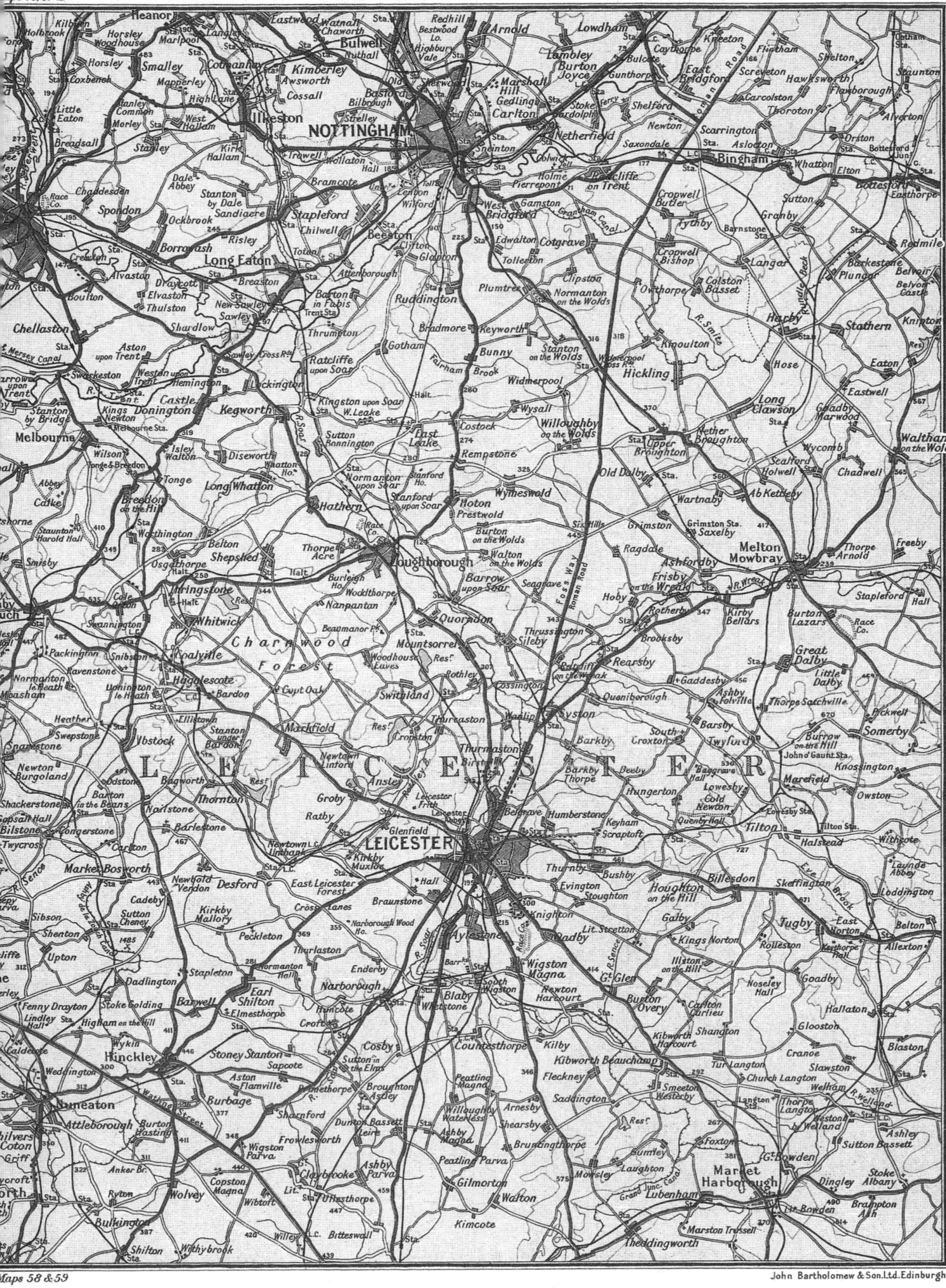

NOTTINGHAM

LEICESTER

Charnwood Forest

Loughborough

Melton Mowbray

Hinckley

Market Harborough

Continued on Map 50

Maps 58 & 59

John Bartholomew & Son Ltd. Edinburgh

Main Roads ———   Other Roads ———   Railways ———

MAP 50

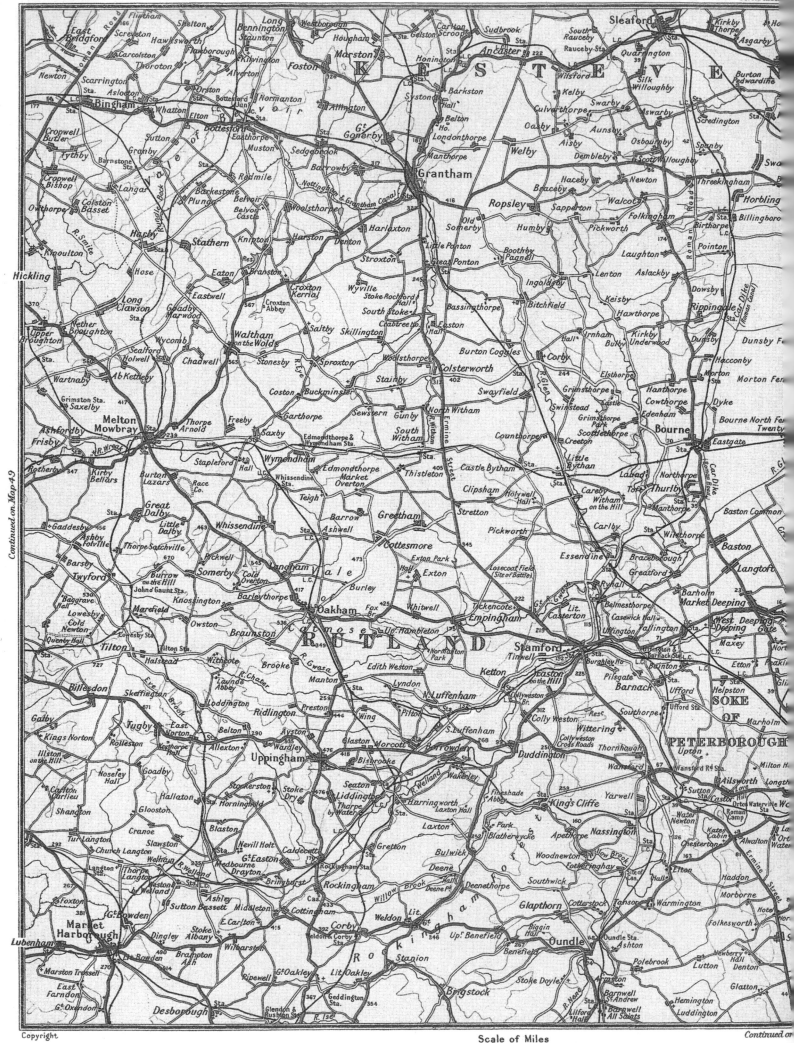

Continued on Map 49

Scale of Miles

0 1 2 3 4 5 6 7 8 9 10

MAP 51

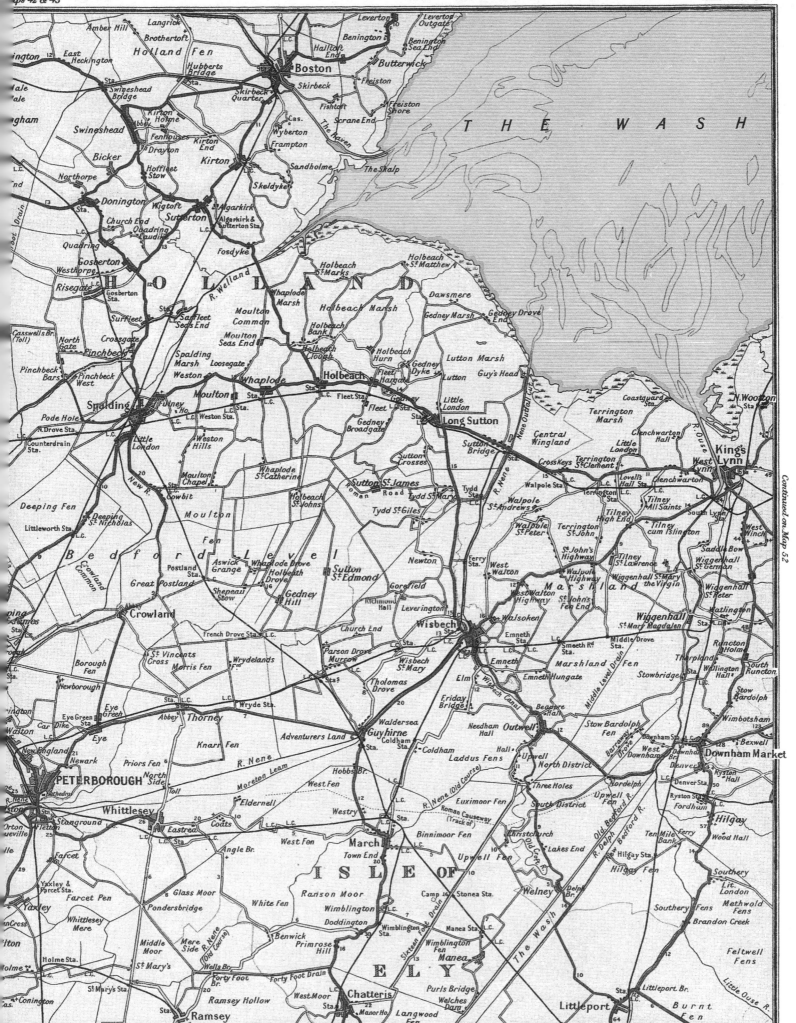

THE WASH

HOLLAND

Bedford Level

ISLE OF

ELY

Main Roads ———— Other Roads ════ Railways ————

Continued on Map 52

MAP 52

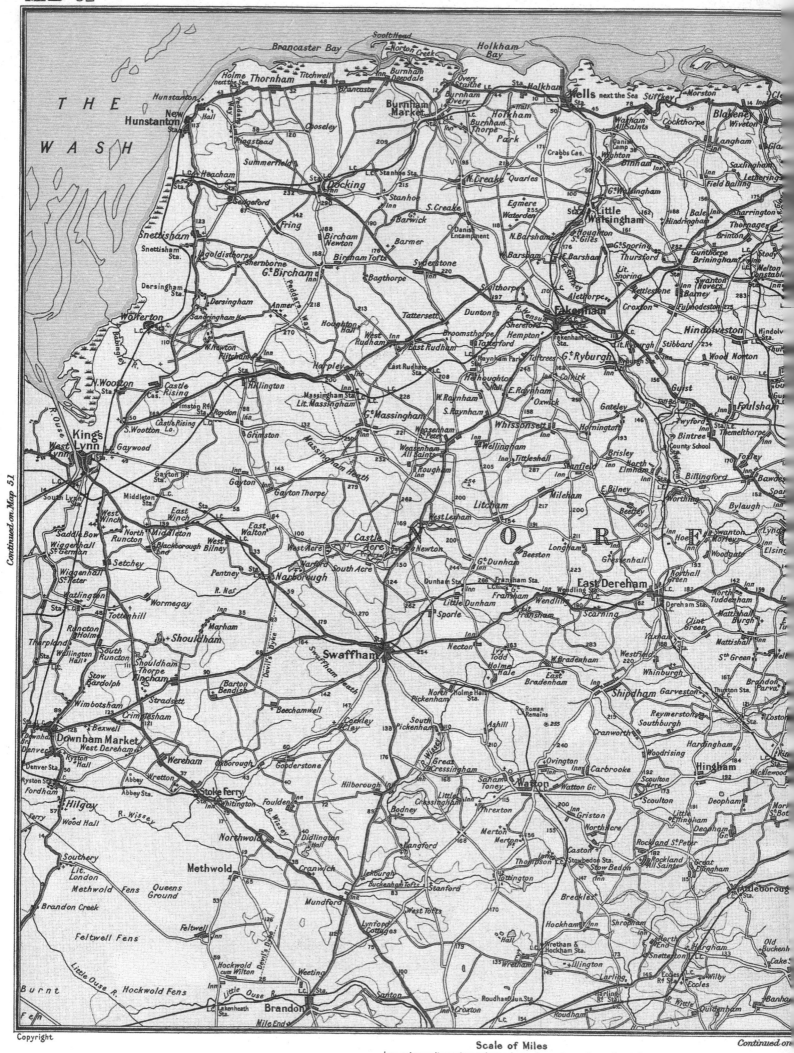

THE WASH

Scale of Miles

0 1 2 3 4 5 6 7 8 9 10

Continued on Map 51

Continued on

MAP 53

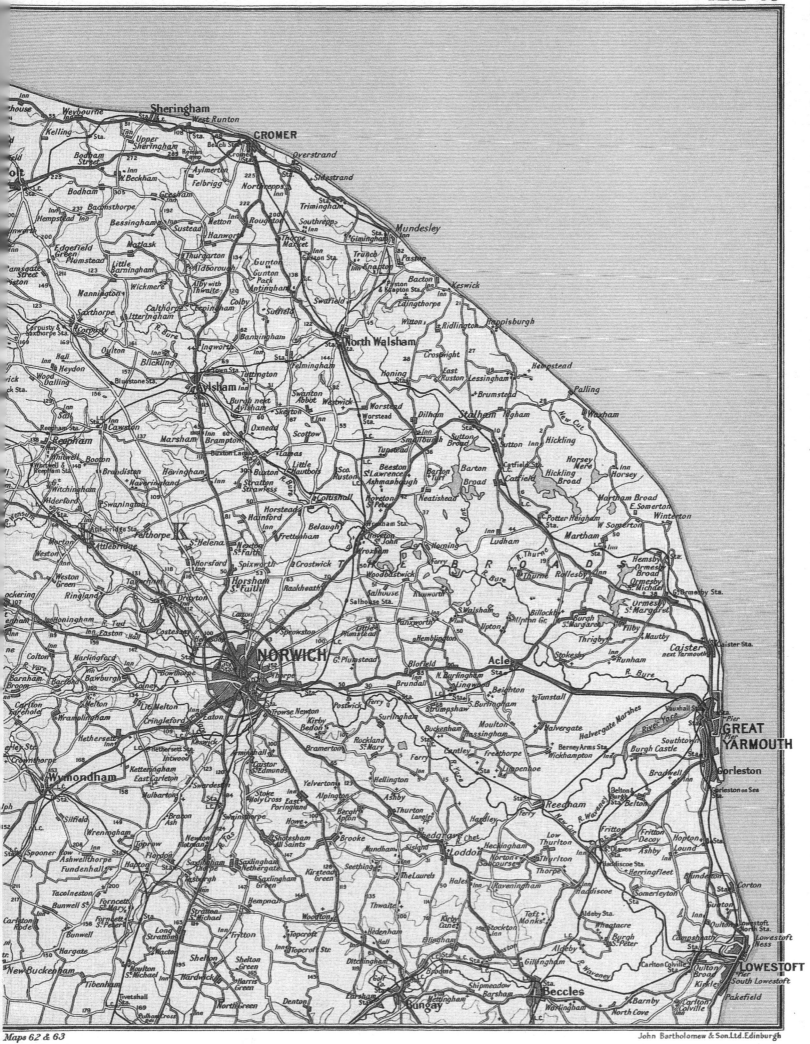

John Bartholomew & Son Ltd. Edinburgh

Main Roads —————— Other Roads ══════ Railways ——————

MAP 54

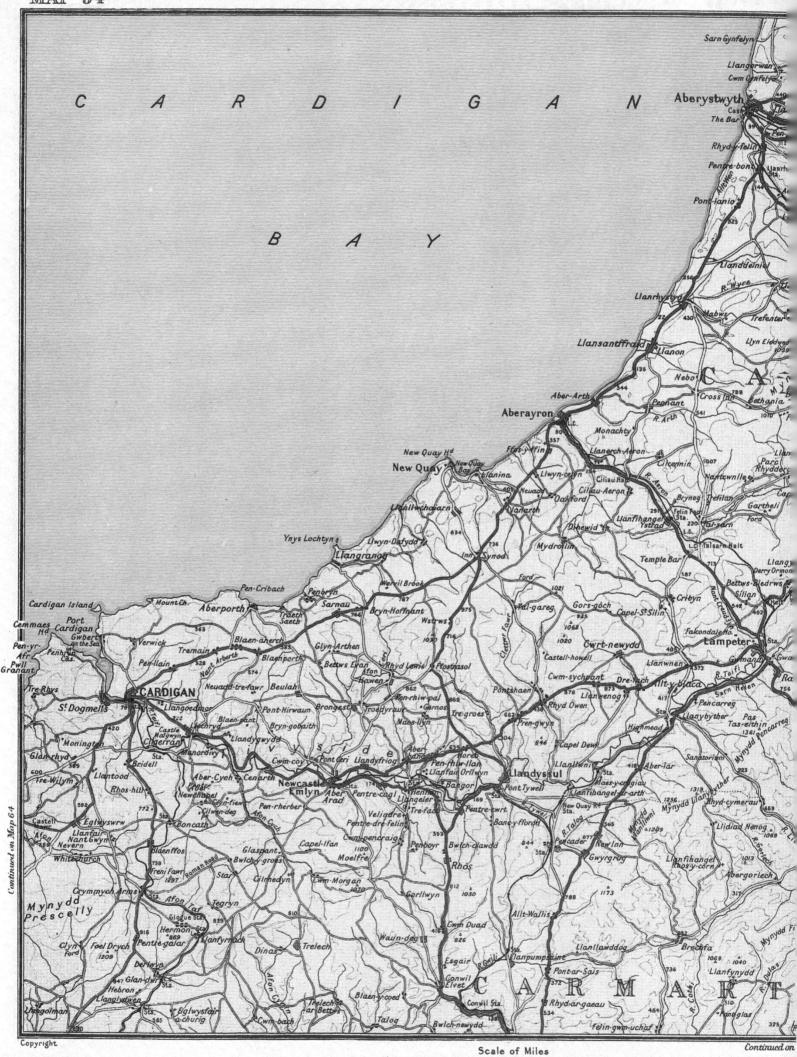

C A R D I G A N

B A Y

Aberystwyth

Sarn Gynfelyn

Llangorwan
Cwm Cynfelyn

Cas
The Bar

Rhyd-y-felin

Pentre-bont

Pont-lanio

Llanddeiniol

R. Wyre

Llanrhystyd

Mabws
Trefenter

Llansantffraid
Llanon

Llyn Eiddwen
1039

Nebo
CA
Cross Inn

Aber-Arth

Peithant
Bethania

Aberayron

Monachty

Cilcennin

Parc
Rhyddech

New Quay Hd
New Quay Bay

Ffos-y-ffin

Llanerch-Aeron

Nantcwnlles

New Quay

Llanina

Llwyn-celyn

Ciliau Hall
R. Aeron

Brynog
Trefilan

Neuadd
Oakford

Ciliau-Aeron

Felin Fach Sta.
Gartheli

Lldallwchoiarn

Nanarth

Dihewid

Llanfihangel
Ystrad

Talsarn

ford

Ynys Lochtyn

Llwyn-Dafydd

Mydroilin

Temple Bar

Llangy
Derry Ormon

Llangranog

Inn
Synod

Ford

Bettws-Bledrws
Silian

Pen-Cribach

Penbryn

Werril Brook

Cribyn

Cardigan Island

S. Mount Ch.

Aberporth

Sarnau

Bryn-Hoffnant

Tal-gareg

Gors-goch

Capel-St-Silin

Falcondale Ho.

Cemmaes Hd
Port
Cardigan

Gwbert
on the Sea

Verwick

Traeth
Saeth

Wstrws

Cletwr Fawr

Cwrt-newydd

Lampeter
Sta.

Pen-yr-
Afr
Pwll
Granant

Penrhyn
Cas.

Tremain

Blaen-anerch

Glyn-Arthen

Castell-howell

Llanwnen

Pen-llain

Blaenporth

Bettws Evan

Rhyd Lewis
Frostrasol

Pontshaen

Dre-fach

Allt-y-blaca

Tre-Rhys

Neuadd-tre-fawr

Beulah

Afon
Hawen

Rhyd Owen

Llanwenog

Pencarreg

CARDIGAN

Llangoedmor

Pont-Hirwaun

Brongest
Troedyraur

Garnos

Pen-rhiw-pal

Tre-groes

Pren-gwyn

Highmead

St. Dogmells

Blaen-pant
Llechryd

Bryn-gobaith

Maes-llyn

Capel Dewi

Aber-lar

Monington

Castle
Malgwyn
Cilgerran

Llandygwydd

Aber
band

Horeb

Llanllwni

Glan-rhyd

Bridell

Manordivy

Cwm-cou

Pont Ceri

Llandyfriog

Pen-rhiw-llan

Llandyssul

Llanfihangel-ar-arth

Rhyd-cymerau

Llantood

Rhos-hill

Aber-Cych
Cenarth

Newcastle
Emlyn

Llangeler

Bangor
Pont Tywell

New Quay Rd
Sta.

Llanfihangel-ar-arth

Eglwyswrw

Clyn-fiew

Pen-rherber

Aber
Arad

Pentre-cagl

Pencarreg

Boncath

Afon Cych

Velindre

Pentre-cwrt

Bancyffordd

Pencader

New Inn

Llidiad Nenog

Llanfair
Nantbwyn
Nevern

Cilwen-deg

Whitechurch

Blaenffos

Glaspant

Capel-Ifan

Penthe-dre-felin

Cwmpencraig

Penboyr

Bwlch-clawdd

Gwyrgrog

Llanfihangel
Rhos-y-corn

Abergorlech

Crymmych Arms

Freni Fawr
1297

Roman Road

Bwlch-y-groes

Moelfre

Rhos

Gorllwyn

Cwm-Morgan

Allt-Wallis

Llanllawddog

Brechfa

Clyn
Ford

Foel Drych
1208

Star

Cilrhedyn

Cwm Duad

Llanfynydd

Hermon

Dinas

Trelech

Waun-deg

Esgair

Llanpumpsaint

Pont-ar-Sais

Pentre-galar
Llanfyrnach

Derlwyn

Glan-dwr

Blaen-y-coed

Conwil
Elvet

Rhyd-ar-gaeau

felin-gwm-uchaf

Hebron
Llanglydwen

Eglwysfair
a-churig

Trelech
ar Bettws

Talog

Bwlch-newydd

Conwil Sta.

Mynydd
Prescelly

CARMART

Continued on Map 6-4

Continued on

Scale of Miles

0 1 2 3 4 5 6 7 8 9 10

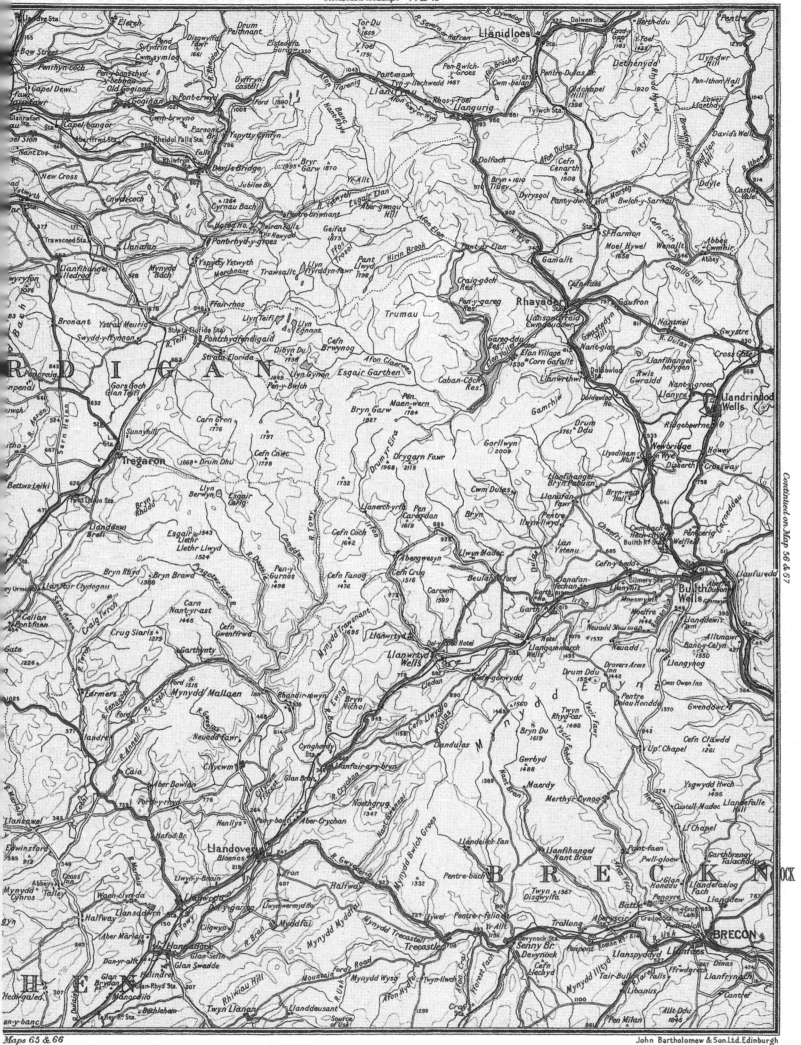

Main Roads ━━━━━ Other Roads ══════ Railways ━━━━━

Continued on Map 56 & 57

MAP 56

Continued o

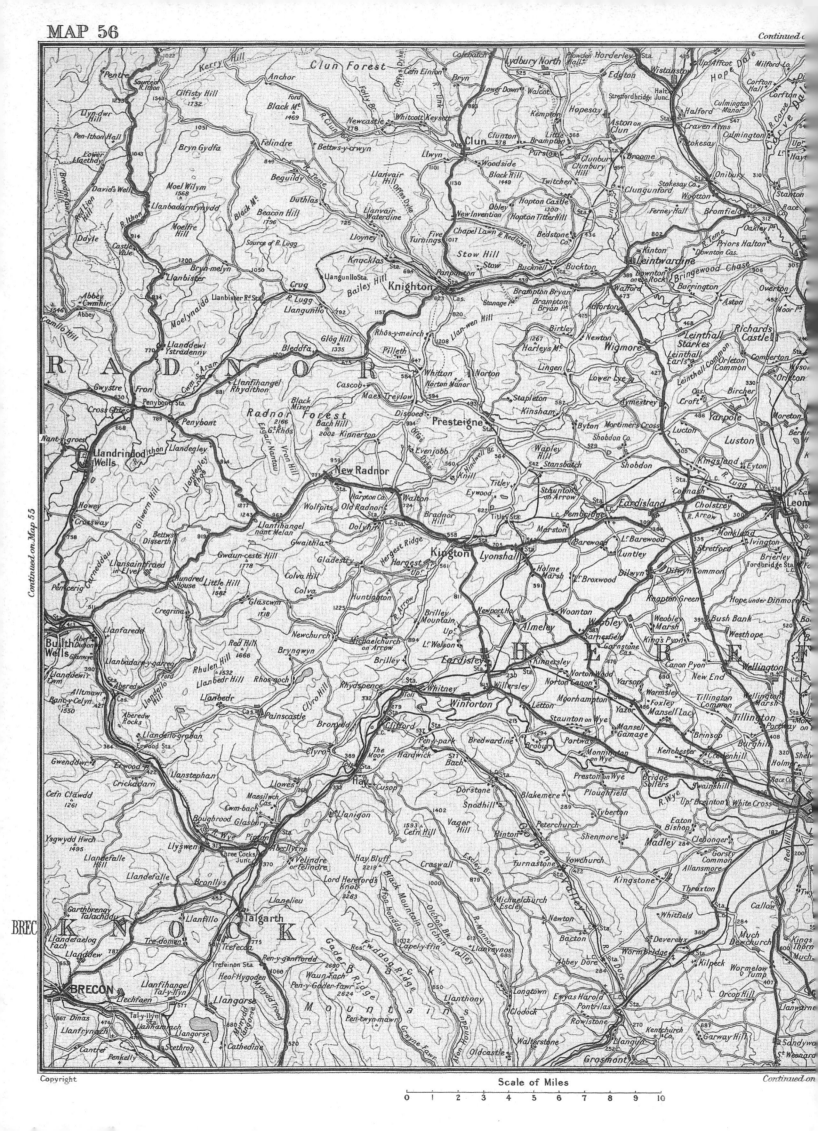

Scale of Miles

0 1 2 3 4 5 6 7 8 9 10

WORCESTER

HEREFORD

Kidderminster
Stourbridge
Halesowen
Bromsgrove
Droitwich
Great Malvern
Malvern Wells
Upton upon Severn
Tewkesbury
Pershore
Ledbury
Newent
Ross
Bromyard
Tenbury
Cleobury Mortimer
Bewdley
Stourport
Clee Hill

John Bartholomew & Son.Ltd.Edinburgh

Continued on Map 58

Main Roads ——— Other Roads ═══ Railways ┼┼┼┼

MAP 58

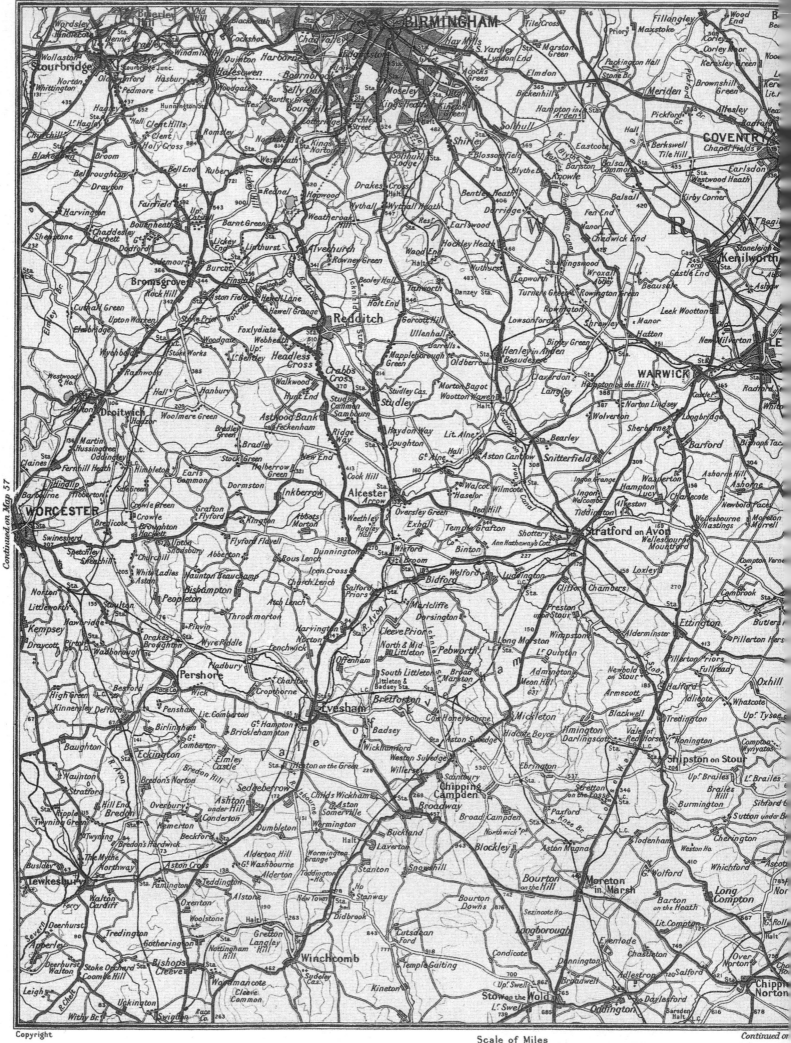

Scale of Miles

0 1 2 3 4 5 6 7 8 9 10

Maps 48 & 49

NORTHAMPT
ON
Lubenham
Walton
Kimcote
Ullesthorpe
Bitteswell
Lutterworth
Misterton
Walcote
N. Kilworth
Husbands Bosworth
Theddingworth
Marston Trussell
East Farndon
Gt. Oxendon
Sibbertoft
Clipston
Desborough
Rothwell
Arthingworth
Kelmarsh
Harrington
Orton
Loddington
Naseby
Welford
S. Kilworth
Swinford
Shawell
Churchover
Cotesbach
Stanford on Avon
Catthorpe
Lilbourne
Yelvertoft
Claycoton
Cold Ashby
Thornby
Haselbech
Maidwell
Draughton
Lamport
Faxton
Cottesbrooke
Hanging Houghton
Scaldwell
Old or Wold
Walgrave
Hannington
Brixworth
Creaton
Spratton
Teeton
Ravensthorpe
Guilsborough
Hollowell
Winwick
West Haddon
Crick
Kilsby
Barby
Hillmorton
RUGBY
Bilton
Dunchurch
Clifton upon Dunsmore
Newbold on Avon
Brinklow
Binley
Stoke
Walsgrave on Sowe
Bell Green
Shilton
Ansty
Withybrook
Monks Kirby
Pailton
Harborough Magna
Easenhall
Newnham Paddox
Wibtoft
Bulkington
Ryton
Brandon
Bretford
Lit. Lawford
Church Lawford
Long Lawford
Wolston
Ryton on Dunsmore
Stretton on Dunsmore
Bubbenhall
Princethorpe
Frankton
Thurlaston
Bourton on Dunsmore
Draycote
Birdingbury
Marton
Leamington Hastings
Grandborough
Kites Hardwick
Willoughby
Braunston
Long Itchington
Broadwell
Wolfhampcote
Napton & Stockton Sta.
Flecknoe Sta.
Flecknoe
Stockton
Southam
Napton on the Hill
Shuckburgh
Daventry
Borough Hill
Staverton
Welton
Norton
Long Buckby
Long Buckby Wharf
Whilton
East Haddon
Holdenby
Althorp Park Sta.
Gt. Brington
Lit. Brington
Harlestone
Church Brampton
Chapel Brampton
Pitsford
Moulton
Boughton
Kingsthorpe
Sywell
NORTHAMPTON
Weston Favell
Lit. Billing
Duston
Upton
Harpole
Kislingbury
Upr. Heyford
Nether
Floore
Weedon Beck
Dodford
Newnham
Brockhall
Badby
Catesby
Hellidon
Priors Marston
Priors Hardwick
Ladbroke
Harbury
Bishops Itchington
Lighthorne
Gaydon
Knightcote
Charwelton
Fawsley
Gt. Everdon
Upper Stowe
Bugbrooke
Rothersthorpe
Milton
Hardingstone
Wootton
Collingtree
Preston Deanery
Quinton
Piddington
Hackleton
Farthingstone
Litchborough
Pattishall
Eastcote
Gayton
Blisworth
Courteenhall
Roade
Salcey Forest
Hartwell
Ashton
Hanslope
Preston Capes
Byfield
Upr. Boddington
Wormleighton
Hinton
Woodford Halse
West Farndon
Aston le Walls
Maidford
Adstone
Foxley
Grimscote
Cold Higham
Tiffield
Blakesley
Duncote
Greens Norton
Towcester
Shutlanger
Stoke Bruerne
Fenny Compton
North End
Kineton
Boddington
Claydon
Avon Dassett
Farnborough
Warmington
Radway
Ratley
Mollington
Cropredy
Shotteswell
Chipping Warden
Eydon
Canons Ashby
Moreton Pinkney
Culworth
Plumpton
Woodend
Bradden
Slapton
Abthorpe
Wood Burcote
Paulerspury
Alderton
Grafton Regis
Yardley Gobion
Long Street
Castle Thorpe
Potterspury
Cosgrove
Wappenham
Weedon Lois
Weston
Sulgrave
Wardington
Williamscot
Gt. Bourton
Hanwell
Horley
Hornton
Alkerton
Shenington
Balscott
Wroxton
Drayton
Chalcombe
Thorpe Mandeville
Marston St. Lawrence
Middleton Cheney
Helmdon
Syresham
Silverstone
Whittlebury
Whittlewood Forest
Wakefield Lo.
Old Stratford
Stony Stratford
Wolverton
Denshanger
Passenham
Calverton
Wicken
Lillingstone Lovell
Lillingstone Dayrell
Biddlesden
Radstone
Whitfield
Greatworth
Warkworth
Banbury
Neithrop
Grimsbury
Farthinghoe
Steane
Brackley
Turweston
Shalstone
Dadford
Stowe
Akeley
Leckhampstead
Chackmore
Maids Moreton
Foscott
Thornton
Beachampton
Upper Weald
Shenley Church End
Nash
Whaddon Chase
Thornborough
Buckingham
Water Stratford
Finmere
Mixbury
Evenley
Westbury
Hinton in the Hedges
Charlton
Kings Sutton
Aynho
Croughton
Adderbury
Bodicote
Bloxham
Milton
Tadmarton
Tadmarton Heath
Broughton
Sibford Ferris
Swalcliffe
N. Newington
Shutford
Milcombe
Wiggington
Newington
Barford St. John
Barford St. Michael
Swerford
Clifton
Deddington
Souldern
Hempton
Nether Worton
Over Worton
Gt. Tew
Lit. Tew
Heythorp
Ledwell
Duns Tew
N. Aston
Mid Aston
Sandford St. Martin
Westcott Barton
Church Enstone
Steeple Aston
Upr. Heyford
Somerton
Fewcott
Fritwell
Ardley
Bucknell
Cottisford
Tusmore Ho.
Hardwick
Baynards Green
Stoke Lyne
Bethe
Fringford
Newton Purcell
Barton Hartshorn
Chetwode
Gawcott
Tingewick
Preston Bissett
Hillesden
Cowley
Steeple Claydon
Mid Claydon
Twyford
Stratton Audley
Padbury
Adstock
Gt. Horwood
Lit. Horwood
The Common
Winslow
Swanbourne
Watling Street
Grand Junc. Canal
Oxford Canal
R. Avon
R. Leam
R. Nene
R. Tove
R. Ouse
R. Cherwell
R. Swere
R. Stour
Fosse Way
Edge Hill
Dunsmore Heath

Continued on Map 60

Maps 68, 69 & 70

John Bartholomew & Son.Ltd.Edinburgh

Main Roads ——— Other Roads ═══ Railways ———

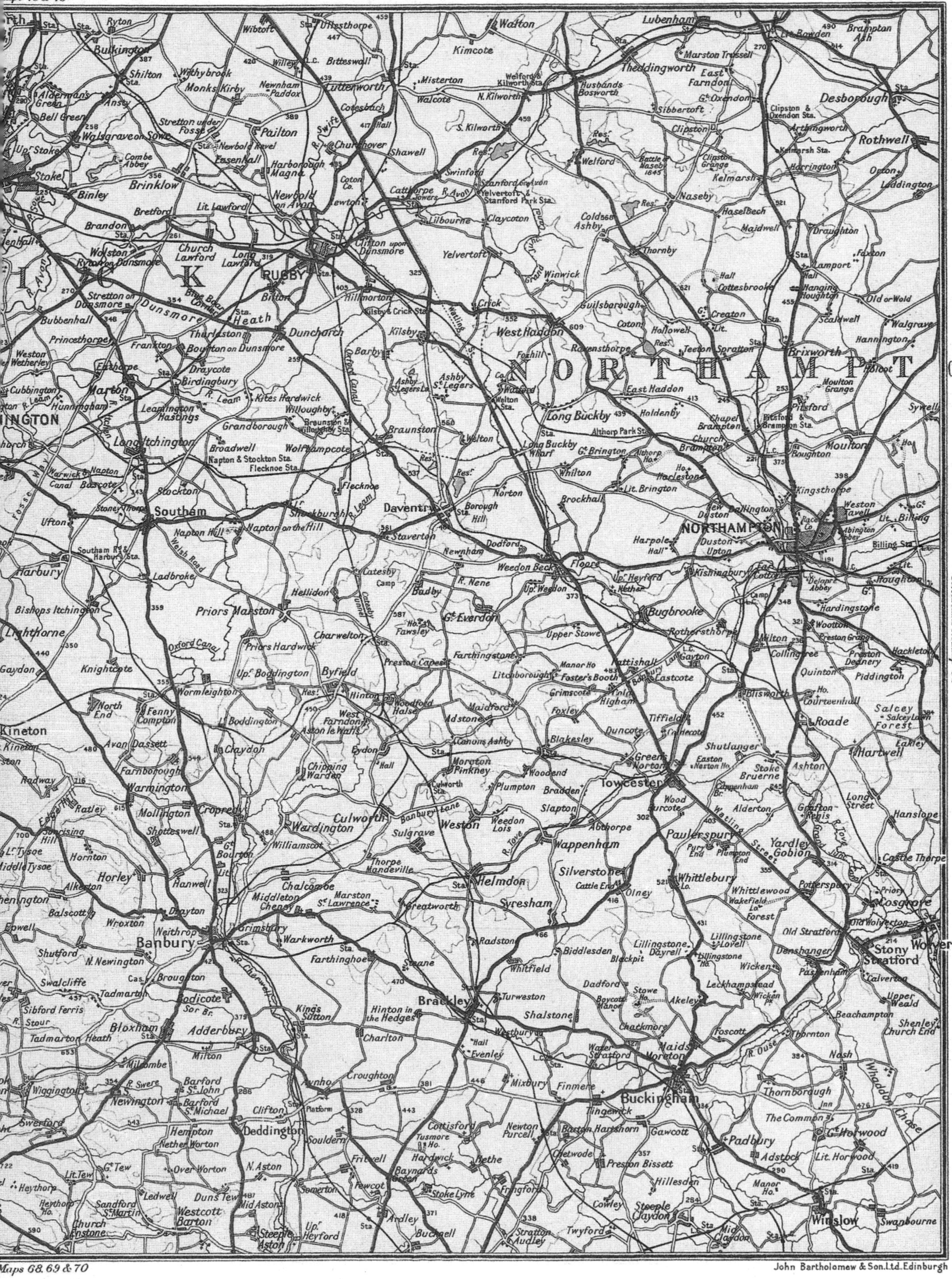

MAP 60

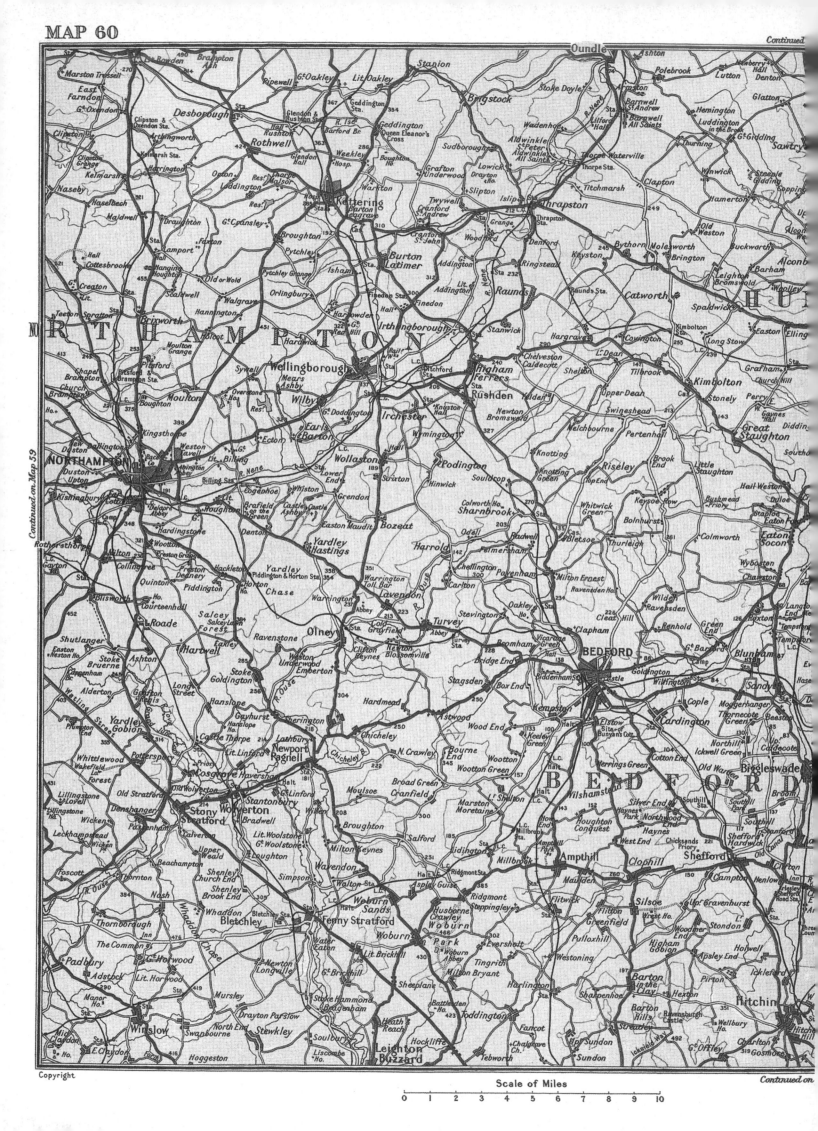

Continued on Map 59

Continued on

Scale of Miles

0 1 2 3 4 5 6 7 8 9 10

MAP 61

John Bartholomew & Son Ltd. Edinburgh

Continued on Map 62

Main Roads —————— Other Roads ══════ Railways ————

MAP 62

Continued

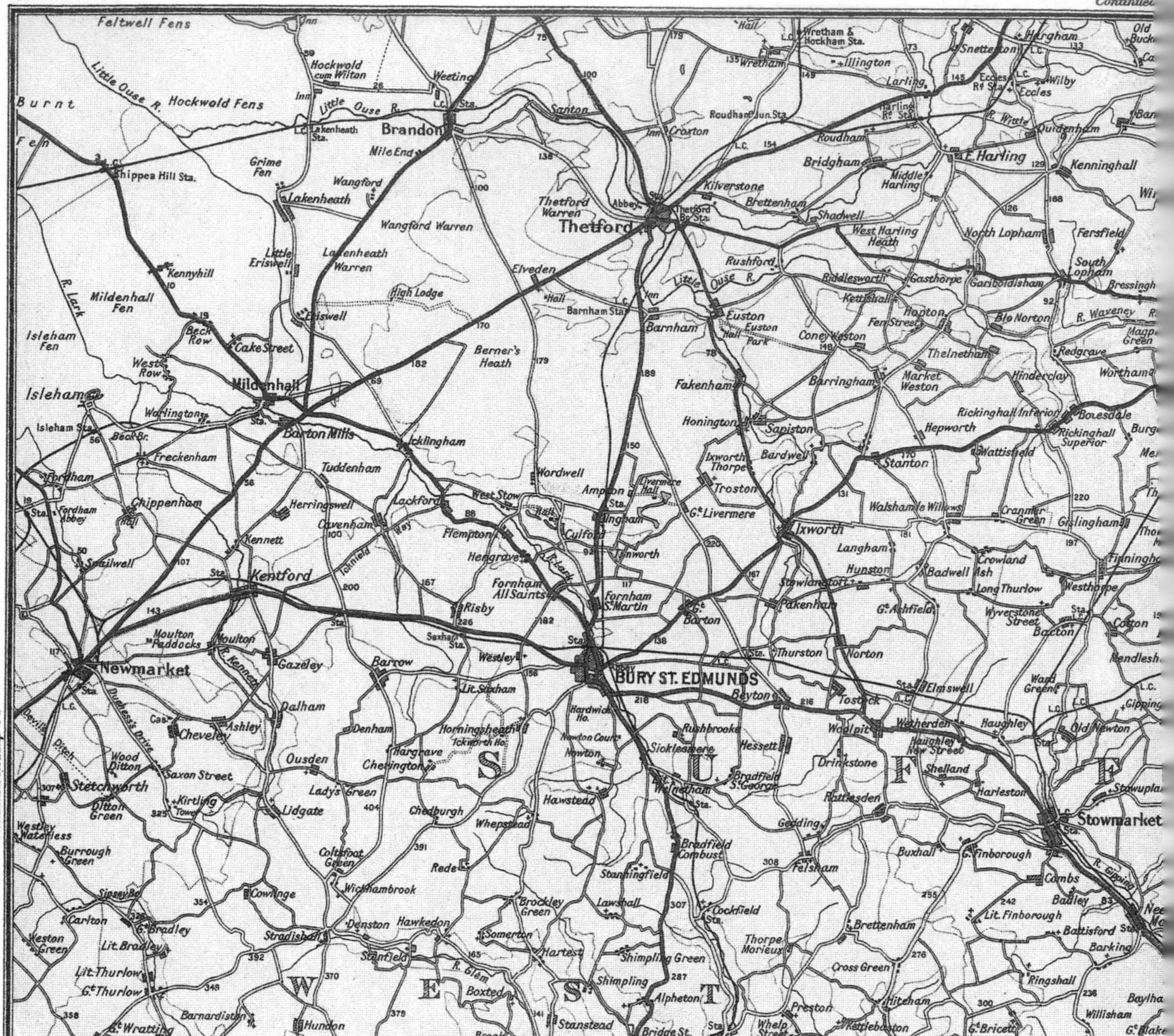

Feltwell Fens

Burnt Fen

Little Ouse R. Hockwold Fens

Hockwold cum Wilton

Weeting

Brandon

Thetford Warren

Thetford

Mile End

Lakenheath

Wangford

Grime Fen

Kennyhill

Shippea Hill Sta.

R. Lark

Mildenhall Fen

Isleham Fen

Little Eriswell

Lakenheath Warren

Eriswell

West Row

Beck Row

Cake Street

Mildenhall

Isleham

Isleham Sta.

Beck Br.

Worlington

Fordham

Fordham Abbey

Chippenham

Freckenham

Barton Mills

Tuddenham

Icklingham

Herringswell

Cavenham

Lackford

West Stow

Wordwell

High Lodge

Berner's Heath

Elveden

Abbey

Euston

Barnham Sta.

Barnham

Euston Park

Fakenham

Kilverstone

Bridgham

Rushford

Little Ouse R.

Riddlesworth

Gasthorpe

Garboldisham

Kettlshall

Honington

Sapiston

Hopton

Blo Norton

Bardwell

Ixworth Thorpe

Troston

Stanton

Wattisfield

Rickinghall Inferior

Rickinghall Superior

Redgrave

Thelnetham

Hinderclay

Wortham

Botesdale

Freckenham

Fordham

Kennett

Kentford

Moulton Paddocks

Moulton

Newmarket

Gazeley

Dalham

Barrow

Saxham Sta.

Westley

Lit. Saxham

BURY ST. EDMUNDS

Fornham All Saints

Risby

Fornham S. Martin

Barton

Thurston

Norton

Elmswell

Beyton

Tostock

Woolpit

Wetherden

Haughley New Street

Haughley

Old Newton

Stowmarket

Combs

Badley

Lit. Finborough

Battisford

Barking

Ashley

Cheveley

Saxon Street

Kirtling

Lidgate

Denham

Chevington

Hargrave

Ousden

Ladys Green

Chedburgh

Whepstead

Hawstead

Hardwick Ho.

Horningsheath

Ickworth Ho.

Newton

Sickleamere

Hessett

Rushbrooke

Bradfield S. George

Drinkstone

Shelland

Harleston

Rattlesden

Felsham

Gedding

Buxhall

Finborough

Brettenham

Thorpe Morieux

Cross Green

Hitcham

Ringshall

Stetchworth

Ditton Green

Burrough Green

Carlton

Gt. Bradley

Lit. Bradley

Weston Green

Lit. Thurlow

Gt. Thurlow

Barnardiston

Hundon

Withersfield

Gt. Wratting

Haverhill

Lit. Wratting

Kedington

Clare

Cavendish

Stradishall

Cowlinge

Wickhambrook

Denston

Hawkedon

Stansfield

Somerton

Hartest

R. Glem

Boxted

Stanstead

Shimpling Green

Shimpling

Alpheton

Bridge St.

Whelp Street

Lavenham

Preston

Kettlebaston

Monks Eleigh

Bildeston

Nedging

Naughton

Chelsworth

Semer

Offton

Somersham

Poslingford

Brook Street

Glemsford

Chilton Street

Long Melford

High Street

Brent Eleigh

Milden

Lindsey

Whatfield

Elmsett

Flowton

Camps Green

Helion Bumpstead

Steeple Bumpstead

Birdbrook

Ridgewell

Ashen

Stoke by Clare

Tilbury juxta Clare

Okington

Puttock End

Belchamp S. Pauls

Belchamp Otton

Belchamp Walter

Bulmer

Borley

Liston

Foxearth

Pentlow

Acton

Lit. Walding Field

Gt. Walding Field

The Heath

Kersey

Aldham

Hadleigh

Hadleigh Heath

Burstall

Hempstead

Spencer Grange

Stambourne

Toppesfield

Gt. Yeldham

Gestingthorpe

Henny Street

Sudbury

Gt. Cornard

Newton

Edwardstone

Groton

Boxford

Layham

Raydon

Cornishhall End

Bar Hall

Highstreet Gr.

Sible Hedingham

Castle Hedingham

Wickham S. Pauls

Lamarsh

Alphamstone

Twinstead

Bures Green

Assington

Polstead

Shelley

Lit. Samford

Finchingfield

Lit. Bardfield

Gt. Bardfield

Howe

Swan Str.

Lit. Maplestead

Gt. Maplestead

Ashford Lo.

Pebmarch

The Howe

Halstead

Gosfield

Colne Engaine

White Colne

Mount Bures

Bures

Wissington

Wormingford

Lit. Horkesley

Gt. Horkesley

Nayland

Stoke by Nayland

Honey Tye

Thorington St.

Holton S. Mary

Stratford S. Mary

Dedham

Langham

Boxted

Lamb Corner

Shalford

Blackmore End

Gosfield Hall

Wethersfield

Continued on Map 61

WEST SUFFOLK

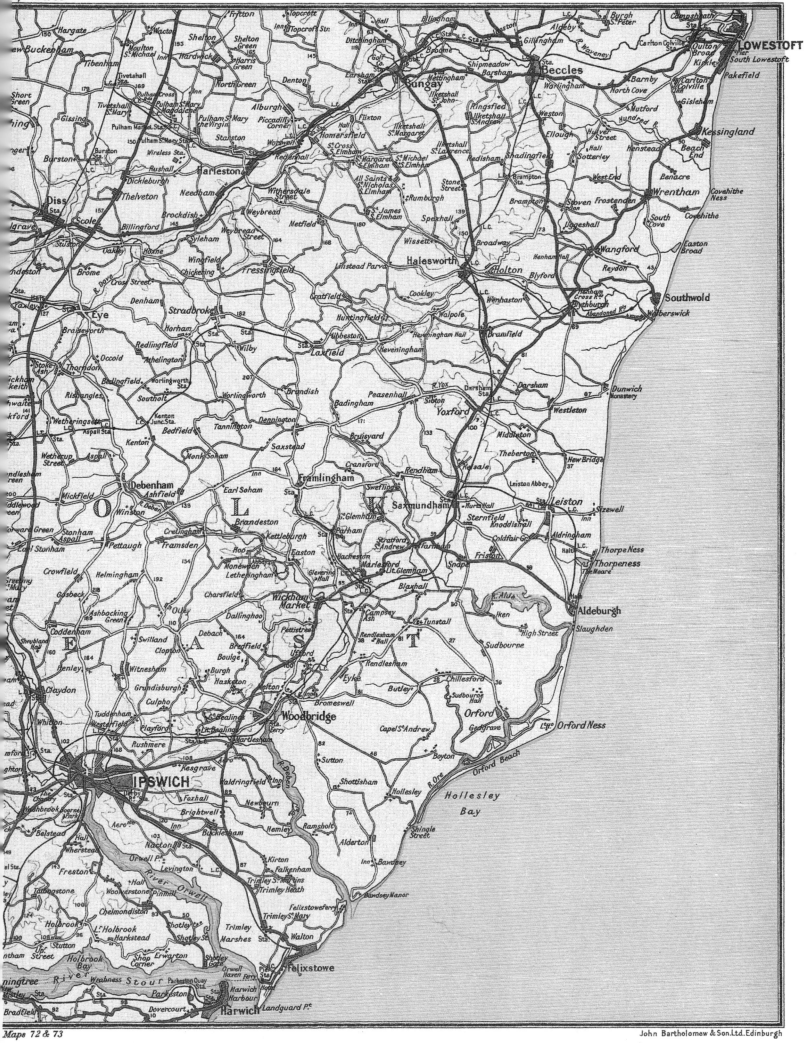

Main Roads ═══ Other Roads ═══ Railways ─────

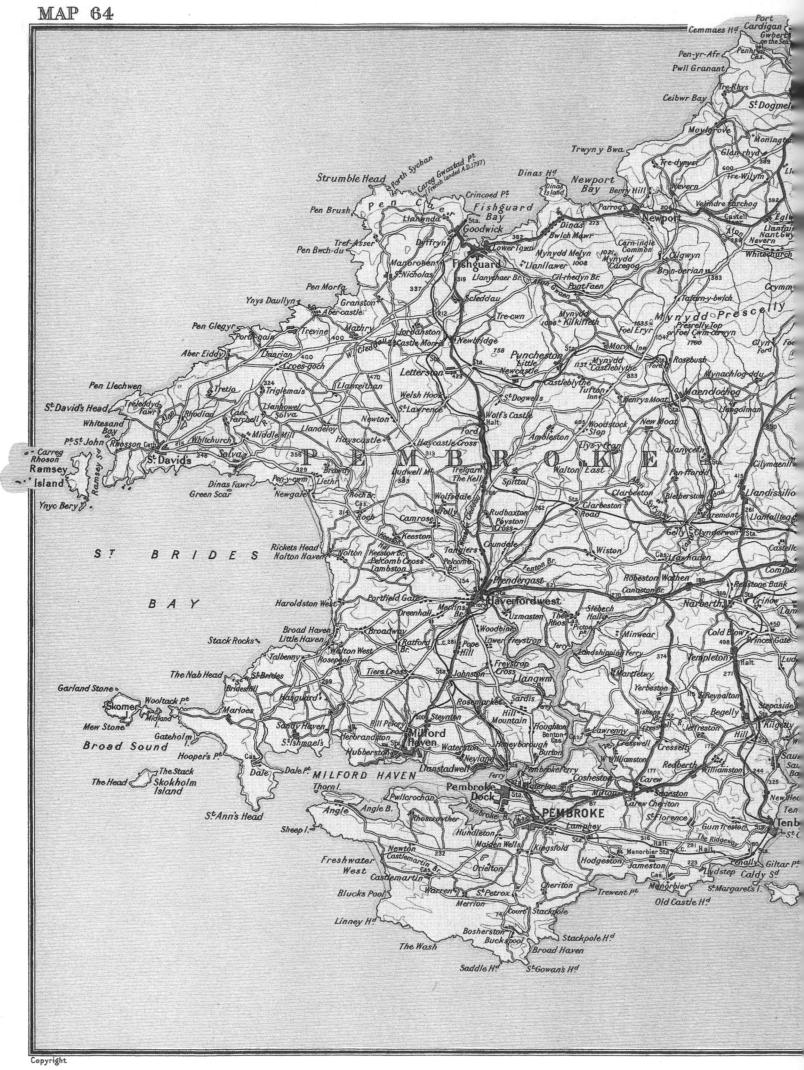

MAP 64

Main Roads ——————   Other Roads ==========   Railways ———————

CARMARTHEN

CARMARTHEN
BAY

Continued on Maps 55 & 66

Scale of Miles
0 1 2 3 4 5 6 7 8 9 10

John Bartholomew & Son, Ltd., Edinburgh

MAP 66

GLAMORGAN

BRECON
Brecon Beacons

SWANSEA · Mumbles · Black Pill · Liliput · West Cross · Cockett · Sketty · Singleton
NEATH · Briton Ferry · Aberavon · Port Talbot · Taibach
Llandilo · Ammanford · Brynamman · Ystalyfera · Pontardawe · Clydach · Morriston · Landore
Aberdare · Merthyr · Dowlais · Mountain Ash · Pontypridd · Treforest
Maesteg · Bridgend · Cowbridge · Porth-cawl · Porthcawl Pt.
Treherbert · Ystrad · Treorky · Ferndale · Pentre · Tonypandy · Porth

Shord Channel
Morgan Burrows
Mumbles Hd.
Breaksea Pt.
Tasker Rocks
Southern Down
Nash Pt.

Continued on Map 65

Scale of Miles
0 1 2 3 4 5 6 7 8 9 10

MAP 67

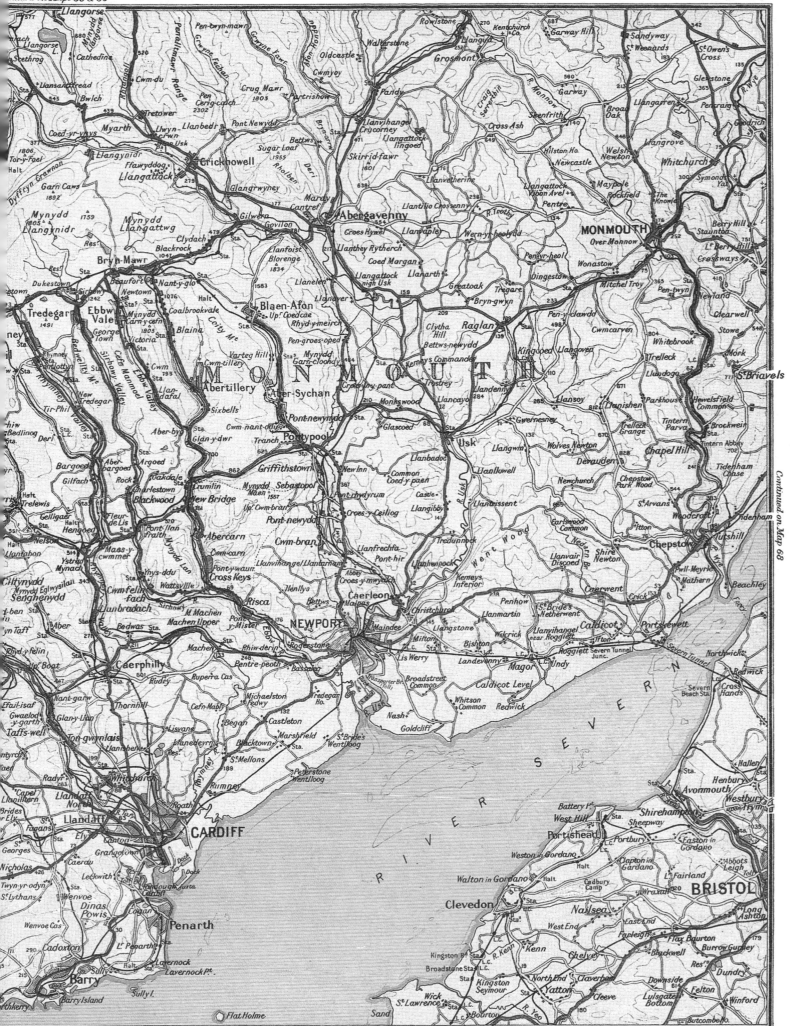

tinued on Maps 55 & 56

Continued on Map 68

Continued on Map 74

John Bartholomew & Son.Ltd.Edinburgh

Main Roads ———— Other Roads ———— Railways ————

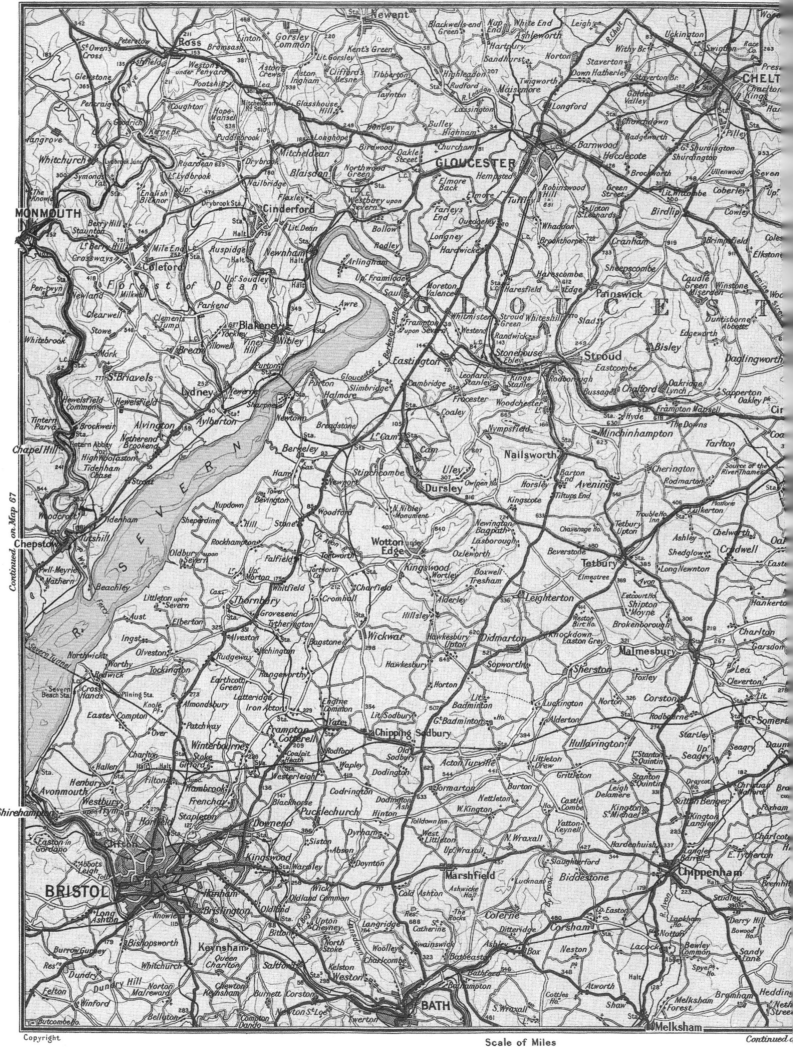

MAP 68

Continue

CHELT

Continued on Map 67

MONMOUTH

GLOUCESTER

Ross

Newent

Forest of Dean

Cinderford

Newnham

Chepstow

Lydney

Blakeney

Berkeley

SEVERN R.

Stroud

Painswick

Nailsworth

Dursley

Wotton under Edge

Tetbury

Malmesbury

Thornbury

Wickwar

Chipping Sodbury

Yate

Sherston

Marshfield

Chippenham

Avonmouth

BRISTOL

Keynsham

BATH

Melksham

Copyright

Continued o

Scale of Miles

0 1 2 3 4 5 6 7 8 9 10

MAP 69

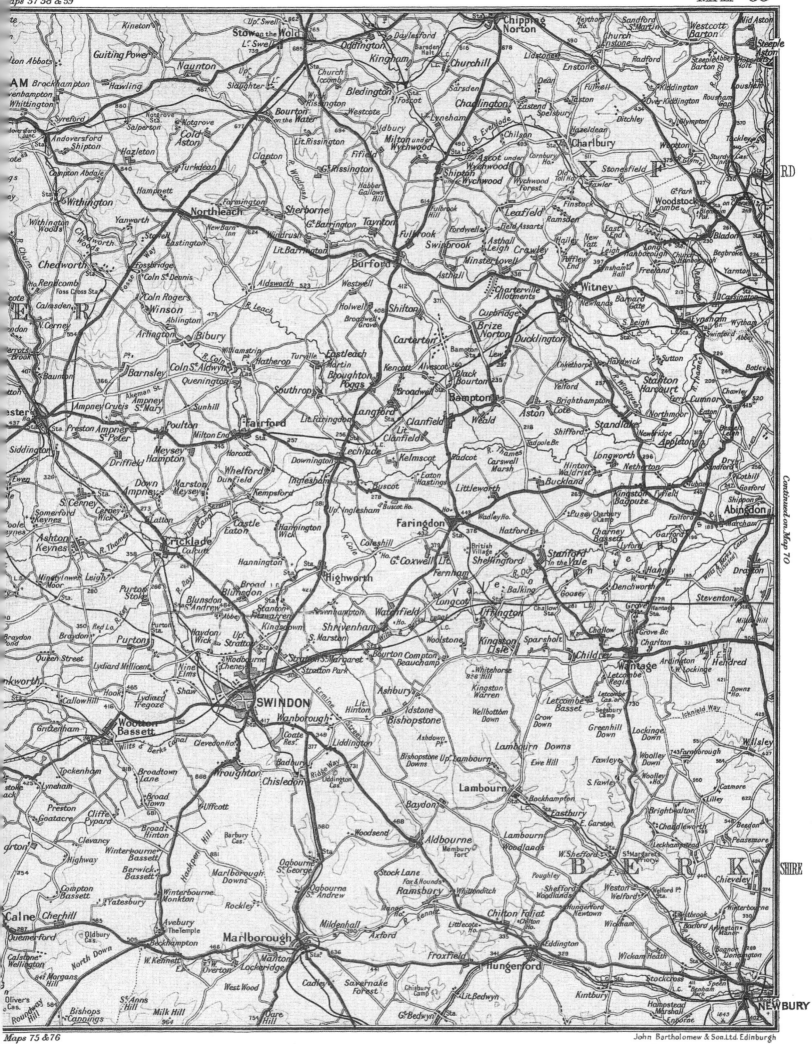

John Bartholomew & Son Ltd. Edinburgh

Main Roads —————— Other Roads ══════ Railways ————————

MAP 70

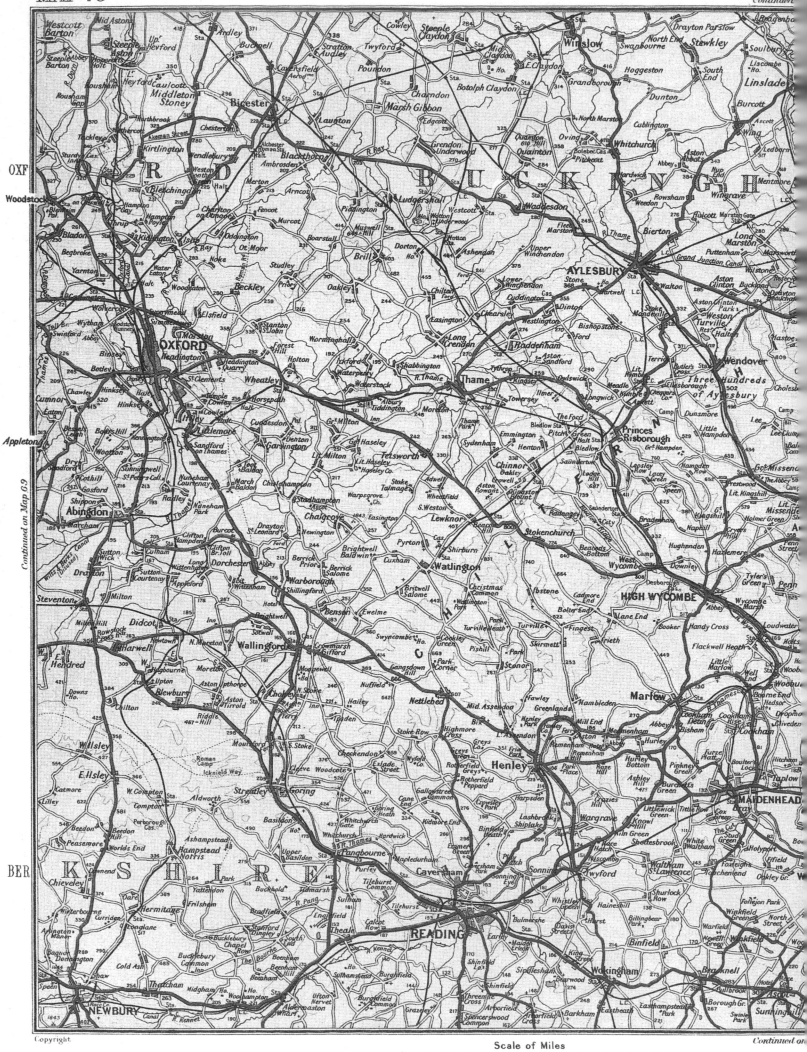

Scale of Miles

0 1 2 3 4 5 6 7 8 9 10

Continued on

MAP 71

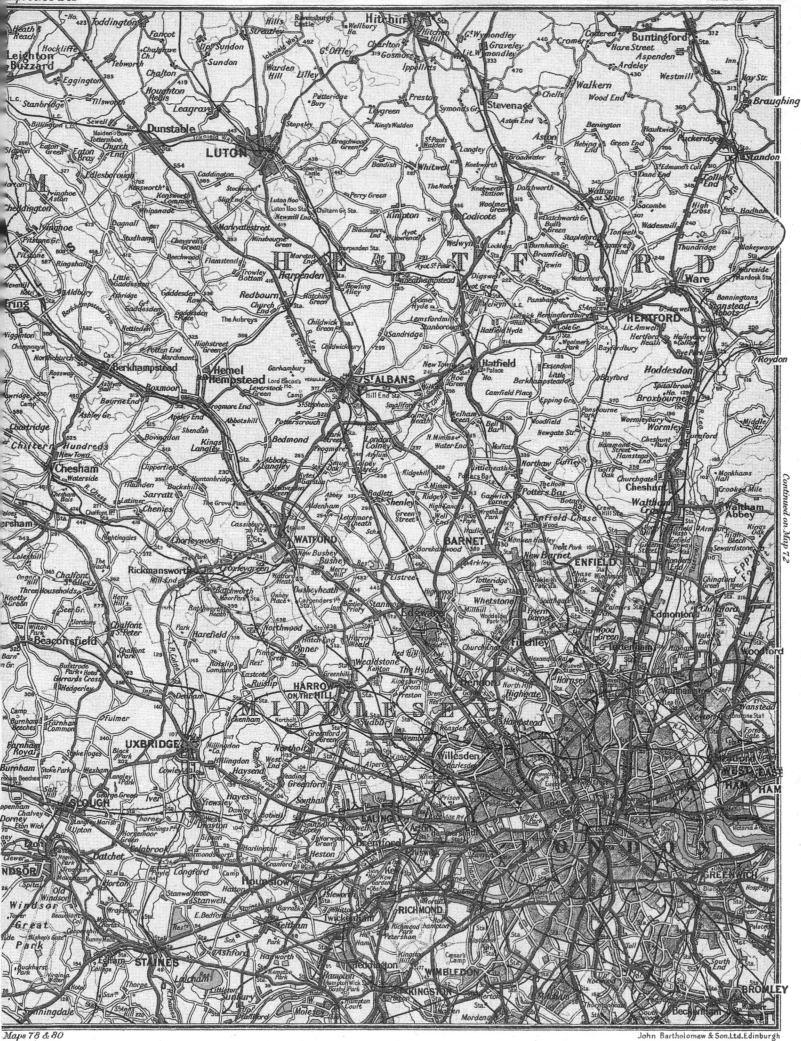

Main Roads —————   Other Roads —————   Railways —————

MAP 72

Continued

Continued on Map 71

Scale of Miles

0 1 2 3 4 5 6 7 8 9 10

Continued on

MAP 73

Main Roads ——— Other Roads ═══ Railways ————

MAP 74
Continued

Continued on Map 67

Continued on Map 85

Senghenydd · Llanbradach · Sirhowy · Risca · Bettws · Caerleon · Malpas · Penhow · St Bride's Netherwent · Crick · Northwick

Aber · M. Machen · Machen Upper · Pont y Mister · Christchurch · Llanmartin · Llanvihangel near Roggiett · Caldicot · Portskewett · North Redwick

Bedwas · Machen · Rhiw derin · Maindee · NEWPORT · Llangstone · Wikrich · Roggiett Severn Tunnel Junc. · Severn Tunnel · Easter

Caerphilly · Rudry · Ruperra Cas · Pentre peoth · Bassaleg · Transporter Br. (Toll) · R. Usk · Milton · Bishton · Undy · Magor · Severn Beach Sta. · Cross Hands · Easter

Nant-gaw · Thornhill · Cefn-Mably · Michaelston Fedwy · Tredegar Ho. · Castleton · Broadstreet Common · Caldicot Level · Whitson Common · Redwick

Glany-Llan · Lisvane · Began · Marshfield · Nash · Goldcliff · Whitson Common · Redwick

Taffs-well · Ton-gwynlais · Llanishen · Blacktown · St Brides Wentlloog · Magor

Radyr · Whitchurch · Roath · Rumney · Petersone Wentlloog · Battery Pt · West Hill · Henbury · Hallen · Westbury

Llandaff North · St Fagans · Ely · Canton · Llandough Cas · Junc. · Portishead · Sheepway · Avonmouth · Shirehampton

CARDIFF · Weston in Gordano · Clapton in Gordano · Abbots Leigh · BRISTOL

Penarth · Lr Penarth · Walton in Gordano · Halt · Cadbury Camp · Wraxall · L. Fairland

Caerau · Leckwith · Dock · Clevedon · West End · Nailsea · East End · Long Ashton

Wenvoe · Dinas Powis · Lavernock · Farleigh · Flax Bourton · Burrow Gurney

Cadoxton · Sully · Lavernock Pt · Kingston B · R. Kenn · Kenn · Chelvey · Blackwell · Downside

Barry · Sully I. · Kingston Seymour · North End · Yatton · Claverham · Cleeve · Lulsgate Bottom · Felton · Winford

Barry Island · Flat Holme · Wick St Lawrence · Bourton · R. Yeo · Congresbury · Redhill · Butcombe · Dundry

Sand Bay · Kewstoke · Puxton Sta. · Wrington · Ridgehill · Butcombe · Chew

Steep Holme · Worle · Milton · East Rolstone · Langford · Yeo Res. · Nempnett Thrubwell · E. Harp

Weston super Mare · Weston Bay · Uphill · Locking · Churchill · Burrington · Blagdon · Ubley · Compton Martin · W. Harp

Hutton · Banwell · Sandford · Rowberrow · Shipham · Mendip · Charterhouse · Castle of Comfort Inn · Miner's Arms

Ferry · Bleadon · Bleadon Hill · Christon · Woodborough · Sidcot · E. Harptree

Brean · R. Axe · Shiplate · Winscombe · Cross · Cheddar Cliffs · Priddy · Hunters Lodge Inn

BRIDGWATER · Loxton · Lr Weare · Axbridge · Caverns · Cheddar · Draycott · Westbury · Wookey Hole

Lympsham · Rooks Bridge · Tarnock · Weare · Nyland Hill · Rodney Stoke

BAY · Berrow · Brent Knoll · East Brent · Stone · Allerton · Clewer · Cocklake · Lodgehill Sta. · Easton · Wedmore

R. Parrett · Burnham · Stert I. · Edington Junc. · Mark Causeway · Stone Allerton Chapel · West Stoughton · Mark · Blackford · Theale · Wells

Highbridge · Huntspill · Bason Bridge · Mark · West Stoughton · Wookey · Henton · Yarley · Dulcote

Stolford · Stert · Huntspill Level · Cote · Tadham Moor · Panborough · Westhay Moor · Polsham · Coxley

Knighton · Stockland Bristol · Otterhampton · Pawlett · Catcott Burtle · Westhay · Lr Godney · Up

Kilve · Kilton · Burton · Fairfield Ho. · Combwich · Down End · Puriton · Woolavington · Edington · Godney · Queens Sedge Moor

East Quantoxhead · Putsham · Shurton · Stringston · Stogursey · Coultings · Rodway · Dunball · Knowle Hall · Cossington · Shapwick Sta. · Meare · Glastonbury

West Quantoxhead · Holford · Dodington · Fiddington · Brymore Ho. · Cannington · Chilton Trinity · Chilton · Catcott · Edington · Ashcott Sta. · Glastonbury Tor · W. Penn

Bicknoller · Over Stowey · Nether Stowey · Bawdrip · Stawell · Chedzoy · Shapwick · Isle of Avalon · Edgarley

SOMERSET · Crowcombe Hill · Quantock · Enmore · Wembdon · BRIDGWATER · Sutton Mallet · Moorlinch · Greinton · Ashcott · Street · Overleigh · Baltonsborough

Lr Vexford · Willett · Merridge · Fourforks · Durleigh · Battle of Sedgemoor 1685 · Weston Zoyland · Drain · Kings Sedge Moor · Nythe · Dundon · Butleigh · Barton St David

Stogumber · Lydeard St Lawrence · West Bagborough · Cothelstone · Spaxton · Goathurst · Woolmersdon · N. Petherton · Huntworth · Middlezoy · Greylake · Henley · Henley Corner · Compton · Kingweston · Copley Wood

Tolland · Combe Florey · Halswell Ho. · Aisholt · Toulton · Thurloxton · North Newton · Othery · High Ham · Littleton · Charlton Mackrell

Pitsford Hill · Ash Priors · Bishops Lydeard · Kingston · Adsborough · Northmoor Green or Moorland · Burrow Bridge · Lyng · Stathe · Pathe · Low Ham · Bramwell · Pitney · Somerton

BRIDGWATER BAY

RIVER SEVERN

QUANTOCK HILLS

MENDIP HILLS

Polden Hills

BATH

Chippenham · Calne · Devizes · Melksham · Trowbridge · Westbury · Warminster

Malmesbury · Wootton Bassett · Sherston · Corston

Thornbury · Wickwar · Chipping Sodbury · Frampton Cotterell · Marshfield · Corsham

Keynsham · Bradford on Avon · Radstock · Midsomer Norton · Shepton Mallet

Frome · Beckington · Norton St. Philip · Mere · Hindon · Tisbury

Bruton · Castle Cary · Wincanton · Maiden Bradley · Longleat · Heytesbury

WILTSHIRE

SALISBURY PLAIN

Continued on Maps 69 & 76

Main Roads ——— Other Roads ═══ Railways ┄┄┄

MAP 76

Continued on Maps 68 & 69

Continued

BASINGSTOKE

NEWBURY

WINCHESTER

HUNGERFORD

Marlborough

Andover

Stockbridge

Amesbury

SALISBURY

Kingsclere

Whitchurch

Ludgershall

Tidworth

WILTSHIRE

HAMPSHIRE

SALISBURY PLAIN

STONEHENGE

Savernake Forest

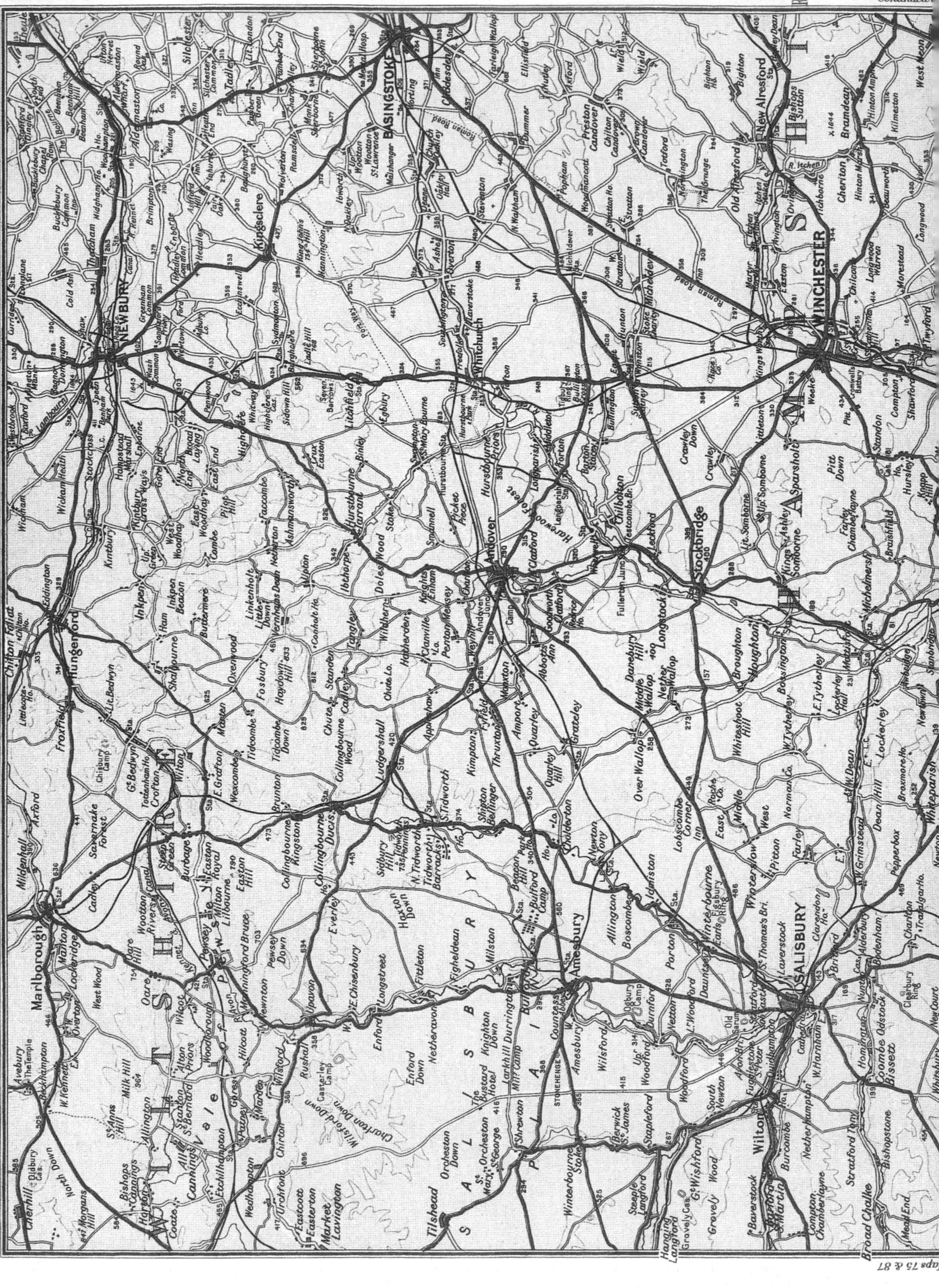

Maps 75 & 87

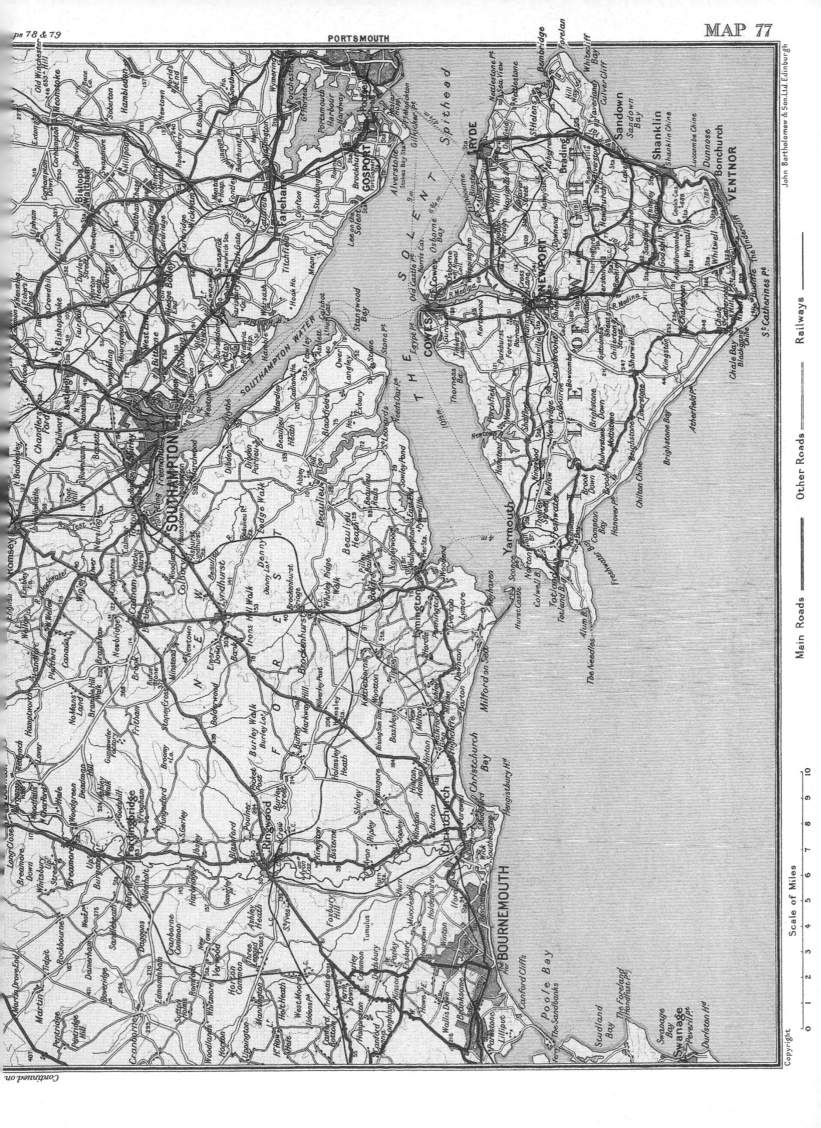

MAP 77

PORTSMOUTH

ps 78 & 79

John Bartholomew & Son Ltd. Edinburgh

SOUTHAMPTON

BOURNEMOUTH

GOSPORT

RYDE

COWES

NEWPORT

ISLE OF WIGHT

VENTNOR

SHANKLIN

SANDOWN

YARMOUTH

CHRISTCHURCH

RINGWOOD

SWANAGE

THE SOLENT

Spithead

SOUTHAMPTON WATER

NEW FOREST

Poole Bay

Scale of Miles
0 1 2 3 4 5 6 7 8 9 10

Main Roads ━━━ Other Roads ═══ Railways

MAP 78

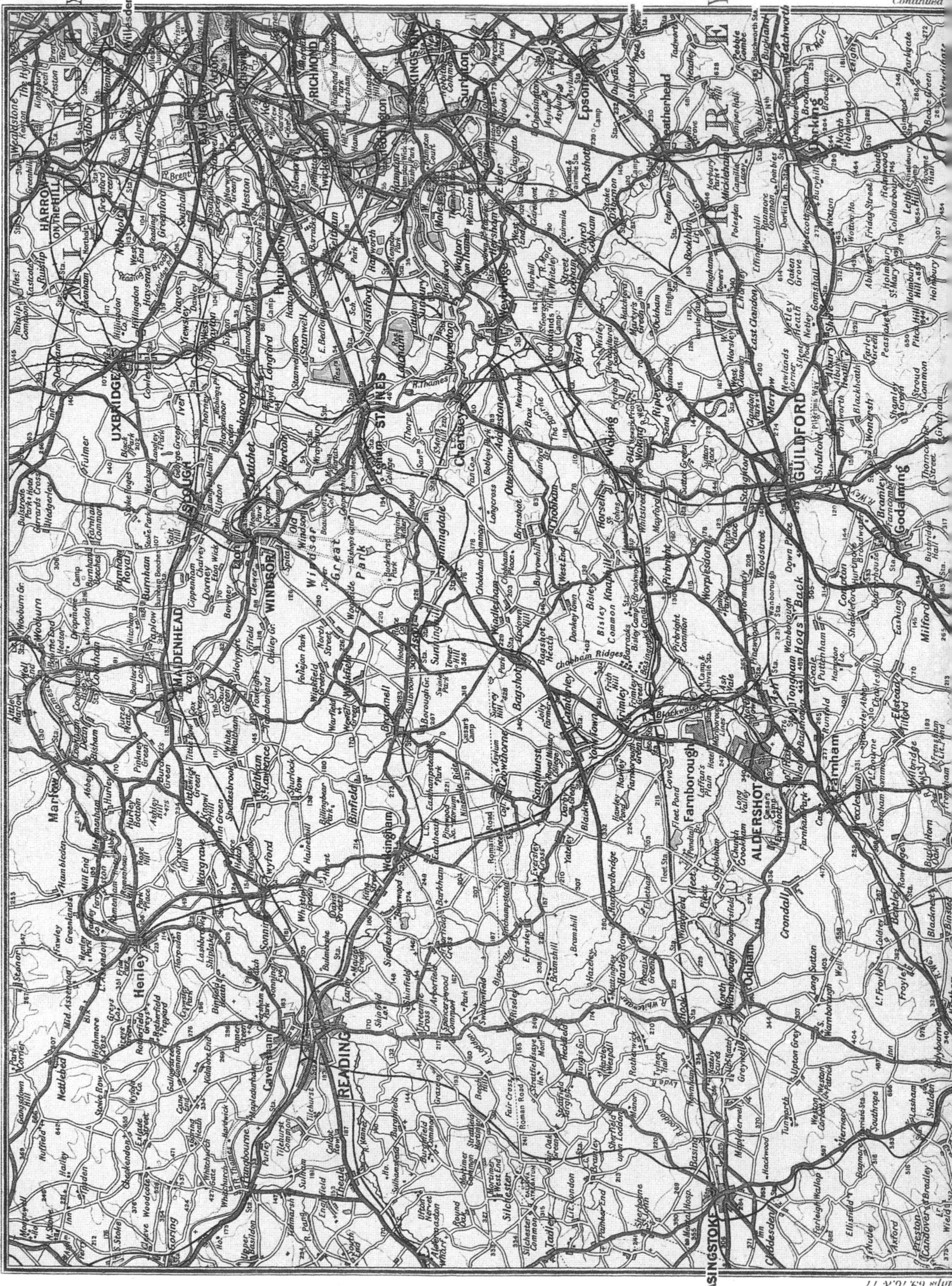

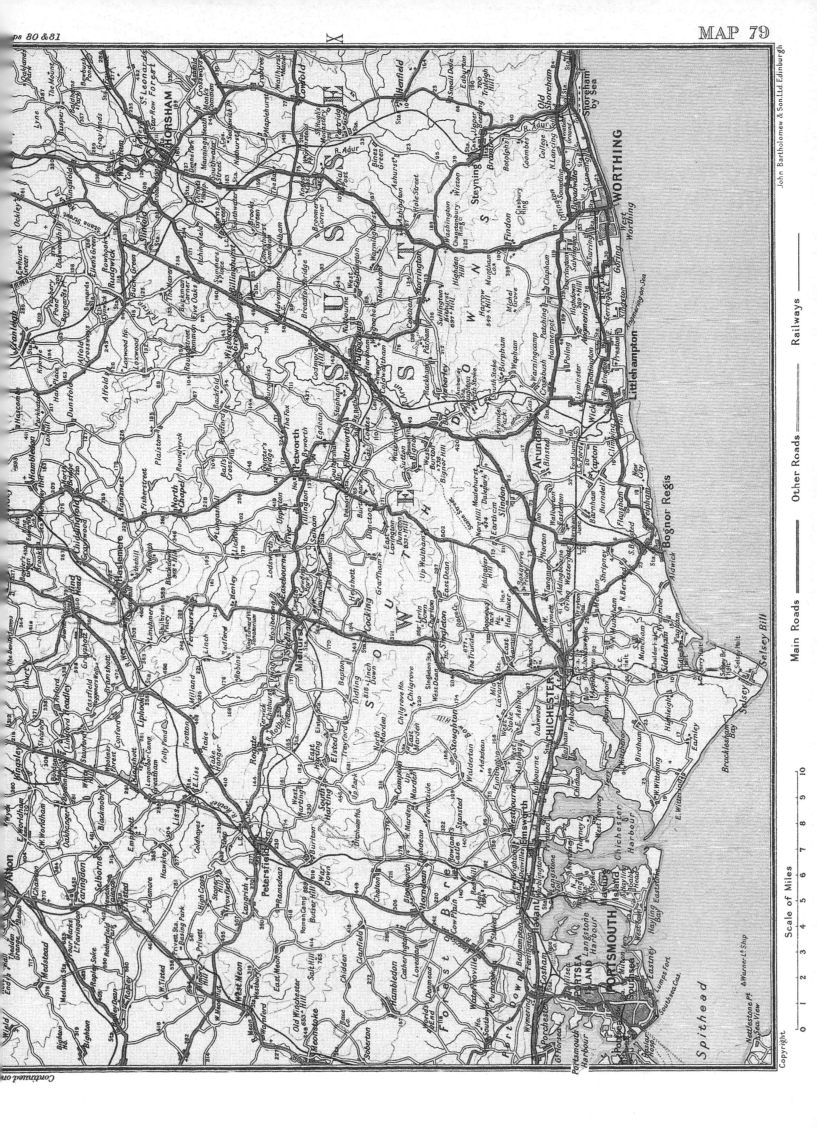

MAP 79

MAP 80

Continued

Continued on Maps 70 71 & 72

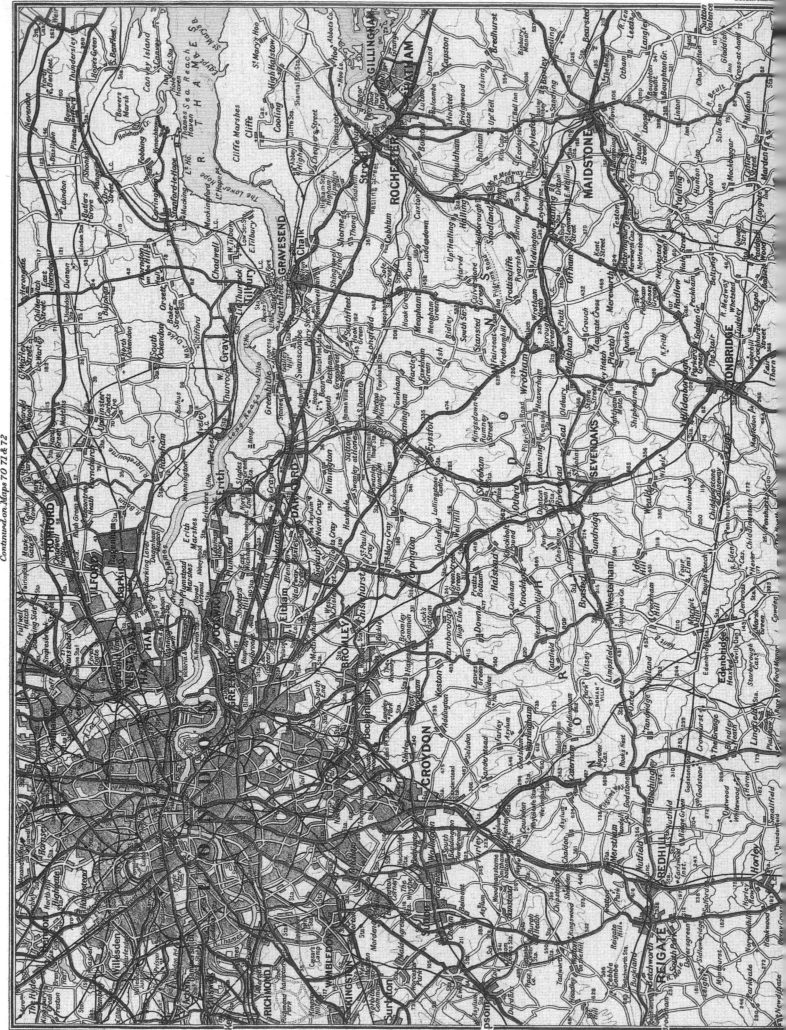

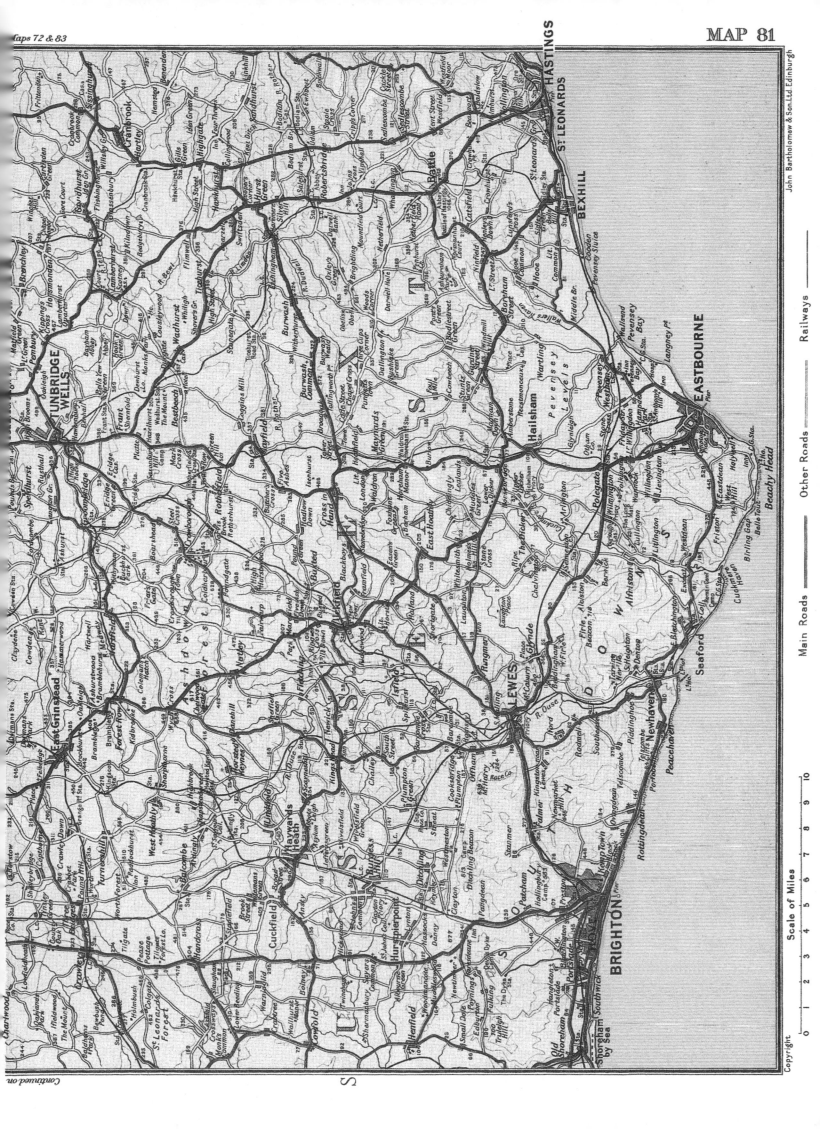

MAP 81

HASTINGS

ST. LEONARDS

BEXHILL

EASTBOURNE

Beachy Head

TUNBRIDGE WELLS

Cranbrook

Battle

BRIGHTON

LEWES

Newhaven

Seaford

East Grinstead

Haywards Heath

Cuckfield

Hurstpierpoint

Scale of Miles

0 1 2 3 4 5 6 7 8 9 10

Main Roads ━━━ Other Roads ━━━ Railways ━━━

MAP 82

Continued o

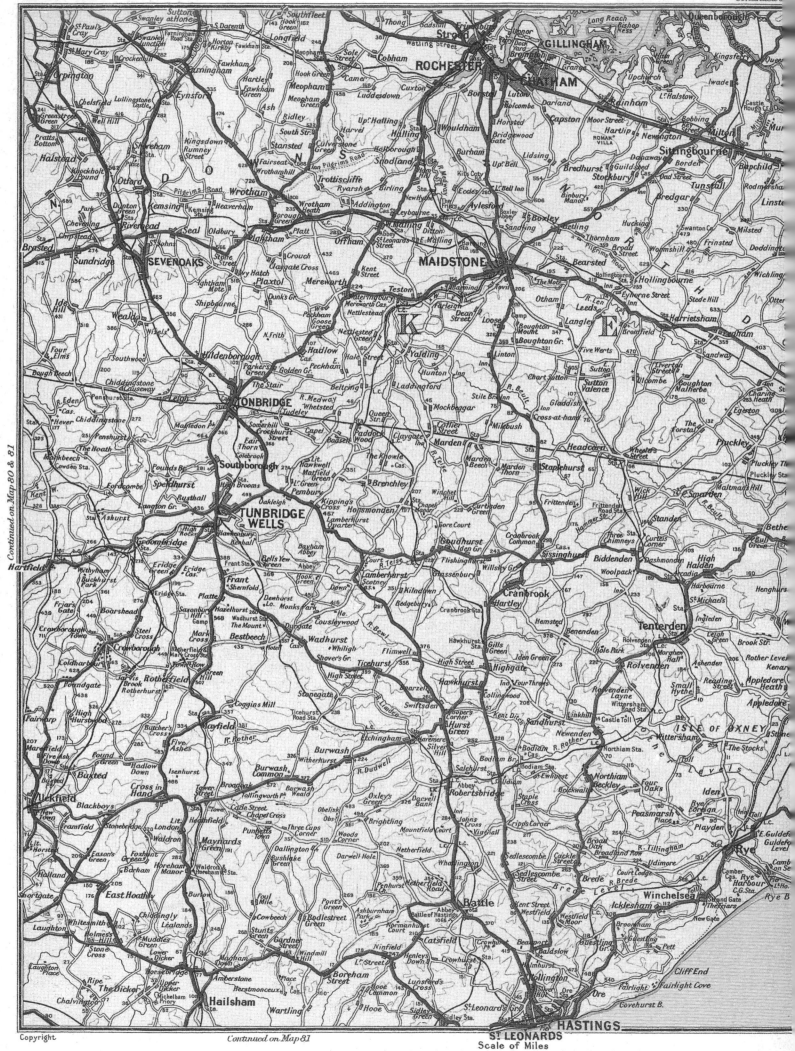

Scale of Miles

0 1 2 3 4 5 6 7 8 9 10

MAP 83

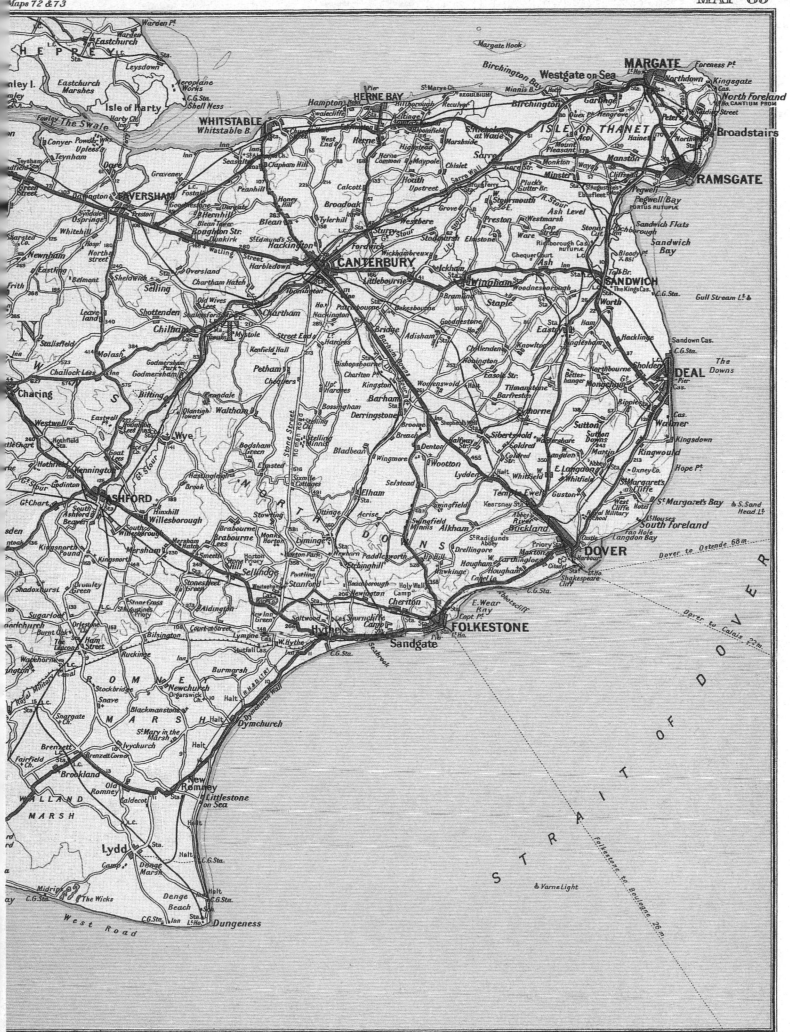

Main Roads ——— Other Roads ═══ Railways ———

John Bartholomew & Son.Ltd.Edinburgh

MAP 84

Scale of Miles

0 1 2 3 4 5 6 7 8 9 10

Continued on Inset Map 91

Continued on

MAP 85

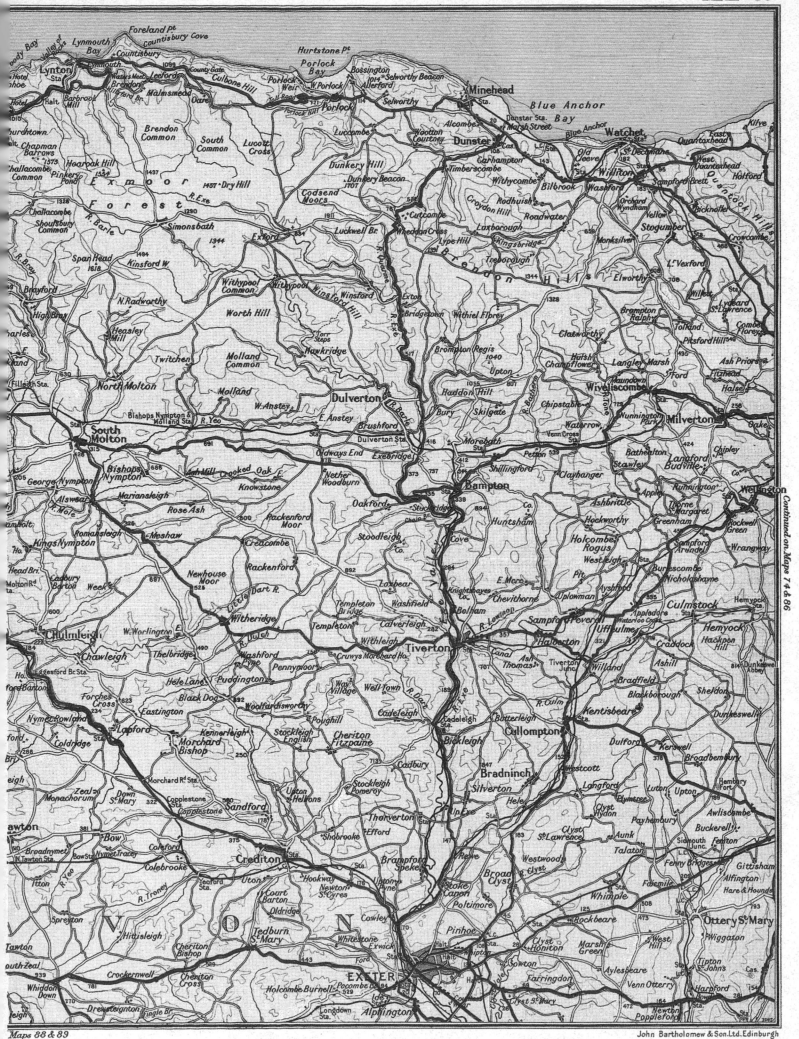

Continued on Maps 74 & 86

Maps 88 & 89

John Bartholomew & Son. Ltd. Edinburgh

Main Roads ——————   Other Roads ============   Railways ——————

MAP 86

Continued

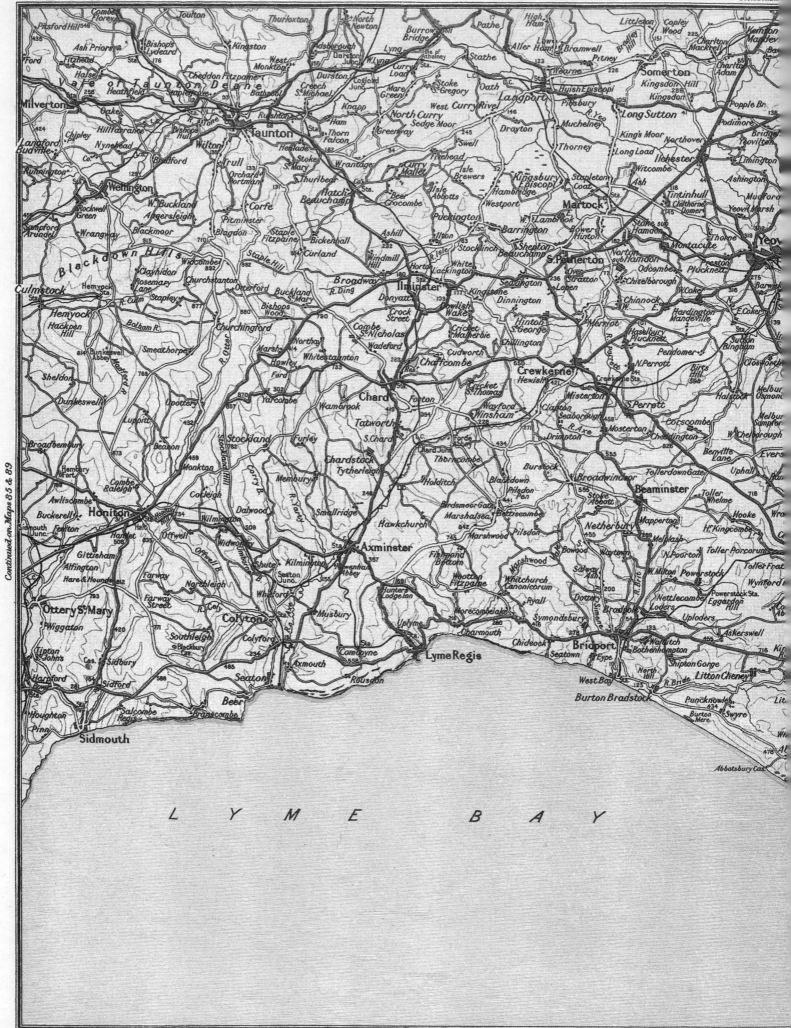

L Y M E   B A Y

Scale of Miles

0 1 2 3 4 5 6 7 8 9 10

MAP 87

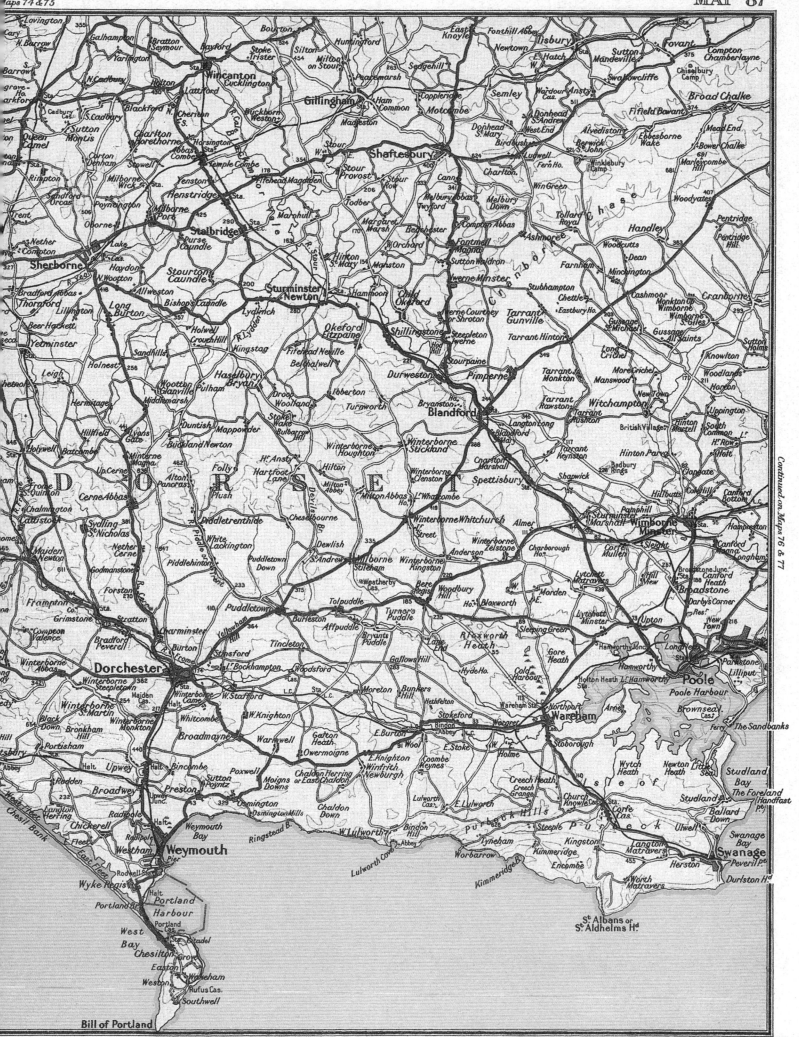

Continued on Maps 76 & 77

John Bartholomew & Son.Ltd.Edinburgh

Main Roads ——— Other Roads ——— Railways ———

MAP 88

Continued o

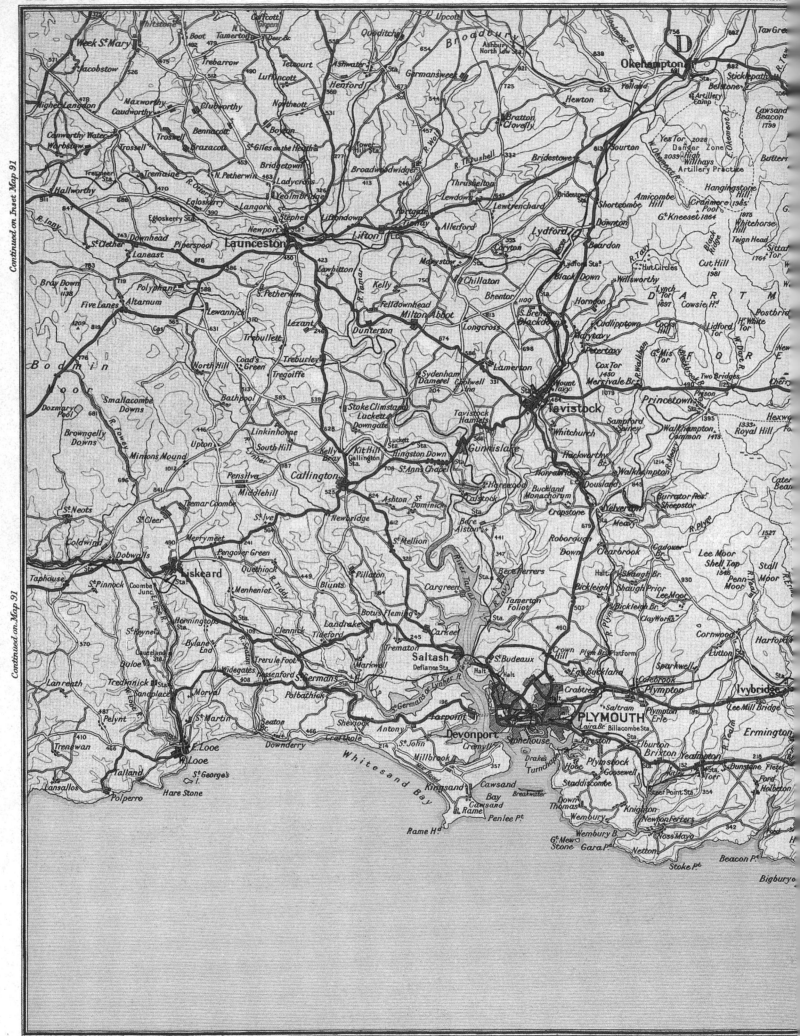

Continued on Inset Map 91

Continued on Map 91

Scale of Miles

0 1 2 3 4 5 6 7 8 9 10

MAP 89

Continued on Map 86

Bartholomew & Son. Ltd. Edinburgh

Main Roads ——————   Other Roads ══════   Railways ——————

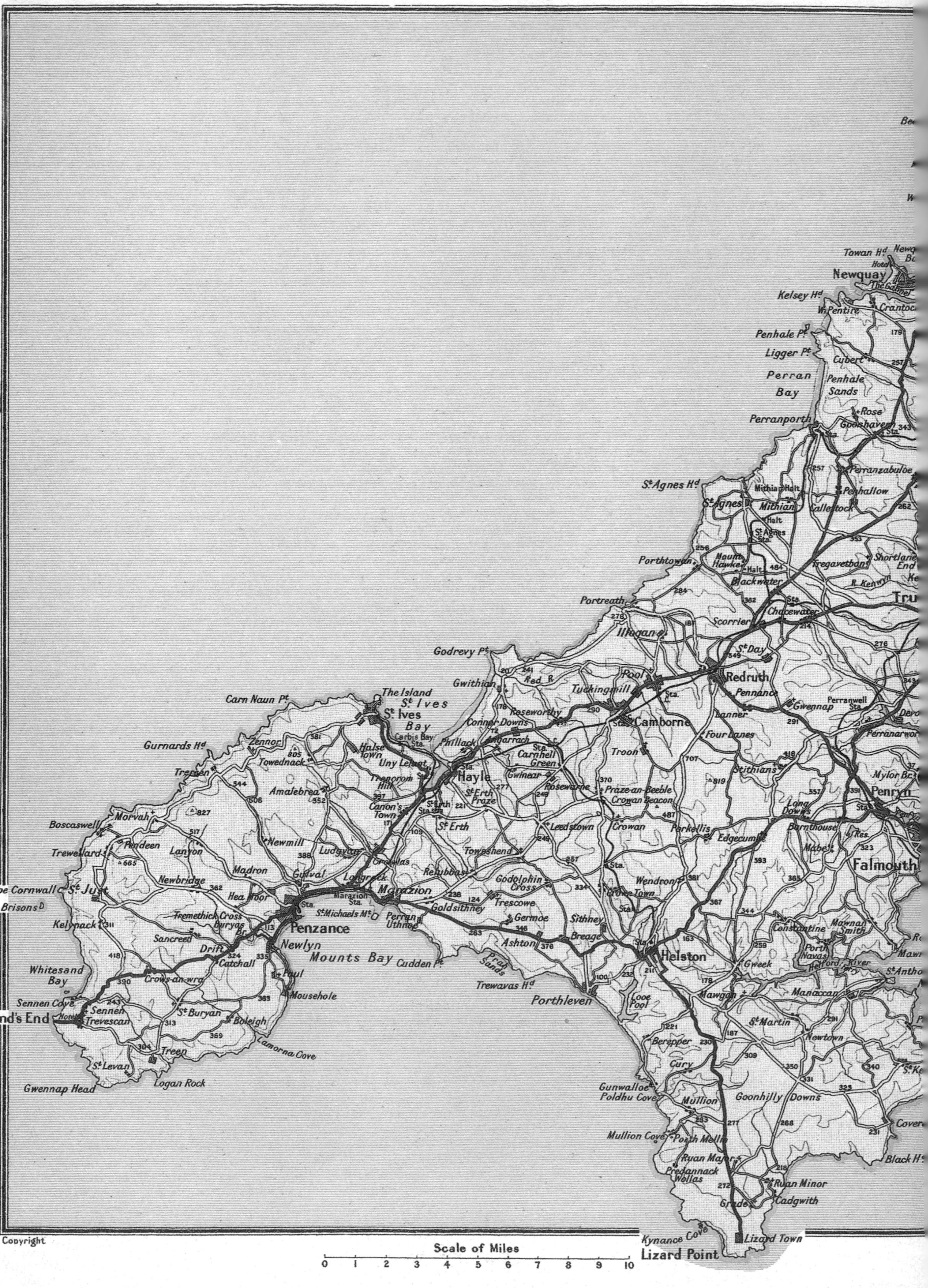

MAP 90

Beacon

Towan Hd   Newquay Bay
Newquay
Hotel   The Gannel
Kelsey Hd
Pentire
Crantock
Penhale Pt
Ligger Pt   Cubert   257
Perran
Bay   Penhale
Sands
Perranporth   Rose
Sta   Goonhavern   Sta   343
St Agnes Hd   Perranzabuloe
Mithian Halt   257   Penhallow
St Agnes   Mithian
Halt   Callestock   262
St Agnes
Sta
Porthtowan   256   Mount
Hawke   Halt   484   Shortlane
End
Blackwater   Tregavethan   Ke
Portreath   284   Sta   Truro
278   Scorrier   362   Chacewater   212
Illogan   187   276
St Day   Pool   349   Redruth   244
Godrevy Pt   Red R   Pennance
Gwithian   20   241   Tuckingmill   290   Pennance   Gwennap   Perranwell
The Island   78   Sta   Camborne   Tanner   Sta   291
St Ives   Roseworthy   Four Lanes   Devo
Bay   Conner Downs   Gwinear   Troon   707   Stithians   318   Perranarwo
Carn Naun Pt   Carbis Bay Sta   Phillack   Gurrach   Carnhell   Rosewarne   370   Praze-an-Beeble   819   Long   557   Mylor Br
St Ives   581   Halse   Sta   Green   277   Crowan Beacon   Downs   339   Penryn
Gurnards Hd   Town   249   487   Parkellis   Penry
Zennor   805   Uny Lelant   St Erth   Leedstown   Crowan   593   Edgcumbe   Burnthouse   Falmouth
Trenon   Towednack   Trencrom   Sta   Praze   221   244   Sta   Mabe   323
544   552   Hill   108   Towshend   257   Res
Amalebrea   Canon's   St Erth   Godolphin   Grove Town   367
508   827   Town   Cross   334   Wendron   Constantine   259
Boscaswell   Newmill   Longrock   Relubbas   238   Trescowe   487   Mawnan   Port
Morvah   Ludgvan   124   Germoe   Sithney   344   Smith   Navas
Trewellard   Pendeen   Lanyon   388   Marazion   Sta   Goldsithney   Germoe   346   Helford River   St Antho
665   Madron   Gulval   Perran   263   Breage   Helston   Gweek   291   Maw
St Just   517   Hea Moor   Marazion Sta   Uthnoe   Ashton   376   211   163   Gear
Cape Cornwall   362   Sta   St Michaels Mt   100   232   Nawgan   178   Manaccan
The Brisons   Tremethick Cross   113   Penzance   Cudden Pt   Porthleven   Loe   221   St Martin   St Ke
Kelynack   311   Buryas   Newlyn   Mounts Bay   Trewavas Hd   Pool   Berepper   230   187   Newtown   240
Sancreed   Br   Paul   Gunwalloe   Cury   350   309   323
418   Drift   Catchall   324   335   Mousehole   Poldhu Cove   353   Goonhilly Downs
Whitesand   390   Crows-an-wra   383   Mullion   271   268   231
Bay   Camorna Cove   Mullion Cove   Porth Mellin   Black Hd
Sennen Cove   243   St Buryan   Boleigh   Ruan Major   219
Land's End   Hotel   Sennen   313   Predannack   Ruan Minor
Trevescan   369   Wellas   272   Cadgwith
304   Treen   Grade
St Levan   Logan Rock   Kynance Cove   Lizard Town
Gwennap Head   Lizard Point

Scale of Miles
0 1 2 3 4 5 6 7 8 9 10

MAP 91

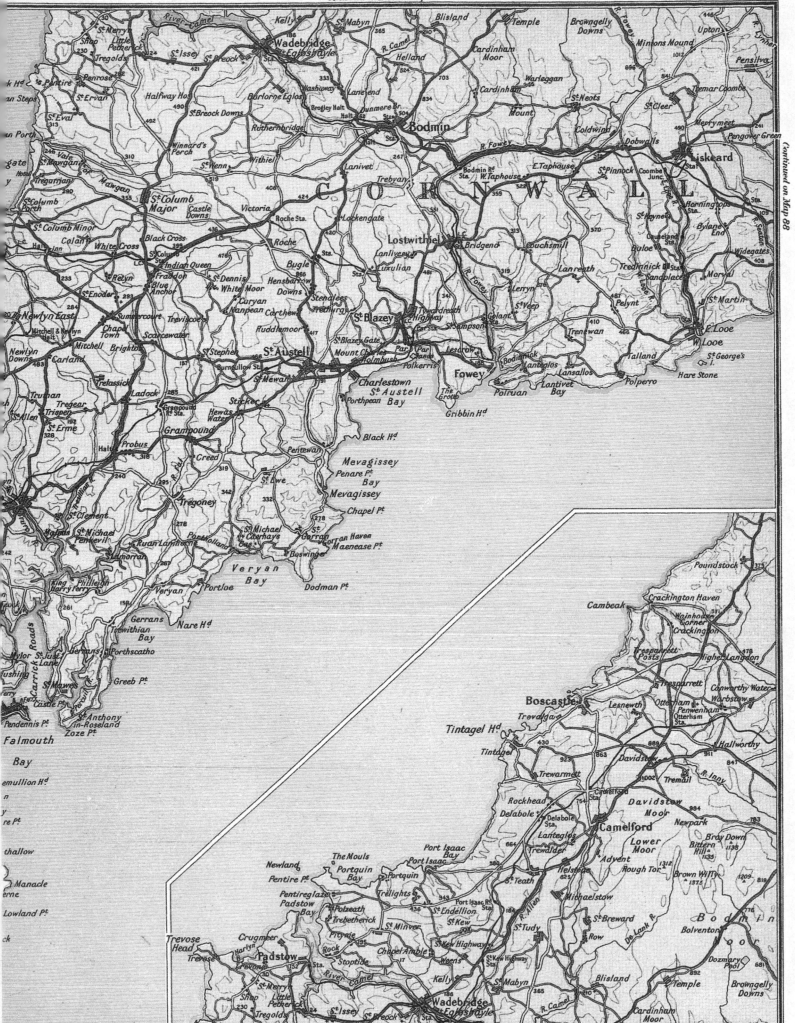

C O R N W A L L

John Bartholomew & Son.Ltd.Edinburgh

Main Roads ━━━━━ Other Roads ═════ Railways ━━━━━

MAP 92

Continued o

Main Roads _____20_____   Other Roads _____   Railways _____

Red Figures indicate distances between places with Black Dots

MAP 93

Scale of Miles

0   4   8   12   16   20   24   28   32   36   40

John Bartholomew & Son Ltd. Edinburgh

MAP 94

Continued

Main Roads ——20——   Other Roads ————   Railways ————
Red Figures indicate distances between places with Black Dots

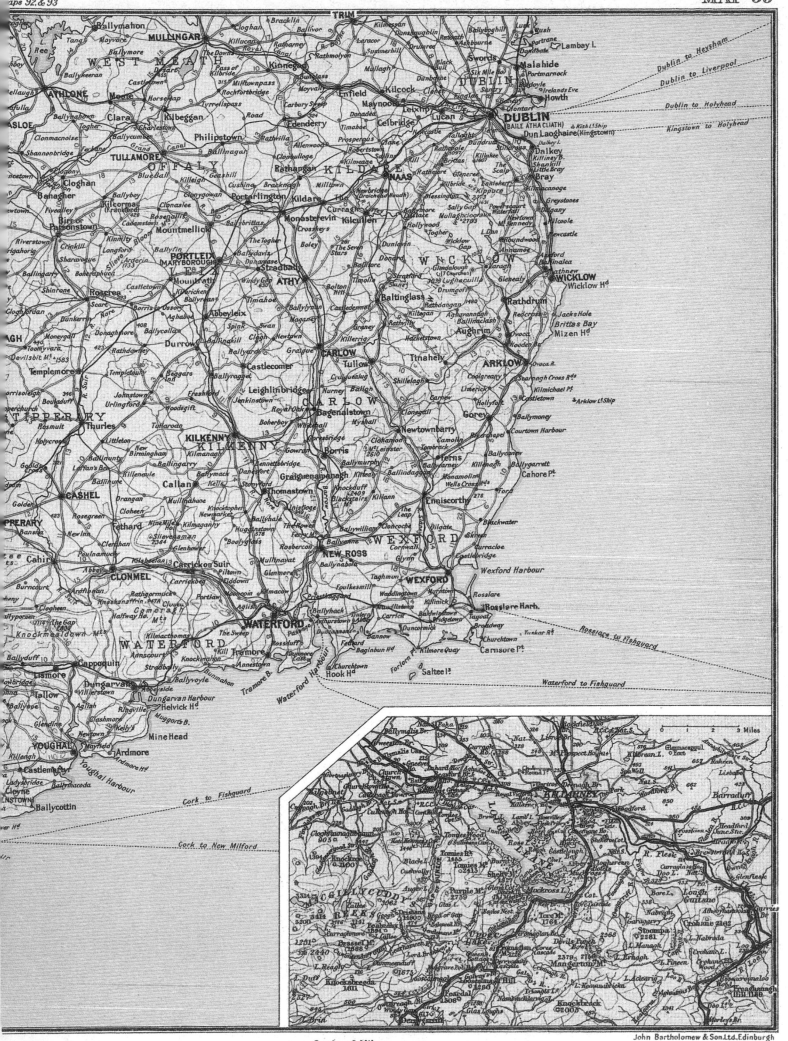

MAP 95

Dublin to Heysham
Dublin to Liverpool
Dublin to Holyhead
Kingstown to Holyhead

Rosslare to Fishguard

Waterford to Fishguard

Cork to Fishguard

Cork to New Milford

Scale of Miles

0   4   8   12   16   20   24   28   32   36   40

John Bartholomew & Son.Ltd.Edinburgh

MAP 96

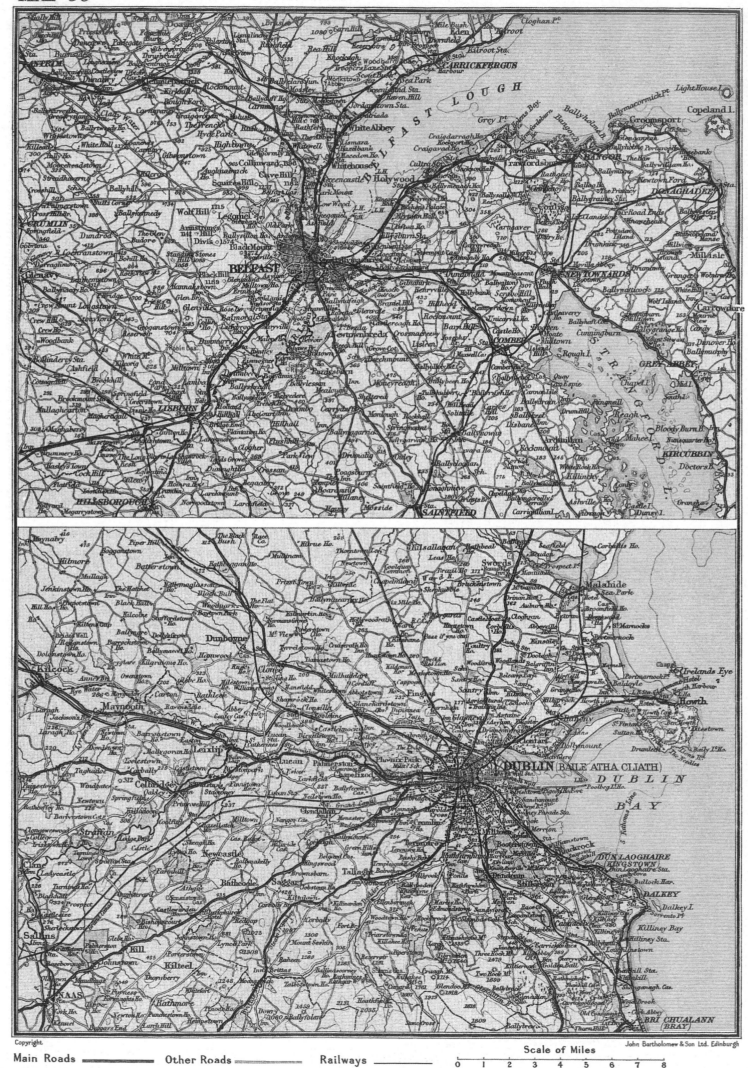

John Bartholomew & Son Ltd. Edinburgh

Scale of Miles

Main Roads ━━━━━ Other Roads ═════ Railways ━━━━━

0 1 2 3 4 5 6 7 8

GAZETTEER INDEX TO PLACES

Abbreviations.—Alt., altitude; bor., borough; bur., burgh (in Scotland); civ., civil; co., county; dist., district; E.R., East Riding; eccl., ecclesiastical; ft., feet; ham., hamlet; isl., island; m., mile or miles; met., metropolitan; mun., municipal; N.R., North Riding; par., parish; pop., population; *q.s., quoad sacra* (in Scotland); r., river; ry. sta., railway station; spt., seaport; tn., town urb., urban; vil., village; W.R., West Riding.

ABBERLEY, par., Worcestershire, 4 m. S.W. of Stourport; pop. 467. Map 57.

Abbeycwmhir, par. and vil., Radnorshire, 6 m. N.E. of Rhayadir; pop. 336. Map 56.

Abbey Town, vil., N.W. Cumberland, 4½ m. E.S.E. of Silloth. Map 20.

Abbots Bromley, par. and town, Staffordshire, 4½ m. N.E. of Rugeley; pop. 1516. Map 48.

Abbotsley, par. and vil., Huntingdonshire, 3½ m. S.E. of St Neots; pop. 321. Map 61.

Aberaman, vil. and ry. sta., Glamorganshire, 2 m. S.E. of Aberdare. Map. 66.

Aberavon, Glamorganshire, now in Port Talbot. Map 66.

Aberayron, urb. dist. and seaport, Cardiganshire, 15 m. S.W. of Aberystwyth; pop. 1155. Map 54.

Abercarn, urb. dist. and par., Monmouthshire, 10½ m. N.W. of Newport; pop. 20,554. Map 67.

Aberdare, par. and urb. dist., Glamorganshire, 4 m. S.W. of Merthyr Tydfil; pop. 48,751. Map 66.

Aberdaron, par. and vil., Carnarvonshire, 14 m. S.W. of Pwllheli; pop. 1075. Map 44.

Aberdeen, parl. and mun. bur. and co. town of Aberdeenshire, 130½ m. N.E. of Edinr.; pop. 167,259. Map 3.

Aberdour, coast par. and vil., Fifeshire, 3 m. W. of Burnt-island; pop. 3063. Map 10.

Aberdovey, seaport, Merionethshire, in urb. dist. and 3¾ m. S. of Towyn. Map 44.

Aberdulais, vil. and ry. sta., Glamorganshire, 1¾ m. N.E. of Neath. Map 66.

Aberfeldy, police burgh, Perthshire, 32½ m. N.W. of Perth; pop. 1505. Map 6.

Aberffraw, par. and seaport vil., S. Anglesey, 12 m. S.E. of Holyhead; pop. 861. Map 36.

Aberffrwd, ry. sta., Cardiganshire, 7 m. S.E. of Aberystwyth. Map 55.

Aberford, par. and vil., W.R. Yorkshire, 5 m. S.W. of Tadcaster; pop. 570. Map 33.

Aberfoyle, par. and vil., Perthshire, 6 m. N.W. of Buchlyvie; pop. 1169. Map 8.

Abergavenny, mun. bor. and par., Monmouthshire, 20 m. N. of Newport; pop. 8608. Map 67.

Abergele, coast par. and market town, Denbighshire, 4½ m. W. of Rhyl; pop. 2651. Map 37.

Aber Glaslyn, mt. pass on boundary between Carnarvon and Merioneth., 1 m. S. of Beddgelert. Map 36.

Abergwili, par. and vil., in co. and 1½ m. N.E. of Carmarthen; pop. 1393. Map. 65.

Aberlady, par. and vil., E. Lothian, 16¼ m. E. of Edinburgh; pop. 1100. Map 10.

Abernethy, par. and police bur., Perthshire, 8½ m. S.E. of Perth; pop. 595. Map 6.

Aberporth, coast par. and vil., in co. and 6½ m. N.E. of Cardigan; pop. 371. Map 54.

Aber-Sychan, urb. dist. and par., Monmouthshire, 2¼ m. N.N.W. of Pontypool; pop. 25,627. Map 67.

Abertillery, urb. dist. and par., Monmouthshire, 15 m. N.W. of Newport; pop. 31,799. Map 67.

Aberystwyth, mun. bor. and seaport, in co. and 38¼ m. N.E. of Cardigan; pop. 9474. Map 54.

Abingdon, mun. bor. and par., Berkshire, 6 m. S. of Oxford; pop. 7240. Map 70.

Abington, vil. and ry. sta., Lanarkshire, 15½ m. S.W. of Carstairs Junction. Map 14.

Aboyne, vil. and ry. sta., Aberdeenshire, 10½ m. E. of Ballater; pop. 890. Map 3.

Abram, urb. dist., Lancashire, 2 m. S.E. of Wigan; pop. 6660. Map 39.

Accrington, par. and mun. bor., market tn. and par., E. Lancs, 20 m. N. of Manchester; pop. 42,973. Map 31.

Achnasheen, ry. sta., Ross and Cromarty, 28 m. W. of Dingwall. Map 2.

Ackworth, par. and seat, W.R. Yorkshire, 3 m. S. of Pontefract; pop. 4831. Map 33.

Acle, par. and vil., Norfolk, 8 m. W.N.W. of Great Yarmouth; pop. 1042. Map 53.

Acton, mun. bor., Middlesex, 4¼ m. W. of Paddington; pop. 70,523. Map 71.

Acton Turville, par. and vil., S.E. Gloucestershire, 9½ m. S.W. of Tetbury; pop. 269. Map 68.

Adderbury, vil. and ry. sta., Oxon, 5¼ m. S. of Banbury. Map 59.

Adderley, par. and ry. sta., Salop, 4 m. N. of Market Drayton; pop. 283. Map 47.

Addiewell, par. and vil., Midlothian, 1½ m. S.W. of West Calder; pop. 2146. Map 9.

Addlestone, eccl. par. and vil., N.W. Surrey, 1½ m. S.E. of Chertsey; pop. 7818. Map 78.

Adlington, urb. dist. and par., N. Lancashire, 3½ m. S.E. of Chorley; pop. 4179. Map 30.

Adwick-le-Street, urb. dist. and par., W.R. Yorkshire, 4 m. N.W. of Doncaster; pop. 20,257. Map 33.

Adwick-upon-Dearne, par., W.R. Yorkshire, 6½ m. N.E. of Rotherham; pop. 751. Map 41.

Aikton, par. and vil., Cumberland, 4 m. N.E. of Wigton; pop. 641. Map 20.

Ainderby Steeple, par., Yorkshire, 3 m. S.W. of Northallerton; pop. 241. Map 27.

Ainstable, par. and vil., E. Cumberland, 11 m. N.E. of Penrith; pop. 363. Map 21.

Aintree, par. and vil., S.W. Lancs, 4¾ m. N.E. of L'pool; well-known racecourse here; pop. 7372. Map 38.

Airdrie, mun. bur., par., and market town, Lanarkshire, 11 m. E. of Glasgow; pop. 25,954. Map 9.

Airth, par. and vil., in co. and 8¼ m. S.E. of Stirling; pop. 1777. Map 9.

Albrighton, par. and vil., Salop, 5 m. S.E. of Shifnal; pop. 1028. Map 47.

Albury, par. and vil., W. Surrey, 4 m. S.E. of Guildford; pop. 1172. Map 78.

Alcester, par. and market town, in co. and 15 m. S.W. of Warwick; pop. 2259. Map 58.

Alconbury, par. and vil., in co. and 4 m. N.W. of Huntingdon; pop. 523. Map 61.

Aldbourne, par. and vil., N. Wiltshire, 6 m. N.E. of Marlborough ; pop. 980. Map 69.

Aldbrough, par. and vil., E.R. Yorkshire, 11½ m. N.E. of Hull, coastguard sta. ; pop. 743. Map 35.

Aldeburgh, mun. bor. and seaport, E. Suffolk, 6 m. S.E. of Saxmundham ; pop. 2480. Map 63.

Aldermaston, par. and vil., S. Berkshire, 9 m. S.W. of Reading ; pop. 533. Map 78.

Aldershot, mun. bor., N. Hants, 3 m. N.E. of Farnham ; pop. 34,281. Map 78.

Aldringham, par. and vil., E. Suffolk, 3 m. N. of Aldeburgh ; pop. 901. Map 63.

Alexandria, *q.s.* par. and town, Dumbartonshire, 3½ m. N. of Dumbarton ; pop. 10,359. Map 8.

Alford, urb. dist. and par., Lindsey, Lincolnshire, 23¼ m. N.E. of Boston ; pop. 2227. Map 43.

Alford, par. and vil., in co. and 29½ m. N.W. of Aberdeen ; pop. 994. Map 3.

Alfreton, urb. dist., Derbyshire, 14 m. N.N.E. of Derby ; pop. 21,232. Map 41.

Alfriston, par. and vil., E. Sussex, 3½ m. N.E. of Seaford ; pop. 667. Map 81.

Allendale, par. and vil., Northumberland, 13½ m. S.W. of Hexham ; pop. 3012. Map 22.

Allerton, eccl. par. and vil., W.R. Yorkshire, 3½ m. N.W. of Bradford ; pop. 4016. Map 32.

Allhallows, par. and vil., Kent, 8 m. N.E. of Rochester ; pop. 314. Map 72.

Alloa, par. and police bur., Clackmannanshire, 6½ m. E. of Stirling ; pop. 13,322. Map 9.

Allonby, par. and seaport, Cumberland, 5 m. N.E. of Maryport ; pop. 660. Map 20.

Almond, Glen, or **Sma' Glen,** Perthshire, 6 m. N. of Crieff. Map 6.

Alness, par. and vil., Ross and Cromarty, 9¾ m. N.E. of Dingwall ; pop. 917. Map 3.

Alnmouth, par. and seaport, Northumberland, 4 m. S.E. of Alnwick ; pop. 933. Map 17.

Alnwick, urb. dist. and par., Northumb., 37¾ m. N.W. of Newcastle-on-Tyne by rail ; pop. 6882. Map 17.

Alpheton, par. and vil., W. Suffolk, 6 m. N. of Sudbury ; pop. 213. Map 62.

Alphington, par. and vil., Devonshire, 2 m. S. of Exeter ; pop. 1053. Map 89.

Alresford, New, par., Hants, 6½ m. N.E. of Winchester ; pop. 1709. Map 76.

Alresford, Old, par., Hants, 1 m. N. of New Alresford ; pop. 499. Map 76.

Alsop-en-le-Dale, vil., N. Derbyshire, 6 m. N. of Ashbourne ; pop. 652. Map 40.

Alston, par. and market town, E. Cumberland, 13 m. S. of Haltwhistle ; pop. 3344. Map 22.

Altcar Rifle Range Station, S.W. Lancashire, 9½ m. N.W. of Liverpool. Map 38.

Altguish Inn, Ross and Cromarty, 13½ m. W.N.W. of Dingall. Map 2.

Althorpe, par. and vil., Lindsey, Lincolnshire, 4½ m. S.E. of Crowle ; pop. 689. Map 34.

Alton, market town and par., N. Hants, 8¾ m. S.W. of Farnham ; pop. 6172. Map 79.

Altrincham, urb. dist. and par., Cheshire, 8 m. S.W. of Manchester ; pop. 21,356. Map 39.

Alva, par. and police bur., Clackmannanshire, 8 m. N.E. of Stirling ; pop. 3820. Map 9.

Alyth, par. and town, Perthshire, 4½ m. E.N.E. of Blairgowrie ; pop. 1662. Map 6.

Amberley, par. and vil., W. Sussex, 4 m. N. of Arundel ; pop. 489. Map 79.

Amble, urb. dist. and par., Northumberland, 7 m. S.E. of Alnwick ; pop. 4208. Map 17.

Ambleside, urb. dist. and par., Westmorland, 12 m. N.W. of Kendal ; pop. 2343. Map 25.

Amersham, market town and par., Buckinghamshire, 15 m. S.E. of Aylesbury ; pop. 4221. Map 70.

Amesbury, town and par., S. Wiltshire, 7¼ m. N. of Salisbury ; pop. 1530. Map 76.

Amlwch, par., urb. dist., and seaport, N. Anglesey, 24 m. N.W. of Bangor ; pop. 2561. Map 36.

Ammanford, urb. dist. and par., Carmarthenshire, 7 m. S. of Llandilo ; pop. 7160. Map 66.

Ampleforth, par. and vil., N.R. Yorkshire, 4 m. S.W. of Helmsley ; pop. 877. Map 28.

Ampthill, urb. dist. and par., in co. and 7 m. S. of Bedford ; pop. 2167. Map 60.

Amulree, *q.s.* par. and vil., Perthshire, 11 m. N.N.E. of Crieff ; pop. 292. Map 6.

Ancaster, par. and vil., Kesteven, Lincolnshire, 6 m. W. of Sleaford ; pop. 566. Map 50.

Ancrum, par. and vil., N. Roxburghshire, 3½ m. N.W. of Jedburgh ; pop. 912. Map 16.

Andover, mun. bor., Hants, on r. Anton, 17¼ m. N.E. of Salisbury ; pop. 9692. Map 76.

Annan, royal bur. and seaport, in co. and 15½ m. S.E. of Dumfries ; pop. 3959. Map 20.

Annfield Plain, urb. dist., Durham, 4 m. E. of Consett ; pop. 15,922. Map 23.

Anstruther, seaport and market town, Fifeshire, 18¼ m. E. of Thornton Junction ; pop. 1673. Map 7.

Antrim, par. and market town, co. Antrim, 27¾ m. N.W. of Belfast ; pop. 4160. Map 93.

Appleby, mun. bor., par. and co. town of Westmorland, 14 m. S.W. of Penrith ; pop. 1618. Map 26.

Applecross, par. and ham., Ross and Cromarty, 11 m. N.W. of Lochcarron ; pop. 1119. Map 2.

Appledore, eccl. par. and seaport vil., N. Devon, 3 m. N. of Bideford ; pop. 2706. Map 84.

Arbirlot, coast par. and vil., Angus, 2½ m. W. of Arbroath ; pop. 789. Map 7.

Arbroath, mun. bur. and seaport, Angus, 17 m. N.E. of Dundee ; pop. 17,637. Map 7.

Ardee, par. and town, co. Louth, 14 m. N.W. of Drogheda ; pop. of town, 1730. Map 93.

Ardlui, vil. with ry. sta. at N. end of Loch Lomond, Dumbartonshire. Map 12.

Ardmore, par. and vil., Waterford, 5¼ m. E. of Youghal ; pop. 2197. Map 95.

Ardnadam, vil., Argyllshire, on Holy Loch, 2 m. N. of Dunoon. Map 12.

Ardnamurchan, par., W. Argyllshire, with lighthouse on **Ardnamurchan Point** ; pop. 1369. Map 2.

Ardrishaig, par. and seaport, Argyllshire, 2 m. S. of Lochgilphead ; pop. 1244. Map 12.

Ardrossan, par., police bur. and seaport, Ayrshire, 6 m. N.W. of Irvine ; pop. 6888. Map 12.

Arklet, Loch, Stirlingshire, ¾ m. S.W. of Loch Katrine, depth 67 feet. Map 5.

Arklow, par., market town and seaport, co. Wicklow, 49 m. S.E. of Dublin ; pop. 4526. Map 95.

Armadale, par. and town, W. Lothian, 2½ m. W. by S. of Bathgate ; pop. (town) 4854. Map 9.

Armagh, parl. bur. and co. town of Armagh, 35¼ m. S.W. of Belfast ; pop. 7356. Map 93.

Arncliffe, par. and vil., W.R. Yorkshire, 9 m. N.E. of Settle ; pop. 101. Map 27.

Arnold, urb. dist., Nottinghamshire, 3 m. N.E. of Nottingham ; pop. 14,470. Map 49.

Arran, Isle of, in Firth of Clyde, forms part of Buteshire ; pop. 8294. Map 12.

Arrochar, vil. and pier, Dumbartonshire, at head of Loch Long, 17¼ m. N. of Helensburgh. Map 12.

Artney, Glen, traversed by the Ruchill Water, Perthshire, 8 m. S.W. of Comrie. Map 5.

Arundel, mun. bor. and par., W. Sussex, 10 m. E. of Chichester ; pop. 2489. Map 79.

Ascot, vil., S.E. Berks., 6¼ m. S.W. of Windsor. Map 78.

Ash, par. and vil., W. Surrey, 2 m. E. of Aldershot ; pop. 5479. Map 78.

Ashbourne, urb. dist. and par., in co. and 13 m. N.W. of Derby ; pop. 4507. Map 40.

Ashburton, urb. dist. and par., Devon, 9½ m. N. of Totnes ; pop. 2505. Map 89.

Ashby-de-la-Zouch, urb. dist. and par., in co. and 21¼ m. N.W. of Leicester ; pop. 5093. Map 49.

Ashford, par. and vil., Middlesex, 2 m. E. of Staines; pop. 7673. Map 71.
Ashford, urb. dist. and par., Kent, 14 m. S.W. of Canterbury; pop. 15,239. Map 83.
Ashington, urb. dist. and par., Northumberland, 4 m. E.N.E. of Morpeth; pop. 29,418. Map 17.
Ashperton, par. and vil., Herefordshire, 5 m. N.W. of Ledbury; pop. 352. Map 57.
Ashprington, par. and vil., Devon, 2¾ m. S.E. of Totnes; pop. 387. Map 89.
Ashridge, Bonar Law Unionist College, Herts, 3 m. N. of Berkhamsted. Map 71.
Ashtead, par. and vil., mid Surrey, 2 m. S.W. of Epsom; pop. 3226. Map 78.
Ashton-in-Makerfield, par. and urb. dist., S.W. Lancs., 7 m. N.W. of Warrington; pop. 20,541. Map 39.
Ashton-under-Lyne, par., parl. and mun. bor., Lancashire, 6 m. E. of Manchester; pop. 51,573. Map 39.
Ashton-upon-Ribble, eccl. dist., N. Lancashire, 2 m. W. of Preston; pop. 8042. Map 30.
Ashwell, par. and vil., Hertfordshire, 4½ m. N.E. of Baldock; pop. 1163. Map 61.
Askam, vil. with ry. sta., Lancashire, 6 m. N.N.E. of Barrow-in-Furness. Map 25.
Askeaton, par. and town, in co. and 16¼ m. W.S.W. of Limerick; pop. 594. Map 94.
Askrigg, par. and vil., N.R. Yorkshire, 12 m. W. of Leyburn; pop. 481. Map 27.
Aspatria, urb. dist., Cumberland, 7½ m. N.E. of Maryport; pop. 3239. Map 20.
Aston Cantlow, par. and vil., Warwickshire, 5½ m. N.W. of Stratford-on-Avon; pop. 878. Map 58.
Aston-on-Clun, vil., Salop, 3 m. W.S.W. of Craven Arms. Map 56.
Athenry, market town, in co. and 12 m. E. of Galway; pop. 791. Map 94.
Atherstone, market town and par., Warwickshire, 8 m. S.E. of Tamworth; pop. 5957. Map 48.
Atherton, urb. dist., town and par., S.W. Lancashire, 11 m. N.W. of Manchester; pop. 19,985. Map 39.
Athleague, par. and vil., cos. Galway and Roscommon, 6 m. S.W. of Roscommon; pop. 155. Map 92.
Athlone, urb. dist., cos. Roscommon and Westmeath, 48½ m. E. of Galway; pop. 7546. Map 95.
Athy, urb. dist., co. Kildare, 44¾ m. S.W. of Dublin; pop. 3549. Map 95.
Attleborough, eccl. dist. and vil., Warwickshire, 1 m. S.S.E. of Nuneaton; pop. 4782. Map 49.
Attleborough, par. and market town, Norfolk, 16 m. S.W. of Norwich; pop. 2453. Map 52.
Attlebridge, par. and ry. sta., Norfolk, 8 m. N.W. of Norwich; pop. 88. Map 53.
Auchterarder, par. and market town, S.E. Perthshire, 14 m. S.W. of Perth; pop. 2254. Map 6.
Auchterderran, par. and vil., Fifeshire, 5 m. N.W. of Kirkcaldy; pop. 19,088. Map 10.
Auchtermuchty, par., bur. and market town, N.W. Fifeshire, 4½ m. W. of Ladybank Jct.; pop. 1253. Map. 6.
Auchtertool, par. and vil., Fifeshire, 4 m. W. of Kirkcaldy; pop. 257. Map 10.
Audlem, par. and town, Cheshire, 5½ m. S. of Nantwich; pop. 1394. Map 39.
Audley, urb. dist., Staffordshire, 4½ m. N.W. of Newcastle-under-Lyme; pop. 13,619. Map 39.
Aughrim, vil. and ry. sta., co. Wicklow, 8 m. S.S.W. of Rathdrum; pop. 291. Map 95.
Aveley, par. and vil., S. Essex, 7 m. S.E. of Romford; pop. 1567. Map 80.
Avening, par. and vil., Gloucestershire, 5 m. S.E. of Stroud; pop. 828. Map 68.
Aviemore, vil. and ry. sta., Inverness-shire, 12½ m. S.W. of Grantown. Map 3.
Avonmouth, eccl. par. and seaport, Gloucestershire, 6¼ m. N.W. of Bristol; pop. 2949. Map 67.
Awe, Loch, N. Argyllshire, extends 24 m. N.N.E. to the base of Ben Cruachan. Map 12.
Axbridge, par. and small town, N.W. Somerset, 9½ m. N.W. of Wells; pop. 919. Map 74.
Axminster, urb. dist. and par., Devonshire, 27 m. N.E. of Exeter; pop. 2327. Map 86.
Axmouth, par. and fishing vil., Devonshire, 6 m. S.W. of Axminster; pop. 594. Map 86.
Aycliffe, par. and vil., S. co. Durham, 5½ m. N. of Darlington; pop. 820. Map 27.
Aylesbury, mun. bor. and par., in co. and 17 m. S.E. of Buckingham; pop. 13,382. Map 70.
Aylesford, par. and vil., Kent, 3½ m. N.W. of Maidstone; pop. 3113. Map 82.
Aylsham, par. and market town, Norfolk, 12 m. N. of Norwich; pop. 2466. Map 53.
Ayr, seaport, parl. and mun. bur., and co. town of Ayrshire, 41½ m. S.W. of Glasgow; pop. 36,784. Map 12.
Ayton, par. and vil., Berwickshire, 7¼ m. N.W. of Berwick-on-Tweed; pop. 1521. Map 11.
Ayton, Great, and **Little**, 2 pars., N.R. Yorkshire, 3 m. N.E. of Stokesley, pop. 2708 and 144. Map 28.
BACTON, coast par. and vil., Norfolk, 4½ m. N.E. of N. Walsham; pop. 585. Map 53.
Bacup, mun. bor., par. and market town, Lancashire, 21¾ m. N. of Manchester; pop. 20,606. Map 31.
Bagenalstown, market town, in co. and 10 m. S. of Carlow; pop. 1825. Map 95.
Bagshot, eccl. par. and town, W. Surrey, 3 m. S. of Ascot; pop. 2198. Map 78.
Baildon, urb. dist., Yorkshire, 1½ m. N.E. of Shipley; pop. 7794. Map 32.
Bainbridge, par., N.R. Yorkshire, 1½ m. S.W. of Askrigg; pop. 632. Map 27.
Bakewell, urb. dist., par. and market town, in co. and 25 m. N.W. of Derby; pop. 3012. Map 40.
Bala, urb. dist. and par., Merionethshire, 10¾ m. S.W. of Corwen; pop. 1395. Map 45.
Bala Lake, Merionethshire, 4 m. long by ½ m. broad. Map 45.
Balbriggan, seaport town, in co. and 21¾ m. N.N.E. of Dublin; pop. 2278. Map 93.
Baldock, urb. dist. and par., Hertfordshire, 4¾ m. N.E. of Hitchin; pop. 3171. Map 61.
Balerno, vil., Midlothian, 7½ m. S.W. of Edinburgh pop. 651. Map 10.
Balfron, par. and vil., W. Stirlingshire, 3 m. N.E. of Killearn; vil. pop. 873. Map 8.
Ballachulish, vil., Argyllshire, on Loch Leven, 16½ m. S. of Fort William; pop. 714. Map 12.
Ballaghaderreen, town, Roscommon, 12¼ m. N.W. of Castlerea; pop. 1317. Map 92.
Ballantree, coast vil., Ayrshire, 13 m. S.W. of Girvan. Map 18.
Ballater, police bur., in co. and 43¼ m. S.W. of Aberdeen; pop. 1198. Map 3.
Ballaugh, par. and vil., Isle of Man, 7 m. W. of Ramsey; pop. 648. Map 24.
Ballina, urb. dist. and seaport, co. Mayo, 7¾ m. S. of Killala; pop. 4872. Map 92.
Ballinasloe, urb. dist., co. Roscommon, 12 m. S.W. of Athlone; pop. 5243. Map 92.
Ballinluig, village and ry. junct., Perthshire, 8 m. N.W. of Dunkeld. Map 6.
Ballinrobe, market town and par., co. Mayo, 12½ m. S.W. of Claremorris; pop. 1585. Map 92.
Balloch, vil., Dumbartonshire, at foot of Loch Lomond, 19½ m. N.W. of Glasgow. Map 12.
Ballybofey, vil. and ry. sta., in E. of co. Donegal. Map 92.
Ballycastle, vil., co. Mayo, 18 m. N.W. of Ballina. Map 92.
Ballycastle, seaport and market town, co. Antrim, 16½ m. N. of Ballymoney; pop. 1485 Map 93.
Ballyclare, market town, W. Antrim, 12½ m. N.E. of Belfast; pop. 3369. Map 95.

Ballycottin, vil., co. Cork, 11½ m. S.E. of Midleton; pop. 431.   Map 95.

Ballyhaise, vil., in co. and 4½ m. N.E. of Cavan ; pop. 92.   Map 93.

Ballylongford, vil., co. Kerry, 8 m. N. of Listowel; pop. 484.   Map 94.

Ballymahon, market town, in co. and 13½ m. S. of Longford ; pop. 661.   Map 93.

Ballymena, urb. dist. and market town, in co. and 11½ m. N. of Antrim ; pop. 11,381.   Map 93.

Ballymoney, urb. dist. and market town, co. Antrim, 20 m. N.W. of Ballymena ; pop. 3100.   Map 93.

Ballynahinch, market town, co. Down, 21¼ m. S. of Belfast ; pop. 1667.   Map 93.

Ballyshannon, seaport town, in co. and 14 m. S.W. of Donegal ; pop. 2112.   Map 92.

Ballyvaughan, fishing vil., co. Clare, 10 m. N.E. of Lisdoonvarna ; pop. 116.   Map 94.

Balmerino, par. and vil., Fifeshire, 3½ m. W. of Wormit ; pop. 699.   Map 7.

Balmoral, royal residence, on r. Dee, in co. and 52½ m. W. of Aberdeen.   Map 3.

Balquhidder, par. and vil., Perthshire, 3 m. S.W. of Lochearnhead ; pop. 875.   Map 12.

Baltinglass, market town, co. Wicklow, 10½ m. N. of Tullow ; pop. 860.   Map 95.

Bamber Bridge, vil., N.E. Lancashire, 3 m. S.E. of Preston ; pop. 3018.   Map 30.

Bamburgh, coast par., Northumberland, 5 m. E. of Belford ; pop. 734.   Map 17.

Bampton, par. and vil., N.W. Westmorland, 3 m. N.W. of Shap ; pop. 424.   Map 26.

Bampton, urb. dist. and par., Devonshire, 7 m. N.W. of Tiverton ; pop. 1392.   Map 85.

Bampton, market town and par., Oxon, 5 m. S.W. of Witney ; pop. 1104.   Map 69.

Banagher, market town, Offaly co., 8 m. N.W. of Birr ; pop. 891.   Map 95.

Banavie, vil., Inverness-shire, 2½ m. N.N.E. of Fort William.   Map 2.

Banbridge, urb. dist., co. Down, 24½ m. S.W. of Belfast ; pop. 5101.   Map 93.

Banbury, mun. bor. and par., in co. and 22 m. N. of Oxford ; pop. 13,953.   Map 59.

Banchory, police bur., Kincardineshire, 16¾ m. S.W. of Aberdeen ; pop. 1690.   Map 3.

Bandon, market town on r. Bandon, in co. and 20 m. S.W. of Cork ; pop. 2816.   Map 94.

Banff, mun. bur., par. and cap. of Banffshire, 64¼ m. N.W. of Aberdeen ; pop. 3489.   Map 3.

Bangor, par., bor. and city, Carnarvonshire, nr. Menai Strait, 59¾ m. W. of Chester ; pop. 10,959.   Map 36.

Bangor, par., urb. dist. and seaport, co. Down, 12 m. N.E. of Belfast ; pop. 11,515.   Map 93.

Bankfoot, vil., S.E. Perthshire, 4 m. N.W. of Strathord ; pop. 713.   Map 6.

Bannockburn, par. and town, in co. and 2½ m. S.E. of Stirling ; town pop. 4223.   Map 9.

Banstead, par. and vil., mid Surrey, 3 m. E. of Epsom ; pop. 7337.   Map 80.

Bantry, seaport tov , co. Cork, 17¾ m. N.W. of Skibbereen ; pop. 2681.   Map 94.

Banwell, par. and vil., N.W. Somersetshire, 3½ m. N.W. of Axbridge ; pop. 1416.   Map 74.

Bapchild, par. and vil., Kent, 1½ m. E.S.E. of Sittingbourne ; pop. 486.   Map 82.

Bardsey, isl. in Cardigan Bay, S.W. Carnarvonshire; pop. 58.   Map 44.

Bardwell, par. and vil., Suffolk, 8 m. N.E. of Bury St. Edmunds ; pop. 653.   Map 62.

Bargoed, ward of Gelligaer urb. dist., Glamorganshire, 18½ m. N. of Cardiff.   Map 67.

Barham, par. and ham., Kent, 6 m. S.E. of Canterbury ; pop. 905.   Map 83.

Barking, mun. bor., S.W. Essex, 7½ m. E. of London ; pop. 51,277.   Map 80.

Barkisland, urb. dist. and par., W.R. Yorkshire, 5 m. S.W. of Halifax ; pop. 1552.   Map 31.

Barkway, par. and vil., Hertfordshire, 4¼ m. S.E. of Royston ; pop. 568.   Map 61.

Barlby, par. and vil., E.R. Yorkshire, 1¼ m. N.E. of Selby ; pop. 2593.   Map 33.

Barmouth, urb. dist., par. and seaport, Merionethshire, 9¼ m. W.S.W. of Dolgelley ; pop. 2491.   Map 44.

Barnack, par. and vil., Soke of Peterborough, Northants, 3½ m. S.E. of Stamford ; pop. 548.   Map 50.

Barnard Castle, urb. dist. and par., S.W. Durham, 15½ m. W. of Darlington ; pop. 3883.   Map 27.

Barnes, urb. dist., Surrey, 7 m. S.W. of Waterloo Sta., London ; pop. 42,439.   Map 71.

Barnet, urb. dist. and market town, Hertfordshire, 11¼ m. N. of London ; pop. 14,721.   Map 71.

Barnham, par. and ry. sta., W. Suffolk, 2¼ m. S. of Thetford ; pop. 384.   Map 62.

Barnoldswick, urb. dist., W.R. Yorkshire, 9¼ m. S.W. of Skipton ; pop. 11,915.   Map 31.

Barnsley, parl. and co. bor. and market town, W.R. Yorks, 16 m. N. of Sheffield ; pop. 71,522.   Map 32.

Barnstaple, mun. bor. and seaport town, N. Devon, 39¼ m. N.W. of Exeter ; pop. 14,693.   Map 84.

Barnwood, par. and vil., in co. and 2 m. E. of Gloucester ; pop. 1333.   Map 68.

Barrasford, vil., Northumberland, 8¼ m. N.W. of Hexham.   Map 22.

Barrhead, police bur., Renfrewshire, 7½ m. S.W. of Glasgow ; pop. 12,308.   Map 8.

Barrington, par. and vil., Somersetshire, 3 m. N.E. of Ilminster ; pop. 358.   Map 86.

Barrowby, par. and vil., Kesteven, Lincolnshire, 2 m. W. of Grantham ; pop. 812.   Map 50.

Barrowford, urb. dist., N.E. Lancashire, 2 m. W. of Colne ; pop. 5299.   Map 31.

Barrow-in-Furness, parl. and co. bor. and seaport, Lancs, 50 m. N.W. of Liverpool ; pop. 66,366.   Map 25.

Barry, coast par., vil. and military camp, Angus, 9¼ m. N.E. of Dundee ; pop. 6133.   Map 7.

Barry, urb. dist., Glamorganshire, 7 m. S.W. of Cardiff ; pop. 38,916.   Map 67.

Barton-in-the-Clay, par. and vil., Bedfordshire, 6 m. N. of Luton ; pop. 783.   Map 60.

Barton Mills, par. and vil., W. Suffolk, 1 m. S.E. of Mildenhall ; pop. 464.   Map 62.

Barton-upon-Humber, par., urb. dist. and market town, N. Lincs, 6 m. S.W. of Hull ; pop. 6330.   Map 35.

Baschurch, par. and vil., Salop, 7½ m. N.W. of Shrewsbury ; pop. 1435.   Map 46.

Basingstoke, mun. bor., N. Hants, 48 m. S.W. of London ; pop. 13,862.   Map 78.

Baslow-with-Bubnell, Derbyshire, 3 m. N.E. of Bakewell ; pop. 854.   Map 40.

Bassenthwaite, par., lake and sta., Cumberland, 7½ m. N.W. of Keswick ; pop. 437.   Map 20.

Bassett, vil., Hampshire, 2 m. N. of Southampton.   Map 77.

Bath, city, co. and parl. bor., N.E. Somersetshire, 11¼ m. S.E. of Bristol ; pop. 68,801.   Map 75.

Bathgate, par. and market town, W. Lothian, 18½ m. W.S.W. of Edinburgh ; pop. 10,097.   Map 9.

Batley, mun. bor. and par., W.R. Yorkshire, 8 m. S.W. of Leeds ; pop. 34,573.   Map 32.

Battle, urb. dist. and par., E. Sussex, 6¼ m. N.W. of Hastings ; pop. 3490.   Map 82.

Battlesbridge, vil., S.E. Essex, 9¾ m. S.W. of Maldon. Map 72.

Bawtry, par. and market town, W.R. Yorkshire, 9 m. S.E. of Doncaster ; pop. 1219.   Map 41.

Beachy Head, prom. on S. Coast of Sussex, 3 m. N.W. of Eastbourne ; alt. 530 ft.   Map 81.

Beaconsfield, urb. dist. and par., Buckinghamshire, 5½ m. S. of Amersham ; pop. 4843.   Map 71.

Beaminster, market town and par., Dorsetshire, 6 m. N. of Bridport; pop. 1651. Map 86.
Bearsden, town, S.E. Dumbartonshire, 5 m. N.W. of Glasgow; pop. 3362. Map 8.
Beattock, vil. and ry. sta., Dumfriesshire, 2 m. S.W. of Moffat. Map 15.
Beaulieu, par. and vil., Hants, 6 m. N.E. of Lymington; pop. 1011. Map 77.
Beauly, town and ry. sta., in co. and 10 m. W. of Inverness; pop. 805. Map 3.
Beaumaris, mun. bor., par. and seaport, Anglesey, 7 m. N.E. of Bangor; pop. 1708. Map 36.
Bebington and Bromborough, urb. dist., Cheshire, 5 m. S.E. of Birkenhead; pop. 26,742. Map 38.
Bebside, colliery vil., Northumberland, 1 m. S.E. of Bedlington. Map 17.
Beccles, mun. bor. and par., E. Suffolk, 8½ m. W. of Lowestoft; pop. 6544. Map 63.
Beckenham, urb. dist., N.W. Kent, 2 m. W. of Bromley; pop. 43,834. Map 80.
Beckfoot, vil., Cumberland, 3½ m. S. of Silloth. Map 20.
Beckington, par. and vil., E. Somersetshire, 3 m. N.E. of Frome; pop. 727. Map 75.
Bedale, par. and market town, N.R. Yorkshire, 7½ m. S.W. of Northallerton; pop. 1064. Map 27.
Beddgelert, par. and vil., in co. and 12½ m. S.E. of Carnarvon; pop. 1055. Map 36.
Beddington and Wallington, urb. dist., Surrey, 1½ m. W. of Croydon; pop. 26,249. Map 80.
Bedford, mun. bor. and co. town of Bedfordshire, 49¾ m. N.W. of London; pop. 40,573. Map 60.
Bedlington, par. co-extensive with **Bedlingtonshire** urb. dist., Northumberland, 5 m. S.E. of Morpeth; pop. 27,315. Map 17.
Bedrule, par. and ham., Roxburghshire, 4 m. S.W. of Jedburgh; pop. 180. Map 16.
Bedwas and Machen, urb. dist., Monmouthshire, 9 m. W. of Newport; pop. 9190. Map 67.
Bedwellty, urb. dist., Monmouthshire, 3½ m. S. of Tredegar; pop. 30,069. Map 67.
Bedworth, par. and town, Warwickshire, 3½ m. S. of Nuneaton; pop. 12,058. Map 49.
Beer, coast par. and vil., Devonshire, 5½ m. S.W. of Axminster; pop. 1257. Map 86.
Beeston, urb. dist. and par., in co. and 3¼ m. S.W. of Nottingham; pop. 16,016. Map 49.
Beith, par. and market town, Ayrshire, 18½ m. S.W. of Glasgow; town pop. 4098. Map 8.
Belfast, parl. and co. bor. on **B. Lough,** cos. Antrim and Down, 113 m. N. of Dublin; pop. 414,844. Map 93.
Belford, par. and market town, Northumberland, 15¼ m. S.E. of Berwick; pop. 663. Map 17.
Belleek, par. and vil., co. Fermanagh, 22 m. N.W. of Enniskillen; pop. 1276. Map 92.
Bellingham, par. and vi., Northumberland, 17 m. N.W. of Hexham; pop. 1392. Map 16.
Belmullet, fishing vil., N.W. co. Mayo, 38¾ m. W.N.W. of Ballina; pop. 681. Map 92.
Belper, urb. dist., par. and market town in co. and 7¾ m. N. of Derby; pop. 13,023. Map 41.
Belton, par. and vil., Lincolnshire, in Isle of Axholme, 1½ m. N.E. of Epworth; pop. 1528. Map 42.
Bembridge, par. and vil., S. Hants, 2½ m. N.E. of Brading, Isle of Wight; pop. 1973. Map 77.
Bempton, coast par. and vil., E.R. Yorkshire, 3½ m. N. of Bridlington; pop. 300. Map 29.
Benfieldside, urb. dist., Durham, 13 m. S.W. of Gateshead; pop. 9193. Map 22.
Benfleet, urb. dist., Essex, 3 m. S.W. of Rayleigh; pop. 12,091. Map 72.
Benfleet, South, coast par., S. Essex, 6 m. W. of Southend; pop. 1918. Map 72.
Bennington, Long, par. and vil., Kesteven, Lincolnshire, 8 m. N.W. of Grantham; pop. 756. Map 50.
Bentley, Gt., par. and vil., N.E. Essex, 8 m. S.E. of Colchester; pop. 1093. Map 73.
Bentley with Arksey, urb. dist., W.R. Yorkshire, 2 m. N. of Doncaster; pop. 16,458. Map 41.
Bentworth, par. and vil., N.E. Hants, 3½ m. N.W. of Alton; pop. 522. Map 78.
Berkeley, town in co. and 15 m. S.W. of Gloucester. Map 68.
Berkhamsted, urb. dist., W. Herts, 10 m. N.W. of Watford; pop. 8053. Map 71.
Berriew, par. and vil., in E. of co. and 3½ m. N.W. of Montgomery; pop. 1479. Map 46.
Bervie, par., parl. and royal bur., mkt. tn., Kincardineshire, 13 m. N.E. of Montrose; pop. 2153. Map 3.
Berwick-upon-Tweed, co. of a town, mun. bor., par. and seaport town, Northumberland, 57½ m. E.S.E. of Edinburgh; pop. 12,299. Map 11.
Bessingby, par., vil. and seat, E.R. Yorkshire, 1½ m. S.W. of Bridlington; pop. 429. Map 29.
Betchworth, par. and vil., mid Surrey, 2¾ m. W.S.W. of Reigate; pop. 1908. Map 80.
Bethersden, par. and vil., S. Kent, 5 m. S.W. of Ashford; pop. 922. Map 82.
Bethesda, urb. dist. and par., Carnarvonshire, 5 m. S.E. of Bangor; pop. 4476. Map 37.
Bettws Garmon, par. and ham., in N.W. of co. and 5 m. S.E. of Carnarvon; pop. 340. Map 36.
Bettwys-y-Coed, urb. dist. and par., E. Carnarvonshire, 4 m. S. of Llanrwst; pop. 912. Map 37.
Beverley, mun. bor. and market town, E.R. Yorkshire, 8¼ m. N.N.W. of Hull; pop. 14,011. Map 35.
Bewdley, mun. bor., Worcestershire, 3 m. W.S.W. of Kidderminster; pop. 2868. Map 57.
Bexhill, mun. bor. and coast par., E. Sussex, 5 m. S.W. of Hastings; pop. 21,229. Map 81.
Bexley, urb. dist., Kent, 4½ m. W. of Dartford; pop. 32,940. Map 80.
Bexleyheath, eccl. par. and vil., N.W. Kent, 3 m. W.N.W. of Dartford; pop. 11,140. Map 80.
Bicester, urb. dist., seat and market town, in N.E. of co. and 12 m. N.E. of Oxford; pop. 3109. Map 70.
Bickleigh, par. and seat, E. Devon, on r. Exe, 10 m. N. of Exeter; pop. 191. Map 85.
Biddenham, par. and vil., in co. and 2 m. W. of Bedford; pop. 460. Map 60.
Biddestone, par. and vil., N. Wiltshire, 4 m. W. of Chippenham; pop. 418. Map 68.
Biddulph, urb. dist., Staffordshire, 4 m. S.E. of Congleton; pop. 8346. Map 39.
Bideford, mun. bor. and seaport, N. Devon, 8¾ m. S.W. of Barnstaple; pop. 8782. Map 84.
Biggar, par. and town, Lanarkshire, 13½ m. S.E. of Lanark; pop. 1323. Map 15.
Biggleswade, urb. dist. and par., in co. and 9 m. E.S.E. of Bedford; pop. 5844. Map 60.
Billericay, eccl. par. and market town, S. Essex, 5¼ m. E. of Brentwood; pop. 1500. Map 72.
Billesdon, par. and vil., in S. of co. and 8½ m. S.E. of Leicester; pop. 514. Map 49.
Billinge and Winstanley, urb. dist., Lancashire, 4½ m. S.W. of Wigan; pop. 5111. Map 39.
Billingham, urb. dist., Durham, 2½ m. N.E. of Stockton-on-Tees; pop. 17,972. Map 23.
Billinghay, par. and vil., S. Lincolnshire, 8 m. N.E. of Sleaford; pop. 1226. Map 43.
Billingshurst, par. and vil., W. Sussex, 6 m. S.W. of Horsham; pop. 1873. Map 79.
Bilston, urb. dist., par. and market town, S. Staffs, 2½ m. S.E. of Wolverhampton; pop. 31,248. Map 47.
Bingham, par. and market town, in co. and 8½ m. E. of Nottingham; pop. 1576. Map 49.
Bingley, urb. dist., par. and mkt. town, W.R. Yorkshire, 5½ m. N.W. of Bradford; pop. 20,553. Map 32.
Birchington, coast par. and vil., N.E. Kent, 3½ m. W.S.W. of Margate; pop. 3503. Map 83.

Birkenhead, co. and parl. bor., seaport town and par., Cheshire, on left bank of Mersey, opp. Liverpool, 13 m. N.N.W. of Chester; pop. 147,946. Map 38.
Birkenshaw, urb. dist., W.R. Yorkshire, 3½ m. S.E. of Bradford; pop. 2816. Map 32.
Birmingham, city, parl., mun. and co. bor., Warwicksh., 113 m. N.W. of London; pop. 1,002,413. Map 48.
Birnam, vil., E. Perths., ¾ m. S.E. of Dunkeld; pop. 711. Map 6.
Birr, or **Parsonstown,** par., market town and urb. dist., 11¾ m. N. of Roscrea; pop. 5405. Map 95.
Birstall, urb. dist. and par. town, W.R. Yorkshire, 2 m. N.W. of Batley; pop. 7205. Map 32.
Birtley, par., vil. and seat, Durham, 5¼ m. S.E. of Gateshead; pop. 11,279. Map 23.
Bishop Auckland, urb. dist., par. and mkt. tn., S. Durham, 11 m. S.W. of Durham; pop. 12,269. Map 23.
Bishopbriggs, now a district in Glasgow, 3½ m. N.E. of Queen Street ry. sta. Map 8.
Bishop's Castle, mun. bor., Salop, 18 m. S.W. of Shrewsbury; pop. 1352. Map 46.
Bishop's Cleave, par. and vil., N. Gloucestershire, 3 m. N. of Cheltenham; pop. 615. Map 57.
Bishop's Frome, par., Herefordshire, 4 m. S. of Bromyard; pop. 696. Map 57.
Bishop's Nympton, par. and vil., N. Devon, 4½ m. S.E. of South Molton; pop. 843. Map 85.
Bishop's Stortford, urb. dist., par. and mkt. tn., in E. of co. and 14 m. N.E. of Hertford; pop. 9509. Map 72.
Bishops-Tawton, par. and vil., N. Devon, 2 m. S.E. of Barnstaple; pop. 779. Map 84.
Bishopsteignton, par. and vil., E. Devon, 2 m. W. of Teignmouth; pop. 1066. Map 89.
Bishopstone, par. and vil., N. Wiltshire, on verge of co., 6 m. E. of Swindon; pop. 427. Map 69.
Bishop's Waltham, par. and mkt. town, S.E. Hampshire, 9½ m. S.E. of Winchester; pop. 2597. Map 77.
Bishopthorpe, par., W.R. Yorkshire, on r. Ouse, 2½ m. S. of York; contains **B. Palace**; pop. 486. Map 33.
Bishopton, vil., N. Renfrewshire, 5¾ m. N.W. of Paisley; pop. 739. Map 8.
Bitterne, par. and seat, S. Hampshire, in co. bor. of Southampton; pop. 3882. Map 77.
Blackawton, par. and vil., S. Devon, 4 m. W. of Dartmouth; pop. 943. Map 89.
Black Borong, hotel, in co. and 4½ m. N. of Peebles. Map 10.
Blackburn, parl., co. bor. and par., mid Lancashire, 11 m. E. of Preston; pop. 122,695. Map 30.
Blackford, par. and vil., S. Perthshire, 10 m. N.E. of Dunblane; pop. 1593. Map 6.
Black Hill, eccl. dist. and vil., N.W. Durham, between Consett and Shotley Bridge; pop. 5342. Map 22.
Blackpool, parl. and co. bor., par., seaport and lifeboat sta., N. Lancashire, 16½ m. N.W. of Preston; pop. 101,543. Map 30.
Blackrod, urb. dist., Lancashire, 5 m. S.E. of Chorley; pop. 3599. Map 30.
Blackwater, vil., N.E. Hants, 3½ m. N.W. of Farnborough. Map 78.
Blackwood, vil., W. Monmouthshire, 7½ m. W.N.W. of Pontypool. Map 67.
Blackwood, vil. and ry. sta., Lanarkshire, 2 m. S. of Stonehouse. Map 14.
Blaenau Ffestiniog, vil., N.W. Merionethshire, 2½ m. N. of Ffestiniog Duffws. Map 37.
Blaen-Avon, urb. dist. and par., N.W. Monmouthshire, 5½ m. N.W. of Pontypool; pop. 11,075. Map 67l
Blaengarw, mining vil., S. Glamorganshire, 9½ m. N. of Bridgend. Map 66.
Blaengwynfi, vil., N. Glamorganshire, 10 m. N.E. of Port Talbot. Map 66.
Blagdon, par. and vil., N. Somersetshire, 11 m. S.W. of Bristol; pop. 958. Map 74.
Blair-Atholl, par. and vil., N. Perthshire, 35¼ m. N.W. of Perth; pop. 1824. Map 3.
Blairgowrie and Rattray, burgh, E. Perthshire, 4¾ m. N.W. of Coupar-Angus; pop. 4676. Map 6.
Blakeney, eccl. dist. and vil., W. Gloucestershire, 3½ m. S.W. of Newnham; pop. 849. Map 68.
Blakeney, par. and vil., Norfolk, 5½ m. N.W. of Holt; pop. 662. Map 52.
Blanchland, eccl. dist. and vil., Northumberland, 9 m. S.E. of Hexham; pop. 222. Map 22.
Blandford, par., mun. bor. and market town, E. Dorset, 16 m. N.E. of Dorchester; pop. 3371. Map 87.
Blanefield, vil., S.W. Stirlingshire, 16¾ m. N.W. of Glasgow. Map 8.
Blantyre, town, Lanarkshire, 3½ m. W. by N. of Hamilton. Map 9.
Blaydon, urb. dist., Durham, 4½ m. W. of Newcastle; pop. 32,259. Map 23.
Blean, par., E. Kent, 2 m. N.W. of Canterbury; pop. 601. Map 83.
Bleasby, par. and vil., in co. and 11 m. N.E. of Nottingham; pop. 288. Map 41.
Bletchingdon, par. and seat, Oxfordshire, 7 m. N. of Oxford; pop. 492. Map 70.
Bletchingley, par. and vil., Surrey, 3 m. E. of Redhill; pop. 2190. Map 80.
Bletchley, ham., N. Shropshire, 3½ m. W. of Market Drayton. Map 47.
Bletchley, urb. dist., Buckinghamshire, 45¾ m. N.W. of London; pop. 6169. Map 60.
Bloxham, par. and vil., Oxon, 3½ m. S.W. of Banbury; pop. 1384. Map 59.
Bloxwich, eccl. dist. and vil., Staffordshire, 2¾ m. N.N.W. of Walsall; pop. 8662. Map 48.
Blundell Sands, eccl. dist., Lancashire, 6¼ m. N.W. of Liverpool; pop. 3991. Map 38.
Blunham, par. and vil., in co. and 6 m. E. of Bedford; pop. 603. Map 60.
Blunsdon Broad, eccl. dist. and vil., N. Wiltshire, 4 m. N. of Swindon; pop. 750. Map 69.
Bluntisham cum Earith, par. and vil., Huntingdonshire, 3¾ m. N.E. of St Ives; pop. 1006. Map 61.
Blyth, mun. bor., seaport and par., Northumberland, 9 m. S.E. of Morpeth; pop. 31,808. Map 17.
Blyth, par. and vil., N. Notts, 7 m. N.E. of Worksop; pop. 600. **B. Hall,** seat of Lord Barnby. Map 41.
Blyth, river, S. Northumberland, flows 20 miles to North Sea at Blyth. Map 23.
Blythburgh, par. and vil., E. Suffolk, 3½ m. W.S.W. of Southwold; pop. 673. Map 63.
Blythebridge, ham. and ry. sta., Staffordshire, 5½ m. S.E. of Stoke-on-Trent. Map 47.
Boat of Garten, vil., Inverness-shire, 5 m. N.E. of Aviemore; pop. 322. Map 3.
Bodenham, par. and vil., Herefordshire, 5½ m. S.E. of Leominster; pop. 685. Map 56.
Bodmin, mun. bor. and par., Cornwall, 29 m. N.W. of Plymouth; pop. 5526. Map 91.
Bodorgan, seat and ry. sta., S.W. Anglesey, 12 m. S.E. of Holyhead. Map 36.
Bognor Regis, urb. dist., par. and watering place, S.W. Sussex, 6¾ m. S.E. of Chichester; pop. 13,510. Map 79.
Boldon, E. and W., par., N. Durham, 3½ m. N.W. of Sunderland; pop. 4179. Map 23.
Boldre, par., S.W. Hampshire, 2½ m. N. of Lymington; pop. 2395. Map 77.
Bollington, urb. dist. and par., Cheshire, 2½ m. N.E. of Macclesfield; pop. 5027. Map 39.
Bolsover, urb. dist. and par., E. Derbyshire, 5¾ m. E. of Chesterfield; pop. 11,811. Map 41.
Bolton, par., co. and parl. bor., and mfr. town, S. Lancs, 10½ m. N.W. of Manchester; pop. 177,253. Map 31.

Bolton Abbey, par., W.R. Yorkshire, 5½ m. N.W. of Ilkley; pop. 186. Map 31.
Bolton-by-Bowland, par., W.R. Yorkshire, 6 m. N.E. of Clitheroe; pop. 633. Map 31.
Bolton-le-Sands, par. and vil., N.W. Lancashire, 4¾ m. N. of Lancaster; pop. 994. Map 25.
Bolton-upon-Dearne, urb. dist. and par., W.R. York., 7 m. N. of Rotherham; pop. 14,242. Map 41.
Bonar Bridge, vil., S.E. Sutherlandshire, 13½ m. N.W. of Tain; pop. 331. Map 3.
Bonawe, vil. and seat, N. Argyllshire, on r. Awe, 13½ m. E.N.E. of Oban. Map 12.
Boncath, vil. and ry. sta., Pembrokeshire, 4½ m. N.N.E. of Crymmych Arms. Map 65.
Bonchurch, par. and vil., in S.E. of Isle of Wight, Hampshire, 1 m. E. of Ventnor; pop. 501. Map 77.
Bo'ness, par. and seaport, W. Lothian, 24 m. W.N.W. of Edinburgh; pop. 10,095. Map 9.
Bonhill, par. and town, Dumbartonshire, adjacent to Alexandria; pop. 16,622. Map 8.
Bonnybridge, par. and town, Stirlingshire, 4 m. W. of Falkirk; pop. 5969. Map 9.
Bonnyrigg and Lasswade, town, Midlothian, 9½ m. S.E. of Edinburgh; pop. 4483. Map 10.
Bonsall, urb. dist., Derbyshire, 2 m. S.W. of Matlock; pop. 1173. Map 40.
Boosbeck, eccl. dist. and vil., N.R. Yorkshire, 3 m. E.N.E. of Guisborough; pop. 5866. Map 28.
Boothby Pagnell, par. and vil., Kesteven, Lincolnshire, 5 m. S.E. of Grantham; pop. 136. Map 50.
Bootle, parl. and co. bor. adjg. Liverpool, S.W. Lancs, on r. Mersey; pop. 76,799. Map 38.
Bootle, coast par. and vil., Cumberland, 4½ m. S. of Ravenglass; pop. 806. Map 25.
Boroughbridge, par. and market town, W.R. Yorks, 11 m. N.E. of Harrogate; pop. 807. Map 28.
Borris, vil. and seat, in co. and 18 m. S. of Carlow; pop. 469. Map 95.
Borrowdale, romantic valley, W. Cumberland. Map 25.
Boscastle, vil. and coastguard sta., N. Cornwall, 5 m. N. of Camelford. Map 91.
Boston, mun. bor. and seaport, Holland, Lincolnshire, 30 m. S.E. of Lincoln; pop. 16,597. Map 51.
Bothwell, par. and town, Lanarkshire, 8 m. S.E. of Glasgow; pop. 3511. Map 9.
Botley, par. and vil., S. Hampshire, 3¾ m. S.W. of Bishop's Waltham; pop. 1166. Map 77.
Bottesford, par. and vil., Leicestershire, 7 m. N.W. of Grantham; pop. 1204. Map 50.
Bottisham, par. and vil., in co. and 6 m. E.N.E. of Cambridge; pop. 624. Map 61.
Boughrood, par., Radnor, 11 m. S.E. of Builth; pop. 215. Map 56.
Boulmer, fishing vil., Northumberland, 5 m. E. of Alnwick. Map 17.
Bourne, urb. dist., Kesteven, Lincolnshire, 9½ m. W. of Spalding; pop. 4889. Map 50.
Bournemouth, parl. and co. bor., par. and watering place, S.W. Hants, 3½ m. S.W. of Christchurch; pop. 116,780. Map 77.
Bournville, vil., Worcestershire, 4½ m. S.W. of Birmingham. Map 58.
Bourton-on-the-Hill, par. and vil., Gloucestershire, 4½ m. N.W. of Stow-on-the-Wold; pop. 363. Map 58.
Bourton-on-the-Water, par. and vil., E. Gloucestershire, 17¾ m. E. of Cheltenham; pop. 1073. Map 69.
Bovey Tracey, par. and vil., S.E. Devon, 6¼ m. S.E. of Moreton Hampstead; pop. 2788. Map 89.
Bow, par. and vil., N. Devon, 16 m. W.N.W. of Exeter; pop. 616. Map 85.
Bowden, par. and vil., Roxburghshire, 1 m. W. of St Boswells; pop. 638. Map 16.
Bowdon, urb. dist., Cheshire, 9 m. S. of Manchester; pop. 3285. Map 30.
Bowes, par. and vil., N.R. Yorkshire, 4 m. S.W. of Barnard Castle; pop. 655. Map 27.
Bowness, par., E. Cumberland, on Solway Firth, 2½ m. S. of Annan (Scotland); pop. 1107. Map 20.
Bowness, par., Westmorland, on E. side of Lake Windermere; pop. 3860. Map 25.
Boxford, par. and vil., W. Suffolk, 6 m. E.S.E. of Sudbury; pop. 479. Map 62.
Boyle, par. and market town, N. co. Roscommon, on r. Boyle, 28 m. S.E. of Sligo; pop. 5654. Map 92.
Bozeat, par. and vil., Northamptonshire, 6 m. S. of Wellingborough; pop. 1145. Map 60.
Bracadale, par., and sea loch, Skye, Inverness-shire, 10 m. S.W. of Portree; pop. (incl. Soay isl.) 740. Map 2.
Brackley, mun. bor., par. and mkt. tn., S. Northants, 7 m. W.N.W. of Buckingham; pop. 2181. Map 59.
Bracknell, eccl. par. and vil., S.E. Berkshire, 4½ m. E. of Wokingham; pop. 2696. Map 78.
Braco, vil., S. Perthshire, 7½ m. S. of Crieff. Map 6.
Bradford, parl. and co. bor. and par., W.R. Yorkshire, 9 m. W. of Leeds; pop. 298,041. Map 32.
Bradford-on-Avon, urb. dist. and market town, W. Wiltshire, 9 m. S.E. of Bath; pop. 4735. Map 75.
Brading, par. and town, Isle of Wight, Hants, 4 m. S. of Ryde; pop. 1696. Map 77.
Bradninch, par. and town, E. Devon, 8¼ m. N.E. of Exeter; pop. 1486. Map 85.
Bradpole, par. and vil., S.W. Dorsetshire, 1 m. N.E. of Bridport; pop. 581. Map 86.
Bradwell, par., N. Derbyshire, 2 m. S.E. of Castleton; stalactite cavern here; pop. 1325. Map 40.
Braemar, vil., Crathie and Braemar par., Aberdeensh., 16½ m. W. of Ballater; pop. 1029. Map 3.
Braintree, urb. dist., par. and market town, N.E. Essex, 45 m. N.E. of London; pop. 8912. Map 72.
Bramber, par. and vil., N. Sussex, 4 m. N.W. of New Shoreham; pop. 255. Map 79.
Bramfield, par., E. Suffolk, 2½ m. S. of Halesworth; pop. 530. Map 63.
Bramham, vil., W.R. Yorkshire, 3½ m. W. of Tadcaster; pop. 984. Map 33.
Bramley, par., S. W. Surrey, 5 m. S.S.E. of Guildford; pop. 2006. Map 78.
Brampton, ham., N Westmorland, 2 m. N. of Appleby. Map 22.
Brampton, par. and market town, N.E. Cumberland, 9 m. N.E. of Carlisle; pop. 2590. Map 21.
Brampton and Walton, urb. dist., Derbyshire, 3 m. S.W. of Chesterfield; pop. 2323. Map 41.
Brampton Bryan, par. and vil., Herefordshire, 5½ m. E. of Knighton; pop. 280. Map 56.
Brancaster, par. and fishing vil., Norfolk, 8½ m. W. of Wells; pop. 974. Map 52.
Brancepeth, par. and vil., mid Durham, 4¼ m. S.W. of Durham; pop. 355. Map 19.
Brandesburton, par. and vil., E.R. Yorkshire, 8 m. N.E. of Beverley; pop. 577. Map 35.
Brandon, par. and market town, W. Suffolk, 6 m. N.W. of Thetford; pop. 2462. Map 62.
Brandon and Byshottles, urb. dist., Durham, 3 m. S.W. of Durham; pop. 17,099. Map 23.
Branksome, urb. dist. and par., S.E. Dorsetshire, now in bor. of Poole; pop. 7202. Map 87.
Bran, Strath, valley of r. Bran and vil., Little Dunkele, par. Perthshire. Map 6.
Brant Broughton, par. and vil., Lincolnshire, 7 m. S.E. of Newark; pop. 515. Map 42.
Branxton, par. and vil., Northumberland, 2 m. S.E. of Coldstream; pop. 184. Map 17.
Brassington, par. and vil., N. Derbyshire, 3 m. W. of Wirksworth; pop. 602. Map 40.
Brasted, par. and vil., W. Kent, 1½ m. N.E. of Westerham; pop. 1327. Map 80.

Bratton Fleming, par. and vil., N. Devon, 7 m. N.E. of Barnstaple; pop. 486. Map 84.
Braughing, par. and vil., E. Hertfordshire, 3½ m. S.S.E. of Buntingford; pop. 928. Map 71.
Braunston, par. and vil., Rutland, 2½ m. S.W. of Oakham; pop. 294. Map 50.
Braunton, par. and vil., N.W. Devon, 5¾ m. N.W. of Barnstaple; pop. 2644. Map 84.
Brawnhills, urb. dist., Staffordshire, 6 m. W. of Lichfield; pop. 18,248. Map 48.
Bray (Bri Chualann), urb. dist., cos. Wicklow and Dublin, 12¼ m. S.E. of Dublin; pop. 7691. Map 95.
Bray, par. and vil., E. Berkshire, 1½ m. S.E. of Maidenhead; pop. 3803. Map 78.
Brechin, par., parl., royal and mun. bur., Angus, 9½ m. W. of Montrose; pop. 6838. Map 3.
Brecon, mun. bor. and co. town of Brecknockshire, 40 m. N.E. of Swansea; pop. 5334. Map 55.
Bredbury and Romiley, urb. dist., Cheshire, 2 m. N.E. of Stockport; pop. 10,878. Map 39.
Bredwardine, par. and vil., Herefordshire, 6½ m. E.N.E. of Hay; pop. 244. Map 56.
Breedon-on-the-Hill, par., N.W. Leicestershire, 5 m. N.E. of Ashby-de-la-Zouch; pop. 730. Map 49.
Brentford and Chiswick, urb. dist. and market town, W. Middlesex, 10½ m. W. of London; pop. 62,617. Map 71.
Brentwood, urb. dist., par. and market town, S. Essex, 11 m. S.W. of Chelmsford; pop. 7209. Map 72.
Brewood, par. and town, Staffordshire, 7 m. N.N.W. of Wolverhampton; pop. 2578. Map 47.
Bridgend, urb. dist. and market town, Glamorganshire, 20 m. W. of Cardiff; pop. 10,033. Map 66.
Bridgend, Islay, Argyllshire. Map 12.
Bridge of Allan, *q.s.* par. and town, in co. and 2½ m. N.W. of Stirling; pop. 2897. Map 9.
Bridge of Earn, vil., S.E. Perthshire, on r. Earn, 4½ m. S.E. of Perth. Map 6.
Bridge of Weir, *q.s.* par. and town, Renfrewshire, 6 m. W.N.W. of Paisley; town pop. 2487. Map 8.
Bridgham, par. and vil., Norfolk, 6 m. N.E. of Thetford; pop. 235. Map 62.
Bridgnorth, mun. bor., Salop, 14½ m. W.S.W. of Wolverhampton; pop. 5151. Map 47.
Bridgwater, mun. bor. and seaport, W. Somersetshire, 33¼ m. S.W. of Bristol; pop. 17,139. Map 74.
Bridlington, mun. bor. and par., E.R. Yorkshire, 31 m. N.N.E. of Hull; pop. 19,704. Map 29.
Bridlington Quay, port of Bridlington; favourite seacoast resort. Map 29.
Bridport, seaport town, mun. bor. and par., S.W. Dorsetshire, 15½ m. W. of Dorchester; pop. 5917. Map 86.
Brierfield, urb. dist. and par., N.E. Lancashire, 2¼ m. N.E. of Burnley; pop. 7696. Map 31.
Brierley Hill, urb. dist. and par., Staffordshire, 2½ m. N.E. of Stourbridge; pop. 14,344. Map 47.
Brigg, urb. dist. and par., Lindsey, Lincs, 10 m. S. of Barton upon Humber; pop. 4019. Map 35.
Brigham, par. and vil., Cumberland, 2½ m. W. of Cockermouth; pop. 772. Map 20.
Brighouse, mun. bor. and par., W.R. Yorkshire, 5¼ m. N. of Huddersfield; pop. 19,756. Map 32.
Brightlingsea, urb. dist., par. and seaport, N.E. Essex, 8 m. S.E. of Colchester; pop. 4145. Map 73.
Brighton, parl. and co. bor., par. and watering place, Sussex, 50½ m. S. of London; pop. 147,427. Map 81.
Brill, par., vil. and seat, W. Buckinghamshire, 6 m. N.W. of Thame; pop. 1019. Map 70.
Brinklow, par. and vil., Warwickshire, 5½ m. N.W. of Rugby; pop. 681. Map 59.
Brinkworth, par. and ham., N. Wiltshire, 4 m. N.W. of Wootton Bassett; pop. 932. Map 68.
Brislington, par. and vil., N. Somersetshire, 2 m. S.E. of Bristol; pop. 3493. Map 75.
Bristol, city, co. bor. and seaport, Glos. and Somersetshires, 117½ m. W. of London; pop. 396,918. Map 74.
Briton Ferry, par., S.W. Glamorganshire, 7¼ m. E. of Swansea; pop. 9165. Map 66.
Brixham, urb. dist., par. and seaport town, S.E. Devon, 6 m. S. of Torquay; pop. 8147. Map 89.
Brixworth, par. and vil., in co. and 7½ m. N. of Northampton; pop. 1184. Map 59.
Brize Norton, par. and vil., S.W. Oxon, 4¼ m. S.W. of Witney; pop. 492. Map 69.
Broad Chalk, par. and vil., S. Wiltshire, 5 m. S.W. of Wilton; pop. 661. Map 75.
Broad Clyst, par. and vil., E. Devon, 5¼ m. N.E. Exeter; pop. 1859. Map 85.
Broadford, fishing vil., Isle of Skye, 8¼ m. W. of Kyle of Lochalsh; pop. 151. Map 2.
Broadmayne, par., S. Dorsetshire, 4½ m. S.E. of Dorchester; pop. 343. Map 87.
Broadstairs and St Peter's, urb. dist. and par., E. Kent, 2 m. N.E. of Ramsgate; pop. 12,748. Map 83.
Broadstone, eccl. dist. and vil., S.E. Dorsetshire, 3½ m. N.N.W. of Poole; pop. 1537. Map 87.
Broadway, par. and vil., S.E. Worcestershire, 5 m. S.E. of Evesham; pop. 1860. Map 58.
Broadway, par. and vil., S. Somersetshire, 2 m. W. of Ilminster; pop. 307. Map 86.
Broadwinsor, par. and vil., W. Dorsetshire, 3 m. N.W of Beaminster; pop. 901. Map 86.
Brockenhurst, par. and vil., S.W. Hampshire, 5 m. N. of Lymington; pop. 2159. Map 77.
Brodick, par., vil., pier and bay, Arran I., Buteshire, 4 m. N.W. of Lamlash; pop. 1760. Map 12.
Bromborough, port and urb. dist., N.W. Cheshire, 5 m. S.E. of Birkenhead; pop. 2557. Map 38.
Bromfield, par. and vil., Salop, 2½ m. N.W. of Ludlow; pop. 545. Map 56.
Bromley, mun. bor., N.W. Kent, 5½ m. N.E. of Croydon; pop. 45,348. Map 80.
Brompton, par. and seat, N.R. Yorkshire, 7 m. S.W. of Scarborough; pop. 598. Map 29.
Brompton, par., N.R. Yorkshire, 3 m. N. of Northallerton; pop. 1452. Map 28.
Brompton-on-Swale, par. and vil., N.R. Yorkshire, 3½ m. E. of Richmond; pop. 362. Map 27.
Bromsgrove, urb. dist. and par., in co. and 12 m. N.E. of Worcester; pop. 9520. Map 58.
Bromsgrove, North, urb. dist., Worcestershire, 7 m. N.E. of Droitwich; pop. 10,982. Map 57.
Bromyard, urb. dist., Herefordshire, 10½ m. E.S.E. of Leominster; pop. 1571. Map 57.
Brora, vil. and loch, Sutherlandshire, 6½ m. N.E. of Golspie; pop. 744; loch 66 ft. deep. Map 3.
Broseley, par. in mun. bor. of Wenlock, S.E. Shropshire, 13½ m. S.E. of Shrewsbury; pop. 3037. Map 47.
Brotton, par., N.R. Yorkshire, 2 m. S.E. of Saltburn; pop. 4428. Map 28.
Brough, par. and market town, E. Westmorland, 5 m. N. of Kirkby Stephen; pop. 620. Map 26.
Broughton, vil., in co. and 11 m. S.W. of Peebles; alt. 636 ft. Map 15.
Broughton, urb. dist., par. and vil., Lincolnshire, 3 m. N.W. of Brigg; pop. 1744. Map 35.
Broughton, par. and vil., N.R. Yorkshire, 2 m. S.E. of Stokesley; pop. 659. Map 28.
Broughton, par., N.E. Lancashire, 7 m. N.E. of Ulverston; pop. 210. Map 25.
Broughty Ferry, *q.s.* par. and dist. in E. of Dundee; pop. 5278. Map 7.
Brownhills, urb. dist., Staffordshire, 6 m. W. of Lichfield; pop. 18,368. Map 48.
Broxbourne, par. and vil., in co. and 5 m. S.E. of Hertford; pop. 790. Map 71.
Broxburn, *q.s.* par. and mining town, W. Lothian, 10½ m. W. of Edinburgh; pop. 7578. Map 9.
Bruisyard, par. and vil., E. Suffolk, 4 m. N.W. of Saxmundham; pop. 212. Map 63.

Bruton, par. and market town, S.E. Somersetshire, 10½ m. S.W. of Frome; pop. 1724. Map 75.
Brydekirk, *q.s.* par. and vil., Dumfriesshire, 3 m. N. of Annan; pop. 701. Map 20.
Brynamman, vil., S.E. Carmarthenshire, 5¾ m. E.N.E. of Ammanford. Map 66.
Bryn-Mawr, urb. dist. and par., S.E. Brecon, 8 m. W.N.W. of Abergavenny; pop. 7247. Map 67.
Buchanty, vil., mid Perthshire, on r. Almond, 10 m. N.E. of Crieff. Map 6.
Buchlyvie, vil. and par., N.W. Stirlingshire, 4½ m. N.N.E. of Balfron; pop. 409. Map 8.
Buckfastleigh, urb. dist., Devonshire, 3¾ m. N.W. of Totnes; pop. 2406. Map 89.
Buckhaven, parl. and police bur., Fifeshire, 1¼ m. S.W. of Methil; pop. 17,643. Map 10.
Buckhurst Hill, urb. dist. and par., S.W. Essex, 10¾ m. N.E. of London; pop. 5486. Map 72.
Buckie, *q.s.* par. and fishing town, Banffshire, 13¾ m. N. of Keith; pop. 8688. Map 3.
Buckingham, mun. bor. and par., Bucks, on r. Ouse, 17 m. N.W. of Aylesbury; pop. 3082. Map 59.
Buckland, vil. and paper mill, E. Kent, 1½ m. N.W. of Dover; pop. 10,087. Map 83.
Buckland, par., N.E. Hertfordshire, 3 m. N. of Buntingford; pop. 237. Map 61.
Bucklesham, par. and vil., E. Suffolk, 5 m. S.E. of Ipswich; pop. 272. Map 63.
Buckley, urb. dist. and ry. sta., Flintshire, 2 m. E. of Mold; pop. 6900. Map 38.
Bucknell, par. and vil., Salop, 5½ m. S.E. of Clun; pop. 419. Map 56.
Bude, ward of Stratton and Bude urb. dist., Cornwall, 10½ m. W.N.W. of Holsworthy; pop. 2069. Map 84.
Budleigh, E., par. and vil., E. Devon, 5 m. S.W. of Sidmouth; pop. 756. Map 89.
Budleigh Salterton, urb. dist., par. and watering pl., Devon, 4½ m. E. of Exmouth; pop. 3162. Map. 89.
Bugbrooke, par. and vil., in co. and 5½ m. S.W. of Northampton; pop. 734. Map 59.
Buglawton, urb. dist., Cheshire, 1 m. N.E. of Congleton; pop. 1651. Map 39.
Bugsworth, Derbyshire. *See* Buxworth.
Builth Road, ry. sta., Radnorshire, 2 m. W.N.W. of Builth Wells. Map 55.
Builth Wells, urb. dist., Brecknock, 16 m. N. of Brecon; pop. 1663. Map 55.
Bulford, par. and vil., Wiltshire, 2 m. N.E. of Amesbury; pop. 3797. Map 76.
Bulkington, urb. dist. and par., Warwickshire, 3½ m. S.S.E. of Nuneaton; pop. 2749. Map 49.
Buncrana, market town, co. Donegal, 12 m. N.W. of Londonderry; pop. 1848. Map 93.
Bungay, urb. dist. and par., E. Suffolk, 6 m. W. of Beccles; pop. 3098. Map 63.
Buntingford, town on r. Rib, Hertfordshire, 7 m. S. of Royston. Map 61.
Bures, par. and vil., N.E. Essex, 6 m. S.E. of Sudbury; pop. 423. Map 62.
Burford, par. and town, in co. and 18½ m. W.N.W. of Oxford; pop. 987. Map 69.
Burgess Hill, urb. dist., E. Sussex, 9 m. N. of Brighton; pop. 5975. Map 81.
Burgh-by-Sands, par. and vil., N.W. Cumberland, 5 m. N.W. of Carlisle; pop. 754. Map 21.
Burghead, spt., Morayshire, 10¾ m. N.W. of Elgin; pop. 1255. Map 3.
Burgh-next-Aylsham, par. and ham., Norfolk, 2 m. S.E. of Aylsham; pop. 212. Map 53.
Burley-in-Wharfedale, urb. dist., W.R. Yorkshire, 3¼ m. E.S.E. of Ilkley; pop. 3960. Map 32.
Burnham, par. and vil., Bucks., 2½ m. N.E. of Maidenhead; pop. 4113. Contains **B. Beeches.** Map 71.
Burnham, urb. dist. and coast par., W. Somersetshire, 7½ m. N. of Bridgwater; pop. 5120. Map 74.
Burnham Market, vil., Norfolk, 6 m. W. of Wells. Map 52.
Burnham-on-Crouch, urb. dist. and seaport, E. Essex, 9 m. S.E. of Maldon; pop. 3395. Map 73.
Burnley, parl. and co. bor. and par., N.E. Lancashire, 23 m. E. of Preston; pop. 98,259. Map 31.
Burntisland, par., parl., royal and mun. bur., spt., Fife, 5 m. by ferry N. of Edinburgh; pop. 5389. Map 10.
Burringham, par. and vil., Lincolnshire, on r. Trent, 4½ m. S.E. of Crowle; pop. 706. Map 34.
Burry Port, urb. dist., par. and seaport, Carmarthenshire, 4 m. W. of Llanelly; pop. 5752. Map 65.
Burslem, par., Staffordshire, in Stoke-on-Trent co. bor.; pop. 41,566. Map 39.
Burstwick, par. and vil., E.R. Yorkshire, 7½ m. S.E. of Hull; pop. 586. Map 35.
Burton Agnes, par. and vil., E.R. Yorkshire, 5½ m. S.W. of Bridlington; pop. 342. Map 35.
Burton Bradstock, par., S.W. Dorsetshire, 4 m. S.E. of Bridport; pop. 624. Map 86.
Burton Coggles, par. and vil., Kesteven, Lincolnshire, 7½ m. S.S.E. of Grantham; pop. 192. Map 50.
Burton Constable, seat, E.R. Yorkshire, 7 m. N.E. of Hull. Map 35.
Burton-in-Kendal, par. and town, Westmorland, 10½ m. S. of Kendal; pop. 460. Map 26.
Burton-in-Lonsdale, par., W.R. Yorkshire, 12 m. N.W. of Settle; pop. 565. Map 26.
Burton Joyce, par. and vil., in co. and 5 m. N.E. of Nottingham; pop. 1010. Map 49.
Burton Latimer, par. and vil., Northamptonshire, 3 m. S.E. of Kettering; pop. 3586. Map 60.
Burton Pidsea, par. and vil., E.R. Yorkshire, 7½ m. N.W. of Patrington; pop. 313. Map 35.
Burton-upon-Trent, co. bor. and par., Staffordshire, 11 m. S.W. of Derby; pop. 49,485. Map 48.
Burwash, par., vil. and seat, E. Sussex, 8 m. N.W. of Battle; pop. 1942. Map 82.
Burwell, par. and vil., in co. and 10 m. N.E. of Cambridge; pop. 2108. Map 61.
Bury, parl. and co. bor. and par., S.E. Lancashire, 5¼ m. E. of Bolton; pop. 56,186. Map 31.
Bury St Edmunds, mun. bor. and par., W. Suffolk, 27 m. N.W. of Ipswich; pop. 16,708. Map 62.
Busby, vil., Lanarkshire, 7½ m. S. of Glasgow; pop. 538. Map 8.
Bushey, urb. dist. and par., S.W. Hertfordshire, 16 m. N.W. of London; pop. 11,243. Map 71.
Busheyheath, eccl. dist., Bushey par., Hertfordshire; pop. 2251. Map 71.
Bushmills, market town, co. Antrim, 8 m. N.E. of Coleraine; pop. 970. Map 93.
Buttermere, par., vil. and lake, W. Cumberland, 9½ m. S.W. of Keswick; pop. 130. Map 25.
Buttertubs, pass, N.W. Yorkshire, 5½ m. long, between Hawes and Muker. Map 26.
Butterwick, coast par., Holland, Lincolnshire, 4 m. E. of Boston; pop. 498. Map 51.
Buttington, dist., Montgomeryshire, 2¾ m. N.E. of Welshpool. Map 46.
Buxton, mun. bor. and watering place, Derbyshire, 36 m. N.W. of Derby; pop. 15,353. Map 40.
Buxworth, ham., N.W. Derbyshire, 3 m. W.N.W. of Chapel-en-le-Frith. Map 40.
Bwlch-y-Sarnau, hamlet, Radnorshire, 6½ m. N.E. of Rhayader. Map 55.
Byfleet, par. and vil., N.W. Surrey, 2¼ m. S.S.W. of Weybridge; pop. 4173. Map 78.
Bynea, vil. and ry. sta., Carmarthenshire, 2¾ m. E.S.E. of Llanelly. Map 65.
Byrness, eccl. dist. and ham., N. Northumberland, 9 m. N.W. of Otterburn; pop. 140. Map 16.
Bytham, Little, par. and vil., Kesteven, Lincolnshire, 7 m. N. of Stamford; pop. 390. Map 50.
CADER IRIS, mountain ridge in S.W. of Merionethshire. Map 45.
Cadnam, ham., Hampshire, 4 m. N. of Lyndhurst. Map 77.

Caergwrie, ham., Flintshire, on R. Alyn, 5¼ m. N.W. of Wrexham. Map 38.

Caerlaverock, par. and ruined castle, in co. and 7½ m. S.E. of Dumfries ; pop. 799. Map 20.

Caerleon, urb. dist. and par., Monmouthshire, 2½ m. N.E. of Newport ; pop. 2326. Map 67.

Caerphilly, urb. dist., Glamorganshire, 7 m. N. of Cardiff ; pop. 35,760. Map 74.

Caersws, ham. and ry. sta., Montgomeryshire, 5¾ m. N.W. of Newton. Map 46.

Cahir, market town and par., in co. and 13¼ m. S.E. of Tipperary ; pop. of town 1707. Map 95.

Cahirciveen, market town, co. Kerry, 3½ m. N.E. of Valencia ; pop. 1773. Map 94.

Cairnwell, pass, Perthshire and Aberdeenshire, 10 m. S. of Braemar. Map 3.

Caister-on-Sea, coast par. and vil., Norfolk, 3 m. S. of Yarmouth ; pop. 2346. Map 53.

Caistor, par. and town, Lindsey, Lincolnshire, 8 m. S.E. of Brigg ; pop. 1571. Map 42.

Caldbeck, par. and vil., Cumberland, 6½ m. S.E. of Wigton ; pop. 775. Map 21.

Caldecott, par., Rutland, 4 m. S. of Uppingham ; pop. 264. Map 50.

Caldercruix, q.s. par. and vil., Lanarkshire, 4½ m. N.E. of Airdrie ; pop. 2370. Map 9.

Caldicot, par. and vil., Monmouthshire, 5 m. S.W. of Chepstow ; pop. 1770. Map 67.

Caldy and **St Margaret,** 2 isls. off S.E. coast of Pembrokeshire, 2½ m. S. of Tenby. Map 64.

Callan, market town and par. in co. and 13 m. S.W. of Kilkenny ; pop. 1510. Map 95.

Callander, police bur., Perthshire, 16 m. N.W. of Stirling ; pop. of town, 1572. Map 5.

Callington, urb. dist. and par., Cornwall, 9½ m. S. of Launceston ; pop. 1801. Map 88.

Cally, Bridge of, Perthsh., 4½ m. N.W. of Blairgowrie. Map 6.

Calne, mun. bor., N. Wiltshire, 5½ m. S.E. of Chippenham ; pop. 3463. Map 75.

Calverley, urb. dist. and par., W.R. Yorkshire, 5¾ m. W.N.W. of Leeds ; pop. 3655. Map 32.

Calverton, par. and vil., in co. and 6½ m. N.E. of Nottingham ; pop. 1040. Map 49.

Camberley, place, W. Surrey, 2½ m. S.W. of Bagshot. Here is a Military Staff College. Map 78.

Cambois, colliery vil., Northumberland, 2½ m. N.W. of Blyth. Map 17.

Camborne, urb. dist. and par., Cornwall, 12½ m. S.W. of Truro , pop. 14,157. Map 90.

Cambridge, parl. and mun. bor., and co. town of Cambs., 57 m. N. of London by rail ; pop. 66,803. Map 61.

Cambuslang, town, Lanarkshire, 5 m. S.E. of Glasgow. Map 9.

Cambusnethan, par. and vil., Lanarkshire, 1½ m. N.E. of Wishaw ; pop. 36,737. Map 9.

Camelford, market town, Cornwall, 17½ m. W. of Launceston. Map 91.

Camelon, q.s. par., forming part of Falkirk, Stirlingshire ; pop. 8137. Map 9.

Campbeltown, mun. bur. and spt., Kintyre, Argyllshire, 83 m. S.W. of Glasgow by sea ; pop. 6309. Map 12.

Campsie, par., Stirlingshire, containing Lennoxtown ; pop. 5335. Map 8.

Cannington, par. and vil., W. Somersetshire, 3½ m. N.W. of Bridgwater ; pop. 871. Map 74.

Cannock, urb. dist. and par., Staffordshire, 8 m. N.N.W. of Walsall ; pop. 34,588. Map 48.

Canonbie, par. and vil., S.E. Dumfriesshire, 6 m. S.E. of Langholm ; pop. 1756. Map 21.

Canterbury, city, co. bor. and par., Kent, 16 m. N.W. of Dover ; pop. 24,450. Map 83.

Canvey Island, urb. dist., Essex, 4½ m. S.W. of Rayleigh ; pop. 3530. Map 72.

Capel, par. and vil., S. Surrey, 5½ m. S. of Dorking ; pop. 1459. Map 78.

Capel Bangor, vil. and sta., Cardiganshire, 4½ m. E.S.E. of Aberystwyth. Map 55.

Capel Curig, par. and ham., E. Carnarvonshire, 6 m. W. of Bettws-y-Coed ; pop. 359. Map 37.

Cappamore, vil., in co. and 12 m. S.E. of Limerick ; pop. 531. Map 94.

Cappoquin, town, co. Waterford, 10½ m. W.N.W. of Dungarvan ; pop. 1069. Map 95.

Caputh, par. and vil., Perthshire, 1½ m. N.W. of Murthly sta. ; pop. 1046. Map 6.

Cardiff, co. bor., co. town and seaport, Glamorganshire, 38 m. W. of Bristol ; pop. 223,648. Map 67.

Cardigan, mun. bor. and co. town of Cardiganshire, 42 m. N.W. of Carmarthen by rail ; pop. 3309. Map 54.

Cardington, par. and vil., in co. and 2 m. S.E. of Bedford ; pop. 377. Map 60.

Cardross, coast par. and vil., in co. and 3¾ m. W.N.W. of Dumbarton ; pop. 1662. Map 8.

Carew, par. and ham., in co. and 4¼ m. E.N.E. of Pembroke ; pop. 756. Map 64.

Carham, par. and vil., Northumberland, near boundary with Scotland ; pop. 841. Map 16.

Carisbrooke, par., vil. and castle, Isle of Wight, 1 m. S.W. of Newport ; pop. 4767. Map 77.

Carlisle, city, bor. and co. town of Cumberland, 60 m. W. of Newcastle ; pop. 57,107. Map 21.

Carlops, vil., Peeblesshire, on N. Esk, 15 m. S.W. of Edinburgh. Map 10.

Carlow, urb. dist. and par., co. Carlow, 56 m. S.W. of Dublin ; pop. 7175. Map 95.

Carlton, urb. dist. and par., in co. and 3½ m. N.E. of Nottingham ; pop. 22,336. Map 49.

Carluke, town and par., Lanarkshire, 5½ m. N.W. of Lanark ; town pop. 5436. Map 9.

Carmarthen, par. and mun. bor., Carmarthenshire, 27¾ m. N.W. of Swansea by rail ; pop. 10,310. Map 65.

Carnaby, par. and ham., E.R. Yorkshire, 2¼ m. S.W. of Bridlington ; pop. 194. Map 29.

Carnarvon, co. town of Carnarvonshire, parl. and mun. bor., 8½ m. S.W. of Bangor ; pop. 8469. Map 36.

Carndonagh, vil. and ry. sta., co. Donegal, 18 m. N.E. of Buncrana ; pop. 668. Map 93.

Carnforth, urb. dist. and par., N. Lancashire, 6½ m. N.N.E. of Lancaster ; pop. 3193. Map 26.

Carnoustie, coast town, Angus, 10½ m. N.E. of Dundee ; pop. 4806. Map 7.

Carnwath, par. and vil., Lanarkshire, 26 m. S.W. of Edinburgh ; vil. pop. 964. Map 9.

Carrbridge, vil. and ry. sta., in co. and 28 m. S.E. of Inverness. Map 3.

Carrickfergus, seaport and urb. dist., co. Antrim, 9½ m. N. of Belfast ; pop. 8669. Map 93.

Carrickmacross, urb. dist. and par., co. Monaghan, 14 m. W. of Dundalk ; pop. 2000. Map 93.

Carrick-on-Shannon, market town, co. Leitrim, 37 m. S.E. of Sligo ; pop. 1013. Map 92.

Carrick-on-Suir, urb. dist., co. Tipperary, 13¾ m. E. of Clonmel ; pop. 4675. Map 95.

Carr Shield, vil., Northumberland, 7 m. S.W. of Allendale. Map 22.

Carshalton, urb. dist., Surrey, 1½ m. E. of Sutton ; pop. 28,769. Map 80.

Carstairs, par. and vil., Lanarkshire, 27½ m. S.W. of Edinburgh ; vil. pop. 492. Map 9.

Carter Bar, road summit, Cheviot Hills, between Roxburgh and Northumberland ; alt. 1371 ft. Map 16.

Cartmel, market town, N. Lancashire, 6 m. E. of Ulverston ; pop. 313. Map 25.

Cashel, city and urb. dist., co. Tipperary, 8 m. N. of Cahir ; pop. 2945. Map 95.

Castle Acre, par. and vil., Norfolk, 4 m. N. of Swaffham ; pop. 955. Map 52.

Castle Bar, urb. dist. and cap. of co. Mayo, 11 m. N.E. of Westport ; pop. 4256. Map 92.

Castleblayney, urb. dist., co. Monaghan, 18 m. N.W. of Dundalk; pop. 1553. Map 93.
Castle Carrock, par. and vil., N.E. Cumberland, 4 m. S. of Brampton; pop. 346. Map 21.
Castle Cary, par. and market town, Somersetshire, 12 m. N.E. of Yeovil; pop. 1646. Map 75.
Castlecomer, market town and par., in co. and 11¼ m. N.N.E. of Kilkenny; pop. of town 872. Map 95.
Castlederg, vil. and ry. sta., co. Tyrone, 10 m. S.W. of Strabane; pop. 835. Map 93.
Castle Donington, par. and town, Leicestershire, 11 m. S.W. of Nottingham; pop. 2736. Map 49.
Castle Douglas, police bur., Kirkcudbrightshire, 10½ m. S.W. of Dumfries; pop. 3008. Map 19.
Castleford, urb. dist. and par., W.R. Yorkshire, 10 m. S.E. of Leeds; pop. 21,781. Map 33.
Castle Hedingham, par. and vil., Essex, 5 m. N. of Halstead; pop. 961. Map 62.
Castleisland, par. and town, co. Kerry, 11½ m. S.E. of Tralee; pop. 1333. Map 94.
Castlemartyr, vil., co. Cork, 1¼ m. S. of Mogeely ry. sta.; pop. 274. Map 95.
Castlemorris, vil., Pembrokeshire, 5 m. S.S.W. of Fishguard. Map 64.
Castlerea, market town, in co. and 16½ m. N.W. of Roscommon; pop. 1224. Map 92.
Castle Rising, par. and vil., Norfolk, 4 m. N.E. of King's Lynn; pop. 236. Map 52.
Castleton, par. and vil., Derbyshire, 10 m. N.E. of Buxton; pop. 646. Map 40.
Castleton, par. and vil., S. Roxburghshire, 21½ m. S. of Hawick; pop. 1853. Map 16.
Castleton, vil. and ry. sta., N.R. Yorkshire, 6½ m. S.E. of Guisborough. Map 28.
Castletown, seaport town and coastguard station, Isle of Man, 10 m. S.W. of Douglas; pop. 1898. Map 24.
Castlewellan, market town, co. Down, 4 m. N.W. of Newcastle; pop. 819. Map 93.
Castor, par. and vil., Soke of Peterborough, Northants, 4 m. W. of Peterborough; pop. 576. Map 50.
Catcleugh, ham. and reservoir, N. Northumberland, on r. Rede, 12 m. N.W. of Otterburn. Map 16.
Caterham and Warlingham, urb. dist., E. Surrey, 7 m. S. of Croydon; pop. 19,503. Map 80.
Catterall, par. and vil., N. Lancashire, 2 m. S.E. of Garstang; pop. 330. Map 30.
Catterick, par. and vil., N.R. Yorkshire, 4½ m. S.E. of Richmond; pop. 564. Map 27.
Cattistock, par. and vil., Dorsetshire, 4½ m. W.S.W. of Cerne Abbas; pop. 434. Map 87.
Catwick, par. and vil., E.R. Yorkshire, 5½ m. W.S.W. of Hornsea; pop. 213. Map 35.
Catworth, par. and vil., Huntingdonshire, 4 m. N. of Kimbolton; pop. 384. Map 60.
Cavan, urb. dist. and co. town of Cavan, 79¾ m. S.W. of Belfast; pop. 2961. Map 93.
Caversham, eccl. par. in N. of co. bor. of Reading, Berkshire; pop. 10,432. Map 78.
Cawood, par. and vil., W.R. Yorkshire, 5¼ m. N.W. of Selby; pop. 983. Map 34.
Cawston, par. and vil., Norfolk, 4 m. S.W. of Aylsham; pop. 970. Map 53.
Caxton, par. and vil., in co. and 9 m. W. of Cambridge; pop. 398. Map 61.
Caythorpe, par. and vil., Kesteven, Lincolnshire, 8½ m. N.N.E. of Grantham; pop. 764. Map 50.
Cefn-Coed-y-Cymmer, vil. and ry. sta., Brecon, 2½ m. N.W. of Merthyr-Tydfil. Map 66.
Celbridge, vil., co. Kildare, 10¼ m. W. of Dublin. Map 93.
Cellardyke, fishing vil. and *q.s.* par., Fifeshire, adjoining Anstruther; pop. 1472. Map 7.
Ceres, par. and vil., Fifeshire, 2½ m. S.E. of Cupar; pop. 1445. Map 7.
Cerne Abbas, market town and par., Dorsetshire, 7 m. N. of Dorchester; pop. 511. Map 87.
Cerney, South, par. and vil., Gloucestershire, 4 m. S.E. of Cirencester; pop. 873. Map 69.
Cerrig-y-Druidion, par. and vil., in co. and 13 m. S.W. of Denbigh; pop. 1072. Map 37.
Chadderton, urb. dist., Lancashire, 1 m. W. of Oldham; pop. 27,455. Map 31.
Chadlington, par. and vil., Oxon, 3½ m. S. of Chipping Norton; pop. 496. Map 69.
Chaffcombe, par. and vil., Somersetshire, 3 m. S. of Ilminster; pop. 230. Map 86.
Chagford, market town and par., Devonshire, 3 m. N.W. of Moreton Hampstead; pop. 1715. Map 89.
Chalfont St Giles, par. and vil., Buckinghamshire, 3 m. S.E. of Amersham; pop. 2074. Map 71.
Chalford, par. and vil., Gloucestershire, 3½ m. S.E. of Stroud; pop. 2985. Map 68.
Chalgrove, par. and vil., Oxon, 5 m. S.W. of Tetsworth; pop. 359. Map 70.
Chalk, par. and vil., N. Kent, on r. Thames, 1½ m. S.E. of Gravesend; pop. 517. Map 80.
Chandler's Ford, par. and vil., Hants, 5 m. E. of Romsey; pop. 1831. Map 77.
Chapel-en-le-Frith, market town and par., Derbyshire, 5¼ m. N. of Buxton; pop. 5283. Map 40.
Chard, mun. bor. and par., Somersetshire, 12 m. S.E. of Taunton; pop. 4053. Map 86.
Chardstock, par. and vil., Devonshire, 4 m. N. of Axminster; pop. 916. Map 86.
Charing, town and par., mid Kent, 5½ m. N.W. of Ashford; pop. 1207. Map 83.
Charlbury, market town and par., in co. and 13¼ m. N.W. of Oxford; pop. 1231. Map 69.
Charlestown, seaport vil., Fifeshire, 3½ m. S.W. of Dunfermline. Map 9.
Charlestown, seaport, Cornwall, 2 m. S.E. of St Austell; pop. of eccl. dist. 2973. Map 91.
Charlestown of Aberlour, town, Banffshire, 2¼ m. S.W. of Craigellachie; pop. 1175. Map 3.
Charlesworth, par. and vil., N. Derbyshire, 2 m. W.S.W. of Glossop; pop. 1772. Map 40.
Charleville, market town, in co. and 33 m. N. of Cork; pop. 1684. Map 94.
Charlton Kings, urb. dist., Gloucestershire, sub. of Cheltenham; pop. 4764. Map 68.
Charminster, par. and vil., Dorsetshire, 2 m. N.W. of Dorchester; pop. 1762. Map 87.
Charmouth, par. and watering place, Dorsetshire, 6 m. S.E. of Axminster; pop. 668. Map 86.
Chatburn, par., Lancashire, 2 m. N.E. of Clitheroe; pop. 1168. Maps 26 and 31.
Chatham, mun. bor. and seaport town, N. Kent, 7¾ m. N. of Maidstone; pop. 42,996. Map 80.
Chat Moss, peat bog, Lancashire, 7 m. W. of Manchester; area 12 sq. m., 30 ft. deep in places. Map 39.
Chatsworth, par., N. Derbyshire, on r. Derwent, 2½ m. N.E. of Bakewell; pop. 50. Map 40.
Chatteris, urb. dist. and par., Isle of Ely, Cambs, 8 m. S. of March; pop. 5153. Map 51.
Chatton, par. and vil., Northumberland, 3 m. E. of Wooler; pop. 891. Map 17.
Cheadle and Gatley, urb. dist., Cheshire, 2½ m. S.W. of Stockport; pop. 18,469. Map 39.
Cheddar, par. and vil., N. Somersetshire, 1¾ m. S.E. of Axbridge; pop. 2007. Map 74.
Chedworth, par. and vil., Gloucestershire, 6¾ m. N.E. of Cirencester; pop. 671. Map 69.
Chelmondiston, par. and vil., E. Suffolk, 5 m. S.S.E. of Ipswich; pop. 801. Map 63.
Chelmsford, mun. bor. and co. town of Essex, 29¾ m. N.E. of London by rail; pop. 26,537. Map 72.
Cheltenham, parl. and mun. bor., Gloucestershire, 7 m. N.E. of Gloucester; pop. mun. bor. 49,385. Map 68.
Chepstow, urb. dist. on r. Wye, in co. and 14¾ m. S. of Monmouth; pop. 4303. Map 67.

Cheriton, coast par. and urb. dist., Kent, 2 m. W.N.W. of Folkestone; pop. 8089. Map 83.
Cherry Burton, par. and vil., E.R. Yorkshire, $3\frac{1}{2}$ m. N.W. of Beverley; pop. 378. Map 35.
Cherry Hinton, par., in co. and $2\frac{1}{2}$ m. S.E. of Cambridge; pop. 1164. Map 61.
Chertsey, market town and par., N. Surrey, on r. Thames, $9\frac{1}{2}$ m. W.S.W. of Kingston; pop. 17,130. Map 78.
Chesham, urb. dist. and par., Buckinghamshire, 5 m. S.W. of Berkhampstead; pop. 8809. Map 71.
Cheshunt, urb. dist. and par., Hertfordshire, $16\frac{1}{4}$ m. N. of London; pop. 14,651. Map 71.
Chesilton, vil., on W. side of Portland Isle, Dorsetshire. Map 87.
Chester, co. bor., city and co. in itself and par., 16 m. S. of Liverpool; pop. 41,438. Map 38.
Chesterfield, mun. bor. and par., Derbyshire, $12\frac{1}{4}$ m. S. of Sheffield; pop. 64,146. Map 41.
Chesterford, Great and **Little,** 2 pars., Essex, 4 m. N.W. of Saffron Walden; pop. 766 and 176. Map 61.
Chester-le-Street, urb. dist. and par., in co. and $5\frac{1}{2}$ m. N. of Durham; pop. 16,639. Map 23.
Chesterton, par. and ward of Wolstanton United, Staffordshire; pop. 7439. Map 39.
Cheveley, par. and vil., Cambridgeshire, 3 m. S.E. of Newmarket; pop. 599. Map 61.
Chevington, East, par. and vil., Northumberland, $3\frac{1}{2}$ m. S. of Amble; pop. 3671. Map 17.
Chevington, West, par. and vil., Northumberland, $7\frac{1}{2}$ m. N.N.E. of Morpeth; pop. 359. Map 17.
Cheviot Hills, mtn. range, extending about 35 m. along border of England and Scotland. Map 16.
Chew Magna, par. and vil., E. Somersetshire, 7 m. S. of Bristol; pop. 1594. Map 74.
Chew Stoke, par. and vil., N. Somerset, 8 m. S. of Bristol; pop. 622. Map 74.
Chichester, city and mun. bor., W. Sussex, 28 m. W. of Brighton; pop. 13,911. Map 79.
Chickerell, par. and vil., Dorsetshire, 3 m. N.W. of Weymouth; pop. 1016. Map 87.
Chiddingfold, par. and vil., S.W. Surrey, $4\frac{1}{4}$ m. N.E. of Haslemere; pop. 2156. Map 79.
Chigwell, par. and vil., W. Essex, $13\frac{1}{2}$ m. N.E. of London; pop. 2943. Map 72.
Childrey, par. and vil., Berkshire, $2\frac{1}{2}$ m. W. of Wantage; pop. 476. Map 69.
Childwall, par., S.W. Lancashire, in S.E. of co. bor. of Liverpool; pop. 1970. Contains **C. Hall.** Map 38.
Chillingham, par., vil. and seat (**C. Castle**), Northumberland, $4\frac{1}{2}$ m. S.E. of Wooler; pop. 95. Map 17.
Chilton Foliat, par. and vil., E. Wiltshire, 2 m. N.W. of Hungerford; pop. 336. Map 69.
Chingford, mun. bor. and par., W. Essex, $12\frac{1}{4}$ m. N.E. of London; pop. 22,051. Map 71.
Chinnor, par. and vil., Oxon, 5 m. S.E. of Thame; pop. 973. Map 70.
Chippenham, par. and vil., Cambridgeshire, $4\frac{1}{2}$ m. N.E. of Newmarket; pop. 481. Map 62.
Chippenham, mun. bor., N.W. Wiltshire, 13 m. N.E. of Bath; pop. 8493. Map 68.
Chipping Campden, par. and market town, Gloucestershire; $9\frac{1}{2}$ m. S.E. of Evesham; pop. 1627. Map 58.
Chipping Norton, mun. bor. and par., Oxon, 13 m. S.W. of Banbury; pop. 3489. Map 58.
Chipping Ongar, par. and vil., Essex, $23\frac{1}{4}$ m. N.E. of London; pop. 1142. Map 72.
Chipping Sodbury, par. and market town, Gloucestershire, 11 m. N.E. of Bristol; pop. 952. Map 68.
Chirk, par. and vil., Denbighshire, 9 m. S. of Wrexham; pop. 2576. Map 46.
Chirnside, par. and vil., Berwickshire, $4\frac{3}{4}$ m. N.E. of Duns; pop. 1402. Map 11.
Chisledon, par. and vil., Wiltshire, 3 m. S.E. of Swindon; pop. 1688. Map 69.
Chislehurst, urb. dist., N.W. Kent, $11\frac{1}{4}$ m. S.E. of London; pop. 9876. Map 80.
Chiswick. *See* Brentford and Chiswick.
Chobham, par. and vil., W. Surrey, 3 m. N.W. of Woking ry. sta.; pop. 4085. Map 78.
Chorley, mun. bor., market town and par., N. Lancashire, 9 m. S.E. of Preston; pop. 30,795. Map 30.
Chorleywood, urb. dist., Herts, 2 m. N.W. of Rickmansworth; pop. 3296. Map 71.
Christchurch, mun. bor., seaport and par., Hants, $25\frac{1}{2}$ m. S.W. of Southampton by rail; pop. 9183. Map 77.
Chryston, *q.s.* par., Cadder par., Lanarkshire, 7 m. N.E. of Glasgow; pop. 6837. Map 8.
Chudleigh, market town and par., Devonshire, $14\frac{3}{4}$ m. S.W. of Exeter by rail; pop. 1869. Map 89.
Chulmleigh, market town and par., Devonshire, 8 m. S. of S. Molton; pop. 1143. Map 85.
Church, urb. dist., Lancs, 1 m. W. of Accrington; pop. 6185. Map 31.
Churchingford, vil. in Somersetshire, $7\frac{1}{2}$ m. S. of Taunton. Map 86.
Church Lawford, par. and vil., Warwickshire, $3\frac{1}{2}$ m. W.N.W. of Rugby; pop. 271. Map 59.
Church Stretton, urb. dist., Salop, $12\frac{3}{4}$ m. S.S.W. of Shrewsbury; pop. 1705. Map 46.
Cilfynydd, vil. and ry. sta., Glamorganshire, $2\frac{1}{4}$ m. N. of Pontypridd. Map 67.
Cilgerran, par. and vil., Pembrokeshire, 3 m. S.S.E. of Cardigan; pop. 904. Map 54.
Cinderford, vil. and ry. sta., Gloucestershire, 3 m. N.W. of Newnham. Map 68.
Cirencester, urb. dist. and par., Gloucestershire, $20\frac{3}{4}$ m. S.E. of Cheltenham by rail; pop. 7200. Map 68.
Clackmannan, par. and co. town of Clackmannanshire, 2 m. S.E. of Alloa; pop. 2373. Map 9.
Clacton-on-Sea, urb. dist. and par., Essex, 19 m. S.E. of Colchester; pop. 15,851. Map 73.
Clapham, vil., W.R. Yorkshire, 4 m. S.E. of Ingleton; pop. 642. Map 26.
Clare, par. and market town, W. Suffolk, 7 m. W.N.W. of Sudbury; pop. 1340. Map 62.
Clare, town and ry. sta. (**C. Castle**), mid co. Clare, 2 m. S.E. of Ennis; pop. 538. Map 94.
Clavering, par., Essex., $6\frac{1}{2}$ m. S.W. of Saffron Walden; pop. 799. Map 61.
Claybrook, vil., Leicestershire, $3\frac{1}{2}$ m. N.W. of Lutterworth. Map 49.
Clay Cross, urb. dist., Derbyshire, $4\frac{1}{2}$ m. S. of Chesterfield; pop. 8493. Map 41.
Claydon, par. and vil., E. Suffolk, 5 m. N.W. of Ipswich; pop. 613. Map 63.
Claypole, par. and vil., Kesteven, Lincolnshire, 4 m. S.E. of Newark; pop. 547. Map 42.
Clayton, urb. dist. and par., Yorkshire $3\frac{1}{2}$ m. S.W. of Bradford; pop. 5043. Map 31.
Clayton-le-Moor, urb. dist. and par., N.E. Lancashire, $5\frac{1}{2}$ m. N.E. of Blackburn; pop. 7910. Map 31.
Clayton, West, urb. dist., W.R. Yorkshire, 12 m. S.E. of Huddersfield; pop. 1846. Map 32.
Cleator, par. and urb. dist. (**C. Moor**), Cumberland, $4\frac{1}{4}$ m. S.E. of Whitehaven; pop. 6582. Map 24.
Cleckheaton, W.R. Yorkshire, $5\frac{1}{2}$ m. S.E. of Bradford, now part of Spenborough. Map 32.
Cleethorpes, urb. dist. and par., ry. terminus, N. Lincs, $2\frac{1}{4}$ m. S.E. of Gt. Grimsby; pop. 28,624. Map 43.
Cleobury Mortimer, market town, Salop, 7 m. N.E. of Tenbury; pop. 1487. Map 57.
Clevedon, seaside town and par., N.W. Somersetshire, $15\frac{1}{4}$ m. W.S.W. of Bristol; pop. 7033. Map 74.
Cliddesden, par. and vil., N. Hants, 3 m. S. of Basingstoke; pop. 316. Map 78.
Clifden, seaport and market town, in co. and 49 m. N.W. of Galway; pop. 809. Map 92.
Cliffe, par. and vil., N. Kent, $5\frac{1}{2}$ m. E.N.E. of Gravesend; pop. 2581. Map 72.
Clifford, par. and vil., Herefordshire, $2\frac{1}{4}$ m. N.E. of Hay; pop. 729. Map 56.

Clifton, par. and vil., N. Lancashire, 3 m. S.E. of Kirkham; pop. 460. Map 30.
Clifton, par. and vil., Westmorland, 2½ m. S.E. of Penrith; pop. 397. Map 21.
Clifton, watering place, forming W. suburb of Bristol. Map 68.
Clifton, par., N.R. Yorkshire, 1 m. N. of York city; pop. 808. Map 33.
Clitheroe, mun. bor. and market town, N.E. Lancashire, 10¼ m. N.E. of Blackburn; pop. 12,008. Map 31.
Cloghan, vil. and ry. sta., Offaly co., 5 m. N.E. of Banagher; pop. 256. Map 95.
Clogheen, market town, Tipperary, 8 m. S. of Cahir ry. sta.; pop. 734. Map 95.
Clonakilty, urb. dist. and seaport, co. Cork, 13 m. S.W. of Bandon; pop. 2771. Map 94.
Clones, urb. dist. and market town, co. Monaghan, 39½ m. N.W. of Dundalk; pop. 2358. Map 93.
Clonmel, mun. bor., cos. Tipperary and Waterford, 28 m. N.W. of Waterford; pop. 8989. Map 95.
Clophill, par. and vil., Bedfordshire, 3½ m. E. of Ampthill; pop. 909. Map 60.
Clovelly, coast par. and vil., Devonshire, 11 m. S.W. of Bideford; pop. 634. Map 84.
Clovenfords, ham., N.E. Selkirkshire, 3½ m. W. of Galashiels. Map 16.
Clun, market town and par., Salop, 5½ m. N.N.E. of Knighton; pop. 1774. Map 56.
Clydach-on-Tawe, vil. and ry. sta., Glamorganshire, 5 m. N. of Swansea. Map 66.
Clydebank, police bur., Dumbartonshire, 6¼ m. N.W. of Glasgow; pop. 46,963. Map 8.
Clynderwen, vil. and ry. sta., Pembroke and Carmarthen, 6½ m. E. of Clarbeston Road sta. Map 64.
Coalville, urb. dist. and par., Leicestershire, 5 m. S.E. of Ashby-de-la-Zouch; pop. 21,886. Map 49.
Coatbridge, mun. bur., Lanarkshire, 8¾ m. E. of Glasgow; pop. 43,056. Map 9.
Cobh (Queenstown), seaport town, in co. and 13 m. S.E. of Cork; pop. 7070. Map 94.
Cobham, or **Church Cobham**, par. and vil., Surrey, 6½ m. W. of Epsom; pop. 5103. Map 78.
Cockburnspath, par. and vil., Berwickshire, 7¼ m. S.E. of Dunbar; pop. 941. Map 11.
Cockenzie and Port Seton, seaport, E. Lothian, 9¾ m. E. of Edinburgh; pop. 2526. Map 10.
Cockerham, par. and vil., N. Lancashire, 6 m. S. of Lancaster; pop. 569. Map 30.
Cockermouth, urb. dist. and par., Cumberland, 32 m. S.W. of Carlisle; pop. 4789. Map 20.
Cockfield, par. and vil., Durham, 7 m. N.E. of Barnard Castle; pop. 2693. Map 22.
Cockfield, par., W. Suffolk, 7 m. S.E. of Bury St Edmunds; pop. 816. Map 62.
Cocking, par. and vil., W. Sussex, 2½ m. S. of Midhurst; pop. 427. Map 79.
Coddenham, par. and vil., E. Suffolk, 3 m. E. of Needham Market; pop. 671. Map 63.
Coggeshall, town, Essex, 6 m. E. of Braintree; pop. of par. (**Great C.**) 2300. Map 72.
Colbury, par. and vil., Hants, 3 m. N.E. of Lyndhurst; pop. 1066. Map 77.
Colby, vil., Isle of Man, 3 m. N.W. of Castletown. Map 24.
Colchester, mun. bor. and river-port, Essex, 22 m. N.E. of Chelmsford; pop. 48,607. Map 73.
Coldingham, par. and vil., Berwickshire, 3 m. N.W. of Eyemouth; pop. 2830. Map 11.
Coldstream, police bur. and par., Berwickshire, 13½ m. S.W. of Berwick-on-Tweed; pop. 1233. Map 16.
Coleford, urb. dist. and par., Gloucestershire, 4½ m. E.S.E. of Monmouth; pop. 2777. Map 68.
Coleraine, seaport, urb. dist. and par., in co. and 33½ m. N.E. of Londonderry; pop. 7785. Map 93.
Colerne, par. and vil., N. Wiltshire, 8 m. W.S.W. of Chippenham; pop. 912. Map 75.
Coleshill, market town and par., Warwickshire, 8½ m. E.N.E. of Birmingham; pop. 3177. Map 48.
Colinsburgh, vil., Fifeshire, 2 m. N.W. of Kilconquhar sta.; pop. 304. Map 7.
Colinton, eccl. par., in S.W. of city of Edinburgh; pop. 4778. Map 10.
Coll Island, par., Argyllshire, 9½ m. W.S.W. of Ardnamurchan Point; pop. 383. Map 2.
Collace, par. and vil., in co. and 8 m. N.E. of Perth; pop. 349. Map 6.
Collessie, par. and vil., Fifeshire, 2½ m. N.W. of Ladybank Junction; pop. 2014. Map 6.
Collingbourne Ducis, par. and vil., Wiltshire, 2½ m. N.W. of Ludgershall; pop. 366. Map 76.
Collingbourne Kingston, par. and vil., Wiltshire, 3½ m. N.W. of Ludgershall; pop. 669. Map 76.
Collingham, vil., Nottinghamshire, 5½ m. N.E. of Newark. Map 42.
Collooney, vil., in co. and 6½ m. S. of Sligo; pop. 330. Map 92.
Colne, mun. bor., market town and par., N.E. Lancashire, 5¼ m. N.E. of Burnley; pop. 23,790. Map 31.
Coln St Aldwyn, par. and vil., Gloucestershire, 6½ m. S.E. of Northleach; pop. 325. Map 69.
Colsterworth, par. and vil., Kesteven, Lincolnshire, 7½ m. S. of Grantham; pop. 764. Map 50.
Coltishall, par. and vil., Norfolk, 8 m. N.E. of Norwich; pop. 955. Map 53.
Colwyn Bay, watering place with ry. sta., Denbighshire, 6 m. W. of Abergele; pop. 20,885. Map 37.
Colyton, market town and par., Devonshire, 2¾ m. N. of Seaton; pop. 1886. Map 86.
Combe Martin, coast par. and vil., N. Devonshire, 5 m. E. of Ilfracombe; pop. 2004. Map 84.
Combe St Nicholas, par. and vil., Somersetshire, 2 m. N.W. of Chard; pop. 929. Map 86.
Commercial, ham., Pembrokeshire, 3 m. N.E. of Narberth. Map 64.
Compstall, urb. dist., Cheshire, 5 m. E. of Stockport; pop. 865. Map 40.
Compton, par. and vil., W. Sussex, 6 m. S.E. of Petersfield; pop. 249. Map 79.
Comrie, par. and town, Perthshire, 6¾ m. W. of Crieff; pop. 2208. Map 5.
Congleton, mun. bor., mkt. town and par., E. Cheshire, 8½ m. S.S.W. of Macclesfield; pop. 12,885. Map 39.
Congresbury, par. and vil., N.W. Somersetshire, on r. Yeo, 11½ m. S.W. of Bristol; pop. 1258. Map 74.
Coningsby, par. and vil., Lindsey, Lincolnshire, 7 m. S.S.W. of Horncastle; pop. 1031. Map 43.
Conisborough, urb. dist., W.R. Yorkshire, 5 m. S.W. of Doncaster; pop. 18,179. Map 41.
Coniston, par., vil. and lake, Lancashire, 6 m. N.W. of Ambleside; pop. 1098. Map 25.
Connah's Quay, par. and urb. dist. on Dee estuary, in co. and 3¼ m. S.E. of Flint; pop. 5982. Map 38.
Connel Ferry, vil. and ry. sta., Argyllshire, 6 m. N.E. of Oban; pop. 458. Map 12.
Consett, urb. dist. and par., Durham, 12 m. S.W. of Newcastle; pop. 12,251. Map 22.
Conway, market town and spt., Carnarvonshire, 3½ m. S. of Llandudno; pop. 8769. Map 37.
Conwil Elvet, par. and vil., in co. and 5¼ m. N.N.W. of Carmarthen; pop. 1225. Map 65.
Cookham, par. and vil., Berkshire, 3 m. N. of Maidenhead; pop. 5848. Map 70.
Coombe Bissett, par., S. Wiltshire, 3 m. S.W. of Salisbury; pop. 248. Map 76.
Cootehill, urb. dist., co. Cavan, 33½ m. N.W. of Dundalk; pop. 1534. Map 93.
Corbridge, par. and town, Northumberland, 3½ m. E. of Hexham; pop. 2415. Map 22.
Corby, par. and vil., Kesteven, Lincolnshire, 8 m. S.E. of Grantham; pop. 664. Map 50.

Corby, par. and vil., Northants, 7½ m. N. of Kettering. Map 50.
Corfe, par. and vil., Somersetshire, 3½ m. S. of Taunton; pop. 230. Map 86.
Corfe Castle, par. and town, Isle of Purbeck, Dorsetshire, 6 m. S.E. of Wareham; pop. 1402. Map 87.
Cork, seaport, mun. bor. and co. town of Cork, 166½ m. S.W. of Dublin by rail; pop. 78,468. Map 94.
Cornhill, par. and vil., Northumberland, adjoining Coldstream. Map 17.
Cornworthy, par. and vil., Devonshire, 4 m. S.E. of Totnes; pop. 355. Map 89.
Corpusty, par. and vil., Norfolk, 5 m. N.W. of Aylsham; pop. 424. Map 53.
Corsham, market town and par., N. Wiltshire, 4½ m. S.W. of Chippenham; pop. 3940. Map 68.
Corwen, market town and par., Merionethshire, 11 m. N.E. of Bala; pop. 2690. Map 37.
Coseley, urb. dist., Staffordshire, 2¾ m. S.E. of Wolverhampton; pop. 25,137. Map 47.
Cosgrove, par. and vil., Northamptonshire, 1½ m. N. of Stony Stratford; pop. 584. Map 60.
Cosheston, par. and vil., in co. and 2 m. N.E. of Pembroke; pop. 508. Map 64.
Cotherstone, par. and ham., N.R. Yorkshire, 3½ m. N.W. of Barnard Castle; pop. 701. Map 27.
Cotmanhay, eccl. dist. and ham., Derbyshire, 1½ m. N. of Ilkeston; pop. 6636. Map 49.
Cottenham, par. and vil., in co. and 6½ m. N. of Cambridge; pop. 2470. Map 61.
Cottesmore, par. and vil., Rutlandshire, 4½ m. N.E. of Oakham; pop. 363. Map 50.
Cottingham, urb. dist. and par., E.R. Yorkshire, 4 m. N.W. of Hull; pop. 6182. Map 35.
Coulsdon and Purley, urb. dist., Surrey, 5 m. S. of Croydon; pop. 37,666. Map 80.
County School, ry. sta., Norfolk, 6 m. N. of East Dereham. Map 52.
Coupar-Angus, police bur. and par., in co. and 15¾ m. N.E. of Perth; pop. 1883. Map 6.
Cove and Kilcreggan, bur. and wtg. place, Dumbartonshire, 4½ m. N.W. of Greenock; pop. 954. Map 12.
Coventry, city, parl. and co. bor., Warwickshire, 19 m. S.E. of Birmingham; pop. 167,046. Map 58.
Cowbit, par. and vil., Holland, Lincolnshire, 3½ m. S. of Spalding; pop. 528. Map 51.
Cowbridge, mun. bor., Glamorganshire, 12½ m. W. of Cardiff; pop. 1018. Map 66.
Cowden, Great, par., E.R. Yorkshire, 4 m. S.E. of Hornsea; pop. (with **Little Cowden**) 102. Map 35.
Cowdenbeath, police bur., Fifeshire, 5¾ m. N.E. of Dunfermline; pop. 12,731. Map 10.
Cowes, urb. dist. and seaport, Isle of Wight, 4½ m. N. of Newport; pop. 10,179, **E. Cowes** 4595. Map 77.
Cowie, mining vil., 4 m. S.E. of Stirling. Map 9.
Coxwell, Great, par., Berkshire, 1½ m. S.W. of Faringdon; pop. 259. Map 69.
Coxwold, par. and vil., N.R. Yorkshire, 7½ m. S.E. of Thirsk; pop. 251. Map 28.
Craigendoran, pier, Dumbartonshire, 1 m. E. of Helensburgh. Map 8.
Crail, seaport and bur., Fifeshire, 11 m. S.E. of St Andrews; pop. 1058. Map 7.
Crailing, par. and vil., Roxburghshire, 3½ m. N.E. of Jedburgh; pop. 488. Map 16.
Cramlington, urb. dist. and par., Northumberland, 7 m. S.E. of Morpeth; pop. 8238. Map 23.
Cranborne, par. and vil., Dorsetshire, 10 m. N.E. of Wimborne Minster; pop. 657. Map 87.
Cranbrook, market town and par., Kent, 4 m. N. of Hawkhurst; pop. 3829. Map 82.
Cranford, vil. and ry. sta., Northamptonshire, 4½ m. E.S.E. of Kettering. Map 60.
Cranleigh, par. and vil., W. Surrey, 8 m. S.E. of Guildford; pop. 3746. Map 79.
Cranswick, vil., E.R. Yorkshire, 3 m. S. of Great Driffield. Map 35.
Cranwell, par., vil., Kesteven, Lincolnshire, 4 m. N.W. of Sleaford; pop. 2191. Map 42.
Craven Arms and Stokesay, ry. junct., Salop, 7 m. S. of Church Stretton. Map 56.
Crawford, par. and vil., Lanarkshire, 2¾ m. S.E. of Abington; pop. 2041. Map 14.
Crawley, par. and vil., W. Sussex, 7 m. N.E. of Horsham; pop. 453. Map 81.
Crawley, par. and vil., N. Hants, 5½ m. N.W. of Winchester; pop. 563. Map 76.
Crayford, urb. dist., Kent, 15½ m. S.E. of London; pop. 15,887. Map 80.
Creake, North, par., Norfolk, 3 m. S.E. of Burnham Market; pop. 499. Map 52.
Creake, South, par., Norfolk, 3½ m. S. of Burnham Market; pop. 658. Map 52.
Crediton, urb. dist. and par., Devonshire, 7½ m. N.W. of Exeter; pop. 3490. Map 85.
Creeslough, coast vil. and ry. sta., co. Donegal, 20 m. N.W. of Letterkenny; pop. 150. Map 92.
Creetown, seaport, Kirkcudbrightshire, 6½ m. S.E. of Newton Stewart; pop. 757. Map 19.
Cressingham, Great and **Little,** 2 pars., Norfolk, 4 m. W. of Watton; pop. 286 and 197. Map 52.
Crewe, mun. bor., Cheshire, 24½ m. N.W. of Stafford; pop. 46,061. Map 39.
Crewkerne, urb. dist. and par., Somersetshire, 8 m. S.W. of Yeovil; pop. 3509. Map 86.
Crianlarich, vil. and ry. station, Perthshire, 28¾ m. N.W. of Callander. Map 12.
Criccieth, par. and urb. dist., Carnarvonshire, 4 m. W.S.W. of Portmadoc; pop. 1449. Map 44.
Crich, par. and mining vil., N. Derbyshire, 4 m. W.S.W. of Alfreton; pop. 3056. Map 41.
Crickhowel, market town and par., Brecon, 14½ m. S.E. of Brecknock; pop. 1307. Map 67.
Cricklade, market town and par., Wiltshire, 8½ m. N.W. of Swindon; pop. 1425. Map 69.
Crieff, police bur. and par., in co. and 17¾ m. W. of Perth; pop. 5544. Map 6.
Cringleford, par. and vil., Norfolk, 3 m. S.W. of Norwich; pop. 261. Map 53.
Croesgoch, vil., Pembrokeshire, 6 m. N.E. of St Davids. Map 64.
Croft, par. and vil., N.R. Yorkshire, 3 m. S. of Darlington; pop. 509. Map 27.
Crofton, par. and seat, W.R. Yorkshire, 3¾ m. S.E. of Wakefield; pop. 2817. Map 33.
Cromarty, mun. bur., par. and seaport, Ross and Crom., 15½ m. N.E. of Inverness; pop. 837. Map 3.
Cromer, urb. dist. and watering place, Norfolk, 24 m. N. of Norwich; pop. 4177. Map 53.
Crompton, urb. dist., Lancashire, 3 m. N. of Oldham; pop. 14,750. Map 31.
Crook, urb. dist. and par., Durham, 6 m. N.W. of Bishop Auckland; pop. 11,690. Map 23.
Crookham, vil., Northumberland, 8½ m. N.W. of Wooler. Map 17.
Crooklands, ham., Westmorland, 6 m. S.E. of Kendal. Map 26.
Crook of Devon, vil., on r. Devon, in co. and 6 m. S.W. of Kinross. Map 6.
Croom, par. and town, in co. and 12½ m. S.W. of Limerick; pop. of par. 2038. Map 94.
Cropredy, par. and vil., Oxon, 3½ m. N. of Banbury; pop. 409. Map 59.
Crosby Ravensworth, par., N. Westmorland, 6 m. S.W. of Appleby; pop. 722. Map 26.
Crossford, vil., Lanarkshire, 3 m. S.W. of Carluke. Map 9.
Crossgates, mining vil., Fifeshire, 3½ m. N.E. of Dunfermline; pop. 2602. Map 10.

Cross Hands, vil., Carmarthenshire, 4½ m. W. of Ammanford. Map 65.
Cross Keys, ham. and ry. sta., Monmouthshire, 8 m. N.W. of Newport. Map 67.
Crossmolina, market town and par., co. Mayo, 7 m. W. of Ballina; pop. 4065. Map 92.
Croston, urb. dist. and par., S.W. Lancashire, 8 m. N.E. of Ormskirk; pop. 1935. Map 30.
Crowborough, par. and vil., E. Sussex, 7 m. N.E. of Uckfield; pop. 5846. Map 82.
Crowland, market town, Holland, Lincolnshire, 8 m. N.E. of Peterborough; pop. 2707. Map 51.
Crowland, vil., W. Suffolk, 5 m. E. of Ixworth. Map 62.
Crowle, urb. dist. and par., Lincolnshire, 6 m. E. of Thorne; pop. 2833. Map 33.
Crowthorne, par. and vil., Berkshire, 2½ m. S.E. of Wokingham; pop. 3980. Map 78.
Croxleygreen, eccl. par., S.W. Hertfordshire, 2 m. S.W. of Watford; pop. 2649. Map 71.
Croxton, eccl. dist. and ham., Staffordshire, 3 m. N.W. of Eccleshall; pop. 548. Map 47.
Croydon, mun. bor., N.E. Surrey, 10 m. S. of London Bridge; pop. 233,115. Map 80.
Cruden Bay, watering-place, Aberdeenshire, 8 m. S.S.W. of Peterhead. Map 3.
Crymmych Arms, vil. with ry. sta., Pembrokeshire, 11 m. S. of Cardigan. Map 65.
Cuckfield, urb. dist. and par., E. Sussex, 14 m. N. of Brighton; pop. 2114. Map 81.
Cudworth, urb. dist. and par., W.R. Yorkshire, 4¼ m. N.E. of Barnsley; pop. 9380. Map 33.
Culdaff, coast par. and vil., Donegal, 5 m. N.E. of Carndonagh; pop. 3075. Map 93.
Culgaith, par., E. Cumberland, 7 m. N.W. of Appleby; pop. 313. Map 21.
Cullen, mun. bur., par. and seaport, Banffshire, 5½ m. W.N.W. of Portsoy; pop. of bur. 1688. Map 3.
Cullercoats, eccl. dist. and ry. sta., in Tynemouth bor., Northumberland; pop. 5063. Map 23.
Culloden Moor, pl. with ry. sta., in co. and 7 m. E. of Inverness. Map 3.
Cullompton, market town and par., Devonshire, 12½ m. N.E. of Exeter; pop. 2737. Map 85.
Culmington, par. and vil., Salop, 5 m. N.N.W. of Ludlow; pop. 483. Map 56.
Culmstock, par. and vil., Devonshire, 9¾ m. N.E. of Tiverton; pop. 760. Map 85.
Culross, royal and mun. bur. and small seaport, Fifeshire, 7½ m. S.E. of Alloa; pop. 495. Map 9.
Cumbernauld, par. and vil., Dumbartonshire, 13 m. N.E. of Glasgow; pop. 5261. Map 9.
Cumbrae Islands, Buteshire, in Firth of Clyde. Map 8.
Cummertrees, par. and vil., Dumfriesshire, 3¼ m. W. of Annan; pop. 1084. Map 20.
Cumnock, par. and police bur., on r. Lugar, in co. and 16 m. E. of Ayr; pop. 3653. Map 12.
Cumwhitton, par. and vil., N.E. Cumberland, 6½ m. S.E. of Carlisle; pop. 444. Map 21.
Cupar, par., mun. bur. and co. town of Fifeshire, 44½ m. N.E. of Edinburgh by rail; pop. 4596. Map 7.
Curdworth, par. and vil., Warwickshire, 2½ m. N.N.W. of Coleshill; pop. 413. Map 48.
Cushendall, coast vil., co. Antrim, 17 m. N.E. of Ballymena; pop. 306. Map 93.
Cushendun, coast vil., co. Antrim, 4 m. N. of Cushendall. Map 93.
Cwmaman, vil. and ry. sta., Glamorganshire, 2 m. S. of Aberdare. Map 66.
Cwmamman, urb. dist., Carmarthenshire, 4 m. E.N.E. of Ammanford; pop. 5214. Map 66.
Cwmbach, vil., Glamorganshire, 2 m. E. of Aberdare. Map 66.
Cwm-bran, vil., Monmouthshire, 3½ m. S. of Pontypool. Map 67.
Cwm-felin-fach, ham., Monmouthshire, 1¼ m. W.N.W. of N ne M le Point ry. sta. Map 7.
DAGENHAM, par. and urb. dist., Essex, 3 m. E. of Barking; pop. 89,365. Map 72.
Dalbeattie, police bur., Kirkcudbrightshire, 5¼ m. E. of Castle Douglas; pop. 3011. Map 19.
Dalby, vil., Isle of Man, 4 m. S. of Peel. Map 24.
Dale End, vil., N.R. Yorkshire, 6 m. W.N.W. of Egton. Map 28.
Dalkeith, police bur. and par., Midlothian, 6½ m. S.E. of Edinburgh; pop. 7502. Map 10.
Dalkey, urb. dist. and par., in co. and 9 m. S.E. of Dublin; pop. 4135. Map 93.
Dalmally, vil. and ry. sta., Argyllshire, 24½ m. E. of Oban. Map 12.
Dalmellington, par. and vil., in co. and 15 m. S.E. of Ayr; pop. 6155. Map 12.
Dalmeny, par. and vil., West Lothian, 9½ m. N.W. of Edinburgh; pop. 4557. Map 10.
Dalry, par. and town, Ayrshire, 3½ m. N. of Kilwinning; pop. 7243. Map 12.
Dalserf, par. and vil., Lanarkshire, 7 m. S.E. of Hamilton; pop. 19,465. Map 9.
Dalston, par., N.E. Cumberland, 4½ m. S.W. of Carlisle; pop. 1746. Map 21.
Dalton, par. and vil., Dumfriesshire, 6 m. S.S.W. of Lockerbie; pop. 548. Map 20.
Dalton-in-Furness, urb. dist. and par., Lancashire, 3½ m. N.E. of Barrow-in-Furness; pop. 10,338. Map 25.
Danby Wiske, par. and vil., N.R. Yorkshire, 3½ m. N.W. of Northallerton; pop. 297. Map 28.
Darfield, urb. dist., W.R. Yorkshire, 5 m. E.S.E. of Barnsley; pop. 5268. Map 33.
Darlaston, urb. dist., Staffordshire, within Wednesbury; pop. 19,736. Map 47.
Darleydale, locality, Derbyshire, in N. Derby urb. dist. Map 40.
Darlington, parl. and co. bor., market town and par., S. Durham, 9½ m. W.S.W. of Stockton-on-Tees; pop. 72,093. Map 27.
Darliston, ham., Salop, on r. Tern, 5½ m. N.E. of Wem. Map 46.
Dartford, urb. dist. and market town, W. Kent, 6¾ m. W. of Gravesend; pop. 28,928. Map 80.
Dartmoor Forest, upland tract, Devonshire, from Brent to Okehampton. Maps 88, 89.
Dartmouth, mun. bor., par. and seaport, Devonshire, opposite Kingswear; pop. 6707. Map 89.
Darton, urb. dist., W.R. Yorkshire, 3½ m. N.W. of Barnsley; pop. 12,595. Map 32.
Darvel, town, Ayrshire, 9 m. E. of Kilmarnock; pop. 3232. Map 12.
Darwen, mun. bor., mkt. and mfg. town, par., N.E. Lancs, 4 m. S. of Blackburn; pop. 36,010. Map 31.
Darwen, Lower, eccl. dist., N.E. Lancashire, 1½ m. S. of Blackburn; pop. 1874. Map 31.
Datchet, par. and vil., S. Buckinghamshire, on r. Thames, 2 m. E. of Windsor; pop. 2406. Map 78.
Daventry, mun. bor. and par., in co. and 12 m. W.N.W. of Northampton; pop. 3608. Map 59.
Dawley, urb. dist. and par., Salop, 4 m. S.E. of Wellington; pop. 7363. Map 47.
Dawlish, urb. dist., Devonshire, 3 m. N.E. of Teignmouth; pop. 4578. Map 89.
Deal, mun. bor., par. and Cinque port, Kent, 8 m. N.E. of Dover; pop. 13,680. Map 83.
Dearham, par. and vil., Cumberland, 7½ m. N.W. of Cockermouth; pop. 2075. Map 20.
Debenham, par. and market town, E. Suffolk, 8 m. S. of Eye; pop. 1085. Map 63.
Deddington, market town and par., Oxon, 6 m. S. of Banbury; pop. 1339. Map 59.
Deeping St Nicholas, par. and vil., Holland, Lincolnshire, 4½ m. S.W. of Spalding; pop. 1540. Map 51.
Deganwy, ry. sta., Denbighshire, 1 m. N.W. of Llandudno Junction. **D. Castle** in vicinity. Map 37.

Delph, vil., W.R. Yorkshire, 6 m. N.E. of Ashton-under-Lyne. Map 31.
Denbigh, mun. bor., market town and par., Denbighshire, 29½ m. W. of Chester; pop. 7249. Map 37.
Denby and Cumberworth, urb. dist., W.R. Yorkshire, 8 m. W. of Barnsley; pop. 3396. Map 32.
Denholm, vil., Roxburghshire, 5 m. N.E. of Hawick; pop. 384. Map 16.
Denholme, urb. dist., par. and ham., W.R. Yorkshire, 6½ m. W. of Bradford; pop. 2662. Map 31.
Denny, town and par., in co. and 12 m. S. of Stirling; pop. of par. 5512. Map 9.
Dennyloanhead, vil. and ry. sta., Stirlingshire, 1¾ m. S. of Denny; pop. 3378. Map 9.
Dent, par. and vil., W.R. Yorkshire, 5 m. S.E. of Sedbergh; pop. 996. Map 26.
Denton, urb. dist. and par., Lancashire, 7 m. E.S.E. of Manchester; pop. 17,383. Map 39.
Denwick, par. and vil., Northumberland, 1½ m. N.E. of Alnwick; pop. 668. Map 17.
Derby, parl. and co. bor., cap. of Derbyshire, 42½ m. N.E. of Birmingham; pop. 142,406. Map 48.
Dereham, East, urb. dist. and par., Norfolk, 16 m. W.N.W. of Norwich; pop. 5641. Map 52.
Derwent, par., N. Derbyshire, on r. Derwent, 5 m. N.E. of Castleton; pop. 174. Map 40.
Derwent Water, lake, in basin of r. Derwent, Cumberland. Map 20.
Desborough, urb. dist. and par., Northamptonshire, 5¼ m. S.E. of Market Harborough; pop. 4407. Map 60.
Devil's Bridge, ham. and ry. sta., Cardiganshire, 11¾ m. E.S.E. of Aberystwyth. Map 55.
Devil's Elbow, crook on road over the Grampians, 9½ m. S. of Braemar. Map 3.
Devizes, mun. bor., N. Wiltshire, 25½ m. N.W. of Salisbury; pop. 6058. Map 75.
Devonport, dist. in Plymouth, Devonshire. Map 88.
Dewsbury, co. and parl. bor., mkt. town and par., W.R. Yorkshire, 9¼ m. S. of Leeds; pop. 54,303. Map 32.
Dibden, par. and vil., Hants, 1 m. W.N.W. of Hythe; pop. 2144. Map 77.
Diddlebury, par., Salop, 6½ m. N. of Ludlow; pop. 727. Map 56.
Didmarton, par. and ham., Gloucestershire, 5½ m. S.W. of Tetbury; pop. 318. Map 68.
Didsbury, ward in S. Manchester. Map 39.
Digby, par. and vil., Kesteven, Lincolnshire, 6 m. N. of Sleaford; pop. 368. Map 42.
Dilton Marsh, par., S. Wiltshire, 5 m. S. of Trowbridge; pop. 1525. Map 75.
Dinas, coast par. and vil., Pembrokeshire, 3½ m. N.E. of Fishguard; pop. 691. Map 64.
Dinas, ham., in co. and 3 m. S. of Carnarvon. Map 36.
Dinas Mawddwy, market town, Merionethshire, 10 m. S.E. of Dolgelley. Map 45.
Dinas Powis, vil., Glamorganshire, 6 m. S.W. of Cardiff. Map 67.
Dingle, seaport town and par., co. Kerry, 31¼ m. S.W. of Tralee; pop. of town 1998. Map 94.
Dingwall, mun. bur., par. and cap. of Ross and Cromarty, 18½ m. N.W. of Inverness; pop. 2554. Map 3.
Dinnington, par. and vil., Northumberland, 6½ m. N.N.W. of Newcastle; pop. 1078. Map 23.
Dinorwic, vil., 1½ m. N.E. of Llanberis, co. Carnarvon; slate quarries. Map 36.
Dirleton, coast par. and vil., E. Lothian, 20¼ m. E.N.E. of Edinburgh; pop. 2623. Map 10.
Diss, urb. dist. and par., Norfolk, 20 m. S.W. of Norwich; pop. 3422. Map 63.
Distington, par. and vil., Cumberland, 3½ m. S. of Workington; pop. 2093. Map 20.
Ditchingham, par. and vil., Norfolk, 1½ m. N. of Bungay; pop. 997. Map 53.
Ditchling, par. and vil., E. Sussex, 6 m. N. of Brighton; pop. 1414. Map 81.
Ditton Priors, par. and vil., Salop, 7½ m. S.W. of Bridgnorth; pop. 650. Map 47.
Docking, par. and vil., Norfolk, 5¾ m. S.W. of Burnham Market; pop. 1127. Map 52.
Dodworth, urb. dist., W.R. Yorkshire, 2 m. S.W. of Barnsley; pop. 4248. Map 33.
Dolgarrog, par., Carnarvonshire, 7½ m. S. of Conway; pop. 364. Map 37.
Dolgelley, urb. dist. and par., Merionethshire, 9¼ m. E. of Barmouth; pop. 2261. Map 43.
Dollar, police bur. and par., Clackmannanshire, 6½ m. N.E. of Alloa; pop. 1485. Map 9.
Dolphinton, par., Lanarkshire, 11 m. N.E. of Carstairs; pop. 252. Map 9.
Dolton, par. and vil., Devonshire, 7 m. N.E. of Hatherleigh; pop. 359. Map 84.
Dolyhir, ry. sta., Radnorshire, 2½ m. S.E. of New Radnor. Map 56.
Donaghadee, seaport town and par., co. Down, 21½ m. E. of Belfast; pop. of par. 4878. Map 93.
Doncaster, mun. bor., mkt. tn. and par., W.R. Yorks, on r. Don, 32 m. S. of York; pop. 63,308. Map 41.
Donegal, spt., par. and cap. of co. Donegal, 18 m. S.W. of Stranorlar; pop. of town 1104. Map 92.
Donington, par. and vil., Kesteven, Lincolnshire, 8½ m. N.N.W. of Spalding; pop. 1604. Map 51.
Donnington, market town, Salop, 3½ m. S.W. of New port. Map 47.
Dorchester, mun. bor. and capital of Dorsetshire, 6 m. N. of Weymouth; pop. 10,030. Map 87.
Dorking, urb. dist. and par., Surrey, 5½ m. S.W. of Reigate; pop. 10,109. Map 78.
Dornoch, mun. bur., spt. and capital of Sutherlandshire, 8¾ m. N.E. of Tain; pop. 725. Map 3.
Dornock, par. and vil., Dumfriesshire, 3 m. E. of Annan; pop. 2475. Map 20.
Dorrington, par. and vil., Kesteven, Lincolnshire, 5 m. N. of Sleaford; pop. 410. Map 42.
Douglas, spt. and mkt. tn., cap. of I. of Man, 10¾ m. N.E. of Castletown; pop. 27,604. Map 24.
Doune, police bur., Perthshire, 8¾ m. N.W. of Stirling; pop. 822. Map 9.
Dove Holes, vil., N.W. Derbyshire, 3 m. N.N.W. of Buxton. Map 40.
Dover, mun. bor., par. and Cinque port, Kent, 78½ m. S.E. of London by rail; pop. 41,095. Map 83.
Dovercourt, par., Essex, in Harwich mun. bor.; pop. 7695. Map 73.
Dowally, vil., Perthshire, 4½ m. N.W. of Dunkeld. Map 6.
Dowlais, colliery and iron dist., Glamorganshire, round Merthyr-Tydfil. Map 66.
Downend, eccl. par. and vil., S.E. Gloucestershire, 4½ m. N.E. of Bristol; pop. 9448. Map 68.
Downham Market, urb. dist. and par., Norfolk, 11 m. S. of King's Lynn; pop. 2463. Map 51.
Downholland, par. and ry. sta., Lancashire, 6½ m. S.E. of Southport; pop. 618. Map 30.
Downpatrick, market town and cap. of co. Down, 27 m. S.E. of Belfast; pop. 3199. Map 93.
Downton, town and par., Wiltshire, 7 m. S.E. of Salisbury; pop. 1906. Map 77.
Drayton, par. and vil., Norfolk, 4½ m. N.W. of Norwich; pop. 557. Map 53.
Drigg, par. and ham., Cumberland, 2 m. N.W. o Ravenglass; pop. 446. Map 25.
Drighlington, urb. dist., par. and vil., W.R. York shire, 6½ m. S.E. of Bradford; pop. 4064. Map 32.
Drogheda, mun. bor. and seaport, co. Louth, 32 m. N. of Dublin; pop. 12,688. Map 93.
Droitwich, mun. bor., in co. and 6 m. N.E. of Wor cester; pop. 4553. Map 57.
Dromcolliher, par. and vil., co. Limerick, 10 m. S.E. of Newcastle; pop. 948. Map 94.
Dromore, urb. dist. and par., co. Down, 17½ m. S.W. of Belfast; pop. of town, 2364. Map 93.

Dronfield, urb. dist. and par., E. Derbyshire, 6 m. N.W. of Chesterfield; pop. 4530. Map 41.
Dronfield Woodhouse, par., E. Derbyshire, 2 m. N. of Dronfield; pop. 902. Map 41.
Droylsden, urb. dist. and par., S.E. Lancs, 4¾ m. N.E. of Manchester; pop. 13,277. Map 40.
Drymen, par. and vil., in co. and 23½ m. S.W. of Stirling; vil. pop. 279. Map 8.
Dublin (Baile Atha Cliath), city co. bor. and spt., on Dublin Bay, cap. of Ireland, 112¾ m. by rail S. of Belfast; pop., with environs, 419,176. Map 93.
Ducklington, par. and vil., Oxon, 1½ m. S. of Witney; pop. 386. Map 69.
Dudley, parl. and co. bor., Worcestershire, 8 m. N.W. of Birmingham; pop. 59,579. Map 48.
Dufftown, police bur., Banffshire, 64 m. N.W. of Aberdeen; pop. 1454. Map 3.
Dukeries Junction, sta. adjoining Tuxford, Nottinghamshire, 6½ m. S.E. of Retford. Map 41.
Dukinfield, mun. bor. and par., Cheshire, 1½ m. W.S.W. of Stalybridge; pop. 19,309. Map 40.
Duleek, par. and vil., co. Meath, 4¾ m. S.W. of Drogheda; pop. 1810. Map 93.
Dulverton, par. and market town, W. Somersetshire, 20 m. W. of Taunton; pop. 1298. Map 85.
Dumbarton, mun. bur., par. and cap. of Dumbartonshire, 15½ m. N.W. of Glasgow; pop. 21,546. Map 12.
Dumfries, bur., par. and cap. of Dumfriesshire, 33 m. N.W. of Carlisle; pop. 22,795. Map 20.
Dunbar, mun. bur., par. and seaport, E. Lothian, 29½ m. E. of Edinburgh; pop. 3751. Map 11.
Dunblane, police bur. and par., Perthshire, 5 m. N. of Stirling; pop. 2692. Map 9.
Dunchurch, par. and vil., Warwickshire, 2 m. S.W. of Rugby; pop. 963. Map 59.
Dundalk, urb. dist., seaport, par. and cap. of co. Louth, 54 m. N. of Dublin; pop. 14,007. Map 93.
Dundee, parl. and co. bur. and city, Angus, 59½ m. N. of Edinburgh; pop. 175,583. Map 7.
Dundrum, seaport and vil., co. Down, 7 m. S.W. of Downpatrick; pop. 474. Map 93.
Dunfermline, parl. and mun. bur., Fifeshire, 16¾ m. N.W. of Edinburgh; pop. 34,954. Map 9.
Dungannon, urb. dist., co. Tyrone, 40 m. W. of Belfast; pop. 3830. Map 93.
Dungarvan, urb. dist., par. and seaport, in co. and 28½ m. S.W. of Waterford; pop. 4977. Map 95.
Dungeness, headland, S. Kent, 10½ m. E.S.E. of Rye. Map 83.
Dunipace, town and par., Stirlingshire, forms part of Denny and Dunipace. Map 9.
Dunkeld, market town, in co. and 15½ m. N.W. of Perth; pop. 529. Map 6.
Dunlop, par. and vil., Ayrshire, 7½ m. N.W. of Kilmarnock; pop. 1335. Map 8.
Dunmanway, market town, in co. and 37¾ m. S.W. of Cork; pop. 1619. Map 94.
Dunmore, market town and par., co. Galway, 8 m. N.E. of Tuam; pop. of par. 5986. Map 92.
Dunmow, Great, market town and par., Essex, 8½ m. W. of Braintree; pop. 2506. Map 72.
Dunning, par. and vil., in co. and 10 m. S.W. of Perth; pop. 1136. Map 6.
Dunoon, police bur., Argyllshire, on Firth of Clyde, 27 m. by water from Glasgow; pop. 8780. Map 12.
Duns, police bur. and par., Berwickshire, 7½ m. N.E. of Greenlaw; pop. of bur. 1788. Map 11.
Dunshelt, vil., Fifeshire, 1 m. S.E. of Auchtermuchty. Map 6.
Dunstable, mun. bor. and par., Bedfordshire, 4½ m. W. of Luton; pop. 8972. Map 71.
Dunstan, coast par., Northumberland, 6 m. N.E. of Alnwick; pop. 357. Map 17.
Dunstanburgh Castle, ruin, Northumberland, 7 m. N.E. of Alnwick. Map 17.
Dunster, par. and market town, W. Somersetshire, 5 m. W. of Watchet; pop. 705. Map 85.
Dunsyre, par. and vil., Lanarkshire, 8½ m. E.N.E. of Carstairs; pop. 161. Map 9.
Dunvegan, vil. and loch, N.W. Skye Isl., Inverness-shire, 22½ m. N.W. of Portree. Map 2.
Durham, city and cap. of co. Durham, 14½ m. S. of Newcastle; pop. 16,223. Map 23.
Durrow, market town, Leix co., 15 m. N.N.W. of Kilkenny; pop. 548. Map 95.
Dursley, market town and par., in co. and 15 m. S.S.W. of Gloucester; pop. 2792. Map 68.
Duxford, par. and vil., in co. and 8 m. S.S.E. of Cambridge; pop. 734. Map 61.
Dymchurch, coast par. and vil., Kent, 4 m. N.E. of New Romney; pop. 891. Map 83.
Dymock, par. and vil., Gloucestershire, 4 m. S. of Ledbury; pop. 1215. Map 57.
Dysart, seaport, Fifeshire, 2 m. N.E. of Kirkcaldy, to which it has been annexed. Map 10.
EAGLESFIELD, par. and vil., Cumberland, 2½ m. S.W. of Cockermouth; pop. 232. Map 20.
Eaglesham, par. and vil., Renfrewshire, 8½ m. S.S.W. of Glasgow; pop. 1519. Map 8.
Ealing, mun. bor., Middlesex, 5¾ m. W. of Paddington; pop. 117,688. Map 71.
Earby, urb. dist., W.R. Yorkshire, 6½ m. S.W. of Skipton; pop. 5522. Map 32.
Eardington, par. and vil., Salop, 2 m. S. of Bridgnorth; pop. 271. Map 47.
Eardisland, par. and vil., Herefordshire, 5 m. W. of Leominster; pop. 496. Map 56.
Eardisley, par. and vil., Herefordshire, 5 m. S. of Kington; pop. 702. Map 56.
Earith, vil., Huntingdonshire, 5¾ m. N.E. of St Ives. Map 61.
Earls Barton, par. and vil., in co. and 6½ m. E. of Northampton; pop. 2574. Map 60.
Earls Colne, par. and vil., Essex, 2½ m. S.E. of Halstead; pop. 1806. Map 73.
Earlston, market town and par., S.W. Berwickshire, 4½ m. N. of St Boswells; pop. 1061. Map 16.
Earn, Loch, Perthshire, 12 m. W. of Crieff, 6½ m. long by ½ m. broad. Map 5.
Earn, River, Perthshire, from Loch Earn flows 46 m. E. to Tay, 6½ m. S.E. of Perth. Map 6.
Earsdon, urb. dist. and coast par., Northumberland, 4 m. N.W. of North Shields; pop. 13,086. Map 23.
Easebourne, par. and vil., W. Sussex, 1 m. N. of Midhurst; pop. 1514. Map 79.
Easington, coast par., E.R. Yorkshire, 5 m. S.E. of Patrington; pop. 336. Map 35.
Easington, par. and vil., N.R. Yorkshire, 10½ m. N.W. of Whitby; pop. 768. Map 28.
Easingwold, town and par., N.R. Yorkshire, 13 m. N.W. of York; pop. 2045. Map 28.
East Barnet Valley, urb. dist., Hertfordshire, adjoining Barnet; pop. 18,542. Map 71.
Eastbourne, co. bor. and par., E. Sussex, 66 m. S.S.E. of London; pop. 57,435. Map 81.
East Grinstead, urb. dist. and par., E. Sussex, 14 m. N.E. of Horsham; pop. 7981. Map 81.
East Halton, par. and vil., N. Lincolnshire, 7 m. S.E. of Barton; pop. 662. Map 35.
Eastham, par. and vil., N. Cheshire, on r. Mersey, 6 m. S.E. of Birkenhead; pop. 1098. Manchester Ship Canal enters Mersey here. Map 38.
East Ham, co. bor., S.W. Essex, 6 m. E. of Fenchurch St. Sta., London; pop. 142,460. Map 71.
Eastington, par. and vil., Gloucestershire, 5 m. W. of Stroud; pop. 1182. Map 68.
East Kilbride, town and par., Lanarkshire, 12 m. S. of Glasgow; pop. 2046. Map 8.
East Leake, par. and vil., Nottinghamshire, 5 m. N.E. of Loughborough; pop. 1023. Map 49.
Eastleigh and Bishopstoke, urb. dist., Hampshire, 5½ m. N.E. of Southampton; pop. 18,333. Map 77.

East Linton, town, East Lothian, 6 m. W. of Dunbar; pop. 882. Map 10.

East Markham, par. and vil., Nottinghamshire, 1½ m. N. of Tuxford; pop. 737. Map 41.

East Retford, mun. bor., market town and par., Notts, 18½ m. N.W. of Newark; pop. 14,228. Map 41.

Eastrington, par. and vil., E.R. Yorkshire, 3 m. N.E. of Howden; pop. 531. Map 34.

East Wemyss, town, Fifeshire, 1 m. S.W. of Buckhaven; pop. 2805. Map 10.

Eastwood, urb. dist., in co. and 9 m. N.W. of Nottingham; pop. 5360. Map 41.

Eatington or **Ettington,** par. and vil., Warwickshire, 5½ m. S.E. of Stratford-on-Avon; pop. 500. Map 58.

Eaton Bray, par. and vil., Bedfordshire, 3½ m. S.W. of Dunstable; pop. 975. Map 71.

Eaton Socon, par. and vil., Bedfordshire, 1½ m. W.S.W. of St Neots; pop. 2231. Map 60.

Ebberston, par., vil. and seat, N.R. Yorkshire, 6 m. E. of Pickering; pop. 462. Map 29.

Ebbw Vale, urb. dist. and par., Monmouthshire, 6 m. N.W. of Aberbeeg Junction; pop. 31,695. Map 67.

Ebchester, par. and vil., Durham, 12¾ m. S.W. of Newcastle; pop. 710. Map 22.

Ebenezer, vil. in co. and 6 m. S.W. of Carmarthen. Map 65.

Ecclefechan, vil. and ry. sta., Dumfriesshire, 5¾ m. S.E. of Lockerbie; pop. 680. Map 20.

Eccles, parl. and mun. bor. and par., S.E. Lancashire, 4 m. W. of Manchester; pop. 44,415. Map 39.

Eccleshall, market town and par., in co. and 7 m. N.W. of Stafford; pop. 3630. Map 47.

Eckford, par. and vil., Roxburghshire, 6 m. S. of Kelso; pop. 665. Map 16.

Eckington, par. and vil., in co. and 9 m. S.E. of Worcester; pop. 623. Map 57.

Eckington, par. and town, E. Derbyshire, 6 m. S.E. of Sheffield; pop. 12,624. Map 41.

Eddleston, par. and vil., in co. and 4 m. N. of Peebles; pop. 527. Map 10.

Edenbridge, par. and town, W. Kent, 5 m. S. of Westerham; pop. 2890. Map 80.

Edenderry, town, Offaly co., 37 m. W. of Dublin; pop. 2093. Map 93.

Edenfield, eccl. dist. and vil., S.E. Lancashire, 5½ m. N. of Bury; pop. 3385. Map 31.

Edgbaston, parl. div. in S.W. of Birmingham; pop. 71,459. Map 58.

Edgeworthstown, town, in co. and 9 m. E.S.E. of Longford; pop. 654. Map 93.

Edgware, par. and vil., Middlesex, 11¼ m. N.W. of London; pop. 1516. Map 71.

Edgworth, par., S.E. Lancashire, 5 m. N.N.E. of Bolton; pop. 2557. Map 31.

Edinburgh, city, parl. and mun. bur. and capital of Scotland, on Firth of Forth, 392¼ m. N. of London by rail; pop. 438,998. Map 10.

Edington, par., N. Wiltshire, 3½ m. N.E. of Westbury; pop. 748. Map 75.

Edlington, par. and ham., W.R. Yorkshire, 4¼ m. S.W. of Doncaster; pop. 5289. Map 41.

Edmondbyers, par. and vil., Durham, 5½ m. W.S.W. of Consett; pop. 285. Map 22.

Edmonton, urb. dist. and par., Middlesex, 8¾ m. N. of London; pop. 77,652. Map 71.

Ednam, par. and vil., Roxburghshire, 2½ m. N.E. of Kelso; pop. 413. Map 16.

Edzell, par. and vil., Angus, 6½ m. N. of Brechin; pop. 745. Map 3.

Egham, urb. dist. and par., W. Surrey, 1½ m. W. of Staines; pop. 15,915. Map 78.

Egremont, urb. dist., Cumberland, 5 m. S.E. of Whitehaven; pop. 6015. Map 24.

Egremont, eccl. dist., W. Cheshire, on r. Mersey, 2 m. N.W. of Birkenhead; pop. 16,727. Map 38.

Egten, par. and vil., N.R. Yorkshire, 6½ m. S.W. of Whitby; pop. 993. Map 29.

Eigg, isl., Inverness-shire, 5 m. S.W. of Sleat Point; pop. 197. Map 2.

Elan Valley, reservoirs of Birmingham Water Supply, Rhayader, Radnorshire. Map 55.

Elgin, bur., par. and capital of co. Moray, 37 m. N.E. of Inverness; pop. 8810. Map 3.

Elie, police bur., Fifeshire, on Firth of Forth, 5¼ m. S.E. of Largo; pop. 1098. Map 7.

Elland, urb. dist., par. and town, W.R. Yorkshire, 3 m. S.E. of Halifax; pop. 10,327. Map 32.

Ellerby, par. and ham., E.R. Yorkshire, 7½ m. N.E. of Hull; pop. 339. Map 35.

Ellerker, par. and vil., E.R. Yorkshire, 11 m. W. of Hull; pop. 299. Map 34.

Ellerton, vil., E.R. Yorkshire, 3 m. N. of Bubwith. Map 33.

Ellesmere, urb. dist. and par., Salop, 11 m. S.W. of Whitchurch; pop. 1872. Map 46.

Ellesmere Port, urb. dist. and par., W. Cheshire, 7 m. N. of Chester; pop. 18,898. Map 38.

Ellington, par. and vil., Northumberland, 6 m. N.E. of Morpeth; pop. 786. Map 17.

Ellon, police bur. and par., in co. and 19½ m. N.E. of Aberdeen; pop. of town 1300. Map 3.

Elloughton, par. on estuary of r. Ouse, E.R. Yorkshire, 9 m. W. of Hull; pop. 1230. Map 34.

Elphin, par. and town, co. Roscommon, 9 m. S.W. of Carrick-on-Shannon; pop. of par.: 208. Map 92.

Elsham, par. and vil., N. Lincolnshire, on the Wolds, 2¾ m. N.W. of Barnetby; pop. 421. Map 35.

Elstow, par. and vil., in co. and 1¼ m. S. of Bedford; pop. 412. Map 60.

Elstree, par. and vil., S. Herefordshire, 7 m. S. of St Albans; pop. 2238. Map 71.

Elstronwick, par. and vil., E.R. Yorkshire, 3½ m. N.E. of Hedon; pop. 101. Map 35.

Eltham, par. and town in met. bor. of Woolwich, co. of London; pop. 28,308. Map 72.

Elvanfoot, ham., Lanarkshire, 5 m. S.E. of Abington. Map 14.

Ely, city, Isle of Ely, in co. and 15 m. N.E. of Cambridge; pop. 8382. Map 61.

Embleton, par. and vil., Northumberland, 6½ m. N.E. of Alnwick; pop. 639. Map 17.

Emley, urb. dist., W.R. Yorkshire, 7 m. S.E. of Huddersfield; pop. 1635. Map 32.

Empingham, par. and vil., Rutlandshire, 6 m. W.N.W. of Stamford; pop. 559. Map 50.

Emsworth, eccl. dist. and port, Hampshire, 2 m. S.S.E. of Havant; pop. 2459. Map 79.

Enfield, vil., co. Meath, 11 m. S.W. of Trim; pop. 182. Map 93.

Enfield, market town and par., Middlesex, 10¾ m. N. of London; pop. 67,869. Map 71.

Ennerdale Bridge, vil., Cumberland, 6½ m. S.E. of Whitehaven. Map 25.

Ennerdale Water, lake, Cumberland, 7½ m. S.E. of Whitehaven. Map 25.

Ennis, urb. dist., co. Clare, 24¾ m. N.W. of Limerick; pop. 5517. Map 94.

Enniscorthy, urb. dist., co. Wexford, 77½ m. S. of Dublin; pop. 5545. Map 95.

Enniskillen, co. town of co. Fermanagh, 61¾ m. N.W. of Dundalk; pop. 4847. Map 93.

Ennistimon, town, co. Clare, 15 m. N.W. of Ennis pop. 1204. Map 94.

Enterkinfoot, hamlet, Dumfries-shire, 6 m. N.W. of Thornhill. Map 14.

Epping, market town and par., W. Essex, 17 m. N.E. of London; pop. 4956. Map 72.

Epsom, urb. dist. and market town, mid Surrey, 17½ m. S.W. of London; pop. 27,089. Map 78.

Epworth, market town and par., N. Lincolnshire, in Isle of Axholme, 8½ m. N.N.W. of Gainsborough; pop. 1822. Map 42.

Erdington, eccl. par. in N.E. of Birmingham; pop. 35,380. Map 48.

Ericht, River, E. Perthshire, flows 10 m. S.E. to the Isla, 2 m. N.E. of Coupar-Angus. Map 6.
Eriswell, par. and vil., W. Suffolk, 2½ m. N.E. of Mildenhall; pop. 317. Map 62.
Erith, urb. dist., N.W. Kent, 5 m. E. of Woolwich; pop. 32,780. Map 72.
Erpingham, par. and vil., Norfolk, 3 m. N. of Aylsham; pop. 357. Map 53.
Errol, par. and vil., in co. and 10½ m. E. of Perth; pop. 738. Map 6.
Escrick, par. and vil., E.R. Yorkshire, 7 m. S. of York; pop. 597. Map 34.
Esher and the Dittons, urb. dist., N. Surrey, 14½ m. S.W. of London; pop. 17,075. Map 78.
Etal, vil., Northumberland, 8 m. N.W. of Wooler. Map 17.
Eton, urb. dist. and par., S. Buckinghamshire, 21 m. W.S.W. of London; pop. 2005. Map 78.
Ettingshall, ward in Bilston urb. dist., Staffordshire. Map 47.
Euston, par. and vil., W. Suffolk, 4 m. S.E. of Thetford; pop. 248. Map 62.
Evenjobb, par. and vil., Radnorshire, 3½ m. S.W. of Presteigne; pop. 204. Map 56.
Evenlode, par. and vil., Gloucester, 3 m. N.E. of Stow-on-the-Wold. Map 58.
Evercreech, par. and vil., E. Somersetshire, 3½ m. S.E. of Shepton Mallet; pop. 1265. Map 75.
Everdon, Great, par. and vil., Northamptonshire, 4 m. S.E. of Daventry; pop. 436. Map 59.
Evesham, mun. bor., in co. and 15 m. S.E. of Worcester; pop. 8799. Map 58.
Ewell, town and par., N. Surrey, 1½ m. N.E. of Epsom; pop. 4187. Map 80.
Exbourne, par. and vil., Devonshire, 4½ m. S.E. of Hatherleigh; pop. 311. Map 84.
Exeter, bor. and co. town of Devon, 171¾ m. S.W. of London; pop. 66,039. Map 89.
Exminster, par. and vil., Devonshire, 3½ m. S.E. of Exeter; pop. 2404. Map 89.
Exmouth, urb. dist., and seaport, Devonshire, 10½ m. S.E. of Exeter; pop. 14,584. Map 89.
Eye, mun. bor. and par., E. Suffolk, 19 m. N. of Ipswich; pop. 1733. Map 63.
Eyemouth, coast town, Berwickshire, 5½ m. N.W. of Berwick-upon-Tweed; pop. 2231. Map 11.
Eynsford, par. and vil., W. Kent, 6½ m. N. of Sevenoaks; pop. 2567. Map 82.
FAILSWORTH, urb. dist., Lancashire, 3¾ m. N.E. of Manchester; pop. 15,724. Map 39.
Fairford, par. and vil., Gloucestershire, 8 m. E. of Cirencester; pop. 1347. Map 69.
Fakenham, market town and par., Norfolk, 12 m. N.W. of E. Dereham; pop. 2966. Map 52.
Fakenham Magna, par., W. Suffolk, 5½ m. S.E. of Thetford; pop. 163. Map 62.
Falkirk, mun. bur. and par., Stirlingshire, 25½ m. W.N.W. of Edinburgh; pop. 36,565. Map 9.
Falkland, bur. and par., Fifeshire, 10 m. N. of Kirkcaldy; pop. of bur. 791. Map 6.
Fallin, mining vil., in co. and 3 m. S.E. of Stirling. Map 9.
Falmouth, mun. bor., seaport and par., Cornwall, 11¾ m. S. of Truro; pop. 13,492. Map 90.
Falstone, eccl. dist. and vil., S. Northumberland, 8 m. W.N.W. of Bellingham; pop. 834. Map 16.
Fareham, urb. dist. and par., Hampshire, 11 m. S.E. of Eastleigh; pop. 11,575. Map 77.
Faringdon, par. and vil., E. Hampshire, 3 m. S. of Alton; pop. 439. Map 79.
Faringdon, Great, par., Berkshire, 5½ m. S.E. of Lechlade; pop. 2758. Map 69.
Farnborough, urb. dist. and par., N. Hampshire, 33 m. S.W. of London; pop. 16,359. Map 78.
Farnham, market town and par., W. Surrey, 3 m. S.W. of Aldershot; pop. 18,294. Map 78.
Farningham, town and par., W. Kent, 12 m. W. of Rochester; pop. 1395. Map 80.
Farnworth, urb. dist. and par., S.E. Lancashire, 3 m. S.E. of Bolton; pop. 28,711. Map 31.
Farsley, urb. dist. and par., W.R. Yorkshire, 4 m. N.E. of Bradford; pop. 6158. Map 32.
Fauldhouse, town, West Lothian, 6½ m. S.W. of West Calder; pop. 4106. Map 9.
Faversham, mun. bor. and river port, N. Kent, 9¾ m. N.W. of Canterbury; pop. 10,091. Map 83.
Featherstone, urb. dist., W.R. Yorkshire, 2½ m. S.W. of Pontefract; pop. 14,952. Map 33.
Felindre, vil., Radnorshire, 9½ m. N.W. of Knighton. Map 56.
Felixstowe, coast par. and urb. dist., E. Suffolk, 11 m. S.E. of Ipswich; pop. 12,037. Map 63.
Felling, urb. dist., Durham, 1½ m. S.E. of Gateshead pop. 27,041. Map 23.
Felsted, par. and vil., Essex, 3½ m. S.E. of Dunmow pop. 2089. Map 72.
Feltham, urb. dist., Middlesex, 15 m. W.S.W. of London; pop. 16,316. Map 78.
Felton, par. and vil., Northumberland, 8 m. S. of Alnwick; pop. 547. Map 17.
Fen Ditton, par. and vil., in co. and 2 m. N.E. of Cambridge; pop. 781. Map 61.
Fenny Compton, par. and vil., in co. and 12 m. S.E. of Warwick; pop. 443. Map 59.
Fen Stanton, par. and vil., Huntingdonshire, 2 m. S. of St Ives; pop. 798. Map 61.
Fenton, Staffordshire, now in Stoke-on-Trent. Map 40.
Fenwick, par. and vil., Ayrshire, 3½ m. N.E. of Kilmarnock; pop. 330. Map 12.
Fermoy, urb. dist., co. Cork, 16 m. E. of Mallow; pop. 4505. Map 94.
Ferndale, vil., Glamorganshire, 6 m. N.W. of Pontypridd Junction. Map 66.
Ferns, town and par., co. Wexford, 7¾ m. N. of Enniscorthy; pop. 1576. Map 95.
Ferryside, vil., in co. and 7 m. S.S.W. of Carmarthen. Map 65.
Fethard, par. and town, co. Tipperary, 8¾ m. N. of Clonmel; pop. 1599. Map 95.
Fettercairn, par. and vil., Kincardineshire, 4½ m. N.W. of Laurencekirk; pop. 1290. Map 3.
Ffestiniog, urb. dist. and par., Merionethshire, 16 m. S.W. of Llanrwst; pop. 9072. Map 37.
Fife Ness, the Eastern extremity of Fifeshire, 2 m. N.E. of Crail. Map 7.
Filey, urb. dist. and watering place, E.R. Yorkshire, 9½ m. S.E. of Scarborough; pop. 3730. Map 29.
Fillongley, par. and vil., Warwickshire, 6 m. S.W. of Nuneaton; pop. 1408. Map 48.
Finchley, urb. dist. and par., Middlesex, 7¼ m. N. of London; pop. 58,961. Map 71.
Findern, par. and vil., in co. and 5 m. S.W. of Derby; pop. 381. Map 48.
Findochty, seaport, Banffshire, 3½ m. N.E. of Buckie; pop. 1675. Map 3.
Finedon, urb. dist., Northants, 3 m. N.E. of Wellingborough; pop. 4100. Map 60.
Fintona, town, co. Tyrone, 5¼ m. S. of Omagh; pop. 1100. Map 93.
Fishguard, urb. dist., seaport and par., Pembrokeshire, 13 m. N. of Haverfordwest; pop. 2963. Map 64.
Fittleworth, par. and vil., W. Sussex, 2¼ m. S.E. of Petworth; pop. 639. Map 79.
Flamborough, par. and vil., E.R. Yorkshire, 4 m. N.E. of Bridlington; pop. 1325. Map 29.
Fleet, urb. dist. and par., Hampshire, 3½ m. W. of Farnborough; pop. 4528. Map 78.
Fleetwood, urb. dist., seaport and par., Lancashire, 20 m. N.W. of Preston; pop. 22,983. Map 30.
Fletching, par. and vil., E. Sussex, 8 m. N. of Lewes; pop. 1151. Map 81.
Flimby, coast par. and vil., Cumberland, 1¾ m. S.E. of Maryport; pop. 2498. Map 20.
Flint, mun. bor., market town and par., Flintshire, 11½ m. N.W. of Chester; pop. 7635. Map 38.

Flockton, par. and urb. dist., W.R. Yorkshire, 7 m. S.W. of Wakefield; pop. 1471. Map 32.
Floore, par. and vil., Northamptonshire, 5½ m. S.E. of Daventry; pop. 815. Map 59.
Fobbing, par. and vil., S. Essex, 2½ m. E.N.E. of Stanford-le-Hope; pop. 607. Map 72.
Fochabers, vil., Morayshire, 6¼ m. S.E. of Elgin; pop. 867. Map 3.
Folkestone, mun. bor., seaport and par., Kent, 5 m. S.W. of Dover; pop. 35,890. Map 83.
Folkton, par. and vil., E.R. Yorkshire, 5½ m. S. of Scarborough; pop. 419. Map 29.
Fontmell Magna, par. and vil., Dorsetshire, 4 m. S. of Shaftesbury; pop. 460. Map 87.
Ford, ham., Argyllshire, at head of Loch Awe, 13 m. N. of Ardrishaig. Map 12.
Ford, par. and vil., Northumberland, 6½ m. N.W. of Wooler; pop. 950. Map 17.
Ford Bridge, ry. sta., Herefordshire, 2½ m. S.E. of Leominster. Map 56.
Fordham, par. and vil., Cambridgeshire, 5 m. N. of Newmarket; pop. 1461. Map 61.
Fordingbridge, market town and par., Hants, 14¼ m. S. of Salisbury; pop. 3394. Map 77.
Forest Row, par. and vil., E. Sussex, 3¼ m. S.E. of E. Grinstead; pop. 3303. Map 81.
Forfar, bur. and co. town of Angus, 21½ m. N.E. of Dundee; pop. 9660. Map 7.
Forgandenny, par. and vil., Perthshire, 4 m. S.W. of Perth; pop. 678. Map 6.
Forge Valley, resort and ry. stn., N.R. Yorks., 6½ m. S.W. of Scarborough. Map 29.
Formby, urb. dist. and coast par., S.W. Lancashire, 7 m. S.W. of Southport; pop. 7957. Map 30.
Fornham, vil., W. Suffolk, 2 m. N.W. of Bury St Edmunds. Map 62.
Forres, mun. bur. and par., Morayshire, 12½ m. W. of Elgin; pop. 4169. Map 3.
Fort Augustus, vil. and monastery, at head of Loch Ness, Inverness-shire. Map 2.
Fortingall, par. and vil., Perthshire, 8 m. W.S.W. of Aberfeldy; pop. 1629. Map 5.
Fortrose, mun. bur., Ross and Cromarty, 10½ m. N.E. of Inverness; pop. 875. Map 3.
Fort William, police bur., in co. and 65½ m. S.W. of Inverness; pop. 2527. Map 12.
Foston, par. and vil., Kesteven, Lincolnshire, 5½ m. N.W. of Grantham; pop. 279. Map 50.
Foston-on-the-Wolds, par. and vil., E.R. Yorkshire, 5 m. S.E. of Driffield; pop. 211. Map 35.
Foulness, insular par. and vil., Essex, 7 m. N.E. of Shoeburyness; pop. 460. Map 73.
Foulsham, par. and vil., Norfolk, 8 m. N.E of E. Dereham; pop. 869. Map 52.
Fountainhall, ham. and ry. junct., 22½ m. S.E. of Edinburgh. Map 10.
Four Crosses, ry. sta., Montgomeryshire, 7½ m. S.W. of Oswestry. Map 46.
Fovant, par. and vil., S. Wiltshire, 6 m. S.W. of Wilton; pop. 474. Map 87.
Fowey, bor., seaport and par., Cornwall, 10 m. S.S.E. of Bodmin; pop. 2382. Map 91.
Fowlis Wester, par. and vil., Perthshire, 4½ m. N.E. of Crieff; pop. 939. Map 6.
Foyle, Lough, sea inlet between cos. Donegal and Londonderry. Map 93.
Framlingham, par. and market town, E. Suffolk, 7 m. E. of Debenham; pop. 2397. Map 63.
Frampton, Cotterell, par. and vil., Gloucestershire, 3½ m. W.S.W. of Chipping Sodbury; pop. 2122. Map 68.
Frankford, town, Offaly co., 11 m. S.W. of Tullamore; pop. 518. Map 95.
Fraserburgh, police bur., seaport and par., in co. and 47½ m. N. of Aberdeen; pop. of bur. 9720. Map 3.
Freckleton, par. and vil., N. Lancashire, 7½ m. W. of Preston; pop. 1438. Map 30.
Freiston, par. and vil., Holland, Lincolnshire, 3 m. E. of Boston; pop. 984. Map 51.
Freshwater, par. and vil., Isle of Wight, 1½ m. S.W. of Yarmouth; pop. 3439. Map 77.
Fressingfield, par. and vil., E. Suffolk, 8 m. W. of Halesworth; pop. 986. Map 63.
Freuchie, *q.s.* par. and vil., Falkland par., Fifeshire; pop. 1059. Map 6.
Friarton, isle in r. Tay, in co. and 1 m. S. of Perth. Map 6.
Friern Barnet, urb. dist., Middlesex, 1½ m. N. of Finchley; pop. 23,081. Map 71.
Frimley, par. and vil., W. Surrey, 1¾ m. S. of Camberley; pop. 16,472. Map 78.
Frinton-on-Sea, urb. dist., Essex, 1½ m. S. of Walton-on-the-Naze; pop. 2196. Map 73.
Friockheim, *q.s.* par. and vil., Angus, 6½ m. N.W. of Arbroath; pop. 701. Map 7.
Friskney, par. and vil., Lindsey, Lincolnshire, 3 m. S.W. of Wainfleet; pop. 1508. Map 43.
Friston, par. and vil., E. Suffolk, 3 m. S.E. of Saxmundham; pop. 491. Map 63.
Frizington, eccl. dist. and vil., Cumberland, 4 m. E.S.E. of Whitehaven; pop. 3656. Map 24.
Frodingham, North, par. and vil., E.R. Yorkshire, 5½ m. S.E. of Gt. Driffield; pop. 543. Map 35.
Frodsham, market town and par., Cheshire, 10 m. N.E. of Chester; pop. 3025. Map 38.
Frome, market town and par., E. Somersetshire, 24¼ m. S.E. of Bristol; pop. 10,738. Map 75.
Frosterly, eccl. dist. and vil., Durham, 3 m. S.E. of Stanhope; pop. 1315. Map 22.
Froxfield, par. and vil., E. Wiltshire, 3 m. W. of Hungerford; pop. 285. Map 69.
Fulford (Gate Fulford), eastern suburb of York city. Map 33.
Fulwood, urb. dist., Lancashire, in parl. bor. of Preston; pop. 7387. Map 30.
Furnace, vil., Argyllshire, on Loch Fyne, 7 m. S.S.W. of Inverary. Map 12.
Furness Vale, vil., N.E. Cheshire, 4¼ m. N.W. of Chapel-en-le-Frith. Map 40.
Fyne, Loch, sea loch, Argyllshire, 40½ m. long, and from 1 to 5 m. broad. Map 12.
GAINSBOROUGH, urb. dist. and par., Lindsey, in co. and 17¾ m. N.W. of Lincoln; pop. 18,684. Map 42.
Gairloch, par. and vil., Ross and Cromarty, 29½ m. N.W. of Achnasheen; pop. 2781. Map 2.
Galashiels, mun. bur., town and par., Selkirkshire, 33½ m. S.E. of Edinburgh; pop. 13,102. Map 16.
Galloway, Mull of, headland, Wigtown; most southerly point of Scotland. Map 18.
Galston, police bur. and par., Ayrshire, 5½ m. E.S.E. of Kilmarnock; pop. of bur. 4601. Map 14.
Galway, seaport, urb. dist. and co. town of Galway, 20 m. S. of Tuam; pop. 14,223. Map 94.
Gamblesby, par. and vil., Cumberland, 3½ m. S.E. of Kirkoswald; pop. 189. Map 21.
Gamlingay, par. and vil., in co. and 15¾ m. S.W. of Cambridge; pop. 1645. Map 61.
Ganton, par. and vil., E.R. Yorkshire, 7½ m. S.W. of Scarborough; pop. 351. Map 29.
Gareloch, right arm of Firth of Clyde, Dumbartonshire. Map 12.
Garelochhead, par. and vil., with pier, Dumbartonshire, 7½ m. N.W. of Helensburgh; pop. 1116. Map 12.
Garforth, urb. dist. and par., W.R. Yorkshire, 7 m. E. of Leeds; pop. 3774. Map 33.
Gargrave, par. and vil., W.R. Yorkshire, 4 m. N.W. of Skipton; pop. 1166. Map 31.
Gargunnock, par. and vil., in co. and 6 m. W. of Stirling; pop. 586. Map 9.
Garstang, market town and par., N.W. Lancashire, 10½ m. S. of Lancaster; pop. 837. Map 30.
Garston, par., S.W. Lancashire, on r. Mersey, 6½ m. S.E. of Liverpool; pop. 16,645. Map 38.

Garthorpe, par. and vil., Lindsey, Lincolnshire, on r. Old Don, 6½ m. N.E. of Crowle; pop. 453. Map 34.

Gartly, par., Aberdeenshire, 5 m. S. of Huntly; pop. 684. Map 3.

Gartmore, vil., Perthshire, 2 m. S. of Aberfoyle; pop. 351. Map 8.

Garton-on-the-Wolds, par. and vil., E.R. Yorkshire, 3 m. N.W. of Great Driffield; pop. 438. Map 35.

Garvagh, town, co. Londonderry, 12½ m. S. of Coleraine; pop. 494. Map 93.

Gatehouse of Fleet, police bur. and river port, in co. and 9 m. W. of Kirkcudbright; pop. 888. Map 19.

Gateshead, co. bor. and par., Durham, on Tyne, opposite Newcastle; pop. 122,379. Map 23.

Gattonside, vil., Roxburghshire, 1 m. N.W. of Melrose; pop. 272. Map 16.

Gazeley, par. and vil., Suffolk, 4½ m. E. of Newmarket; pop. 430. Map 62.

Geddington, par. and vil., Northamptonshire, 3 m. N.E. of Kettering; pop. 958. Map 60.

Gedney, par. and vil., Holland, Lincolnshire, 3½ m. E. of Holbeach; pop. 1985. Map 51.

Gelligaer, urb. dist., Glamorganshire, 14 m. N. of Cardiff; pop. 41,042. Map 67.

Gerrard's Cross, par. and vil., Buckinghamshire, 3 m. S.E. of Beaconsfield; pop. 2208. Map 71.

Giant's Causeway, promontory of columnar basalt, on N. coast of co. Antrim. Map 93.

Gifford, vil., East Lothian, 4 m. S.S.E. of Haddington; pop. 345. Map 10.

Giggleswick, par. and vil., W.R. Yorkshire, 10 m. S.E. of Ingleton; pop. 954. Map 26.

Gilcrux, par. and vil., Cumberland, 5½ m. N.W. of Cockermouth; pop. 463. Map 20.

Gildersome, urb. dist. and par., W.R. Yorkshire, 5 m. S.W. of Leeds; pop. 3041. Map 32.

Gillingham, market town and par., N. Dorsetshire, 4 m. N.W. of Shaftesbury; pop. 3294. Map 87.

Gillingham, mun. bor., Kent, on r. Medway, 1½ m. N.E of Chatham; pop. 60,983. Map 80.

Gilmerton, vil., Perthshire, 2 m. N.E. of Crieff. Map 6.

Gilsland, eccl. dist. and vil., Northumberland, 7 m. N.E. of Brampton; pop. 781. Map 21.

Girvan, police bur., seaport and par., in co. and 21½ m. S.W. of Ayr; pop. 5292. Map 12.

Gisburn, par. and vil., W.R. Yorkshire, 7½ m. N.E. of Clitheroe; pop. 416. Map 31.

Glamis, par. and vil., Angus, 5½ m. S.W. of Forfar; pop. 1099. Map 7.

Glanton, par. and vil., Northumberland, 11½ m. W. of Alnwick; pop. 421. Map 17.

Glasbury, par. and vil., Radnorshire, 4 m. S.W. of Hay; pop. 468. Map 56.

Glasgow, co. of a city and mun. bur., on r. Clyde, Lanarkshire, 47¼ m. W. of Edinburgh; pop. 1,088,417. Map 8.

Glassonby, par. and vil., E. Cumberland, 7 m. N.E. of Penrith; pop. 147. Map 21.

Glastonbury, mun. bor. and market town, mid Somersetshire, 5 m. S.W. of Wells; pop. 4515. Map 74.

Glemsford, urb. dist., Suffolk, 2½ m. N.W. of Long Melford; pop. 1262. Map 62.

Glenarm, seaport town, co. Antrim, 11 m. N.W. of Larne; pop. 951. Map 93.

Glenboig, vil., Lanarkshire, 2½ m. N. of Coatbridge. Map 9.

Glencaple, vil., in co. and 5 m. S. of Dumfries; pop. 225. Map 20.

Glencoe, vil. and glen, Argyllshire, 2 m. E. of Ballachulish. Map 12.

Glendalough, mtn. vale, co. Wicklow, 8 m. N.W. of Rathdrum. Map 95.

Glen Devon, valley of r. Devon and par., S. Perthshire; pop 134. Map 6.

Gleneagles, Perthshire, 2 m. S.W. of Auchterarder; palatial hotel with golf courses, etc. Map 6.

Glenelg, par. and vil., Inverness-shire, 7 m. S.W. of Lochalsh; pop. 1643. Map 2.

Glenfarg, vil., in co. and 10½ m. S. of Perth; pop. 409. Map 6.

Glenfinnan, ham., Inverness-shire, at head of Loch Shiel, 17 m. W. of Fort William. Map 2.

Glengariff, vil., co. Cork, 8 m. N.W. of Bantry. Map 94.

Glenluce, vil., Wigtownshire, 8¾ m. S.E. of Stranraer; pop. 806. Map 18.

Glenridding, ham. and mt. vale, N.W. border of Westmorland. Map 25.

Glentham, par. and vil., Lindsey, Lincolnshire, 7 m. W.N.W. of Market Rasen; pop. 340. Map 42.

Glenties, vil., co. Donegal, 24½ m. W. of Stranorlar; pop. 425. Map 92.

Glossop, mun. bor., mkt. tn. and par., N. Derbyshire, 13 m. S.E. of Manchester; pop. 19,510. Map 40.

Gloucester, city, co. bor., par. and co. tn. of Gloucestershire, 37 m. N.N.E. of Bristol; pop. 52,937. Map 68.

Glusburn, par. and vil., W.R. Yorkshire, 4 m. S. of Skipton; pop. 2587. Map 31.

Glyncorwg, urb. dist., Glamorganshire, 2 m. N.E. of Cymmer; pop. 10,208. Map 66.

Glynde, par. and vil., E. Sussex, 3 m. S.E. of Lewes; pop. 274. Map 81.

Glyn Neath, vil. and ry. sta., Glamorganshire, 12 m. N.E. of Neath. Map 66.

Goathland, par. and vil., N.R. Yorkshire, 7½ m. S.W. of Whitby; pop. 712. Map 29.

Godalming, mun. bor. and market town, W. Surrey, 34½ m. S.W. of London; pop. 10,400. Map 78.

Godmanchester, mun. bor. and par., in co. and adjoining Huntingdon; pop. 1991. Map 61.

Godshill, par. and vil., Isle of Wight, 5½ m. N.W. of Ventnor; pop. 972. Map 77.

Godstone, par. and vil., E. Surrey, 4½ m. N.E. of Redhill; pop. 2943. Map 80.

Goginan, vil., Cardiganshire, 7 m. E. of Aberystwyth. Map 55.

Gogmagog Hills, in co. and 4 m. S.E. of Cambridge. Map 61.

Goil, sea loch, Argyllshire, west arm of Loch Long. Map 12.

Golborne, urb. dist., Lancashire, 5½ m. S.E. of Wigan; pop. 7322. Map 39.

Golcar, urb. dist., par. and vil., W.R. Yorkshire, 3 m. S.W. of Huddersfield; pop. 9812. Map 32.

Golspie, coast par. and vil., Sutherlandshire, 84 m. N.E. of Inverness; pop. 890. Map 3.

Gomersal, Yorkshire, in Spenborough urb. dist. Map 32.

Goodwick, urb. dist., Pembrokeshire, 1½ m. N.W. of Fishguard; pop. 2279. Map 64.

Goodwood, seat and racecourse, W. Sussex, 3 m. N.E. of Chichester. Map 79.

Goole, urb. dist., par., mkt. tn. and r. port, W.R. Yorks, 23¾ m. S.W. of Hull; pop. 20,238. Map 34.

Gorey, market town, co. Wexford, 10½ m. S.W. of Arklow; pop. 2291. Map 95.

Goring, par. and vil., Oxon, on r. Thames, 8¾ m. N.W. of Reading; pop. 1989. Map 70.

Gorleston, par., in S. of Great Yarmouth bor., Norfolk; pop. 20,391. Map 53.

Gornal, Lower and **Upper,** 2 eccl. dists., Staffs, 4½ m. S. of Wolverhampton; pop. 7399 and 5122. Map 47.

Gornalwood, vil., Staffordshire, 1 m. N.W. of Dudley. Map 47.

Gorseinon, vil. and ry. sta., Glamorganshire, 5 m. N. of Swansea. Map 65.

Gosforth, par. and vil., Cumberland, 6½ m. S.E. of Egremont; pop. 922. Map 25.

Gosforth, urb. dist. and par., Northumberland, 2¼ m. N. of Newcastle; pop. 18,042. Map 23.

Gosport, mun. bor., seaport and par., Hants, on W. side of Portsmouth Harbour; pop. 37,928. Map 77.

Goudhurst, par. and town, Kent, 3½ m. N.W. of Cranbrook; pop. 2967. Map 82.

Gourock, police bur., Renfrewshire, 2 m. below Greenock; pop. 8844. Map 12.

Govan, par. in S.W. of Glasgow. Map 8.

Grafton Underwood, par. and vil., Northamptonshire, 4 m. N.E. of Kettering; pop. 212. Map 60.

Graiguenamanagh, town and par., co. Kilkenny, 5 m. S. of Borris ry. sta.; pop. of town 844. Map 95.

Grainthorpe, par. and vil., Lindsey, Lincolnshire, 7 m. N.E. of Louth; pop. 659. Map 43.

Grampound, par. and vil., Cornwall, 6 m. S.W. of St Austell; pop. 419. Map 91.

Grange-over-Sands, urb. dist. and par., Lancashire, 8 m. E. of Ulverston; pop. 2648. Map 25.

Grangemouth, seaport town, pol. bur. and par., E. Stirlingshire, 3 m. N.E. of Falkirk; pop. 11,798. Map 9.

Grangetown, eccl. dist., N.R. Yorkshire, 3½ m. E. of Middlesbrough; pop. 7021. Map 28.

Grantchester, par. and vil., in co. and 2½ m. S.W. of Cambridge; pop. 489. Map 61.

Grantham, mun. bor., Kesteven, in co. and 25 m. S.S.W. of Lincoln; pop. 19,709. Map 50.

Grantown-on-Spey, police bur., Morayshire, 23½ m. S. of Forres; pop. 1577. Map 3.

Grantshouse, ham., Berwickshire, 16½ m. N.W. of Berwick-on-Tweed. Map 11.

Grappenhall, par. and vil., Cheshire, 2½ m. S.E. of Warrington; pop. 1945. Map 39.

Grasmere, urb. dist., par. and lake, Westmorland, 3½ m. N.W. of Ambleside; pop. 988. Map 25.

Gravesend, mun. bor. on S. bank of r. Thames, 24 m. E. of London; pop. 35,490. Map 72.

Grayrigg, par., Westmorland, 5 m. N.E. of Kendal; pop. 202. Map 26.

Grays Thurrock, urb. dist. and market town, S. Essex, 19½ m. S.E. of London; pop. 18,172. Map 80.

Greasbrough, urb. dist., W.R. Yorkshire, 2 m. N.W. of Rotherham; pop. 3599. Map 41.

Great Coates, par. and vil., N.E. Lincs, on r. Humber, 2½ m. W. of Gt. Grimsby; pop. 493. Map 35.

Great Crosby, coast town, S.W. Lancashire, 6½ m. N.W. of Liverpool; pop. 18,283. Map 38.

Great Dalby, par. and vil., Leicestershire, 3½ m. S.W. of Melton Mowbray; pop. 317. Map 49.

Great Driffield, urb. dist. and par., E.R. Yorkshire, 36 m. E. of York; pop. 5916. Map 35.

Great Gidding, par. and vil., in co. and 10 m. N.W. of Huntingdon; pop. 271. Map 60.

Great Grimsby, parl. and co. bor. and par., Lincolnshire, 15 m. S.E. of Hull; pop. 92,463. Map 35.

Greatham, par. and vil., Durham, 3½ m. S.W. of W. Hartlepool; pop. 1128. Map 23.

Great Haywood, eccl. dist. and vil., in co. and 5 m. E. of Stafford; pop. 618. Map 48.

Great Torrington, mun. bor., Devonshire, 6 m. E. of Bideford; pop. 2913. Map 84.

Greenford, dist., Middlesex, 7½ m. W.N.W. of Paddington; pop. 1461. Map 71.

Greenhead, eccl. dist. and vil., S. Northumberland, 3 m. N.W. of Haltwhistle; pop. 1349. Map 21.

Greenhithe, eccl. par. and vil., W. Kent, 2½ m. E.N.E. of Dartford; pop. 3361. Map 80.

Greenhow, vil., W.R. Yorks, 3½ m. S.W. of Pateley Bridge. Map 27.

Greenlcaning, vil., Perthshire, 5½ m. N.E. of Dunblane. Map 6.

Greenock, mun. bur., par. and seaport, Renfrewshire, 22½ m. N. W. of Glasgow; pop. 78,948. Map 12.

Greenore, coast town, co. Louth, on S. side of Carlingford Lough; pop. 289. Map 93.

Greenwich, met. bor., co. London, 3½ m. S.E. of London Bridge; pop. 100,879. Map 80.

Greetland, urb. dist., par. and town, W.R. Yorks, 2 m. S.W. of Halifax; pop. 4298. Map 31.

Gretna, par. and town, Dumfriesshire, 9½ m. N.W. of Carlisle; pop. 2969. Map 21.

Greystoke, par. and vil., E. Cumberland, 5 m. W. of Penrith; pop. 495. Map 21.

Greystones, coast town, co. Wicklow, 4½ m. S.E. of Bray; pop. 1592. Map 95.

Griffithstown, par. and vil., Monmouthshire, 1½ m. S. of Pontypool; pop. 4151. Map 67.

Grimsthorpe, ham. and seat, Kesteven, Lincolnshire, 3½ m. N.W. of Bourne. Map 50.

Grimston, par. and vil., Norfolk, 6½ m. N.E. of King's Lynn; pop. 1058. Map 52.

Grindon, par. and vil., N. Staffordshire, 13¾ m. E.S.E. of Leek; pop. 325. Map 40.

Grinton, par., vil. and seat, N.R. Yorkshire, 1 m. S.E. of Reeth; pop. 262. Map 27.

Grosmont, eccl. dist. and vil., N.R. Yorkshire, 5½ m. S.W. of Whitby; pop. 879. Map 29.

Grosmont, par. and vil., in co. and 10 m. N.W. of Monmouth; pop. 521. Map 67.

Grundisburgh, par. and vil., E. Suffolk, 3 m. W.N.W. of Woodbridge; pop. 762. Map 63.

Guildford, mun. bor. and co. town of Surrey, 30¼ m. S.W. of London; pop. 30,753. Map 78.

Guisborough, urb. dist. and par., N.R. Yorkshire, 8 m. S. of Middlesbrough; pop. 6306. Map 28.

Guiseley, urb. dist., par. and vil., W.R. Yorkshire, 2 m. S. of Otley; pop. 5607. Map 32.

Gullane, vil., East Lothian, 4 m. S.W. of North Berwick; pop. 1354. Map 12.

Gunnislake, market vil., Cornwall, 3 m. S.W. of Tavistock. Map 88.

Gunthwaite and Ingbirchworth, urb. dist., W.R. Yorkshire, 2½ m. N. of Penistone; pop. 338. Map 40.

Guyhirn, vil. and ry. sta., Cambridgeshire, 3½ m. N.W. of March. Map 51.

Gwaun-cae-Gurwen, ham., Glamorganshire, 1½ m. S.E. of Garnant. Map 66.

Gwbert-on-the-Sea, vil., in co. and 2¾ m. N.W. of Cardigan. Map 54.

Gweedore, vil., co. Donegal, 38 m. N.W. of Letterkenny. Map 92.

Gwytherin, par. and vil., Denbigshire, 5½ m. E. of Llanrwst. Map 37.

HABROUGH, par. and vil., Lindsey, Lincolnshire, 8 m. N.W. of Grimsby; pop. 411. Map 35.

Hacheston, par. and vil., E. Suffolk, 2 m. N. of Wickham Market; pop. 390. Map 63.

Hackington, par., Kent, adjoining Canterbury; pop. 632. Map 83.

Hackthorp, vil., Westmorland, 5 m. S.E. of Penrith. Map 21.

Haddenham, par. and vil., Isle of Ely, Cambridgeshire, 5¾ m. S.W. of Ely; pop. 1655. Map 61.

Haddenham, par. and vil., Buckinghamshire, 3 m. N.E. of Thame; pop. 1403. Map 70.

Haddington, mun. bur., par. and co. town of East Lothian, 18 m. E. of Edinburgh; pop. 4405. Map 10.

Haddon, West, par. and vil., Northamptonshire, 8 m. N.E. of Daventry; pop. 706. Map 59.

Hadleigh, urb. dist. and par., W. Suffolk, 9½ m. W.S.W. of Ipswich; pop. 2952. Map 62.

Hadleigh, par. and vil., S. Essex, 2 m. N.E. of Benfleet sta.; pop. 2246. Map 72.

Hadlow, par. and vil., Kent, 4 m. N.E. of Tonbridge; pop. 2264. Map 82.

Hailsham, par. and town, Sussex, 7 m. N. of Eastbourne; pop. 4907. Map 81.

Hale, par. and vil., Cumberland, 2½ m. S.E. of Egremont; pop. 291. Map 24.

Hale, urb. dist. and par., Cheshire, 1 m. S.E. of Altrincham; pop. 10,669. Map 39.

Halesowen, urb. dist. and par., Worcestershire, 7 m. S.W. of Birmingham; pop. 31,058. Map 58.

Halesworth, urb. dist. and par., E. Suffolk, 9 m. S.W. of Beccles; pop. 2024. Map 63.
Halifax, parl. and co. bor. and par., W.R. Yorks, 7 m. W. of Bradford; pop. 98,122. Map 31.
Halkyn, par. and vil., in co. and 2½ m. S.W. of Flint; pop. 1297. **H. Castle,** seat. Map 38.
Halkirk, par. and vil., Caithness-shire, 8½ m. S.W. of Thurso; pop. 1969. Map 3.
Halstead, urb. dist. and par., Essex, 16 m. N.W. of Colchester; pop. 5878. Map 62.
Halstead, par. and vil., W. Kent, 4½ m. N.N.W. of Sevenoaks; pop. 565. Map 80.
Halton, par. and vil., N. Lancashire, 2½ m. N.E. of Lancaster; pop. 825. Map 26.
Haltwhistle, par. and market town, Northumberland, 16½ m. W. of Hexham; pop. 4500. Map 22.
Ham, urb. dist., Surrey, 1½ m. N.N.W. of Kingston; pop. 2206. Map 71.
Hambledon, par. and vil., Hants, 6½ m. N.E. of Fareham; pop. 2185. Map 79.
Hambledon, par. and vil., S.W. Surrey, 3 m. S. of Godalming; pop. 838. Map 79.
Hambleton, par. and vil., W.R. Yorkshire, 4¼ m. W. of Selby; pop. 526. Map 33.
Hamilton, mun. bur. and par., Lanarkshire, 11½ m. S.E. of Glasgow; bur. pop. 37,863. Map 9.
Hampstead, met. bor., co. of London; pop. 86,153. **Hampstead Heath** is here. Map 71.
Hampstead Norris, par. and vil., Berkshire, 7½ m. N.E. of Newbury; pop. 1321. Map 70.
Hampsthwaite, par. and vil., W.R. Yorkshire, 2 m. S.W. of Ripley; pop. 425. Map 32.
Hampton, urb. dist. and vil., Middlesex, 3½ m. W. of Kingston; pop. 13,053. Map 71.
Hampton, par., Cheshire, 2 m. N.E. of Malpas; pop. 384. Map 38.
Hampton in Arden, par. and vil., Warwickshire, 9 m. N.W. of Coventry; pop. 1157. Map 58.
Hampton Lucy, par. and vil., Warwickshire, 4 m. N.E. of Stratford-on-Avon; pop. 367. Map 58.
Hampton Wick, urb. dist., Middlesex, suburb of Kingston; pop. 2957. Map 71.
Hamstall Ridware, par. and vil., Staffordshire, 4 m. E.N.E. of Rugeley; pop. 312. Map 48.
Handforth, urb. dist., Cheshire, 5 m. S.W. of Stockport; pop. 1031. Map 39.
Handley, par. and vil., Dorsetshire, 5 m. N.W. of Cranborne; pop. 724. Map 87.
Handsworth, par. in N.W. of Birmingham. Map 48.
Hanley, par. and parl. div. of Stoke-on-Trent, in co. and 18½ m. N. of Stafford; par. pop. 67,891. Map 39.
Hanningfield, East, par. and vil., W. Essex, 5 m. S.E. of Chelmsford; pop. 474. Map 72.
Happisburgh, coast par. and vil., Norfolk, 6 m. E. of N. Walsham; pop. 574. Map 53.
Hapton, par. and vil., N.E. Lancashire, 3 m. N.E. of Accrington; pop. 1950. Map 31.
Harborne, a S.W. ward of Birmingham. Map 58.
Harbury, par. and vil., Warwickshire, 5 m. S.E. of Leamington; pop. 1192. Map 58.
Harlech, ancient coast town, Merionethshire, 11¼ m. N. of Barmouth. Map 44.
Harleston, market town, Norfolk, 6½ m. S.W. of Bungay; pop. of par. 1789. Map 63.
Harling, East, par. and town, Norfolk, 7½ m. N.E. of Thetford; pop. 880. Map 62.
Harlow, market town and par., Essex, 24½ m. N.E. of London by rail; pop. 2962. Map 72.
Harpenden, urb. dist. and par., Hertfordshire, 5 m. S.E. of Luton by rail; pop. 8349. Map 71.
Harrietfield, vil., S.E. Perthshire, 3½ m. N.W. of Methven. Map 6.
Harrietsham, par. and vil., Kent, 7 m. S.E. of Maidstone; pop. 722. Map 82.
Harrington, urb. dist. and par., Cumberland, 4½ m. N. of Whitehaven; pop. 4125. Map 20.
Harris, par. and lower part of Lewis Isl., Outer Hebrides, Inverness-shire; pop. 5276. Map 2.
Harrogate, mun. bor., par. and market town, W.R. Yorks, 18 m. N. of Leeds; pop. 39,785. Map 32.
Harrow-on-the-Hill, urb. dist., Middlesex, 10 m. N.W. of London; pop. 26,378. Map 71.
Hartfield, par. and vil., E. Sussex, 6¾ m. S. of East Grinstead; pop. 1861. Map 81.
Hartington, town, N. Derbyshire, 8 m. S.W. of Bakewell; pop. 405. Map 40.
Hartland, par. and vil., N. Devonshire, 13½ m. W. of Bideford; pop. 1483. Map 84.
Hartlepool, mun. bor., par. and seaport, Durham, 11 m. N.E. of Stockton; pop. 20,545. Map 23.
Hartlepool, West, co. bor. and par. within the parl. limits of Hartlepool; pop. 68,134. Map 23.
Hartley, ward of Seaton Delaval, Northumberland, 4 m. S.E. of Blyth. Map 23.
Hartshill, par. and vil., Warwickshire, 3 m. S.S.E. of Atherstone; pop. 2560. Map 48.
Harwich, mun. bor., seaport and par., Essex, 10 m. S.E. of Ipswich; pop. 12,700. Map 73.
Harwood, Great, urb. dist., town and par., N.E. Lancs, 4½ m. N.E. of Blackburn; pop. 12,787. Map 31.
Haselbury Bryan, par., Dorsetshire, 4 m. S.W. of Sturminster Newton; pop. 484. Map 87.
Haslemere, urb. dist. and par., S.W. Surrey, 12¾ m. S.W. of Guildford; pop. 4340. Map 79.
Haslingdon, mun. bor., mkt. tn. and par., N.E. Lancs, 3½ m. S. of Accrington; pop. 16,637. Map 31.
Hastings, co. bor., par. and Cinque port, E. Sussex, 34 m. E. of Brighton; pop. 65,199. Map 82.
Haswell, par. and vil., Durham, 9¼ m. S.S.W. of Sunderland; pop. 6199. Map 23.
Hatfield, market town and par., in co. and 6 m. S.W. of Hertford; pop. 5965. Map 71.
Hatfield, par., W.R. Yorkshire, 7 m. N.E. of Doncaster; pop. 1820. Map 33.
Hatherleigh, par. and vil., Devonshire, 10¾ m. S.S.E. of Torrington; pop. 1206. Map 84.
Hathern, par. and ry. sta., Leicestershire, 3 m. N.W. of Loughborough; pop. 1124. Map 49.
Hathersage, par., N. Derbyshire, on r. Derwent, 10 m. N. of Bakewell; pop. 1694. Map 40.
Hatherton, par. and vil., Staffordshire, 3 m. S.E. of Penkridge; pop. 532. Map 47.
Haughton, par. and vil., in co. and 4 m. S.W. of Stafford; pop. 567. Map 47.
Havant, urb. dist. and par., Hants, 7½ m. N.E. of Portsmouth; pop. 4264. Map 79.
Haverfordwest, mun. bor. and cap. of Pembrokeshire, 9 m. N.N.W. of Pembroke; pop. 6113. Map 64.
Haverhill, urb. dist, and par., W. Suffolk, 12 m. S.S.E. of Newmarket; pop. 3827. Map 61.
Haveringland, par. and vil., Norfolk, 8 m. N.W. of Norwich; pop. 126. Map 53.
Haverrigg, vil., Cumberland, 1¼ m. S.W. of Millom. Map 25.
Hawarden, market town and par., Flintshire, 6 m. N.W. of Chester; pop. 8016. **H. Castle** is a seat. Map 38.
Hawes, par. and market town, N.R. Yorkshire, 16 m. W. of Leyburn; pop. 1437. Map 26.
Hawes Water, lake, Westmorland, 2½ m. long, 694 ft. above sea level. Map 26.
Hawick, mun. bur., town and par., Roxburghshire, 53¾ m. S.E. of Edinburgh; pop. 17,059. Map 16.
Haworth, urb. dist., par. and town, W.R. Yorkshire, 3½ m. S.W. of Keighley; pop. 5912. Map 32.
Hawstead, par. and vil., W. Suffolk, 3 m. S. of Bury St Edmunds; pop. 266. Map 62.
Haxey, par. and vil., Lindsey, Lincolnshire, 7½ m. N.W. of Gainsborough; pop. 1944. Map 42.
Hay, urb. dist. and par., Breconshire, 7 m. N.E. of Brecon; pop. 1509. Map 56.
Haydock, urb. dist. and par., S.W. Lancashire, 3 m. N.E. of St Helens; pop. 10,352. Map 39.

Haydon Bridge, town and ry. sta., Northumberland, 6 m. W. of Hexham; pop. of eccl. dist. 2464. Map 22.

Hayes, par. and vil., Kent, 2 m. S. of Bromley; pop. 1010. Map 80.

Hayes and Harlington, urb. dist. and par., Middlesex, 3 m. S.E. of Uxbridge; pop. 23,646. Map 71.

Hayesend, ham., Middlesex, 2 m. S.E. of Uxbridge. Map 71.

Hayfield, par. and vil., N. Derbyshire, 9 m. S.E. of Stockport; pop. 2644. Map 40.

Hayle, urb. dist. and seaport, Cornwall, 7 m. N.E. of Penzance; pop. 915. Map 90.

Hayling Island, Hants, comprising the pars. of N. and S. Hayling, 4 m. S. of Havant; pop. 3288. Map 79.

Hayton, par. and vil., Cumberland, 3 m. S.W. of Brampton; pop. 1210. Map 21.

Hayton, vil., Cumberland, 5 m. N.E. of Maryport. Map 20.

Haywards Heath, urb. dist. and par., E. Sussex, 13 m. N. of Brighton; pop. 5382. Map 81.

Hazel Grove and Bramhall, urb. dist., Cheshire, 2½ m. S.E. of Stockport; pop. 13,300. Map 39.

Headcorn, par. and vil., Kent, 9 m. S.E. of Maidstone; pop. 1492. Map 82.

Headford, vil., co. Galway, 12 m. W. of Tuam ry. sta. Map 94.

Headley, par. and vil., E. Hants, 3 m. E. of Bordon sta.; pop. 4888. Map 79.

Heage, urb. dist. and par., Derbyshire, 2½ m. N.E. of Belper; pop. 4054. Map 41.

Heasor, urb. dist. and par., Derbyshire, 3½ m. N.W. of Ilkeston; pop. 22,386. Map 41.

Hebburn, urb. dist. and par., Durham, 4 m. W.S.W. of South Shields; pop. 24,125. Map 23.

Hebden Bridge, urb. dist. and par., W.R. Yorkshire, 4 m. N.E. of Todmorden; pop. 6312. Map 32.

Heckington, par. and vil., Kesteven, Lincolnshire, 5 m. E.S.E. of Sleaford; pop. 1551. Map 50.

Heckmondwike, urb. dist. and par., W.R. Yorkshire, 2 m. N.W. of Dewsbury; pop. 8991. Map 32.

Heddon-on-the-Wall, par. and vil., Northumberland, 7 m. W.N.W. of Newcastle; pop. 676. Map 22.

Hednesford, eccl. dist. and ward in Cannock urb. dist., Staffordshire; pop. 11,868. Map 48.

Hedon, mun. bor. and par., E.R. Yorkshire, 5½ m. E. of Hull; pop. 1509. Map 35.

Hele Bridge, place, Devonshire, on r. Torridge, 1½ m. N. of Hatherleigh. Map 84.

Helensburgh, police bur., Dumbartonshire, on Firth of Clyde, opposite Greenock; pop. 8893. Map 8.

Helmdon, par. and vil., Northamptonshire, 7¾ m. S.W. of Towcester; pop. 409. Map 59.

Helmsdale, seaport, Sutherlandshire, 17¼ m. N.E. of Golspie; pop. 691. Map 3.

Helmsley, town and par., N.R. Yorkshire, 20 m. N. of York; pop. 1303. Map 28.

Helperthorpe, par., E.R. Yorkshire, 9 m. N.W. of Great Driffield; pop. 124. Map 29.

Helpringham, par. and vil., Kesteven, Lincolnshire, 5 m. S.E. of Sleaford; pop. 733. Map 50.

Helston, mun. bor. and par., Cornwall, 10 m. S.W. of Falmouth; pop. 2544. Map 90.

Hemel Hempstead, mun. bor. and par., Hertfordshire, 12 m. S.W. of Luton; pop. 15,122. Map 71.

Hempstead with Eccles, coast par., Norfolk, 8 m. S.E. of N. Walsham; pop. 125. Map 53.

Hemsworth, urb. dist. and par., W.R. Yorkshire, 8¼ m. S.E. of Wakefield; pop. 13,001. Map 33.

Hemyock, par. and vil., Devonshire, 7½ m. E. of Tiverton Junction; pop. 882. Map 85.

Henbury, par. and vil., S. Gloucestershire, 7¾ m. N.W. of Bristol; pop. 2260. Map 74.

Hendon, urb. dist., Middlesex, 8 m. N.W. of St Paul's, London; pop. 115,682. Map 71.

Hendy, vil., Carmarthenshire, 5¾ m. N.E. of Llanelly. Map 65.

Henfield, par. and vil., W. Sussex, 4 m. N.E. of Steyning; pop. 1948. Map 79.

Hengrave, par. and vil., W. Suffolk, 3 m. N.W. of Bury St Edmunds; pop. 186. Map 62.

Henham, par. and vil., Essex, 6 m. N.E. of Bishop's Stortford; pop. 726. Map 72.

Henley-in-Arden, eccl. par. and town, in co. and 8½ m. W. of Warwick; pop. 1192. Map 58.

Henley-on-Thames, mun. bor., S.E. Oxon, 35½ m. W. of London; pop. 6618. Map 78.

Herbrandston, par. and vil., Pembrokeshire, 2½ m. W.N.W. of Milford; pop. 267. Map 64.

Hereford, city, mun. bor. and co. town of Herefordshire, 144 m. N.W. of London; pop. 24,159. Map 57.

Herne, par. and vil., Kent, 5½ m. N.N.E. of Canterbury; pop. 1964. Map 83.

Herne Bay, urb. dist. and par., Kent, 11 m. S.W. of Margate; pop. 11,244. Map 83.

Hersham, eccl. par. and vil., N. Surrey, 2½ m. E. of Weybridge; pop. 6110. Map 78.

Hertford, mun. bor. and capital of Hertfordshire, 24½ m. N. of London; pop. 11,376. Map 71.

Hesketh Bank, ham., on coast of W. Lancashire, 9 m. N.E. of Southport. Map 30.

Hessle, urb. dist., E.R. Yorkshire, 4½ m. S.W. of Hull; pop. 6430. Map 35.

Heston and Isleworth, urb. dist., Middlesex, 1½ m. N.N.W. of Hounslow; pop. 75,446. Map 71.

Hethersett, par. and vil., Norfolk, 6¼ m. S.W. of Norwich; pop. 1119. Map 53.

Hetton-le-Hole, urb. dist. and par., Durham, 7 m. S. of Sunderland; pop. 17,672. Map 23.

Hevingham, par. and vil., Norfolk, 8½ m. N.N.W. of Norwich; pop. 698. Map 53.

Hexham, urb. dist. and par., Northumberland, 20 m. W. of Newcastle-on-Tyne; pop. 8888. Map 22.

Heybridge, par. and vil., Essex, 9 m. E. of Chelmsford; pop. 1934. Map 73.

Heysham, dist. in bor. of Morecambe, Lancaster; pop. 5027. Map 30.

Heytesbury, par. and vil., S. Wiltshire, 4 m. S.E. of Warminster; pop. 496. Map 75.

Heywood, mun. bor. and par., S.E. Lancashire, 3 m. E. of Bury; pop. 25,967. Map 31.

Higham Ferrers, mun. bor. and par., Northamptonshire, 4½ m. E. of Wellingborough; pop. 2928. Map 60.

High Bentham, par. and market town, W.R. Yorkshire, 14¾ m. N.W. of Hellifield; pop. 2463. Map 31.

High Bickington, par. and vil., Devonshire, 7½ m. E. of Torrington; pop. 56. Map 84.

Highbridge, urb. dist., N.W. Somersetshire, 6¼ m. N. of Bridgwater; pop. 2584. Map 74.

Highclere, par. and vil., N. Hants, 4 m. S.W. of Newbury sta.; pop. 529. Map 76.

High Crompton, eccl. dist. and vil., S.E. Lancashire, 3 m. N. of Oldham; pop. 1873. Map 31.

Higher Newton, ham., N. Lancashire, 3 m. N.E. of Cartmel. Map 25.

Highgate, N. suburb of London, in Hornsey mun. bor., E. Middlesex. Map 71.

High Halden, par. and vil., Kent, 2½ m. N.N.E. of Tenterden; pop. 632. Map 82.

High Ongar, par. and vil., Essex, 6 m. E. of Epping; pop. 1209. Map 72.

High Roding, par., Essex, on r. Roding, 4 m. S.W. of Dunmow; pop. 351. Map 72.

Highworth, town and par., Wiltshire, 6 m. N.E. of Swindon; pop. 2072. Map 69.

Hildenborough, par. and vil., W. Kent, 2 m. N.W. of Tonbridge; pop. 1727. Map 82.

Hilderstone, par. and vil., Staffordshire, 3 m. E. of Stone; pop. 377. Map 47.

Hilgay, par. and vil., Norfolk, 3 m. S. of Downham; pop. 1491. Map 51.

Hillsborough, market town and par., co. Down, 12 m. S.S.W. of Belfast; pop. (town) 544. Map 93.

Hilmarton, par. and vil., N. Wiltshire, 3½ m. N.E. of Calne; pop. 718. Map 75.

Hinckley, urb. dist. and par., in co. and 14½ m. S.W. of Leicester; pop. 16,030. Map 49.

Hinderwell, urb. dist. and par., N.R. Yorkshire, 7½ m. N.W. of Whitby; pop. 2147. Map 29.

Hindhead, eccl. dist., Surrey, 2 m. N.W. of Haslemere; pop. 1536. Map 79.

Hindley, urb. dist. and par., Lancashire, 2½ m. S.E. of Wigan; pop. 21,629. Map 39.

Hindlow, ry. sta., N.W. Derbyshire, 3½ m. S. of Buxton. Map 40.

Hindolveston, par. and vil., Norfolk, 8 m. E. of Fakenham; pop. 571. Map 52.

Hindon, par. and vil., S. Wiltshire, 9 m. S.E. of Warminster; pop. 415. Map 75.

Hingham, par. and vil., Norfolk, 6 m. W. of Wymondham; pop. 1413. Map 52.

Hinton-on-the-Green, par., vil. and ry. stn., Worcestershire, 2½ m. S.S.W. of Evesham. Map 58.

Hinton St George, par. and vil., Somersetshire, 2 m. N.W. of Crewkerne; pop. 433. Map 86.

Hipperholme, urb. dist. and par., W.R. Yorkshire, 2 m. N.E. of Halifax; pop. 5383. Map 31.

Hirnant, par. and vil., Montgomeryshire, 6½ m. N.W. of Llanfyllin; pop. 208. Map 46.

Hirwain, vil. and ry. sta., Glamorganshire, 3½ m. N.W. of Aberdare. Map 66.

Hitchin, urb. dist. and par., in co. and 13½ m. N.W. of Hertford; pop. 14,382. Map 71.

Hoath, par. and vil., Kent, 5 m. N.E. of Canterbury; pop. 317. Map 83.

Hobkirk, par., Roxburghshire, 6 m. S.E. of Hawick; pop. 555. Map 16.

Hoddesdon, urb. dist. and par., in co. and 4 m. S.E. of Hertford; pop. 6811. Map 71.

Holbeach, urb. dist., Holland, Lincolnshire, 7½ m. E.N.E. of Spalding; pop. 6111. Map 51.

Holcombe, vil., S. Devonshire, 1½ m. S.W. of Dawlish. Map 89.

Holkham, par. and vil., Norfolk, 2¼ m. W. of Wells; pop. 426. Map 52.

Holland Arms, ry. sta., 2½ m. S.E. of Llangefni, Anglesey. Map 36.

Hollington Rural, par. and vil., E. Sussex, 2½ m. N.W. of Hastings; pop. 451. Map 82.

Hollingworth, urb. dist., Cheshire, 3½ m. S.E. of Stalybridge; pop. 2299. Map 40.

Holme, par. and vil., Westmorland, 1½ m. N. of Burton in Kendal; pop. 626. Map 26.

Holme, urb. dist., W.R. Yorkshire, 9 m. S.W. of Huddersfield; pop. 368. Map 32.

Holme Cultram, urb. dist., Cumberland pop. 4735. Map 20.

Holme Hale, par. and vil., Norfolk, 5 m. E.S.E. of Swaffham; pop. 343. Map 52.

Holme-on-the-Wolds, par. and vil., E.R. Yorkshire, 6½ m. N.W. of Beverley; pop. 136. Map 35.

Holmes Chapel, vil., mid Cheshire, 4 m. N.E. of Sandbach. Map 39.

Holme upon Spalding Moor, par. and vil., E.R. Yorks, 5½ m. S.W. of Market Weighton; pop. 1596. Map 34.

Holmfirth, urb. dist. and par., W.R. Yorkshire, 6 m. S. of Huddersfield; pop. 10,407. Map 31.

Holsworthy, urb. dist. and par., Devonshire, 15 m. W. of Hatherleigh; pop. 1403. Map 84.

Holt, market town and par., Norfolk, 10 m. W.S.W. of Cromer; pop. 2249. Map 53.

Holt, par. and vil., N. Wiltshire, 3 m. N.E. of Bradford-on-Avon; pop. 991. Map 75.

Holt, par., Denbighshire, on r. Dee, 5½ m. N.E. of Wrexham; pop. 1265. Map 38.

Holton, par. and vil., E. Suffolk, 1 m. E. of Halesworth; pop. 500. Map 63.

Holyhead, spt., urb. dist., par., coastguard and lifeboat sta., Holyhead I., Anglesey; pop. 10,707. Map 36.

Holyhead Island, on W. side of and forming part of co. of Anglesey, 8 m. long, 3½ m. wide. Map 36.

Holy Island, or **Lindisfarne,** par. off coast of N. Northumberland; pop. 586. Map 17.

Holy Loch, arm of Clyde, Dunoon and Kilmun par., Argyllshire. Map 12.

Holytown, town and *q.s.* par., Lanarkshire, 11 m. S.E. of Glasgow; town pop. 12,537. Map 9.

Holywell, urb. dist. and par., on Dee estuary, Flintshire, 4¼ m. N.W. of Flint; pop. 3423. Map 38.

Honeyborough, vil., Pembrokeshire, 3 m. E. of Milford Haven. Map 64.

Honiton, mun. bor. and par., Devonshire, 16½ m. N.E. of Exeter; pop. 3008. Map 86.

Honley, urb. dist., W.R. Yorkshire, 6 m. S. of Huddersfield; pop. 4619. Map 32.

Hook, ham., Hants, 5½ m. N.E. of Basingstoke. Map 78.

Hoole, urb. dist., adjoining Chester; pop. 5889. Map 38.

Hope Bowdler, par. and vil., Salop, 2 m. S.E. of Church Stretton; pop. 121. Map 46.

Hopton, par. and vil., W. Suffolk, 8 m. E.S.E. of Thetford; pop. 420. Map 62.

Horbury, urb. dist., par. and vil., W.R. Yorkshire, 3¾ m. S.W. of Wakefield; pop. 7791. Map 32.

Horley, par. and residential vil., S. Surrey, 5 m. S.S.E. of Reigate; pop. 6100. Map 80.

Hornby, par. and vil., N. Lancashire, 8½ m. N.E. of Lancaster; pop. 421. Map 26.

Horncastle, urb. dist. and par., Lindsey, Lincolnshire, 21 m. E. of Lincoln; pop. 3496. Map 43.

Hornchurch, urb. dist., Essex, 2 m. S.E. of Romford; pop. 28,417. Map 72.

Horndon-on-the-Hill, par. and vil., S. Essex, 2 m. N.E. of Orsett; pop. 683. Map 72.

Hornsea, urb. dist. and par., E.R. Yorkshire, on N. sea, 15½ m. N.E. of Hull; pop. 4450. Map 35.

Hornsey, mun. bor., Middlesex, 4½ m. N. of King's Cross sta.; pop. 95,524. Map 71.

Horsforth, urb. dist. and par., W.R. Yorkshire, 5 m. N.W. of Leeds; pop. 11,770. Map 32.

Horsham, urb. dist. and par., W. Sussex, 26 m. N.W. of Brighton; pop. 13,579. Map 79.

Horsham St Faith with Newton St Faith, par. and vil., Norfolk, 4 m. N. of Norwich; pop. 843. Map 53.

Horton in Ribblesdale, par. and vil., W.R. Yorkshire, 6 m. N.N.W. of Settle; pop. 704. Map 26.

Horwich, urb. dist. and par., S.E. Lancashire, 18 m. N.W. of Manchester; pop. 15,680. Map 30.

Hospital, par. and vil., co. Limerick, 3 m. N. of Knocklong sta.; pop. 1235. Map 94.

Hotham, par. and vil., E.R. Yorkshire, 5 m. S.E. of Market Weighton; pop. 279. Map 34.

Hoton, par. and vil., Leicestershire, 3 m. N.E. of Loughborough; pop. 250. Map 49.

Houghton, vil., in co. and 5¾ m. N. of Pembroke. Map 64.

Houghton, par. and vil., S. Hants, 8½ m. W.N.W. of Winchester; pop. 391. Map 76.

Houghton-le-Spring, urb. dist. and par., in co. and 6½ m. N.E. of Durham; pop. 10,492. Map 23.

Hounslow, town, Heston and Isleworth pars., S.W. Middlesex, 2½ m. S.W. of Brentford. Map 71.

Houston, vil., Renfrewshire, 6 m. N.W. of Paisley. Map 8.

Hove, mun. bor. adjoining Brighton on the west, Sussex; pop. 54,994. Map 81.

Hovingham, par. and vil., N.R. Yorkshire, 8 m. W.N.W. of Malton; pop. 411. Map 28.

Howden, market town and par., E.R. Yorkshire, 21 m. W. of Hull; pop. 2052. Map 34.

Howick, coast par. and vil., Northumberland, 5 m. N.E. of Alnwick; pop. 245. Map 17.

Hoxne, par. and vil., E. Suffolk, 3½ m. N.E. of Eye; pop. 769. Map 63.

Hoylake, urb. dist. and par., Cheshire, 6 m. W. of Birkenhead. Golfing, watering place, racecourse; pop. 16,628. Map 38.

Hoyland, Nether, urb. dist., W.R. Yorkshire, 5½ m. S.E. of Barnsley; pop. 15,215. Map 41.

Hoyland Swaine, urb. dist., W.R. Yorkshire, 5¼ m. W.S.W. of Barnsley; pop. 793. Map 32.

Hubberston, par. and vil., Pembrokeshire, on Milford Haven; pop. 255. Map 64.

Hucknall Torkard, urb. dist. and par., in co. and 8 m. N.W. of Nottingham; pop. 17,338. Map 41.

Huddersfield, parl. and co. bor. and par., W.R. Yorks, 16½ m. S.W. of Leeds; pop. 113,467. Map 31.

Huggate, par. and vil., E.R. Yorkshire, on the Wolds, 7 m. N.E. of Pocklington; pop. 403. Map 34.

Hull, parl. and co. bor., city, spt. and co. in itself, E.R. Yorkshire; pop. 313,366. Map 35.

Hullavington, par. and vil., N. Wiltshire, 5 m. S.W. of Malmesbury; pop. 478. Map 68.

Hulton, Little, urb. dist., Lancashire, 3½ m. S. of Bolton; pop. 7878. Map 31.

Humshaugh, par. and vil., Northumberland, 5 m. N.N.W. of Hexham; pop. 487. Map 22.

Hungerford, mkt. tn. and par., Berks., on r. Kennet, 27 m. W.S.W. of Reading; pop. 2784. Map 76.

Hunmanby, par. and vil., E.R. Yorkshire, 12 m. S.E. of Scarborough by rail; pop. 1501. Map 29.

Hunstanton, New, urb. dist. and par., N.W. Norfolk, on the Wash; pop. 3131. Map 52.

Hunsworth, urb. dist., W.R. Yorkshire, 3½ m. S.E. of Bradford; pop. 1318. Map 32.

Hunter's Quay, part of Dunoon, Argyllshire. Map 12.

Huntingdon, mun. bor. and co. town of Huntingdonshire, 59 m. N. of London; pop. 4108. Map 61.

Huntington, par., N.R. Yorkshire, 3 m. N. of York; pop. 2219. Map 34.

Huntly, town and par., in co. and 41 m. N.W. of Aberdeen; pop. of bur. 3778. Map 3.

Hurstbourne Priors, par. and vil., N. Hants, 3½ m. N.E. of Andover; pop. 394. Map 76.

Hurstbourne Tarrant, par. and vil., N. Hants, 5½ m. N. of Andover; pop. 619. Map 76.

Hurst Green, eccl. dist. and ham., E. Sussex, 2½ m. N. of Robertsbridge; pop. 703. Map 82.

Hurstpierpoint, par. and market town, E. Sussex, 8 m. N. of Brighton; pop. 3099. Map 81.

Hurworth, par. and vil., S. Durham, 3 m. S. of Darlington; pop. 1444. Map 27.

Husbands Bosworth, par. and vil., Leicestershire, 6 m. S.W. of Market Harborough; pop. 732. Map 59.

Husthwaite, par. and vil., N.R. Yorkshire, 4 m. N. of Easingwold; pop. 376. Map 28.

Huthwaite, urb. dist., Nottinghamshire, 3 m. S.W. of Mansfield; pop. 5092. Map 41.

Hutton Bushel, par. and vil., N.R. Yorkshire, 5 m. S.W. of Scarborough; pop. 313. Map 29.

Hutton-le-Hole, par. and vil., N.R. Yorkshire, 2½ m. N.N.E. of Kirkby Moorside; pop. 242. Map 28.

Hutton Rudby, par. and vil., N.R. Yorkshire, 4 m. S.W. of Stokesley; pop. 894. Map 28.

Huyton, urb. dist., par. and vil., S.W. Lancashire, 5½ m. E. of Liverpool; pop. (with Roby) 5198. Map 38.

Hyde, mun. bor., mkt. tn. and par., E. Cheshire, 7½ m. E. of Manchester; pop. 32,066. Map 39.

Hythe, parl. and mun. bor., E. Kent, 68 m. S.E. of London; mun. bor. pop. 8397. Map 83.

Hythe, eccl. dist. and vil., S. Hants, 2½ m. S. of Southampton sta.; pop. 1076. Map 77.

IBSLEY, par. and vil., Hampshire, 3 m. N. of Ringwood; pop. 220. Map 77.

Ibstock, par. and vil., Leicestershire, 14 m. S.W. of Loughborough; pop. 5211. Map 49.

Ibstone, par. and vil., Buckinghamshire, 8 m. W. of High Wycombe; pop. 241. Map 70.

Icklesham, par. and vil., E. Sussex, 1½ m. W. of Winchelsea; pop. 1474. Map 82.

Icklingham, par. and vil., W. Suffolk, 4 m. S.E. of Mildenhall; pop. 285. Map 62.

Iddesleigh, par. and vil., S. Devon, 3 m. N.E. of Hatherleigh. Map 84.

Idridgehay, ham., N. Derbyshire, in par. and 3 m. S. of Wirksworth; pop. 572. Map 40.

Iffley, par. and vil., Oxon, 1½ m. S.E. of Oxford; pop. 405. Map 70.

Ightham, par. and vil., W. Kent, 4½ m. N.E. of Sevenoaks; pop. 1596. Map 82.

Ilchester, par. and vil., S. Somersetshire, 5 m. N.W. of Yeovil; pop. 449. Map 86.

Ilford, urb. dist., S. Essex, 3½ m. N.E. of Stratford; pop. 131,046. Map 72.

Ilfracombe, urb. dist. and market town, N. Devonshire, 14 m. N.W. of Barnstaple; pop. 9174. Map 84.

Ilkeston, mun. bor., market town and par., in co. and 8 m. N.E. of Derby; pop. 32,809. Map 49.

Ilkley, urb. dist., par. and watering place, W.R. Yorkshire, 9 m. S.E. of Skipton; pop. 9721. Map 32.

Ilminster, urb. dist. and par., S. Somersetshire, 5 m. N.E. of Chard; pop. 2232. Map 86.

Ilsley, East, small town and par., Berkshire, 9 m. N. of Newbury; pop. 429. Map 70.

Immingham Dock, par. and port, Lincolnshire, 4¼ m. N.W. of Grimsby; pop. 2150. Map 35.

Ince Blundell, par. and seat, S.W. Lancashire, 8 m. N. of Liverpool; pop. 440. Map 38.

Ince-in-Makerfield, urb. dist. Lancashire, sub. of Wigan; pop. 21,763. Map 30.

Inchcolm, isl. in Firth of Forth, Fifeshire. Map 10.

Inchkeith, isl. in Firth of Forth, Fifeshire. Map 10.

Inchnadamff, ham., S.W. Sutherlandshire, at S.E. end of Loch Assynt. Map 2.

Inchture, par. and vil., Perthshire, 8 m. S.W. of Dundee; pop. 490. Map 6.

Ingatestone, par. and vil., W. Essex, 6 m. S.W. of Chelmsford; pop. 2012. Map 72.

Ingleby Cross, ham., N.R. Yorkshire, 7 m. N.E. of Northallerton. Map 28.

Ingleton, par. and vil., W.R. Yorkshire, 4 m. N.W. of Clapham; pop. 2464. Map 26.

Ingoldsby, par. and vil., Kesteven, Lincolnshire, 8 m. S.E. of Grantham; pop. 239. Map 50.

Ingrow, vil., W.R. Yorks, 1 m. S.W. of Keighley. Map 31.

Ingworth, par. and vil., Norfolk, 2 m. N. of Aylsham; pop. 143. Map 53.

Inkberrow, par. and vil., Worcestershire, 5 m. W. of Alcester; pop. 1360. Map 58.

Inkpen, par. and vil., S.W. Berkshire, 4 m. S.E. of Hungerford; pop. 575. Map 76.

Innellan, q.s. par. and vil., Argyllshire, 3¾ m. S. of Dunoon; pop. 1409. Map 12.

Innerleithen, town and par., in co. and 6¼ m. S.E. of Peebles; bur. pop. 2359. Map 15.

Innerwick, par. and vil., East Lothian, 5 m. S.E. of Dunbar; pop. 146. Map 11.

Insch, par. and vil., Aberdeenshire, 13½ m. S.E. of Huntly; pop. 1377. Map 3.

Inveraray, mun. bur., par. and co. town of Argyllshire, 15 m. S.W. of Dalmally; bur. pop. 455. Map 12.

Inverbervie, mun. bur., Kincardineshire, 13 m. N.E. of Montrose; pop. 1032. Map 3.

Invergarry, ham., Inverness-shire, 7 m. S.W. of Fort Augustus. Map 2.

Invergordon, police bur. and tn., E. Ross and Cromarty, 13 m. N.E. of Dingwall; pop. 1417. Map 3.

Inverkeilor, coast par. and vil., Angus, 6 m. N. of Arbroath; pop. 1297. Map 7.

Inverkeithing, mun. bur. and par., Fifeshire, 13¼ m. N.W. of Edinburgh; pop. 3185. Map 10.

Inverkip, par. and vil., Renfrewshire, 6 m. S.W. of Greenock; pop. 12,901. Map 12.

Inverness, mun. bur., spt. and mkt. tn., Inverness-shire, 108 m. from Aberdeen; pop. 22,582. Map 3.

Inverurie, police bur. and par., in co. and 16½ m. N.W. of Aberdeen; pop. 4524. Map 3.

Iona, isl., off S.W. coast of Mull Isl., Argyllshire. Map 12.

Ipstones, par. and vil., Staffordshire, 4½ m. N. of Cheadle; pop. 1757. Map 40.

Ipswich, parl. and co. bor. and seaport, E. Suffolk, 68¾ m. N.E. of London; pop. 87,557. Map 63.

Irchester, par. and vil., Northamptonshire, 2 m. S.E. of Wellingborough; pop. 2304. Map 60.

Ireby, par., N. Lancashire, 3½ m. S.E. of Kirkby Lonsdale; pop. 71. Map 26.

Irlam, urb. dist., Lancashire, 8 m. S.W. of Manchester; pop. 12,898. Map 39.

Ironbridge, eccl. dist. and town, Shropshire, 13¾ m. S.E. of Shrewsbury; pop. 2371. Map 47.

Irthington, par. and vil., Cumberland, 2 m. N.W. of Brampton; pop. 671. Map 21.

Irthlingborough, urb. dist. and par., Northamptonshire, 2 m. N.W. of Higham Ferrers; pop. 4715. Map 60.

Irvine, mun. bur., market town and par., Ayrshire, 30¼ m. S.W. of Glasgow; pop. of bur. 12,032. Map 12.

Isfield, par. and vil., Sussex, 3 m. S.W. of Uckfield; pop. 478. Map 81.

Islay, Isle of, in Argyllshire, 13 m. W. of Kintyre; pop. 5743. Map 12.

Isleham, par. and vil., Cambridgeshire, 6½ m. N. of Newmarket; pop. 1490. Map 61.

Isleworth, par. and suburban town, Middlesex, 12 m. W.S.W. of London; pop. 29,908. Map 71.

Ivinghoe, market vil. and par., Buckinghamshire, 2 m. S.E. of Cheddington Junction; pop. 810. Map 71.

Ivybridge, urb. dist. and par., Devonshire, 10½ m. E.N.E. of Plymouth; pop. 1609. Map 88.

Iwerne Minster, par. and vil., Dorsetshire, 5 m. N. of Blandford; pop. 501. Map 87.

Ixworth, par. and vil., W. Suffolk, 7 m. N.E. of Bury St Edmunds; pop. 779. Map 62.

JACOBSTOW, par. and vil., Cornwall, 11 m. N.W. of Launceston; pop. 312. Map 84.

Jamestown, vil., in S. co. Leitrim, 3 m. S.E. of Carrick-on-Shannon. Map 92.

Jamestown, town and *q.s.* par., Dumbartonshire, 1 m. S.E. of Balloch; pop. 2389. Map 12.

Jarrow, mun. bor. and par., Durham, 4¼ m. W.S.W. of South Shields; pop. 32,018. Map 23.

Jeantown, vil., on W. side of Loch Carron, Ross and Cromarty. Map 2.

Jedburgh, bur., par. and co. town of Roxburghshire, 56 m. S.E. of Edinburgh; pop. 3057. Map 16.

Jeffreston, par. and vil., Pembrokeshire, 5½ m. S.S.W. of Narberth; pop. 419. Map 64.

Jemimaville, vil., Ross and Cromarty, 2 m. S.S.E. of Invergordon. Map 3.

Jervaulx Abbey, N.R. Yorkshire, 5 m. S.E. of Leyburn. Map 27.

Johnby, vil. and seat, Cumberland, 6 m. N.W. of Penrith. Map 21.

John o' Groats, house, Caithness-shire, 1½ m. W. of Duncansby Head. Map 3.

Johnshaven, fishing vil., Kincardineshire, 8½ m. N.E. of Montrose. Map 3.

Johnston, par. and vil., Pembrokeshire, 4½ m. W.S.W. of Haverfordwest; pop. 322. Map 64.

Johnstone, manufacturing town and police bur., Renfrewshire, 9½ m. W. of Glasgow; pop. 12,837. Map 8.

Juniper Green, *q.s.* par., in city and 4¾ m. from Princes Street sta., Edinburgh; pop. 1865. Map 10.

Jura, Isle of, isl. and par., Argyllshire; pop. 446. Map 12.

Jurby, par. and vil., Isle of Man, 6 m. N.W. of Ramsey; pop. 448. Map 24.

KAMES, vil., on Kyles of Bute, Argyllshire, 1½ m. S.W. of Tighnabruaich. Map 12.

Kanturk, market town, N. co. Cork, 36¼ m. N.W. of Cork; pop. 1630. Map 94.

Katrine, Loch, Perthshire and Stirlingshire, 8½ m. W. of Callander. Map 12.

Keadby, par. and vil., Lindsey, Lincolnshire, 4 m. S.E. of Crowle; pop. 681. Map 34.

Keady, town and par., in co. and 8 m. S.W. of Armagh; pop. 5202. Map 93.

Kearsley, urb. dist., Lancashire, 4 m. S.E. of Bolton; pop. 9736. Map 31.

Keelby, par. and vil., Lincolnshire, 6½ m. N.E. of Caistor; pop. 635. Map 43.

Kegworth, par. and town, Leicestershire, 5½ m. N.W of Loughborough; pop. 2139. Map 49.

Keighley, mun. bor., mkt. tn. and par., W.R. Yorkshire, 9 m. N.W. of Bradford; pop. 40,440. Map 32.

Keiss, fishing vil., Caithness-shire, 8 m. N. of Wick; pop. of *q.s.* par. 857. Map 3.

Keith, police bur. and par., Banffshire, 53½ m. N.W. of Aberdeen; pop. 4424. Map 3.

Kelso, market town and par., Roxburghshire, 52½ m. S.E. of Edinburgh; pop. 3855. Map 16.

Kelton, small port and seat, in co. and 3½ m. S. of Dumfries. Map 20.

Kelty, *q.s.* par. and mining town, Fifeshire, 5 m. S.E. of Kinross; pop. 7315. Map 10.

Kelvedon, par. and vil., Essex, 9 m. S.W. of Colchester; pop. 1547. Map 72.

Kelvedon Hatch, par. and vil., Essex, 3 m. S.E. of Chipping Ongar; pop. 469. Map 72.

Kempston, urb. dist. and par., in co. and 2 m. S. of Bedford; pop. 5390. Map 60.

Kendal, market town and par., Westmorland, 8¼ m. S.E. of Windermere; pop. 15,575. Map 26.

Kenfig, par. and ancient town, Glamorganshire, 3½ m. N. of Porthcawl; pop. 519. Map 66.

Kenilworth, urb. dist. and par., Warwickshire, 4 m. N. of Warwick; pop. 7592. Map 58.

Kenmare, town and par., Kerry, 19¾ m. S.E. of Headford Junction; pop. 2739. Map 94.

Kenmore, par. and vil., Perthshire, on r. Tay at its efflux from Loch Tay; pop. 1009. Map 5.

Kennoway, par. and vil., Fifeshire, 3 m. N.W. of Leven; pop. 1783. Map 7.

Kentford, par. and vil., W. Suffolk, 4½ m. N.E. of Newmarket; pop. 245. Map 62.

Kentisbeare, par. and vil., Devonshire, 3½ m. N.E. of Cullompton; pop. 724. Map 85.

Kenton, par. and vil., Devonshire, 6½ m. S.E. of Exeter; pop. 1826. Map 89.

Kenton, par. and vil., Northumberland, 3 m. N.W. of Newcastle-on-Tyne. Map 23.

Kessingland, coast par. and vil., E. Suffolk, 4½ m. S.W. of Lowestoft; pop. 2056. Map 63.

Keswick, urb. dist. and par., Cumberland, 12½ m. S.E. of Cockermouth; pop. 4635. Map 20.

Kettering, urb. dist. and par., Northamptonshire, 8 m. N. of Wellingborough; pop. 31,220. Map 60.

Kettlebridge, vil., Fifeshire, 2 m. S. of Ladybank Junction. Map 7.

Kettleholmbridge, ham., Dumfriesshire, 3 m. S.S.W. of Lockerbie. Map 20.

Kettlewell, par., W.R. Yorkshire, 13 m. N. of Skipton; pop. 374. Map 27.

Kew, eccl. par. and vil., on r. Thames, Surrey, 6 m. W. of London; pop. 4362. Map 71.

Keyingham, par. and vil., E.R. Yorkshire, 10 m. S.E. of Hull; pop. 595. Map 35.

Keynsham, market town and par., Somersetshire, 5 m. S.E. of Bristol; pop. 3837. Map 75.

Kidderminster, mun. bor., Worcestershire, 19 m. S.W. of Birmingham; pop. 28,914. Map 57.

Kidlington, par. and vil., Oxon, 5 m. N. of Oxford; pop. 1073. Map 70.

Kidsgrove, urb. dist., Staffordshire, 2½ m. N.N.W. of Tunstall; pop. 9937. Map 39.
Kidwelly, par., mun. bor. and port, Carmarthenshire, 9¼ m. N.W. of Llanelly; pop. 3161. Map 65.
Kilbarchan, town and par., Renfrewshire, 5 m. W. of Paisley; pop. 7492. Map 8.
Kilbeggan, town and par., Westmeath, 4 m. S.E. of Horseleap ry. sta.; pop. 1265. Map 93.
Kilbirnie, town and par., Ayrshire, 20½ m. S.W. of Glasgow; pop. 8032. Map 8.
Kilcock, market town and par., Kildare, 3½ m. N.W. of Maynooth; pop. 986. Map 93.
Kilconquhar, par. and vil., Fifeshire, 4 m. E. of Largo; pop. 1319. Map 7.
Kilcreggan, watering place, Dumbartonshire, 6 m. N.W. of Greenock. Map 12.
Kilcullen, town and par., in co. and 5 m. E.S.E. of Kildare; pop. 1293. Map 95.
Kildare, market town, par. and cap. of co. Kildare, 30 m. S.W. of Dublin; pop. 1971. Map 95.
Kilfenora, par. and vil., co. Clare, 5 m. N.E. of Ennistimon; pop. 1278. Map 94.
Kilfinan, par. and vil., Argyllshire, on E. shore of Loch Fyne; pop. 2199. Map 12.
Kilfinnane, par. and town, co. Limerick, 5 m. S.E. of Kilmallock; pop. 890. Map 94.
Kilgarvan, par. and vil., co. Kerry, 6¾ m. N.E. of Kenmare; pop. 2350. Map 94.
Kilgetty, ham. and ry. sta., Pembrokeshire, 5 m. N. of Tenby. Map 64.
Kilham, par. and vil., E.R. Yorkshire, 5½ m. N.E. of Great Driffield; pop. 853. Map 35.
Kilkee, watering place with ry. sta. in co. Clare, 9 m. N.W. of Kilrush; pop. 1682. Map 94.
Kilkeel, seaport town and par. in co. Down, 10 m. S.E. of Warrenpoint ry. sta.; pop. 1620. Map 93.
Kilkenny, mun. bor. with ry. sta., cap. of Kilkenny, 80 m. S.W. of Dublin; pop. 10,056. Map 95.
Kilkieran, ham. and bay, in co. and 28 m. W. of Galway. Map 92.
Killala, seaport town and par., co. Mayo, 8 m. N.N.W. of Ballina; pop. 872. Map 92.
Killaloe, town and par., Clare, 17 m. N.E. of Limerick; town pop. 821. Map 94.
Killarney, par. and urb. dist., Kerry, 185¼ m. S.W. of Dublin; pop. 5325. Map 94.
Killearn, par. and vil., Stirlingshire, 9½ m. N.W. of Lennoxtown; pop. 1054. Map 8.
Killeshandra, par. and town, in co. and 5 m. W. of Cavan; pop. of town 561. Map 93.
Killester, par. and vil., in co. and 2 m. N.E. of Dublin; pop. 5325. Map 95.
Killin, par. and vil., Perthshire, 39¼ m. N.W. of Stirling; pop. 1502. Map 12.
Killiney and Ballybrack, urb. dist. and par., co. Dublin, 2 m. S.E. of Dun-Laoghaire; pop. 2069. Map 95.
Killinghall, par. and vil., W.R. Yorkshire, 1 m. S. of Ripley; pop. 1237. Map 33.
Killorglin, par. and town, co. Kerry, 13 m. N.W. of Killarney; pop. of town 1087. Map 94.
Killybegs, seaport town and ry. sta., in co. and 19 m. W. of Donegal; pop. 634. Map 92.
Killyleagh, seaport town and par., co. Down, 4 m. E. of Crossgar ry. sta.; pop. 1610. Map 93.
Kilmacolm, par. and town, Renfrewshire, 17½ m. W. of Glasgow; pop. 2852. Map 8.
Kilmacow, par. and vil., co. Kilkenny, 6 m. N.W. of Waterford; pop. 988. Map 95.
Kilmacrenan, par. and vil., co. Donegal, 7 m. N.W. of Letterkenny; pop. 4375. Map 92.
Kilmallock, market town with ry. sta., in co. and 20¾ m. S. of Limerick; pop. 1101. Map 94.
Kilmany, par. and vil., Fifeshire, 5 m. N. of Cupar; pop. 514. Map 7.
Kilmarnock, mun. bur. and par., Ayrshire, 24¼ m. S.W. of Glasgow; pop. 38,099. Map 12.
Kilmaurs, town and par., Ayrshire, 2¼ m. N.W. of Kilmarnock; pop. 1843. Map 12.
Kilmun, *q.s.* par. and vil., Argyllshire, 7½ m. W. of Greenock; pop. 1351. Map 12.
Kilrea, town and par., Londonderry, 5¾ m. S.E. o Garvagh; pop. 783. Map 93.
Kilrenny, mun. bur. and par., Fifeshire, on Firth of Forth; pop. 3325. Map 7.
Kilronan, vil., Inishmore Isl., co. Galway; pop. 459. Map 94.
Kilrush, seaport town, urb. dist. and par., Clare, 9 m. S.E. of Kilkee; pop. 3346. Map 94.
Kilsby, par. and vil., Northamptonshire, 7 m. N. of Daventry; pop. 518. Map 59.
Kilspindie, par. and vil., S.E. Perthshire, 2 m. N.W. of Errol sta.; pop. 437. Map 6.
Kilsyth, town, police bur. and par., Stirlingshire, 12¾ m. N.E. of Glasgow; pop. 7551. Map 9.
Kilwinning, town and par., Ayrshire, 26½ m. S.W. of Glasgow; pop. 5324. Map 12.
Kilworth, par. and vil., co. Cork, 3 m. N. of Fermoy; pop. 990. Map 94.
Kimberley, par. and town, in co. and 5 m. N.W. of Nottingham; pop. 5158. Map 49.
Kimbolton, market town and par., in co. and 10½ m. W.S.W. of Huntingdon; pop. 902. Map 60.
Kimbolton, par. and vil., Herefordshire, 2½ m. N.E. of Leominster; pop. 526. Map 57.
Kimpton, par. and vil., Hampshire, 5 m. W.N.W. of Andover; pop. 387. Map 76.
Kincardine, small seaport town, Fifeshire, 5½ m. S.E. of Alloa; pop. 2112. Map 9.
Kinder Scout, mtn., Peak dist., Derbyshire; height 2088 ft. Map 40.
Kineton, market town and par. Warwickshire, 6 m. W. of Fenny Compton; pop. 950. Map 59.
Kingham, par. and vil., Oxon, 4½ m. S.W. of Chipping Norton; pop. 713. Map 59.
Kinghorn, parl., mun. bur. and par., Fifeshire, 22½ m. N. of Edinburgh; pop. 2001. Map 10.
Kinglassie, par. and vil., Fifeshire, 6 m. N.W. of Kirkcaldy; pop. 836. Map 10.
Kingsand, vil., Cornwall, 4 m. S.W. of Plymouth. Map 88.
Kingsbarns, par. and vil., Fifeshire, 8 m. S.E. of St Andrews; pop. 640. Map 7.
Kingsbridge, urb. dist. and par., Devonshire, 11 m. S.W. of Totnes; pop. 2978. Map 89.
Kingsbury, urb. dist., Middlesex, on r. Brent; pop. 16,636. Map 71.
Kingsbury Episcopi, par. and vil., Somersetshire, 4 m. S. of Langport; pop. 1114. Map 86.
Kingsclere, market town and par., Hampshire, 9 m. N.W. of Basingstoke; pop. 2243. Map 76.
King's Cliffe, par. and vil., Northamptonshire, 12 m. W. of Peterborough; pop. 974. Map 50.
Kingscourt, town with ry. sta., Cavan, 47 m. N.W. of Dublin; pop. 788. Map 93.
Kingsheath, eccl. par. in S. of Birmingham; pop. 14,765. Map 58.
Kingskettle, ry. sta., Fifeshire, 1 m. S. of Ladybank Junction. Map 7.
Kings Langley, par. and vil., Hertfordshire, 5 m. N. of Watford; pop. 2504. Map 71.
Kingsley, par. and vil., N.E. Hampshire, 4 m. S.E. of Alton; pop. 1051. Map 79.
King's Lynn, mun. bor. and seaport, Norfolk, 48½ m. N.W. of Norwich; pop. 20,580. Map 51.
Kings Norton, ward and eccl. par. in S. of Birmingham; pop. 7490. Map 58.
Kings Nympton, par. and vil., Devonshire, 3½ m. N. of Chulmleigh; pop. 444. Map 85.
Kings Somborne, par. and vil., Hampshire, 7 m. W.N.W. of Winchester; pop. 1203. Map 76.
Kingston-on-Soar, par. and vil., in co. and 10 m. S.S.W. of Nottingham; pop. 241. Map 49.
Kingston-on-Thames, mun. bor., Surrey, 3¼ m. S. of Richmond; pop. 39,052. Map 80.

Kingstown (Dun Laoghaire), seaport and watering place, 6 m. S.E. of Dublin ; pop. 18,992. Map 93.

Kingswear, par. and vil., Devonshire, 35 m. S. of Exeter ; pop. 862. Map 89.

Kingswinford, par. and vil., Staffordshire, 3½ m. N. of Stourbridge ; pop. 22,067. Map 57.

Kingswood, par. and vil., Gloucestershire, 1½ m. S.W. of Wotton-under-Edge ; pop. 850. Map 68.

Kingswood, urb. dist., Gloucestershire, 3½ m. N.E. of Bristol ; pop. 13,297. Map 68.

Kingswood, par. and vil., Surrey, 3½ m. N.W. of Reigate ; pop. 1140. Map 80.

Kington, urb. dist., Herefordshire, 13¾ m. W. of Leominster ; pop. 1742. Map 56.

Kingussie, eccl. par. and police bur., Inverness-shire, 46½ m. S. of Inverness ; pop. bur. 1067. Map 3.

Kinlochewe, ham., Ross and Cromarty, 10 m. N.W. of Achnasheen ry. sta. Map 2.

Kinlochmoidart, seat and deer forest, Ardnamurchan par., Inverness-shire. Map 2.

Kinloch Rannoch, vil. and q.s. par., Perthshire, 21 m. W. of Pitlochry ; pop. 665. Map 12.

Kinnaird, par. and vil., Perthshire, 2½ m. W. of Inchture ; pop. 193. Map 6.

Kinnerley, par. and vil., Salop, 6 m. S.E. of Oswestry ; pop. 1022. Map 46.

Kinnesswood, vil. in co. and 5 m. E. of Kinross. Map 6.

Kinross, police bur., market tn. and par., Kinrossshire, 13¾ m. N. of Dunfermline ; pop. 2525. Map 6.

Kinsale, seaport, par. and urb. dist., in co. and 24 m. S. of Cork ; pop. 2881. Map 94.

Kintbury, par. and vil., S.W. Berkshire, 3½ m. E. of Hungerford ; pop. 1648. Map 76.

Kintore, police bur. and par., Aberdeenshire, 16 m. E. of Alford ; bur. pop. 756. Map 3.

Kinvarra, vil., Galway, 8 m. N.W. of Gort ; pop. 347. Map 94.

Kinver, town and par., Staffordshire, 3½ m. W.S.W. of Stourbridge ; pop. 2886. Map 57.

Kippen, par. and vil., in co. and 9 m. W. of Stirling ; pop. 1518. Map 8.

Kirby Grindalythe, par. and vil., E.R. Yorkshire, 8 m. S.E. of Malton ; pop. 146. Map 29.

Kirby-le-Soken, par. and vil., Essex, 2 m. W. of Walton-on-the-Naze ; pop. 1160. Map 73.

Kirby Malzeard, par. and vil., W.R. Yorkshire, 6 m. N.W. of Ripon ; pop. 523. Map 27.

Kirkbampton, par. and vil., Cumberland, 6½ m. W. of Carlisle ; pop. 387. Map 21.

Kirkbean, par. and vil., Kirkcudbrightshire, 12 m. S. of Dumfries ; pop. 679. Map 20.

Kirkbride, par. and vil., Cumberland, 12¾ m. W. of Carlisle ; pop. 408. Map 20.

Kirkburton, urb. dist., W.R. Yorkshire, 5 m. S.E. of Huddersfield ; pop. 3184. Map 32.

Kirkby, par., S.W. Lancashire, 7 m. N.E. of Liverpool ; pop. 1429. Map 38.

Kirkby Fleetham, par. and vil., N.R. Yorkshire, 4 m. N.N.E. of Bedale ; pop. 515. Map 28.

Kirkby-in-Ashfield, urb. dist., Nottinghamshire, 12 m. N.W. of Nottingham ; pop. 17,798. Map 41.

Kirkby Lonsdale, urb. dist., mkt. tn. and par., Westmorland, 4¾ m. N.W. of Ingleton ; pop. 1370. Map 26.

Kirkby Moorside, par. and market town, N.R. Yorkshire, 6½ m. W. of Pickering ; pop. 1695. Map 28.

Kirkby Stephen, market town and par., Westmorland, 10 m. S.E. of Appleby ; pop. 1542. Map 26.

Kirkby Thore, par. and vil., N. Westmorland, 4½ m. N.W. of Appleby ; pop. 469. Map 21.

Kirkcaldy, mun. bur. and par., Fifeshire, 26 m. N. of Edinburgh ; pop. 43,874. Map 10.

Kirkcudbright, mun. bur. and co. town, Kirkcudbrightshire, 30 m. S.W. of Dumfries ; pop. 2311. Map 19.

Kirkfieldbank, vil., in co. and 1 m. W. of Lanark. Map 14.

Kirkham, urb. dist., market town and par., N. Lancashire, 8 m. W. of Preston ; pop. 4031. Map 30.

Kirkheaton, urb. dist., W.R. Yorkshire, 2½ m. E. of Huddersfield ; pop. 2610. Map 32.

Kirkintilloch, police bur. and par., Dumbartonshire, 8 m. N.E. of Glasgow ; bur. pop. 11,817. Map 8.

Kirklington, urb. dist., par. and vil., N.R. Yorkshire, 5½ m. S.E. of Bedale ; pop. 251. Map 27.

Kirkliston, vil, with ry. sta., West Lothian, 10 m. W. of Edinburgh ; pop. 961. Map 10.

Kirkmaiden, par., Wigtown, 15 m. S. of Stranraer. Map 18.

Kirkmichael, par. and vil., Isle of Man, 6 m. N.E. of Peel ; pop. 809. Map 24.

Kirknewton, par. and vil., Midlothian, 10 m. S.W. of Edinburgh ; pop. 3000. Map 9.

Kirkoswald, par. and vil., Cumberland, 8 m. N.E. of Penrith ; pop. 475. Map 21.

Kirkpatrick, ry. sta. and vil., Dumfries, 7 m. S.E. of Ecclefechan. Map 20.

Kirkton of Auchterhouse, par. and vil., Angus, 12½ m. N.W. of Dundee by rail ; pop. 643. Map 7.

Kirkwall, cap. of Orkney Islands ; pop. 3517.

Kirkwhelpington, par. and vil., Northumberland, 12½ m. W. of Morpeth ; pop. 230. Map 17.

Kirn, q.s. par., Argyllshire, part of Dunoon. Map 12.

Kirriemuir, police bur. and par., Angus, 5 m. N.W. of Forfar ; pop. 3326. Map 7.

Kirtlebridge, vil., S.E. Dumfriesshire, 3 m. S.E. of Ecclefechan. Map 20.

Kirton, par. and vil., Holland, Lincolnshire, 4 m. S.S.W. of Boston ; pop. 2700. Map 51.

Kirton Lindsey, market town and par., Lincolnshire, 6¼ m. S.W. of Brigg ; pop. 1651. Map 42.

Knapton, par. and vil., Norfolk, 3 m. N.E. of N. Walsham ; pop. 348. Map 53.

Knapton, par., E.R. Yorkshire, 6 m. N.E. of Malton ; pop. 244. Map 29.

Knaresborough, urb. dist., mkt. tn., par., W.R. Yorks, 3½ m. N.E. of Harrogate ; pop. 5942. Map 33.

Knarsdale, par. and vil., Northumberland, 6½ m. S.S.W. of Haltwhistle ; pop. 379. Map 21.

Knighton, urb. dist., Radnorshire, 5½ m. N.N.W. of Presteigne ; pop. 1836. Map 56.

Knightsford Bridge, on r. Teme, Worcestershire, 5½ m. E.N.E. of Bromyard. Map 57.

Knott End, place, W. Lancashire, on r. Wyre, opposite Fleetwood. Map 30.

Knottingley, urb. dist. and par., W. R. Yorkshire, 2½ m. N.E. of Pontefract ; pop. 6842. Map 33.

Knowesgate, ry. sta., Northumberland, 10¼ m. N.E. of Reedsmouth. Map 17.

Knowsley, par. and vil., S.W. Lancashire, 3 m. N.W. of Prescot ; pop. 1175. 1 m. S.E. of vil. is **K. Hall**, seat of Earl of Derby. Map 38.

Knutsford, urb. dist., market town and par., N. Cheshire, 6 m. E.N.E. of Northwich ; pop. 5878. Map 39.

Kyle of Lochalsh, vil., Ross and Cromarty, 10½ m. S.W. of Strome Ferry ; pop. 505. Map 2.

LACEBY, par. and vil., Lindsey, Lincolnshire, 4 m. S.W. of Grimsby ; pop. 1102. Map 35.

Ladbroke, par. and vil., Warwickshire, 2 m. S. of Southam ; pop. 169. Map 59.

Ladybank, police bur., Fifeshire, 5½ m. S.W. of Cupar ; pop. 1128. Map 7.

Ladykirk, par. and ham., Berwickshire, 6 m. N. of Coldstream ; pop. 338. Map 11.

Laindon, par. and vil. Essex, 3½ m. S.S.E. of Billericay ; pop. 1205. Map 72.

Lairg, par. and vil., Sutherlandshire, 11 m. N. of Bonar Bridge ; pop. 328. Map 3.

Lakenheath, par. and vil., Suffolk, 4½ m. S.W. of Brandon ; pop. 1713. Map 62.

Laleham, par. and vil., Middlesex, 2 m. S.E. of Staines ; pop. 755. Map 71.

Lamberhurst, par. and town, Kent, 6½ m. S.E. of Tunbridge Wells; pop. 1508. Map 82.
Lambourn, town and par., Berkshire, 8 m. N. of Hungerford; pop. 2193. Map 69.
Lamerton, par. and vil., Devonshire, 2½ m. N.W. of Tavistock; pop. 545. Map 88.
Lamington, vil., Lanarkshire, 10 m. S. of Carstairs by rail. Map 15.
Lamlash, vil., Arran, 4 m. S.E. of Brodick. Map 12.
Lammermuir Hills, E. Lothian and Berwickshire. **Lammer Law,** 1733 ft. Map 12.
Lamonby, vil., Cumberland, 7½ m. N.W. of Penrith. Map 21.
Lampeter, mun. bor. and par., Cardiganshire, 12 m. S.E. of Aberayron; pop. 1742. Map 54.
Lampeter Velfrey, par., Pembrokeshire, 3 m. E. of Narberth; pop. 909. Map 64.
Lamport, par. and vil., in co. and 10 m. N. of Northampton; pop. 166. Map 59.
Lanark, mun. bur., par. and co. town of Lanarkshire, 32¼ m. S.E. of Glasgow by rail; bur. pop. 6178. Map 14.
Lancaster, mun. bor., spt., par. and co. town of Lancashire, 21 m. N. of Preston; pop. 43,396. Map 30.
Lanchester, par. and vil., Durham, 7½ m. N.W. of Durham; pop. 5091. Map 23.
Landore, vil., Glamorganshire, 1½ m. N.E. of Swansea. Map 66.
Lands End, Cornwall, the extreme S.W. point of Britain. Map 90.
Lanesborough, vil., in co. and 10 m. N.E. of Roscommon; pop. 254. Map 92.
Langbank, *q.s.* par. and vil., Renfrewshire, 4½ m. E. of Port Glasgow; pop. 457. Map 12.
Langdon, East, par. and vil., Kent, 3 m. N.N.E. of Dover; pop. 336. Map 83.
Langford, par. and vil., Oxon, 3 m. N.E. of Lechlade; pop. 268. Map 69.
Langham, par. and vil., Rutlandshire, 1½ m. N.W. of Oakham; pop. 558. Map 50.
Langholm, town and par., Dumfriesshire, 91½ m. S. of Edinburgh; pop. 2448. Map 15.
Langport, market town and par., Somersetshire, 11 m. N.W. of Yeovil; pop. 781. Map 86.
Langsett, par. and vil., W.R. Yorkshire, 3½ m. S.W. of Penistone; pop. 366. Map 40.
Langtoft, par. and vil., E.R. Yorkshire, 6½ m. N.W. of Great Driffield; pop. 470. Map 35.
Langton Matravers, par. and vil., Dorsetshire, 8 m. S.E. of Wareham; pop. 948. Map 87.
Langwathby, par. and vil., Cumberland, 4 m. N.E. of Penrith; pop. 272. Map 21.
Langworth, vil. and ry. sta., in co. and 6¼ m. N.E. of Lincoln. Map 42.
Lapford, par. and vil., Devonshire, 6 m. N.W. of Yeoford Junction; pop. 451. Map 85.
Larbert, par. and town, Stirlingshire, 2½ m. N.W. of Falkirk; pop. 12,301. Map 9.
Largo, par., Fifeshire, 3 m. N.E. of Leven; pop. 3215. Map 7.
Largs, police bur. and par., Ayrshire, 11 m. N. of Ardrossan by rail; pop. 6115. Map 12.
Larkhall, town and *q.s.* par., Lanarkshire, 3½ m. S.E. of Hamilton; pop. 14,055. Map 9.
Larne, town, par. and urb. dist., co. Antrim, 24 m. N. of Belfast; pop. 8036. Map 93.
Lasswade, bur. and par., Midlothian, 6 m. S.E. of Edinburgh; pop. 467. Map 10.
Latchingdon, par. and vil., N.E. Essex, 5 m. S.S.E. of Maldon; pop. 420. Map 73.
Latheron, coast par. and vil., Caithness-shire, 18 m. S.W. of Wick; pop. 3866. Map 3.
Lathom and Burscough, dist., Lancashire, now in Ormskirk. Map 30.
Latimer, par. and vil., Buckinghamshire, 3½ m. S.E. of Chesham; pop. 684. Map 71.
Lauder, royal and mun. bur., W. Berwickshire, 10½ m. E. of Fountainhall; pop. 628. Map 10.
Laugharne, par. and market town, in co. and 9 m. S.W. of Carmarthen; pop. 992. Map 65.
Laughton, par. and vil., E. Sussex, 6 m. N.E. of Lewes; pop. 634. Map 81.
Launceston, mun. bor. and market town, Cornwall, 18½ m. N.W. of Tavistock; pop. 4071. Map 88.
Laurencekirk, small market town and par., S. Kincardineshire; pop. 1316. Map 3.
Lavant, par. and vil., W. Sussex, 2½ m. N. of Chichester; pop. 697. Map 79.
Lavendon, par. and vil., Buckinghamshire, 2 m. N.E. of Olney; pop. 667. Map 60.
Lavenham, par. and vil., Suffolk, 10 m. N.E. of Bury St Edmunds; pop. 1620. Map 62.
Laxey, vil., Isle of Man, 6 m. N.E. of Douglas; pop. 1639. Map 24.
Laxfield, par. and vil., E. Suffolk, 6 m. N. of Framlingham; pop. 787. Map 63.
Laxton, par. and vil., Nottinghamshire, 3½ m. S.W. of Tuxford; pop. 396. Map 41.
Lazonby, par. and vil., Cumberland, 7 m. N.E. of Penrith; pop. 707. Map 21.
Leadburn, ham. and ry. sta., Midlothian, 9½ m. N. of Peebles. Map 10.
Leadgate, urb. dist., Durham, 1½ m. E.N.E. of Consett; pop. 6395. Map 22.
Leadhills, vil. and ry. sta., Lanarkshire, 5 m. S.W. of Elvanfoot sta.; pop. 820. Map 14.
Leafield, par. and vil., Oxfordshire, 4 m. N.W. of Witney; pop. 606. Map 69.
Lealholm Bridge, vil. and ry. sta., N.R. Yorkshire, 9 m. W.S.W. of Whitby. Map 28.
Leamington, mun. bor. and watering place, in co. and 2 m. E. of Warwick; pop. 29,662. Map 58.
Leasingham, par. and vil., Kesteven, Lincolnshire, 2 m. N. of Sleaford; pop. 299. Map 42.
Leatherhead, urb. dist. and town, Surrey, 4 m. S.W. of Epsom; pop. 6916. Map 78.
Leathley, par. and vil., W.R. Yorkshire, 3 m. N.E. of Otley; pop. 127. Map 32.
Lechlade, par. and market town, Gloucestershire, 3¼ m. E.S.E. of Fairford; pop. 1048. Map 69.
Leconfield, par. and vil., E.R. Yorkshire, 3 m. N.W. of Beverley; pop. 284. Map 35.
Ledbury, urb. dist., in co. and 13 m. S.E. of Hereford; pop. 3283. Map 57.
Leeds, city, parl. and co. bor. and par., W.R. Yorkshire, 25 m. S.W. of York; pop. 482,789. Map 33.
Leek, urb. dist., market town and par., Staffordshire, 12½ m. S.E. of Macclesfield; pop. 18,556. Map 40.
Leeming, eccl. dist. and vil., N.R. Yorkshire, 1½ m. N.E. of Bedale; pop. 487. Map 27.
Lee-on-the-Solent, watering place, Hampshire, 3 m. W. of Fort Brockhurst. Map 77.
Lees, urb. dist., Lancashire, 1½ m. S.E. of Oldham; pop. 4738. Map 31.
Legerwood, par. and ham., Berwickshire, 3½ m. N.E. of Earlston; pop. 379. Map 16.
Leicester, city, parl. and co. bor., par., market town and co. town of Leicestershire, 29 m. N.W. of Northampton; pop. 239,111. Map 49.
Leigh, mun. bor. and par., S.W. Lancashire, 21 m. N.E. of Liverpool; pop. 45,313. Map 39.
Leigh, par. and vil., in co. and 4½ m. S.W. of Worcester; pop. 1094. Map 57.
Leighlinbridge, town, in co. and 8 m. S. of Carlow; on r. Barrow. Map 95.
Leigh-on-Sea, ward of Southend-on-Sea, co. bor., Essex. Map 72.
Leighterton, vil., W. Gloucestershire, 4½ m. E.S.E. of Wotton-under-Edge. Map 68.
Leighton Buzzard, urb. dist., par. and mkt. tn., Beds, 7 m. N.W. of Dunstable; pop. 7031. Map 71.
Leintwardine, par. and vil., Herefordshire, 7 m. W. of Ludlow; pop. 846. Map 56.

Leiston, urb. dist. and par., E. Suffolk, 4 m. E. of Saxmundham; pop. 4184. Map 63.
Leith, parl. bur. and seaport, forming 4 wards of city of Edinburgh. Map 10.
Leith Hill, Surrey, 4 m. S.W. of Dorking; alt. 965 ft., highest point in co. Map 78.
Leitholm, vil., Berwickshire, 5 m. N.W. of Coldstream. Map 12.
Leixlip, town, N. co. Kildare, par. partly also in co. Dublin; pop. 1528. Map 93.
Lelant, par. and vil., Cornwall, 3¼ m. S.E. of St Ives; pop. 1167. Map 90.
Lenham, town and par., Kent, 9 m. E.S.E. of Maidstone; pop. 1947. Map 82.
Lennoxtown, town, Stirlingshire, 11½ m. N. of Glasgow; pop. 2182. Map 8.
Lenzie, *q.s.* par. and S. sub. of Kirkintilloch, Dumbartonshire, 6¼ m. N.E. of Glasgow; pop. 3432. Map 8.
Leominster, mun. bor., in co. and 12 m. N. of Hereford; pop. 5707. Map 56.
Lepton, urb. dist., W.R. Yorkshire, 4¾ m. S.E. of Huddersfield; pop. 3322. Map 32.
Lerwick, seaport and cap. of Shetland Islands; pop. 4221.
Lesbury, par. and vil., Northumberland, 3½ m. E.S.E. of Alnwick; pop. 988. Map 17.
Leslie, market town and par., Fifeshire, 4¼ m. W. of Markinch; pop. 2477. Map 6.
Lesmahagow, par. and vil., Lanarkshire, 6 m. S.W. of Lanark; pop. 12,931. Map 14.
Letchworth, urb. dist., par., N. Herts, 2 m. N.E. of Hitchin; pop. 14,454. Map 61.
Letham, vil., Angus, 5 m. E. of Forfar. Map 7.
Letterkenny, urb. dist., mid co. Donegal, 25 m. S.W. of Londonderry; pop. 2194. Map 92.
Leuchars, par. and vil., Fifeshire, 5 m. N.W. of St Andrews; pop. 2765. Map 7.
Leven, town, Fifeshire, 5¾ m. N.E. of Thornton Junct.; pop. 7411. Map 10.
Leven, Loch, in co. Kinross, about 8½ m. in circuit; max. depth 83 ft. Map 6.
Lever, Little, urb. dist., Lancashire, 3 m. S.E. of Bolton; pop. 4944. Map 31.
Levisham, par. and vil., N.R. Yorkshire, 5 m. N.E. of Pickering; pop. 118. Map 29.
Lewes, mun. bor., par., mkt. tn. and co. tn. of Sussex, 8 m. N.E. of Brighton; pop. 10,785. Map 81.
Lewis, isl., largest and most northerly of Outer Hebrides; pop. 28,378. Map 2.
Leybourne, par. and vil., Kent, 5 m. N.W. of Maidstone; pop. 335. Map 82.
Leyburn, par. and small market town, N.R. Yorkshire, 16 m. W. of Northallerton; pop. 868. Map 27.
Leyland, urb. dist. and par., N. Lancashire, 4½ m. S. of Preston; pop. 10,573. Map 30.
Leysdown, par. and vil., Sheppey, Kent, 6 m. N.N.E. of Faversham; pop. 221. Map 83.
Leyton, urb. dist. and par., Essex, 1 m. N. of Stratford; pop. 128,317. Map 71.
Lezayre, par. and vil., Isle of Man, 1¾ m. S.W. of Ramsey; pop. 2643. Map 24.
Libberton, par. and vil., Lanarkshire, 5 m. N.W. of Biggar; pop. 541. Map 15.
Lichfield, mun. bor., city and co. in itself, 17 m. S.E. of Stafford; pop. 8508. Map 48.
Liddesdale, the valley of Liddel Water, Roxburghshire. Map 16.
Liddington, par. and vil., Wiltshire, 3 m. S.E. of Swindon; pop. 396. Map 69.
Lidgate, par. and vil., W. Suffolk, 6½ m. S.E of Newmarket; pop. 268. Map 62.
Lifford, town, Donegal, 15 m. S.W. of Londonderry; pop. 419. Map 93.
Lifton, par. and vil., Devonshire, 3½ m. E. of Launceston; pop. 830. Map 88.
Lilliesleaf, par. and vil., Roxburghshire, 5 m. S.E. of Selkirk; pop. 246. Map 16.
Limavady, market town and urb. dist., in co. and 12½ m. N.E. of Londonderry; pop. 2667. Map 93.
Limerick, co. bor., city and co. in itself, 62 m. N. of Cork; pop. 39,690, parl. bor. pop. 62,403. Map 94.
Limpsfield, par. and vil., Surrey, 7 m. W. of Sevenoaks; pop. 2522. Map 80.
Lincoln, parl. and co. bor., co. town and co. in itself, 33 m. N.E. of Nottingham; pop. 66,246. Map 42.
Lindfield, par. and vil., E. Sussex, 1½ m. N.E. of Hayward's Heath; pop. 3061. Map 81.
Lindisfarne (or **Holy Island**), insular par., Northumberland, 6 m. N. of Belford; pop. 586. Map 17.
Lingdale, vil., N.R. Yorkshire, 4 m. E. of Guisborough. Map 28.
Lingfield, par. and vil., Surrey, 3½ m. N. of East Grinstead; pop. 4905. Map 80.
Linlithgow, royal and mun. bur. and co. tn., W. Lothian, 17½ m. W. of Edinburgh; pop. 3666. Map 9.
Linnhe, Loch, sea loch, Argyllshire and Inverness-shire, extends 21 m. N.E. from Firth of Lorne. Map 12.
Linslade, urb. dist., Buckinghamshire, 2 m. N.W. of Leighton Buzzard; pop. 2433. Map 70.
Linthwaite, urb. dist., W.R. Yorkshire, on S. side of Huddersfield; pop. 9689. Map 31.
Lintrathen, par. and vil., Angus, 10 m. W.N.W. of Forfar; pop. 500. Map 3.
Liphook, vil., Hants, 8½ m. N.E. of Petersfield. Map 79.
Lisburn, town and urb. dist., cos. Antrim and Down, 7½ m. S.W. of Belfast. Map 93.
Liskeard, mun. bor. and par., Cornwall, 15 m. S.W. of Launceston; pop. 4266. Map 88.
Lismore, market town, Waterford, 14½ m. W. of Dungarvan; pop. 1474. Map 95.
Liss, par. and vil., Hants, 4 m. N.E. of Petersfield; pop. 2322. Map 79.
Listowel, urb. dist. and par., co. Kerry, 20 m. N.E. of Tralee; pop. 4392. Map 94.
Litcham, par. and vil., Norfolk, 8 m. N.E. of Swaffham; pop. 575. Map 52.
Litherland, urb. dist. and par., S.W. Lancashire, 1½ m. N. of Bootle; pop. 15,967. Map 38.
Littleborough, urb. dist., par. and town, S.E. Lancashire, 3¼ m. N.E. of Rochdale; pop. 12,028. Map 32.
Little Crosby, urb. dist., Lancashire, adjacent to Great Crosby; pop. 1086. Map 38.
Littlehampton, urb. dist. and par., Sussex, 3½ m. S. of Arundel; pop. 10,181. Map 79.
Littleport, par. and vil., Isle of Ely, Cambridgeshire, 4½ m. N.E. of Ely; pop. 604. Map 61.
Litton Cheney, par. and vil., Dorsetshire, 5 m. S.E. of Bridport; pop. 253. Map 86.
Liverpool, parl. and co. bor., city and seaport, Lancashire, 31 m. W. of Manchester; pop. 855,539. Map 38.
Liversedge, par., in Spenborough urb. dist., W.R. Yorkshire, 6½ m. S.E. of Bradford. Map 32.
Liverton, par. and vil., N.R. Yorkshire, 6½ m. E. of Guisborough; pop. 1057. Map 28.
Lizard, The, peninsula, S.W. Cornwall, most southerly promontory in England. Map 90.
Llanarmon, par. and vil., Denbighshire, 5 m. S.E. of Ruthin; pop. 1157. Map 38.
Llanarth, par. and vil., Cardiganshire, 4 m. S.W. of Aberayron; pop. 1592. Map 54.
Llanbadarnfawr, vil., Cardiganshire, 1 m. E. of Aberystwyth. Map 54.
Llanbeblig, par. coterminous with bor. of Carnarvon; pop. 8469. Map 36.
Llanberis, small town and par., in co. and 9 m. S.E. of Carnarvon; pop. 2373. Map 36.

Llanbister, par. and vil., Radnorshire, 9¼ m. W.S.W. of Knighton ; pop. 638. Map 56.

Llanbradach, vil., 9½ m. N. of Cardiff. Map 67.

Llandaff, par. and city, S.E. Glamorganshire, 2 m. N.W. of Cardiff ; pop. 13,277. Map 74.

Llanddarog, par. and vil., in co. and 6 m. S. of Carmarthen ; pop. 953. Map 65.

Llandilo, urb. dist. and par., in co. and 15 m. N.E. of Carmarthen ; pop. 1886. Map 65.

Llandilo Abercowin, par., Carmarthenshire, 3 m. S.E. of St Clears ; pop. 46. Map 65.

Llandissilio, par., Pembrokeshire, 2 m. N. of Clynderwen ; pop. 346. Map 64.

Llandovery, mun, bor., Carmarthenshire, 11¼ m. N.E. of Llandilo ; pop. 1980. Map 55.

Llandowror, par. and vil., Carmarthenshire, 2 m. S.W. of St Clears ; pop. 194. Map 65.

Llandre, ry. sta., Cardiganshire, 6 m. N.E. of Aberystwyth. Map 45.

Llandrillo, par. and vil., Merionethshire, 5 m. S.W. of Corwen ; pop. 556. Map 45.

Llandrindod Wells, urb. dist., Radnorshire, 5¾ m. N.N.E. of Builth Road ; pop. 2925. Map 56.

Llandudno, Carnarvonshire, 3½ m. N.E. of Conway, wtg. place and lifeboat sta. ; pop. 13,677. Map 37.

Llandybie, par. and vil., Carmarthenshire, 4½ m. S. of Llandilo ; pop. 8019. Map 65.

Llandyfriog, par. and ham., Cardiganshire, 1½ m. E.N.E. of Newcastle Emlyn ; pop. 777. Map 54.

Llandyssul, par. and town, Cardiganshire, 7 m. E. of Newcastle Emlyn ; pop. 2688. Map 54.

Llanelly, mun. bor., par. and spt., Carmarthenshire, 10½ m. N.W. of Swansea ; pop. 38,393. Map 65.

Llanerch-Aeron, par., Cardiganshire, 2 m. S.E. of Aberayron ; pop. 133. Map 54.

Llanerchymedd, small town and par., Anglesey, 6½ m. S. of Amlwch ; pop. 782. Map 36.

Llanfaes, locality, Breconshire, in Brecknock borough. Map 55.

Llanfair Caereinion, mkt. tn. and par., Montgomeryshire, 8 m. W. of Welshpool ; pop. 1715. Map 46.

Llanfairfechan, urb. dist. and par., Carnarvonshire, 7¾ m. S.W. of Conway ; pop. 3162. Map 37.

Llanfair Orllwyn, par., Cardiganshire, 3½ m. E. of Newcastle Emlyn ; pop. 438. Map 54.

Llanfihangel Aberbythych, par., Carmarthenshire, 3 m. S.W. of Llandilo ; pop. 1336. Map 65.

Llanfihangel-geneu'r-glynn, vil., Cardiganshire, 4 m. N.E. of Aberystwyth. Map 44.

Llanfihangel Ystrad, par. and ham., Cardiganshire, 6 m. S.E. of Aberayron ; pop. 813. Map 54.

Llanfrechfa, Upper, urb. dist., Monmouthshire, 2½ m. N.W. of Caerleon ; pop. 4482. Map 67.

Llanfyllin, mun. bor., Montgomeryshire, on r. Cain ; pop. 1449. Map 46.

Llanfyrnach, par. and vil., Pembrokeshire, 15 m. S.S.E. of Cardigan ; pop. 960. Map 65.

Llangadock, par. and town, Carmarthenshire, 6 m. N.E. of Llandilo ; pop. 1545. Map 55.

Llangammarch Wells, vil. and sta., Breconshire, 7 m. W.S.W. of Builth. Map 55.

Llangathen, par. and vil., Carmarthenshire, 3 m. W. of Llandilo ; pop. 619. Map 65.

Llangattock, par. and vil., Breconshire, near Crickhowell ; pop. 921. Map 67.

Llangefni, urb. dist., Anglesey, 13 m. S. of Amlwch ; pop. 1782. Map 36.

Llangennech, par. and vil., Carmarthenshire, 4 m. E.N.E. of Llanelly ; pop. 2817. Map 65.

Llangerniew, par. and vil., Denbighshire, on r. Elwy, 7 m. N.E. of Llanrwst ; pop. 817. Map 37.

Llangollen, mkt. tn., urb. dist. and par., Denbighshire, 22 m. S.W. of Chester ; pop. 2937. Map 46.

Llangorse, par. and vil., Breconshire, 6 m. E. of Brecon ; pop. 360 (**L. Lake**, 5 m. in circuit). Map 56.

Llangranog, coast par. and vil., Cardiganshire, 4 m. N.E. of Aberporth ; pop. 763. Map 54.

Llangunilo, par. and sta., Radnorshire, 5¾ m. W. of Knighton ; pop. 452. Map 56.

Llangunnor, par. and vil., in co. and 1 m. E. of Carmarthen ; pop. 830. Map 65.

Llangurig, par. and vil., Montgomeryshire, 4½ m. S.W. of Llanidloes ; pop. 1015. Map 55.

Llangybi, par. and vil., Carnarvonshire, 2½ m. N.W. of Afon Wen sta. ; pop. 455. Map 44.

Llangybi, par. and vil., Cardiganshire, 4 m. N.E. of Lampeter ; pop. 252. Map 54.

Llanidloes, mun. bor. and par., Montgomeryshire, 10½ m. S.W. of Newtown ; pop. 2356. Map 45.

Llanilar, par. and vil., Cardiganshire, 6 m. S.E. of Aberystwyth ; pop. 585. Map 54.

Llanllwchaiarn, coast par., Cardiganshire, 1¾ m. S. of New Quay ; pop. 407. Map 54.

Llanllyfni, par. and vil., in co. and 7 m. S. of Carnarvon ; pop. 4417. Map 36.

Llanpumpsaint, par. and vil., in co. and 5½ m. N. of Carmarthen ; pop. 686. Map 65.

Llanrhaiadr-ym-Mochnant, par., Montgomeryshire ; pop. 741. Map 41.

Llanrhystyd, vil., Cardiganshire, 8 m. S. of Aberystwyth. Map 54.

Llanrhystyd Road, ry. sta., Cardiganshire, 2½ m. S.S.E. of Aberystwyth. Map 54.

Llanrug, par., in co. and 3 m. E. of Carnarvon ; pop. 2504. Map 36.

Llanrwst, mkt. tn. and urb. dist., Denbighshire, 12 m. S. of Llandudno Jun. ; pop. 2366. Map 37.

Llansaintfraed-in-Elvel, par., Radnorshire, 4½ m. N.E. of Builth ; pop. 218. Map 56.

Llansantffraid, par. and ham., Cardiganshire, 4½ m. N.E. of Aberayron ; pop. 946. Map 54.

Llansantffraid Glan Conway, par. and vil., Denbighshire, 2 m. S.E. of Conway ; pop. 1268. Map 37.

Llanstadwell, par. and vil., Pembrokeshire, 2 m. E. of Milford ; pop. 1059. Map 64.

Llanstephan, par. and vil., in co. and 7 m. S.S.W. of Carmarthen ; pop. 1131. Map 65.

Llantarnam, urb. dist., Monmouthshire, 3½ m. N. of Newport ; pop. 7284. Map 67.

Llantrisant, par. and mkt. tn., S.E. Glamorganshire, 10½ m. N.W. of Cardiff ; pop. 21,946. Map 66.

Llanwnda, par., in co. and 4¼ m. S. of Carnarvon pop. 1855. Map 36.

Llanwnda, par. and ham., Pembrokeshire, 2½ m. N.W. of Fishguard ; pop. 2751. Map 64.

Llanwrda, par. and vil., E. Carmarthenshire, 4 m. S.W. of Llandovery ; pop. 460. Map 55.

Llanwrtyd, urb. dist. and par., Breconshire, 10 m. S.W. of Builth ; pop. 742. Map 55.

Llanymynech, par. and vil., Shropshire, 6 m. S.S.W. of Oswestry ; pop. 557. Map 46.

Llwchwr (Loughor), urb. dist., Glamorganshire, 8 m. N.W. of Swansea ; pop. 26,595. Map 65.

Llyswen, par., Breconshire, 7 m. S.W. of Hay ; pop. 219. Map 56.

Loanhead, town, Midlothian, 5 m. S.W. of Edinburgh ; pop. 3940. Map 10.

Lochawe, vil. and ry. sta., Argyllshire, 2½ m. W. of Dalmally. Map 12.

Lochboisdale, ham. in S.E. of South Uist Island, Outer Hebrides, on Loch Boisdale. Map 2.

Loch Buy, ham. and loch in S. of Mull Island, Argyllshire. Map 12.

Lochcarron, or **Jeantown**, par. and vil., Ross and Crom., 5 m. N.E. of Stromeferry ; pop. 1066. Map 2.

Lochearnhead, vil., Perthshire, at head of Loch Earn, 13 m. N.W. of Callander. Map 12.

Lochee, par. and dist., Angus, in N.W. of Dundee; pop. 2613. Map 7.

Lochgelly, town, police bur. and par., Fifeshire, $7\frac{1}{2}$ m. N.E. of Dunfermline; pop. 9297. Map 10.

Lochgilphead, police bur. and par., Argyllshire, 2 m. N. of Ardrishaig; pop. 939. Map 12.

Lochgoilhead, par., Argyllshire, 18 m. (by water) N.W. of Greenock; pop. 974. Map 12.

Loch Indail, sea loch, on S. of Islay, Argyllshire. Map 12.

Lochington, par. and vil., E.R. Yorkshire, 8 m. S. of Great Driffield; pop. 448. Map 35.

Lochinver, vil., with pier, Sutherlandshire, on Loch Inver; pop. 260. Map 2.

Lochluichart, ham. and ry. sta., Ross and Cromarty, 17 m. W. of Dingwall. Map 2.

Lochmaben, royal and mun. bur., in co. and 9 m. N. of Dumfries; pop. 1014. Map 15.

Lochmaddy, seaport vil., North Uist, Outer Hebrides, on W. shore of Loch Maddy; pop. 219. Map 2.

Lochranza, *q.s.* par. and vil., on N. of Arran Island, Buteshire; pop. 1038. Map 12.

Lochwinnoch, par. and town, Renfrewshire, $8\frac{1}{2}$ m. S.W. of Paisley; pop. 4224. Map 8.

Lockerbie, market tn. and police bur., Dumfriesshire, $14\frac{1}{2}$ m. N.E. of Dumfries; pop. 2574. Map 20.

Lockerley, par. and vil., Hants, 5 m. N.W. of Romsey; pop. 563. Map 76.

Loddington, par. and vil., Northamptonshire, 4 m. W. of Kettering; pop. 333. Map 60.

Loddiswell, par. and vil., Devonshire, on r. Avon, 3 m. N.W. of Kingsbridge; pop. 641. Map 89.

Loddon, market town and par., Norfolk, $10\frac{1}{2}$ m. S.E. of Norwich; pop. 1019. Map 53.

Loftus, urb. dist., N.R. Yorkshire, 4 m. S.E. of Saltburn; pop. 7631. Map 28.

Logierait, par. and vil., Perthshire, $\frac{3}{4}$ m. W. of Ballinluig sta., 8 m. N.W. of Dunkeld; pop. 1680. Map 6.

Lomond, Loch, largest loch in Scotland, 24 m. long, 5 m. broad, greatest depth 623 feet. Map 12.

Londesborough, par., E.R. Yorkshire; pop. 297. Map 34.

London, capital of England, in co. of London; administrative co. pop. 4,396,821, Greater London 8,202,818. Map 71.

London Colney, eccl. dist. and vil., on S.E. border of Hertfordshire, 3 m. S.E. of St Albans. Map 71.

Londonderry, city, spt. and co. bor., N.W. co. Londonderry, on W. side of r. Foyle; pop. 45,165. Map 93.

Longbenton, urb. dist. and par., Northumberland, $3\frac{1}{2}$ m. N.E. of Newcastle; pop. 14,072. Map 23.

Longborough, par. and vil., Gloucestershire, 3 m. S.W. of Moreton-in-the-Marsh; pop. 423. Map 58.

Longbridge Deverill, par., Wiltshire, 3 m. S. of Warminster; pop. 624. Map 75.

Long Buckby, par. and vil., in co. and 10 m. N.W. of Northampton; pop. 2430. Map 59.

Long Compton, par. and vil., S. Warwickshire, 5 m. S.E. of Shipston-on-Stour; pop. 525. Map 58.

Long Eaton, urb. dist. and par., Derbyshire, 7 m. S.E. of Derby; pop. 22,339. Map 49.

Longford, market town and urb. dist., co. Longford, 76 m. N.W. of Dublin; pop. 3760. Map 93.

Longforgan, par. and vil., E. Perthshire, $5\frac{1}{2}$ m. S.W. of Dundee; pop. 2032. Map 7.

Longformacus, par. and vil., Berwickshire, $6\frac{1}{2}$ m. N.W. of Duns; pop. 250. Map 11.

Longframlington, par. and vil., Northumberland, $5\frac{1}{2}$ m. E. of Rothbury; pop. 531. Map 17.

Longhirst, par. and vil., Northumberland, $2\frac{1}{2}$ m. N.E. of Morpeth; pop. 417. Map 17.

Longhope, par. and vil., in co. and 9 m. W. of Gloucester; pop. 964. Map 68.

Longhorsley, eccl. par. and vil., Northumberland, 6 m. N.W. of Morpeth; pop. 652. Map 17.

Longhoughton, par. and vil., Northumberland, $5\frac{1}{2}$ m. N.E. of Alnwick; pop. 600. Map 17.

Long Itchington, par. and vil., Warwickshire, $6\frac{1}{2}$ m. E. of Leamington; pop. 1227. Map 59.

Long, Loch, sea loch, Argyllshire and Dumbartonshire, strikes 17 m. N. and N.E. from Firth of Clyde at Holy Loch to Arrochar. Map 12.

Long Marton, par., Westmorland, $3\frac{1}{2}$ m. N.W. of Appleby; pop. 619. Map 21.

Long Melford, par. and town, W. Suffolk, 3 m. N.W. of Sudbury; pop. 2635. Map 62.

Longniddry, vil., East Lothian, $4\frac{3}{4}$ m. N.W. of Haddington; pop. 382. Map 10.

Longnor, par. and vil., Staffordshire, on r. Manifold, 6 m. S.E. of Buxton; pop. 444. Map 40.

Long Preston, par. and vil., W.R. Yorkshire, 4 m. S.E. of Settle; pop. 690. Map 34.

Longridge, urb. dist., N. Lancashire, 7 m. N.E. of Preston; pop. 4158. Map 31.

Long Riston, par. and vil., E.R. Yorkshire, 6 m. N.E. of Beverley; pop. 278. Map 35.

Longstock, par. and vil., Hants, 1 m. N. of Stockbridge; pop. 413. Map 76.

Long Sutton, urb. dist., Holland, Lincolnshire, $4\frac{1}{2}$ m. E.S.E. of Holbeach; pop. 2902. Map 51.

Long Sutton, par. and vil., Somersetshire, $2\frac{3}{4}$ m. S.W. of Somerton; pop. 698. Map 86.

Longton, par. and vil., N. Lancashire, 5 m. S.W. of Preston; pop. 2543. Map 30.

Longton, par., Staffordshire, within the parl. and co. bor. of Stoke-upon-Trent; pop. 37,812. Map 39.

Longtown, market town, Cumberland, on r. Esk, 9 m. N.W. of Carlisle. Map 21.

Long Whatton, par. and vil., Leicestershire, $4\frac{1}{2}$ m. N.W. of Loughborough; pop. 604. Map 49.

Looe, East, urb. dist., fishing port, Cornwall, $8\frac{3}{4}$ m. S. of Liskeard; pop. 2878. Map 88.

Looe, West, coast tn., Cornwall, 7 m. S. of Liskeard, opposite East Looe. Map 88.

Loose, par. and vil., Kent, $2\frac{1}{2}$ m. S. of Maidstone; pop. 1910. Map 82.

Lorton, par. and vil., Cumberland, 4 m. S.E. of Cockermouth; pop. 326. Map 20.

Lossiemouth, seaport town and police bur., Morayshire, $5\frac{1}{2}$ m. N.E. of Elgin; pop. 3014. Map 3.

Lostwithiel, mun. bor., par. and market town, Cornwall, $3\frac{1}{4}$ m. S. of Bodmin Road sta.; pop. 1325. Map 91.

Loughborough, mun. bor. and par., Leicestershire, $10\frac{1}{2}$ m. N.W. of Leicester; pop. 26,945. Map 49.

Loughor, Glamorganshire. *See* Llwchwr. Map 65.

Loughrea, market town and par., co. Galway, on Lough Rea, 9 m. S.S.E. of Attymon; pop. 2778. Map 94.

Loughton, urb. dist. and par., Essex, 5 m. S.W. o Epping; pop. 7390. Map 72.

Louth, mun. bor., mkt. town and par., Lincolnshire, $30\frac{3}{4}$ m. N.E. of Lincoln; pop. 9678. Map 43.

Louth, par. and vil., co. Louth, on r. Glyde, 6 m. S.W. of Dundalk; pop. 3039. Map 93.

Lowdham, par. and vil., in co. and $7\frac{1}{2}$ m. N.E. of Nottingham; pop. 985. Map 41.

Lowestoft, mun. bor. and seaport, E. Suffolk, 10 m. S. of Yarmouth; pop. 41,768. Map 53.

Lowick, par. and vil., Northumberland, 7 m. N.W. of Belford; pop. 874. Map 17.

Lowick, par., Lancashire, 5 m. N. of Ulverston; pop. 313. Map 25.

Loxley, par. and vil., Warwickshire, 4 m. S.E. of Stratford-on-Avon; pop. 221. Map 58.

Loyal, Loch, on E. side of Ben Loyal, Sutherlandshire, 5 m. S.E. of Tongue. Map 3.

Lubenham, par. and vil., Leicestershire, $3\frac{1}{2}$ m. W. of Market Harborough; pop. 597. Map 49.

Lubnaig, Loch, Perthshire, 4 m. N.W. of Callander; length 4 m. Map 5.

Lucan, small town, par. and seat, in co. and 7 m. W. of Dublin; pop. 1121. Map 93.
Luccombe, par. and vil., Somersetshire, 4 m. S.W. of Minehead; pop. 581. Map 85.
Luddenden Foot, urb. dist. and par., W.R. Yorkshire, 6 m. W. of Halifax; pop. 2881. Map 31.
Luddington, par. and vil., Lincolnshire, on r. Old Don, 4½ m. N.E. of Crowle; pop. 431. Map 34.
Ludgershall, par. and vil., Buckinghamshire, 6 m. S.E. of Bicester; pop. 240. Map 70.
Ludgershall, par. and vil., E. Wiltshire, 6½ m. N.W. of Andover; pop. 1090. Map 76.
Ludgvan, urb. dist., Cornwall, 3 m. N.E. of Penzance; pop. 1897. Map 90.
Ludlow, mun. bor., Salop, 27¼ m. S. of Shrewsbury; pop. 5642. Map 57.
Luffenham, North and **South,** 2 pars., Rutlandshire, 7 m. S.E. of Oakham; pop. 441 and 317. Map 50.
Lugwardine, par. and vil., in co. and 3 m. E.N.E. of Hereford; pop. 686. Map 57.
Lulworth, West, coast par. and vil., Dorsetshire, 8½ m. S.W. of Wareham; pop. 797. Map 87.
Lumphanan, par. and vil., in co. and 7 m. W. of Aberdeen; pop. 852. Map 3.
Lunan, par., Angus, and ry. sta. (**L. Bay**), 5 m. S.S.W. of Montrose; pop. 327. Map 7.
Lundin Links, place and summer resort, Fifeshire, 7¼ m. E. of Thornton Junction. Map 7.
Lurgan, town and urb. dist., co. Armagh, 20 m. S.W. of Belfast; pop. 12,553. Map 93.
Lurgashall, par. and vil., W. Sussex, 4 m. N.W. of Petworth; pop. 610. Map 79.
Lusk, par. and vil., in co. and 14 m. N. of Dublin; pop. 3742. Map 93.
Luss, par. and vil., Dumbartonshire, W. side of Loch Lomond; pop. 670. Map 12.
Luton, mun. bor., par. and market town, Bedfordshire, 4½ m. E.S.E. of Dunstable; pop. 68,526. **Map 71.**
Lutterworth, par. and market town, Leicestershire, 7¼ m. N.E. of Rugby; pop. 2092. Map 59.
Lybster, par. and vil., Caithness-shire, 13 m. S.W. of Wick; pop. 1726. Map 3.
Lydbury North, par. and vil., Salop, 2½ m. S.E. of Bishop's Castle; pop. 710. **Map 46.**
Lydd, mun. bor., market town and par., Kent, 3½ m. S.W. of New Romney; pop. 2778. Map 83.
Lydford, par. and vil., S.W. Devonshire, 6¾ m. N. of Tavistock; pop. 2232. Map 88.
Lydham, par., seat and vil., Shropshire, 2 m. N.E. of Bishop's Castle; pop. 146. Map 46.
Lydney, par. and town, Gloucestershire, 8 m. N.E. of Chepstow; pop. 3775. Map 68.
Lye and Wollescote, urb. dist., Worcestershire, 1½ m. E. of Stourbridge; pop. 12,245. Map 57.
Lyme Regis, mun. bor., seaport and par., Dorsetshire, 6½ m. S.E. of Axminster; pop. 2620. Map 86.
Lyminge, par. and vil., Kent, 4 m. N. of Hythe; pop. 1398. Map 83.
Lymington, mun. bor., spt. and par., Hampshire, 20 m. S.W. of Southampton; pop. 5157. Map 77.
Lymm, urb. dist. and par., Cheshire, 5 m. E.S.E. of Warrington; pop. 5642. Map 39.
Lympstone, par. and vil., Devonshire, 8½ m. S.E. of Exeter; pop. 1068. Map 89.
Lyndhurst, par. and vil., Hampshire, New Forest, 9 m. W.S.W. of Southampton; pop. 2562. Map 77.
Lynmouth, vil., Devonshire, 18 m. N.E. of Barnstaple. Map 84.
Lynton, urb. dist. and watering place, Devonshire, 18 m. N.E. of Barnstaple; pop. 2012. Map 85.
Lyon, River, Perthshire, rises near W. border of co. and flows 34 m. E. through Glen Lyon. Map 5.
Lyonshall, par. and vil., Herefordshire, 2 m. E. of Kington; pop. 692. Map 56.
Lytham St Anne's, urb. dist., Lancashire, 7 m. S.E. of Blackpool; pop. 25,760. Map 30.
Lythe, par. and vil., N.R. Yorkshire, 3½ m. N.W. of Whitby; pop. 931. Map 29.
MABLETHORPE, urb. dist., watering place and par., Lincs, 13 m. E.S.E. of Louth; pop. 3928. Map 43.
Macclesfield, mun. bor. and par., Cheshire, on r. Bollin, 17½ m. S. of Manchester; pop. 34,902. Map 39.
Macduff, bur., spt. and *q.s.* par., Banffshire, on r. Deveron, opposite Banff; pop. 3276. Map 3.
Machrihanish, watering place, Kintyre, Argyllshire, 6 m. W. of Campbeltown. Map 12.
Machynlleth, par. and urb. dist., Montgomeryshire, 20¾ m. N.E. of Aberystwyth; pop. 1892. Map 45.
Macroom, market town and par., co. Cork, 24½ m. W. of Cork; pop. 3556. Map 94.
Madron, urb. dist. and par., Cornwall, 1½ m. N.N.W. of Penzance; pop. 3276. Map 90.
Maenclochog, par. and vil., Pembrokeshire, 10 m. E.S.E. of Fishguard; pop. 419. Map 64.
Maesteg, urb. dist., Glamorganshire, 8 m. N.W. of Bridgend; pop. 25,552. Map 66.
Maghera, market town and par., co. Londonderry, 49½ m. N.W. of Belfast; pop. 6584. Map 93.
Magherafelt, market town and par., co. Londonderry, 42½ m. N.W. of Belfast; pop. 3977. Map 93.
Magor, par. and vil., Monmouthshire, 7½ m. E. of Newport; pop. 522. Map 67.
Maidenhead, mun. bor. and market town, Berkshire, 11½ m. N.E. of Reading; pop. 17,520. Map 78.
Maiden Newton, par. and vil., Dorsetshire, 7½ m. N.W. of Dorchester; pop. 597. Map 87.
Maids Moreton, par. and vil., Buckinghamshire, 1 m. N.E. of Buckingham; pop. 351. Map 59.
Maidstone, mun. bor. and co. town of Kent, 41½ m. S.E. of London; pop. 42,259. Map 82.
Malahide, coast par., abbey ruins and vil., in co. and 9 m. N. of Dublin; pop. 1174. Map 93.
Malborough, par. and vil., Devonshire, 3¼ m. S.W. of Kingsbridge; pop. 630. Map 89.
Maldens and Coombe, The, urb. dist., Surrey, 9¾ m. S.W. of Waterloo, London; pop. 23,412. Map 71.
Maldon, mun. bor., market town and r. port, Essex, 17 m. S.W. of Colchester; pop. 6559. Map 72.
Malham, par., vil. and tourist resort, W.R. Yorkshire, 5¼ m. E. of Settle; pop. 142. Map 31.
Malin, coast vil., co. Donegal, 25 m. N. of Londonderry; pop. 129. Map 93.
Mallaig, vil., W. Inverness-shire, at entrance to Loch Nevis, 41¾ m. W. of Fort William. Map 2.
Malling, West, market town and par., Kent, 5 m. W.N.W. of Maidstone; pop. 2365. Map 82.
Mallow, market town and par., co. Cork, on r. Blackwater, 21 m. N.W. of Cork; pop. 5369. Map 94.
Mallwyd, urb. dist., Merionethshire, on r. Dyfi; pop. 679. Map 45.
Malmesbury, mun. bor. and market town, Wiltshire, 16 m. N.W. of Swindon; pop. 2334. Map 68.
Malpas, market town and par., in S.W. Cheshire, 13½ m. S.E. of Chester; pop. 1098. Map 38.
Maltby, urb. dist., W.R. Yorkshire, 6 m. E. of Rotherham; pop. 10,013. Map 41.
Malton, urb. dist. and par., N.R. Yorkshire, 21 m. N.E. of York; pop. 4418. Map 28.
Malvern, Great, urb. dist., in co. and 8½ m. S.W. of Worcester; pop. 15,632. Map 57.
Malvern Wells, par. and vil., Worcestershire, 2½ m. S. of Great Malvern; pop. 1815. Map 57.
Mamore, Gap of, mtn. pass, co. Donegal, 8 m. N.N.W. of Buncrana. Map 92.
Manaccan, par. and vil., Cornwall, 6½ m. S.W. of Falmouth; pop. 350. Map 90.
Manaton, par. and vil., Devonshire, 3½ m. S. of Moreton Hampstead; pop. 387. Map 89.

Manby, par. and vil., Lindsey, Lincolnshire, $4\frac{1}{2}$ m. E.S.E. of Louth; pop. 137. Map 43.

Manchester, parl. and co. bor., city, par. and see of Bishop, S.E. Lancashire, 31 m. E. of Liverpool; pop. 766,333. Map 39.

Manea, par. and vil., Isle of Ely, Cambridgeshire, 10 m. N.W. of Ely; pop. 1463. Map 51.

Man, Isle of, in Irish Sea; area 141,263 acres; pop. 60,284. Capital, Douglas. Map 24.

Mangotsfield, urb. dist., Gloucestershire, 5 m. N.E. of Bristol; pop. 11,251. Map 68.

Manningtree, market town and par., Essex, 8 m. N.E. of Colchester; pop. 870. Map 73.

Manorbier, coast par. and vil., in co. and $5\frac{1}{2}$ m. E.S.E. of Pembroke; pop. 656. Map 64.

Manorcunningham, vil., co. Donegal, 5 m. E. of Letterkenny; pop. 115. Map 93.

Manorhamilton, town, co. Leitrim, $23\frac{1}{2}$ m. E. of Sligo; pop. 1013. Map 93.

Manorowen, coast par., Pembrokeshire, $1\frac{1}{2}$ m. S.W. of Fishguard; pop. 194. Map 64.

Mansergh, par., Westmorland, 2 m. N. of Kirkby Lonsdale; pop. 180. Map 26.

Mansfield, mun. bor., mkt. tn. and par., Notts, 16 m. N. of Nottingham; pop. 46,075. Map 41.

Mansfield Woodhouse, urb. dist. and par., Notts, $1\frac{1}{2}$ m. N. of Mansfield; pop. 13,707. Map 41.

Mapledurham, par. and vil., Oxon, $3\frac{1}{2}$ m. N.W. of Reading; pop. 541. Map 70.

Mapledurwell, par. and vil., Hampshire, 3 m. S.E. of Basingstoke; pop. 209. Map 78.

Marazion, watering place and seaport, Cornwall, 3 m. E. of Penzance; pop. 1114. Map 90.

March, urb. dist., Cambridgeshire, $14\frac{1}{2}$ m. E. of Peterborough; pop. 11,276. Map 51.

Marchington, par. and vil., Staffordshire, $3\frac{1}{2}$ m. S.E. of Uttoxeter; pop. 504. Map 48.

Marden, par. and vil., Kent, 10 m. E.S.E. of Tonbridge; pop. 2484. Map 82.

Maree, Loch, Ross and Cromarty, 19 m. N.W. of Achnasheen. Map 2.

Maresfield, par. and vil., E. Sussex, 2 m. N. of Uckfield; pop. 3610. Map 81.

Margate, mun. bor., par. and pop. seaside resort, Kent, 4 m. N.N.W. of Ramsgate; pop. 31,312. Map 83.

Marhamchurch, par. and vil., Cornwall, 2 m. S.S.E. of Bude Haven; pop. 464. Map 84.

Market Bosworth, par. and market town, Leicestershire, 8 m. N.E. of Nuneaton; pop. 886. Map 49.

Market Deeping, par. and town, Kesteven, Lincolnshire, 7 m. S.S.E. of Bourne; pop. 888. Map 50.

Market Drayton, par., urb. dist. and mkt. tn., Shropshire, 18 m. N.E. of Shrewsbury; pop. 4749. Map 47.

Market Harborough, urb. dist. and par., in co. and 16 m. S.E. of Leicester; pop. 9312. Map 49.

Market Lavington, par. and vil., Wiltshire, $5\frac{1}{2}$ m. S. of Devizes; pop. 904. Map 75.

Market Rasen, urb. dist., mkt. tn. and par., in co. and $13\frac{1}{2}$ m. N.E. of Lincoln; pop. 2048. Map 42.

Market Warsop, urb. dist. and par., Nottinghamshire, 5 m. N.E. of Mansfield; pop. 7238. Map 41.

Market Weighton, market town and par., E.R. Yorkshire, 10 m. N.W. of Beverley; pop. 1717. Map 34.

Market Weston, par. and vil., W. Suffolk, 9 m. S.E. of Thetford; pop. 213. Map 62.

Markinch, police bur., Fifeshire, $4\frac{1}{2}$ m. E. of Leslie; pop. 1988. Map 10.

Marks Tey, par. and vil., Essex, 5 m. W.S.W. of Colchester; pop. 585. Map 73.

Marlborough, mun. bor., Wiltshire, on r. Kennet, 11 m. S. of Swindon; pop. 3492. Map 76.

Marlesford, par. and vil., E. Suffolk, 4 m. S.E. of Framlingham; pop. 379. Map 63.

Marloes, par. and vil., Pembrokeshire, 7 m. W. of Milford Haven; pop. 316. Map 64.

Marlow, urb. dist., mkt. tn., par. and seat, Bucks, 5 m. N.W. of Maidenhead; pop. 5087. Map 70.

Marple, urb. dist. and par., Cheshire, 9 m. S.E. of Manchester; pop. 7390., Map 39.

Marrick, par. and vil., N.R. Yorkshire, $6\frac{1}{2}$ m. W.S.W. of Richmond; pop. 172. Map 27.

Marsden, urb. dist. and par., W.R. Yorkshire, 7 m. S.W. of Huddersfield; pop. 5729. Map 31.

Marsden, coast vil., Durham, $2\frac{1}{2}$ m. S.E. of South Shields. Map 23.

Marshfield, market town and par., Gloucestershire, $11\frac{1}{2}$ m. E. of Bristol; pop. 1030. Map 68.

Marsh Gibbon, par. and vil., Buckinghamshire, $3\frac{1}{2}$ m. E. of Bicester; pop. 521. Map 70.

Marske, par., N.R. Yorkshire, $2\frac{1}{2}$ m. S.E. of Redcar; pop. 3547. Map 28.

Martham, par. and vil., Norfolk, 9 m. N.W. of Yarmouth; pop. 1335. Map 53.

Martin, par. and vil., Hampshire, 6 m. N.W. of Fordingbridge; pop. 384. Map 77.

Martin, vil. and ry. sta., Kent, 4 m. N.E. of Dover. Map 83.

Martindale, par., Westmorland, 10 m. S.W. of Penrith; pop. 195. Map 25.

Martlesham, par. and vil., E. Suffolk, $1\frac{1}{2}$ m. S.W. of Woodbridge; pop. 676. Map 63.

Martock, par. and vil., Somersetshire, 7 m. N.W. of Yeovil; pop. 2065. Map 86.

Marton, par. and vil., Warwickshire, $6\frac{3}{4}$ m. N.E. of Leamington; pop. 392. Map 59.

Marton, par. and vil., N.R. Yorkshire, 3 m. S.S.E. of Middlesbrough; pop. 1062. Map 28.

Maryborough (Port Laoighise), mkt. and co. tn., Leix co., 51 m. S.W. of Dublin; pop. 3272. Map 95.

Maryhill, municipal ward in N.W. of city of Glasgow. Map 8.

Maryport, urb. dist., mkt. tn. and spt., Cumberland, $5\frac{1}{4}$ m. N.E. of Workington; pop. 10,182. Map 20.

Masham, urb. dist., par. and mkt. tn., N.R. Yorkshire, 8 m. N.W. of Ripon; pop. 1995. Map 27.

Massingham, Great and **Little,** 2 pars., Norfolk, 11 m. N.E. of King's Lynn; pop. 726 and 235. Map 52.

Matlock, urb. dist. and par., 17 m. N.W. of Derby pop. **(The Matlocks)** 10,599. Map 40.

Matlock Bath, urb. dist. and par., Derbyshire, 1 m. S. of Matlock. Map 40.

Matterdale, par., Cumberland, 8 m. E. of Keswick; pop. 245. Map 21.

Mauchline, small town and par., Ayrshire, $9\frac{1}{2}$ m. S.E. of Kilmarnock; pop. 2357. Map 12.

Maughold, par. and vil., Isle of Man, $3\frac{1}{2}$ m. S.E. of Ramsey; pop. 3481. Map 24.

Mawdesley, par. and vil., Lancashire, 8 m. N.W. of Wigan; pop. 1280. Map 30.

Maxton, par. and vil., Roxburghshire, 7 m. S.W. of Kelso; pop. 357. Map 16.

Maxwelltown, Kirkcudbrightsh., part of Dumfries. Map 20.

Maybole, market town, police bur. and par., Ayrshire, 9 m. S.W. of Ayr; pop. of par. 4210. Map 12.

Mayfield, par. and vil., Staffordshire, 2 m. S.W. of Ashbourne; pop. 1232. Map 40.

Mayfield, town and par., E. Sussex, 8 m. S. of Tunbridge Wells; pop. 2880. Map 81.

Maynooth, town, co. Kildare, 15 m. W. of Dublin; pop. 886. Map 95.

Mealsgate, vil., Cumberland, $5\frac{3}{4}$ m. S.W. of Wigton. Map 20.

Measham, par. and vil., Leicestershire, 8 m. N.W. of Market Bosworth; pop. 2425. Map 49.

Medbourne, par. and vil., Leicestershire, 6 m. N.E. of Market Harborough; pop. 380. Map 50.

Medina, r., Isle of Wight, flowing 12 m. N. to the Solent. Map 77.

Medmenham, par. and vil., Buckinghamshire, 3 m. S.W. of Marlow; pop. 425. Map 70.

Medomsley, par. and vil., Durham, 2¼ m. N.N.E. of Consett; pop. 6522. Map 22.

Medstead, par. and vil., Hampshire, 4¼ m. S.W. of Alton; pop. 776. Map 79.

Medway, r., Sussex and Kent, flowing 70 m. to the Thames. Map 80.

Meeth, par. and vil., Devonshire, 2½ m. N. of Hatherleigh; pop. 202. Map 84.

Meifod, par. and vil., Montgomeryshire, 5 m. N.W. of Welshpool; pop. 1226. Map 46.

Meigle, par. and vil., Perthshire, 1¼ m. S.E. of Alyth; pop. 808. Map 7.

Meikleour, vil., Perthshire, 4 m. S. of Blairgowrie. Map 6.

Melbourn, par. and vil., in co. and 10 m. S.W. of Cambridge; pop. 1294. Map 61.

Melbourne, par. and vil., E.R. Yorkshire, 4 m. S.W. of Pocklington; pop. 365. Map 34.

Melbourne, town and par., in co. and 7½ m. S.E. of Derby; pop. 3467. Map 49.

Melchbourne, par. and vil., Bedfordshire, 5 m. S.E. of Higham Ferrers; pop. 164. Map 60.

Meldon, par. and vil., Northumberland, 5 m. W.S.W. of Morpeth; pop. 134. Map 17.

Melksham, urb. dist. and market town, Wiltshire, 6¼ m. S. of Chippenham; pop. 3881. Map 75.

Melling, vil., N. Lancashire, 1¼ m. N.W. of Wennington Junction. Map 26.

Mellis, par. and vil., E. Suffolk, 3½ m. S.W. of Diss; pop. 390. Map 62.

Melmerby, par. and vil., Cumberland, 8½ m. N.E. of Penrith; pop. 219. Map 21.

Melrose, market town and par., Roxburghshire, 3¾ m. S.E. of Galashiels; pop. 2052. Map 16.

Melsonby, par. and vil., N.R. Yorkshire, 5½ m. N.E. of Richmond; pop. 458. Map 27.

Meltham, urb. dist. and par., W.R. Yorkshire, 5 m. S.W. of Huddersfield; pop. 5051. Map 31.

Melton Constable, par. and vil., Norfolk, 5½ m. S.W. of Holt; pop. 1034. Map 52.

Melton Mowbray, urb. dist., par. and market town, in co. and 14 m. N.E. of Leicester; pop. 10,437. Map 49.

Melvich, vil., Sutherlandshire, 17 m. W. of Thurso. Map 3.

Menai Bridge, urb. dist., Anglesey, 4 m. S.W. of Beaumaris; pop. 1675. Map 36.

Menstrie, q.s. par. and vil., Clackmannanshire, 4 m. N.W. of Alloa; vil. pop. 774. Map 9.

Meole Brace, par. and vil., Shropshire, 1½ m. S. of Shrewsbury; pop. 2259. Map 46.

Meonstoke, par. and vil., Hants, 4 m. N.E. of Bishops Waltham; pop. 445. Map 77.

Mere, town and par., Wiltshire, 4 m. N.E. of Gillingham; pop. 1847. Map 75.

Mereworth, par. and vil., Kent, 7 m. W.S.W. of Maidstone; pop. 706. Map 82.

Meriden, par. and vil., Warwickshire, 5½ m. N.W. of Coventry; pop. 848. Map 58.

Merrion, vil., in co. and 4 m. S.W. of Pembroke. Map 64.

Mersea Island, Essex, 8 m. S.E. of Colchester; **M. East** pop. 205, **M. West** pop. 2067. Map 73.

Mersey, r. Cheshire and Lancashire, flows 70 m. to the Irish Sea. Map 38.

Merstham, par. and vil., Surrey, 2 m. N.N.E. of Redhill; pop. 3597. Map 80.

Merthyr Tydfil, co. bor., Glamorganshire, 22 m. N.W. of Cardiff; pop. 71,099. Map 66.

Merton and Morden, urb. dist., Surrey, 7½ m. S.W. of Waterloo sta., London; pop. 41,228. Map 71.

Methil, seaport vil. and q.s. par., Fifeshire, 1 m. S.W. of Leven; pop. of par. 12,295. Map 10.

Methley, urb. dist., W.R. Yorkshire, 7 m. S.E. of Leeds; pop. 4606. Map 33.

Methven, par. and vil., Perthshire, 7¾ m. W. of Perth; pop. 1772. Map 6.

Methwold, par. and vil., Norfolk, 3½ m. S.E. of Stoke Ferry; pop. 1195. Map 52.

Mevagissey, fishing town and par., Cornwall, 5 m. S. of St Austell; pop. 1745. Map 91.

Mexborough, urb. dist. and par., W.R. Yorkshire, 5½ m. N.E. of Rotherham; pop. 15,856. Map 41.

Micheldever, par. and vil., Hampshire, 8½ m. N.E. of Winchester; pop. 958. Map 76.

Michelmersh, par. and vil., Hants, 3½ m. N. of Romsey; pop. 1109. Map 76.

Mickleton, par. and vil., N.R. Yorkshire, 2 m. S.E. of Middleton-in-Teesdale; pop. 520. Map 22.

Mickletown, eccl. par., W.R. Yorkshire, 7½ m. S.E. of Leeds; pop. 3293. Map 33.

Mid Calder, par. and vil., Midlothian, 10 m. S.W. of Edinburgh; vil. pop. 634. Map 9.

Middlebie, par. and vil., Dumfriesshire, 6 m. N.E. of Annan; pop. 1547. Map 20.

Middleham, par. and vil., N.R. Yorkshire, 2½ m. S.E. of Leyburn; pop. 652. Map 27.

Middlesbrough, parl. and co. bor. and par., N.R. Yorks, 3 m. E. of Stockton; pop. 138,489. Map 28.

Middleton, mun. bor., mkt. tn. and par., S.E. Lancashire, 3½ m. W. of Oldham; pop. 29,189. Map 31.

Middleton, par. and vil., Westmorland, 5 m. N. of Kirkby Lonsdale; pop. 209. Map 26.

Middleton, par. and vil., N. Lancashire, 4½ m. S.W. of Lancaster; pop. 188. Map 30.

Middleton Cheney, par. and vil., Northamptonshire, 2½ m. N.E. of Banbury; pop. 1093. Map 59.

Middleton-in-Teesdale, market town and par., Durham, 9 m. N.W. of Barnard Castle; pop. 1977. Map 22.

Middleton-on-the-Wolds, par., vil. and seat, E.R. Yorks, 8 m. N.W. of Beverley; pop. 628. Map 35.

Middleton Tyas, par. and vil., N.R. Yorkshire, 5 m. N.E. of Richmond; pop. 423. Map 27.

Middlewich, urb. dist. and par., Cheshire, 5½ m. S.E. of Northwich; pop. 5458. Map 39.

Midgley, urb. dist., W.R. Yorkshire, 4½ m. N.W. of Halifax; pop. 1882. Map 32.

Midhurst, par. and market town, Sussex, 9 m. E.S.E. of Petersfield; pop. 1890. Map 79.

Midlem, vil., N. Roxburghshire, 3½ m. E. of Selkirk; pop. 98. Map 16.

Midsomer Norton, urb. dist. and par., Somersetshire, 10 m. S.W. of Bath; pop. 7490. Map 75.

Milborne Stileham, par., Dorsetshire; pop. 157. Map 87.

Mildenhall, par. and vil., Wiltshire, 1½ m. E. of Marlborough; pop. 457. Map 69.

Mildenhall, market town and par., W. Suffolk, 12 m. N.W. of Bury St Edmunds; pop. 3370. Map 62.

Milford, eccl. par. and vil., Surrey, 1½ m. S.W. of Godalming; pop. 1927. Map 78.

Milford Haven, urb. dist. and seaport, in co. and 6 m. W.N.W. of Pembroke; pop. 10,116. Map 64.

Milford-on-Sea, coast par. and vil., Hants, 3½ m. S.W. of Lymington; pop. 1876. Map 77.

Millbrook, eccl. dist., par. and vil., Cornwall, 2 m. S.W. of Devonport; pop. 1959. Map 88.

Millom, urb. dist. and par., Cumberland, 6 m. S.W. of Broughton-in-Furness; pop. 7406. Map 25.

Millport, watering place and police bur., Buteshire, 24 m. S.W. of Greenock; pop. 2083. Map 12.

Millstreet, market town, Cork, 19¾ m. W. of Mallow Junction; pop. 1069. Map 94.

Milnathort, market town, Kinross-shire, 1¼ m. N.E. of Kinross Junction; pop. 1207. Map 6.

Milngavie, q.s. par. and town, Dumbartonshire, 7 m. N.W. of Glasgow; town pop. 5056. Map 8.

Milnrow, urb. dist. and par., S.E. Lancashire, 2 m. E.S.E. of Rochdale; pop. 8624. Map 31.
Milnthorpe, par. and market town, Westmorland, 7 m. N. of Carnforth; pop. 1025. Map 26.
Milton, urb. dist., Hants, on Christchurch Bay; pop. 5299. Map 77.
Milton Abbas, par. and vil., Dorsetshire, 6 m. S.W. of Blandford; pop. 578. Map 87.
Milton Abbot, par. and vil., Devonshire, 6 m. N.W. of Tavistock; pop. 619. Map 88.
Milton Ernest, par. and vil., in co. and 4½ m. N.W. of Bedford; pop. 340. Map 60.
Milton Regis, urb. dist., Kent, on N.W. side of Sittingbourne; pop. 7481. Map 82.
Miltown Malbay, market town and watering place, co. Clare, 27 m. W. of Ennis; pop. 995. Map 94.
Milverton, par. and market town, Somersetshire, 6¼ m. W. of Taunton; pop. 1393. Map 86.
Minchinhampton, par. and town, Gloucestershire, 3½ m. S.E. of Stroud; pop. 3722. Map 68.
Minehead, urb. dist. and market town, Somersetshire, 8 m. W.N.W. of Watchet; pop. 6315. Map 85.
Minshull Vernon, par., Cheshire, 4½ m. N.W. of Crewe; pop. 295. Map 39.
Minto, par. and vil., Roxburghshire, 6 m. N.E. of Hawick; pop. 382. Map 16.
Mirfield, urb. dist. and par., W.R. Yorkshire, 4¾ m. N.E. of Huddersfield; pop. 12,099. Map 32.
Missenden, Great, par. and vil., Buckinghamshire, 9 m. S.S.E. of Aylesbury; pop. 2882. Map 70.
Missenden, Little, par. and vil., Buckinghamshire, 2 m. S.E. of Great Missenden; pop. 1518. Map 70.
Misterton, par. and vil., Notts, on Chesterfield Canal, 5 m. N.W. of Gainsborough; pop. 1668. Map 42.
Mitcham, mun. bor., Surrey, on r. Wandle, 2¼ m. S.E. of Wimbledon; pop. 56,856. Map 71.
Mitcheldean, par. and vil., Gloucestershire, 5½ m. S.E. of Ross; pop. 624. Map 68.
Mitchelstown, market town, co. Cork, 12 m. N. of Fermoy; pop. 2268. Map 94.
Mobberley, par. and vil., Cheshire, 2¾ m. N.E. of Knutsford; pop. 1550. Map 39.
Mochdre, par., Montgomeryshire, 3 m. S.W. of Newtown; pop. 371. Map 46.
Modbury, small town and par., Devonshire, 3½ m. S.E. of Ivybridge; pop. 1103. Map 89.
Moffat, watering place, Dumfriesshire, 2 m. N.E. of Beattock; town pop. 2006. Map 15.
Mold, par., urb. dist. and market town, Flintshire, on r. Alyn, 6 m. S. of Flint; pop. 5133. Map 38.
Molesey, urb. dist., Surrey, 3 m. S.W. of Kingston-on-Thames; pop. 8460. Map 78.
Molton, North, par. and vil., Devonshire, 2¾ m. N.E. of South Molton; pop. 993. Map 85.
Molton, South, mun. bor. and market town, Devonshire, 10½ m. S.E. of Barnstaple; pop. 2831. Map 85.
Monaghan, par., urb. dist. and co. town of Monaghan, 52 m. S.W. of Belfast; pop. 6923. Map 93.
Monasterevin, small market town and par., in co. and 6¾ m. W. of Kildare; pop. 2010. Map 95.
Moniaive, vil. and ry. sta., Dumfriesshire, 7 m. S.W. of Thornhill; pop. 573. Map 14.
Monifieth, town, Angus, 2 m. N.E. of Broughty Ferry; pop. of par. 2984. Map 7.
Monkleigh, par. and vil., Devonshire, 3 m. N.W. of Torrington; pop. 324. Map 84.
Monmouth, mun. bor., par. and co. tn., Monmouthshire, 19 m. S. of Hereford; pop. 4731. Map 67.
Montacute, par. and vil., Somersetshire, 4 m. W. of Yeovil; pop. 739. Map 86.
Montgomery, mun. bor., par. and co. tn., Montgomeryshire, 6¼ m. S. of Welshpool; pop. 918. Map 46.
Montrose, parl., royal and mun. bur. and par., Angus, 90 m. N.E. of Edinburgh; pop. 10,196. Map 3.
Monyash, par. and vil., Derbyshire, 5 m. W. of Bakewell; pop. 350. Map 40.
Monzie, eccl. par. and vil., Perthshire, 3 m. N. by E. of Crieff; pop. 447. Map 6.
Moorfoot Hills, chiefly in S.E. of Midlothian; greatest alt. 2136 ft. Map 12.
Moorsholm, par., N.R. Yorkshire, 5 m. E.S.E. of Guisborough; pop. 582. Map 28.
Morar, dist. and ry. sta., Inverness-shire. **Loch M.** is deepest loch in Scotland. Map 2.
Morchard Bishop, par. and vil., Devonshire, 6½ m. N.W. of Crediton; pop. 894. Map 85.
Morda, vil., Shropshire, 1½ m. S. of Oswestry. Map 46.
Morebattle, par. and vil., Roxburghshire, 7 m. S. by E. of Kelso; pop. 238. Map 16.
Morecambe and Heysham, mun. bor. and watering place, N. Lancs, 3½ m. N.W. of Lancaster; pop. 24,586. Map 26.
Moreton Hampstead, town and par., Devonshire, 12¼ m. N.W. of Newton Abbot; pop. 1636. Map 89.
Moreton-in-the-Marsh, market town and par., Glos., 4½ m. N. of Stow-on-the-Wold; pop. 1442. Map 58.
Moreton Pinkney, par. and vil., Northamptonshire, 8 m. W. of Towcester; pop. 362. Map 59.
Moreton Say, par. and vil., Shropshire, 3 m. W. of Market Drayton; pop. 847. Map 47.
Morham, par., East Lothian, 3 m. S.E. of Haddington; pop. 204. Map 10.
Morley, mun. bor. and par., W.R. Yorkshire, 5 m. S.W. of Leeds; pop. 23,397. Map 32.
Morpeth, mun. bor. and par., Northumberland, 16½ m. N. by W. of Newcastle; pop. 7390. Map 17.
Morriston, vil. and ry. stas., Glamorganshire, in N.E. suburbs of Swansea. Map 66.
Mortehoe, par. and vil., Devonshire, 5 m. S.W. of Ilfracombe; pop. 1515. Map 84.
Mortimer, vil. and ry. sta., Berkshire, 7½ m. S.W. of Reading. Map 78.
Mortimers Cross, ham., Herefordshire, 5½ m. N.W. of Leominster. Map 56.
Mortlake, par., Surrey, Barnes urb. dist., 1½ m. N.E. of Richmond; pop. 19,502. Map 71.
Morton, par. and vil., Kesteven, Lincolnshire, 3 m. N. of Bourne; pop. 790. Map 50.
Morville, par. and vil., Shropshire, 3 m. W.N.W. of Bridgnorth; pop. 366. Map 47.
Moss, par. and ry. sta., W.R. Yorkshire, 7 m. N. of Doncaster; pop. 278. Map 34.
Moss Bank, vil., Prescot par., S.W. Lancashire, 1½ m. N.W. of St Helens. Map 38.
Mossend, tn., Lanarksh., 2 m. N. of Motherwell. Map 9.
Mossley, mun. bor., Lancashire, 2½ m. N. of Stalybridge; pop. 12,041. Map 40.
Mostyn, vil., Whitford par., Flintshire, 3¼ m. N.W. of Holywell. Map 38.
Motcombe, par. and vil., Dorsetshire, 1½ m. N.W. of Shaftesbury; pop. 1143. Map 87.
Motherwell and Wishaw, town, Lanarkshire, 2½ m. N.E. of Hamilton; pop. 64,708. Map 9.
Mottingham, par. and vil., Kent, 1 m. S. of Eltham; pop. 1804. Map 80.
Mottisfont, par. and vil., Hampshire, 4 m. N.W. of Romsey; pop. 516. Map 76.
Mottistone, par. and vil., Isle of Wight, 6½ m. S.W. of Newport; pop. 105. Map 77.
Mottram, urb. dist. and par., Cheshire, 3 m. W.N.W. of Glossop; pop. 2636. Map 40.
Moulton, par. and vil., in co. and 4 m. N.E. of Northampton; pop. 1347. Map 60.
Moulton, par. and vil., Holland, Lincolnshire, 4 m. E. of Spalding; pop. 2345. Map 51.
Mountain Ash, urb. dist. and mining town, Glamorgan, 37½ m. S.E. of Aberdare; pop. 38,381. Map 66.

Mount Bellew, small market town, co. Galway, 9 m. N. of Woodlawn; pop. 254. Map 94.

Mountmellick, market town with ry. sta., N. Leix co., 6 m. N. of Maryborough; pop. 2341. Map 95.

Mountnessing, par. and vil., Essex, 3 m. N.E. of Brentwood; pop. 1118. Map 72.

Mountrath, small market town and ry. sta., W. Leix co., 8 m. S.W. of Maryborough; pop. 1259. Map 95.

Mouswald, par. and vil., Dumfriesshire, 7 m. S.E. of Dumfries; pop. 466. Map 20.

Moville, small market town, co. Donegal, 19 m. N. by E. of Londonderry; pop. 1016. Map 93.

Moy, vil. and ry. sta., Inverness-shire, 14¾ m. S.E. of Inverness. Map 3.

Moy, small market town and ry. sta., co. Tyrone, 6¼ m. N. of Armagh; pop. 471. Map 93.

Much Birch, par. and vil., in co. and 6½ m. S. of Hereford; pop. 410. Map 66.

Much Hadham, par. and vil., Hertfordshire, 4 m. S.W. of Bishop's Stortford; pop. 1570. Map 72.

Much Wenlock, par. and ry. sta., Shropshire; pop. 1991. Map 47.

Muckhart, par., Perthshire, on r. Devon, 16 m. S.E. of Crieff; pop. 599. Map 6.

Mucking, par. and vil., Essex, on Thames, 4 m. N. of Tilbury; pop. 561. Map 72.

Muggleswick, par. and vil., Durham, 4 m. W. of Consett; pop. 368. Map 22.

Muirkirk, town and par., Ayrshire, 8 m. N.E. of Cumnock; pop. of par. 4726. Map 14.

Muker, par. and small town, N.R. Yorkshire, 5 m. N.W. of Askrigg; pop. 547. Map 27.

Mulbarton, par. and vil., Norfolk, 4 m. S.S.W. of Norwich; pop. 469. Map 53.

Mull, Isle of, Argyllshire, 7 m. W. of Oban; Isl. pop. 3389. Map 12.

Mullingar, co. town and par., co. Westmeath, 50 m. N.W. of Dublin; pop. of par. 8673. Map 93.

Mullion, par. and vil., Cornwall, 5½ m. N. of Lizard Head; pop. 954. Map 90.

Mumbles, seaport vil., Glamorganshire, 5 m. S.W. of Swansea. Map 66.

Muncaster, par. and vil., Cumberland, 1½ m. E. of Ravenglass; pop. 530. Map 25.

Mundesley, coast par. and vil., Norfolk, 5 m. N.E. of N. Walsham; pop. 1161. Map 53.

Munlochy, vil., Black Isle, Ross and Cromarty, 5½ m. S.W. of Fortrose; pop. 158. Map 3.

Murston, par. and vil., Kent, 1¼ m. N.E. of Sittingbourne; pop. 1603. Map 82.

Murthly, q.s. par., E. Perthshire, 4¼ m. S.E. of Dunkeld; pop. 739. Map 6.

Musgrave, Great, par., Westmorland, 4 m. N.W. of Kirkby Stephen; pop. 196. Map 26.

Musselburgh, parl. and mun. bur. and town, Midlothian, 6 m. E. of Edinburgh; pop. 16,996. Map 10.

Muthill, par. and vil., Perthshire, 3 m. S. of Crieff; pop. of par. 1287. Map 6.

Myddle, par. and vil., Shropshire, 7 m. N.W. of Shrewsbury; pop. 685. Map 46.

Mydroilin, vil., Cardigansh., 6 m. S. of Aberayron. Map 54.

Mynyddislwyn, urb. dist., Monmouthshire, 7 m. S.W. of Pontypool; pop. 16,201. Map 67.

Mytholmroyd, urb. dist. and par., N. div., W.R. Yorks, 1½ m. S.E. of Hebden Bridge; pop. 4467. Map 31.

NAAS, par. and urb. dist., co. Kildare, 20¼ m. S.W. of Dublin; pop. 3343. Map 95.

Naburn, par. and vil., E.R. Yorkshire, on r. Ouse, 4 m. S. of York; pop. 556. Map 34.

Nafferton, par. and vil., E.R. Yorkshire, 2 m. N.E. of Great Driffield; pop. 1237. Map 35.

Nailsea, par. and vil., Somersetshire, 8 m. W.S.W. of Bristol; pop. 1984. Map 74.

Nailsworth, urb. dist. and par., Gloucestershire, 4 m. S. of Stroud; pop. 3129. Map 68.

Nairn, mun. bur., par. and co. town of Nairnshire, 15½ m. E.N.E. of Inverness by rail; pop. 4201. Map 3.

Nannerch, par. and vil., Flintshire, 6½ m. N.W. of Mold; pop. 347. Map 38.

Nantlle, vil. and lake, in co. and 9 m. S.S.E. of Carnarvon. Map 36.

Nantwich, urb. dist. and par., Cheshire, 4 m. S.W. of Crewe; pop. 7132. Map 39.

Nantyglo and Blaina, urb. dist., Monmouthshire, 7½ m. S.W. of Abergavenny; pop. 13,190 Map 67.

Napton-on-the-Hill, par. and vil., Warwickshire, 3 m. E. of Southam; pop. 805. Map 59.

Narberth, urb. dist. and par., Pembrokeshire, 10½ m. N. of Tenby; pop. 1046. Map 64.

Narborough, par. and vil., in co. and 7 m. S.W. of Leicester; pop. 320. Map 49.

Naseby, par. and vil., Northamptonshire, 7 m. S.W. of Market Harborough; pop. 416. Map 59.

Nash, par. and vil., in co. and 5½ m. E. of Buckingham; pop. 237. Map 59.

Nash, par. and vil., Monmouthshire, 3½ m. S.E. of Newport; pop. 331. Map 67.

Nassington, par. and vil., Northamptonshire, 8 m. W.S.W. of Peterborough; pop. 491. Map 50.

Nateby, par. and vil., N. Lancashire, 2 m. S.W. of Garstang; pop. 305. Map 30.

Natland, par. and vil., Westmorland, 2 m. S. of Kendal; pop. 572. Map 26.

Naunton, par. and vil., Gloucestershire, 5 m. S.W. of Stow-on-the-Wold; pop. 404. Map 69.

Navan, urb. dist. and par., co. Meath, 16½ m. S.W. of Drogheda; pop. 3649. Map 93.

Navenby, par. and vil., Kesteven, in co. and 8¾ m. S. of Lincoln; pop. 824. Map 42.

Naver, r., Sutherlandshire, flows 19 m. N. from Loch Naver to the Pentland Firth. Map 3.

Navestock, par. and vil., Essex, 6 m. N. of Romford; pop. 720. Map 72.

Nayland, par. and vil., W. Suffolk, 8½ m. S.E. of Sudbury; pop. 1273. Map 62.

Neagh, Lough, Ulster, largest fresh water lake in British Isles. Map 93.

Neasham, par. and vil., Durham, 4 m. S.E. of Darlington; pop. 323. Map 27.

Neath, mun. bor. and par., Glamorganshire, 8 m. S.E. of Swansea; pop. 33,322. Map 66.

Needham Market, market town and par., Suffolk, 7 m. N.W. of Ipswich; pop. 1349. Map 62.

Needingworth, vil., Huntingdonshire, 2 m. N.E. of St Ives. Map 61.

Needles, The, group of rocks at western extremity of Isle of Wight. Map 77.

Neilston, town and par., Renfrewshire, 10 m. S.W. of Glasgow by rail; town pop. 3499. Map 8.

Nelson, mun. bor. and par., N.E. Lancashire, 3½ m. N.E. of Burnley; pop. 38,306. Map 31.

Nenagh, urb. dist. and par., Tipperary, 27½ m. N.E. of Limerick; pop. 4517. Map 94.

Nenthall, vil., Cumberland, 2 m. E. of Alston. Map 22.

Nenthead, eccl. dist. and vil., Cumberland, 4 m. S.E. of Alston; pop. 780. Map 22.

Nenthorn, par. and vil., S.W. Berwickshire, on Eden Water; pop. 363. Map 16.

Ness, loch and r., Inverness-shire, on line of Caledonian Canal. Map 3.

Neston, urb. dist. and par., Cheshire, on Dee estuary, 12½ m. N.W. of Chester; pop. 5674. Map 38.

Netherbury, par. and vil., Dorsetshire, 12½ m. S.W. of Beaminster; pop. 1110. Map 86.

Nether Stowey, par. and vil., Somersetshire, 7 m. W.N.W. of Bridgwater; pop. 578. Map 74.

Nethybridge, vil., Inverness-shire, 5 m. S.S.W. of Grantown; pop. 478. Map 3.

Netley Marsh, par. and vil., Hampshire, 6 m. W. of Southampton; pop. 1396. Map 77.

Nettleham, par. and vil., Lindsey, in co. and 3 m. N.E. of Lincoln; pop. 381. Map 42.

Nevin, par. and town, Carnarvonshire, 6 m. N.W. of Pwllheli; pop. 1900. Map 36.

New Abbey, par. and vil., Kirkcudbrightshire, 7 m. S. of Dumfries; pop. 779. Map 20.

New Alresford, par., Hants, 6½ m. N.E. of Winchester; pop. 1709. Map 76.

Newark, mun. bor. and par., in co. and 18½ m. N.E. of Nottingham; pop. 18,055. Map 42.

New Barnet, eccl. par. and vil., S. Hertfordshire, 9¼ m. N.N.W. of London; pop. 4574. Map 71.

Newbiggin-by-the-Sea, urb. dist. and par., Northumberland, 7 m. N.E. of Morpeth; pop. 6904. Map 17.

Newbigging, vil., Lanarkshire, 3 m. S.E. of Carnwath. Map 10.

Newbigging, vil., Angus, 7½ m. N.E. of Dundee. Map 7.

Newbold-on-Avon, par. and vil., Warwickshire, 2 m. N.W. of Rugby; pop. 1699. Map 59.

Newborough, par. and vil., Staffordshire, 7 m. W.N.W. of Burton-on-Trent; pop. 496. Map 48.

New Bridge, vil., Monmouthshire, 5½ m. S.W. of Pontypool. Map 67.

Newbridge, place, Pembrokeshire, 3½ m. S. of Fishguard. Map 64.

Newbridge, urb. dist., in co. and 4½ m. N.E. of Kildare; pop. 2250. Map 95.

Newbridge-on-Wye, vil., Radnorshire, 7½ m. S.E. of Rhayader. Map 55.

New Brighton, ward of Wallasey co. bor., Cheshire, 4 m. N. of Birkenhead; watering pl. Map 38.

New Broughton, ham., Denbighshire, 1½ m. N.W. of Wrexham. Map 38.

New Buckenham, par. and vil., Norfolk, 4 m. S.E. of Attleborough; pop. 464. Map 53.

Newburgh, mun. bur. and par., Fifeshire, 7 m. N.W. of Ladybank Junction by rail; pop. 2152. Map 6.

Newburgh, eccl. dist. and ham., S.W. Lancashire, 5 m. N.E. of Ormskirk; pop. 554. Map 30.

Newburn, urb. dist., Northumberland, 5 m. W.N.W. of Newcastle; pop. 19,539. Map 23.

Newbury, mun. bor., Berkshire, on r. Kennet, 17 m. S.W. of Reading; pop. 13,336. Map 76.

Newby Bridge, vil., N. Lancashire, 5 m. N.W. of Cartmel. Map 25.

Newcastle, market town and par., in co. and 27½ m. S.W. of Limerick; pop. 2687. Map 94.

Newcastle, town, co. Down, 11 m. S.W. of Downpatrick; pop. 1765. Map 93.

Newcastle, Little, par. and vil., Pembrokeshire, 5½ m. S.S.E. of Fishguard; pop. 170. Map 64.

Newcastle Emlyn, urb. dist., Carmarthenshire, 9 m. E.S.E. of Cardigan; pop. 762. Map 54.

Newcastle-on-Tyne, city, co. bor. and spt., Northumberland, 268½ m. N. of London; pop. 283,145. Map 23.

Newcastleton, vil., Roxburghshire, 21 m. S.W. of Hawick; pop. 847. Map 16.

Newcastle-under-Lyme, mun. bor. and par., in co. and 16 m. N.N.W. of Stafford; pop. 23,246. Map 39.

Newchurch, par. and vil., Isle of Wight, 2½ m. N.W. of Sandown; pop. 707. Map 77.

New Cumnock, par. and town, Ayrshire, 5½ m. S.E. of Cumnock; pop. 1889. Map 14.

New Deer, par. and vil., Aberdeenshire, 13 m. W. of Peterhead; pop. 761. Map 3.

Newent, par. and market town, in co. and 8½ m. N.W. of Gloucester; pop. 2325. Map 57.

New Ferry, eccl. dist. in Birkenhead co. bor., Cheshire, on r. Mersey; pop. 11,244. Map 38.

New Forest, region, S.W. Hampshire; cap. Lyndhurst. Map 77.

Newgale, place, on coast of Pembrokeshire, 7 m. E.S.E. of St Davids. Map 64.

New Galloway, mun. bur. and town, in co. and 19 m. N. of Kirkcudbright; pop. 307. Map 19.

Newhaven, urb. dist. and par., E. Sussex, 9 m. E. of Brighton by rail; pop. 6790. Map 81.

New Holland, seaport, Lincolnshire, on r. Humber, 3½ m. N.E. of Barton-upon-Humber, opp. Hull. Map 35.

New Hutton, par., Westmorland, 3 m. E.S.E. of Kendal; pop. 246. Map 26.

Newick, par. and vil., E. Sussex, 7 m. N. of Lewes; pop. 965. Map 81.

New Inn, vil., in co. and 11 m. N.N.E. of Carmarthen. Map 65.

Newlyn, eccl. dist. and seaport, Cornwall, 1 m. S.W. of Penzance; pop. 3902. Map 90.

Newlyn, East, par. and vil., Cornwall, 7½ m. S.W. of St Columb; pop. 1097. Map 91.

Newmarket, town, with ry. sta., co. Cork, 5 m. N.W. of Kanturk; pop. 934. Map 94.

Newmarket, urb. dist. and racecourse, W. Suffolk, 14 m. E. of Cambridge; pop. 9753. Map 61.

New Mill, urb. dist., W.R. Yorkshire, 6 m. S.E. of Huddersfield; pop. 4538. Map 32.

New Mills, urb. dist. and par., Derbyshire, on r. Goyt, 6¼ m. N.W. of Chapel-en-le-Frith; pop. 8551. Map 40.

Newmilns, town and police bur., Ayrshire, 7 m. E. of Kilmarnock; pop. 3979. Map 14.

Newnham, urb. dist. and par., in co. and 11 m. S.W. of Gloucester by rail; pop. 1035. Map 68.

Newnham, ham. and ry. sta., Worcestershire, 3 m. N.E. of Tenbury. Map 57.

New Pitsligo, vil., Aberdeenshire, 4 m. W. of Strichen; pop. 1440. Map 3.

Newport, par., town and port, Pembrokeshire, 6¼ m. E.N.E. of Fishguard; pop. 1292. Map 64.

Newport, urb. dist. and par., Salop, 11½ m. W.S.W. of Stafford; pop. 3439. Map 47.

Newport, par. and vil., Essex, 3 m. S.W. of Saffron Walden; pop. 914. Map 61.

Newport, seaport, mun. bur. and q.s. par., Fifeshire, 2 m. N.E. of Wormit; pop. 3275. Map 7.

Newport, co. bor., spt. and par., Monmouthshire, 12 m. N.E. of Cardiff by rail; pop. 89,198. Map 74.

Newport, mun. bor. and par., cap. of Isle of Wight, 91 m. from London; pop. 11,313. Map 77.

Newport Pagnell, urb. dist. and par., in co. and 14 m. N.E. of Buckingham; pop. 3957. Map 60.

Newquay, urb. dist. and par., Cornwall, 11 m. N. of Truro; pop. 5958. Map 90.

New Quay, urb. dist. and seaport, Cardiganshire, 5 m. S.W. of Aberayron; pop. 1112. Map 54.

New Radnor, par. and vil., Radnorshire, 6 m. N.W. of Kington; pop. 368. Map 56.

New Romney, mun. bor., par. and Cinque port, Kent, 8 m. S.W. of Hythe; pop. 1786. Map 83.

New Ross, r. port and urb. dist., Wexford, 13 m. N.E. of Waterford; pop. 5009. Map 95.

Newry, seaport, par. and urb. dist., co. Down, 44¼ m. S. of Belfast by rail; pop. 11,963. Map 93.

Newton Abbot, urb. dist., Devonshire, 20¼ m. S. of Exeter by rail; pop. 15,003. Map 89.

Newton Arlosh, eccl. dist., Cumberland, near Moricambe Bay; pop. 358. Map 20.

Newton-by-the-Sea, par. and vil., Northumberland, 7½ m. N.E. of Alnwick; pop. 243. Map 17.

Newton Heath, town, S. Lancashire, forming N.E. portion of Manchester parl. bor. Map 39.

Newton in Makerfield, urb. dist. and par., S.W. Lancashire, 15¾ m. W. of Manchester; pop. 20,150. Map 39.

Newtonmore, vil., with ry. sta., Inverness-shire, 3 m. S.W. of Kingussie; pop. 884. Map 3.

Newton Reigny, par. and vil., Cumberland, 2½ m. N.W. of Penrith; pop. 165. Map 21.

Newton Stewart, police bur., Wigtownshire, 23½ m. E. of Stranraer; pop. 1914. Map 18.

Newton Tracey, par. and vil., Devonshire, 5 m. S.W. of Barnstaple; pop. 121. Map 84.

Newtown and Llanllwchaiarn, urb. dist., in co. and 7½ m. S.W. of Montgomery; pop. 5152. Map 46.

Newtownards, township and par., co. Down, 9 m. E. of Belfast; pop. 9587. Map 93.

Newtonbarry, market town, Wexford, 12 m. S. of Tullow; pop. 884. Map 95.

Newtown St Boswells, vil., Roxburghshire, 3½ m. S.E. of Melrose; pop. 518. Map 16.

Newtown Stewart, market town, Tyrone, 23¾ m. S.E. of Londonderry; pop. 1012. Map 93.

Newtyle, par. and vil., Angus, 11 m. N.W. of Dundee; pop. 883. Map 7.

Neyland, urb. dist. and seaport, Pembrokeshire, 3½ m. E. of Milford; pop. 2161. Map 64.

Nigg, par. and vil., Ross and Cromarty, 4 m. N.E. of Cromarty; pop. 867. Map 3.

Nocton, par. and vil., Kesteven, in co. and 7 m. S.E. of Lincoln; pop. 553. Map 42.

Norden, urb. dist. and par., Lancashire, 2 m. W.N.W. of Rochdale; pop. 4348. Map 31.

Normanby, par. and vil., N.R. Yorkshire, 4½ m. S.W. of Pickering; pop. 143. Map 28.

Normanby, par. and vil., Lindsey, Lincolnshire, 3½ m. N.E. of Market Rasen; pop. 281. Map 42.

Normanton, ham. and seat, N.E. vicinity of Southwell, Nottinghamshire. Map 41.

Normanton, urb. dist. and par., W.R. Yorkshire, 3 m. N.E. of Wakefield; pop. 15,684. Map 33.

Normanton-upon-Trent, par. and vil., Nottinghamshire, 3½ m. S.E. of Tuxford; pop. 275. Map 42.

Northallerton, urb. dist., par. and mkt. tn., N.R. Yorks, 14 m. S.E. of Darlington; pop. 4787. Map 27.

Northam, urb. dist., Devonshire, 1½ m. N.W. of Bideford; pop. 5561. Map 84.

Northampton, parl. and co. bor. and cap. of Northamptonshire, 65¾ m. N.W. of London by rail; pop. 92,314. Map 59.

North Berwick, mun. bur. and par., E. Lothian, 22½ m. E.N.E. of Edinburgh by rail; pop. 3473. Map 10.

North Burton, par. and vil., E.R. Yorkshire, 7 m. N.W. of Bridlington; pop. 420. Map 29.

North Cave, par. and vil., E.R. Yorkshire, 14½ m. W.N.W. of Hull; pop. 1019. Map 34.

North Chapel, par. and vil., W. Sussex, 5 m. N.N.W. of Petworth; pop. 732. Map 79.

North Coates, par. and vil., Lindsey, Lincolnshire, 9 m. N.N.E. of Louth; pop. 241. Map 43.

North Curry, par. and vil., W. Somersetshire, 6 m. E. of Taunton; pop. 1363. Map 86.

North Darley, urb. dist., Derbyshire, 6 m. S.E. of Bakewell; pop. 4093. Map 40.

Northfleet, urb. dist., Kent, on r. Thames, 21¾ m. S.E. of London; pop. 16,429. Map 80.

North Kelsey, par. and vil., Lindsey, Lincolnshire, 5 m. W. of Caistor; pop. 822. Map 42.

Northleach, par. and vil., Gloucestershire, 10 m. N.E. of Cirencester; pop. 611. Map 69.

North Leverton, par. and vil., Nottinghamshire, 5½ m. E. of East Retford; pop. 374. Map 42.

Northlew, par. and vil., Devonshire, 3½ m. S.W. of Hatherleigh; pop. 628. Map 84.

North Molton, par. and vil., Devonshire, 2¾ m. N.E. of South Molton; pop. 993. Map 85.

Northolt, par. and vil., Middlesex, 4½ m. E. of Uxbridge; pop. 904. Map 71.

Northowram, former urb. dist., W.R. Yorkshire, now included in Halifax; pop. 2425. Map 32.

Northrepps, par. and vil., Norfolk, 3 m. S.S.E. of Cromer; pop. 559. Map 53.

North Shields, town and seaport, Northumberland, now in Tynemouth mun. bor. Map 23.

North Somercotes, par. and vil., Lindsey, Lincolnshire, 8 m. N.E. of Louth; pop. 1031. Map 43.

Northwich, urb. dist., Cheshire, 9½ m. S.E. of Warrington; pop. 18,728. Map 39.

Northwick, ham., Gloucestershire, 5½ m. S.W. of Thornbury. Map 68.

Northwold, par. and vil., Norfolk, 6½ m. N.W. of Brandon; pop. 1105. Map 52.

Northwood, vil., Middlesex, 2¼ m. S.E. of Rickmansworth. Map 71.

Norton, par. and vil., Durham, 2 m. N. of Stockton; pop. 330. Map 23.

Norton, urb. dist., E.R. Yorkshire, opposite Malton; pop. 3934. Map 28.

Norton sub Hamdon, par. and vil., Somersetshire, 5½ m. W. of Yeovil; pop. 428. Map 86.

Norton St Philip, par. and vil., Somersetshire, 6 m. S. of Bath; pop. 448. Map 75.

Norwich, parl. and co. bor., par., city and co. town of Norfolk, 114 m. N.E. of London by rail; pop. 126,207. Map 53.

Nottingham, city, co. bor. and co. town of Nottinghamshire, 123½ m. N.W. of St Pancras, London, by rail; pop. 268,801. Map 49.

Nunburnholme, par. and vil., E.R. Yorkshire, 4 m. N.W. of Market Weighton; pop. 189. Map 34.

Nuneaton, mun. bor. and par., Warwickshire, 9 m. N.N.E. of Coventry; pop. 46,305. Map 49.

Nunnington, par. and vil., N.R. Yorkshire, 4½ m. S.E. Helmsley; pop. 278. Map 28.

Nursling, par. and vil., Hampshire, 5 m. W.N.W. of Southampton; pop. 655. Map 77.

Nutfield, par. and vil., Surrey, 2 m. E. of Redhill; pop. 1828. Map 80.

OADBY, urb. dist., in co. and 3½ m. S.E. of Leicester; pop. 4724. Map 49.

Oakengates, urb. dist., Salop, 13½ m. E. of Shrewsbury; pop. 11,189. Map 47.

Oakham, urb. dist. and co. town of Rutlandshire, 11½ m. W. of Stamford; pop. 3191. Map 50.

Oakhill, vil. and eccl. par., Somersetshire, 2½ m. N.E. of Shepton Mallet; pop. 92. Map 75.

Oakley, par. and vil., in co. and 4 m. N.W. of Bedford; pop. 337. Map 60.

Oakley, Great, par. and vil., Northamptonshire, 5 m. N. of Kettering; pop. 204. Map 60.

Oaksey, par. and vil., Wiltshire, 6 m. S.W. of Cirencester; pop. 308. Map 68.

Oakworth, urb. dist. and par., W.R. Yorkshire, 3 m. S.W. of Keighley; pop. 3984. Map 31.

Oban, mun. bur., seaport and q.s. par., Argyllshire, 101 m. N.W. of Glasgow; pop. 5759. Map 12.

Ockendon, South, par. and vil., Essex, 5½ m. S.E. of Romford; pop. 1432. Map 72.

Oddington, par., Gloucestershire, 2½ m. E. of Stow-on-the-Wold; pop. 388. Map 58.

Odiham, market town and par., N.E. Hampshire, 6½ m. E.S.E. of Basingstoke; pop. 2683. Map 78.

Offham, par. and vil., Kent, 3 m. S.E. of Wrotham; pop. 386. Map 80.

Ogmore and Garw, urb. dist., Glamorganshire, 7 m. N. of Bridgend; pop. 26,979. Map 66.

Okeford Fitzpaine, par. and vil., Dorsetshire, 7 m. N.W. of Blandford; pop. 652. Map 87.

Okehampton, mun. bor. and par., Devonshire, 25¾ m. W. of Exeter; pop. 3352. Map 84.

Oldbury, urb. dist. and par., Worcestershire, 5 m. N.W. of Birmingham; pop. 35,918. Map 48.

Oldcastle, market town and par., Meath, 12¾ m. N.W. of Kells; pop. 673. Map 93.

Oldham, parl. and co. bor. and par., Lancashire, 6 m. N.E. of Manchester; pop. 140,309. Map 31.

Old Meldrum, police bur., Aberdeenshire, 19 m. N.W. of Aberdeen; pop. 980. Map 3.

Old Woking, locality, Surrey, in Woking urb. dist. Map 78.

Ollerton, par. and town, Nottinghamshire, on r. Maun, 9 m. N.E. of Mansfield; pop. 676. Map 41.

Olney, par. and town, Buckinghamshire, 11 m. S.E. of Northampton; pop. 2651. Map 60.

Omagh, urb. dist., Tyrone, 34 m. S.E. of Londonderry; pop. 4836. Map 93.

Ombersley, par. and vil., Worcestershire, 3½ m. W. of Droitwich; pop. 2066. Map 57.

Onchan, or **Conchan,** par., Isle of Man, partly in town of Douglas. Map 24.

Onibury, par. and vil., Salop, 5 m. N.W. of Ludlow; pop. 405. Map 56.

Oranmore, par. and vil., in co. and 5½ m. E. of Galway; pop. 164. Map 94.

Orchy, Bridge of, place, with ry. sta., Argyllshire, 12 m. N.E. of Dalmally. Map 12.

Orford, par. and fishing vil., E. Suffolk, 5½ m. S.W. of Aldeburgh; pop. 818. Map 63.

Orleton, par. and vil., Herefordshire, 5 m. S.S.W. of Ludlow; pop. 505. Map 56.

Ormesby, 2 pars. and vil., Norfolk, 4 m. N. of Yarmouth; pop. 1449. Map 53.

Ormesby, par. and vil., N.R. Yorkshire, 3 m. S.E. of Middlesbrough; pop. 428. Map 28.

Ormes Head, Great, Carnarvonshire, has lighthouse, 325 ft. above high water, seen 24 m. Map 37.

Ormes Head, Little, headland, on coast of Carnarvonshire, 2½ m. E. of Llandudno. Map 37.

Ormiston, par. and vil., East Lothian, 12 m. E.S.E. of Edinburgh; pop. 1841. Map 10.

Ormskirk, urb. dist., mkt. tn. and par., S.W. Lancashire, 12 m. N.E. of Liverpool; pop. 17,121. Map 30.

Orpington, par. and vil., Kent, 2½ m. S.E. of Chislehurst; pop. 7047. Map 80.

Orrell, urb. dist., Lancashire, 3 m. W.S.W. of Wigan; pop. 6951. Map 39.

Orsett, par. and vil., Essex, 3½ m. N. of Tilbury; pop. 1530. Map 72.

Orton, market vil. and par., Westmorland, 8 m. S.W. of Appleby; pop. 798. Map 26.

Osborne, former royal residence, Isle of Wight, 1 m. S.E. of East Cowes. Map 77.

Ossett, mun. bor. and par., W.R. Yorkshire, 2½ m. W. of Wakefield; pop. 14,838. Map 32.

Oswaldkirk, par. and vil., N.R. Yorkshire, 3 m. S. of Helmsley; pop. 191. Map 28.

Oswaldtwistle, urb. dist., Lancashire, 3 m. E.S.E. of Blackburn; pop. 14,221. Map 31.

Oswestry, mun. bor. and par., Salop, 17 m. N.W. of Shrewsbury; pop. 9754. Map 46.

Otford, par. and vil., Kent, 3 m. N. of Sevenoaks; pop. 857. Map 80.

Othery, par. and vil., Somersetshire, 6½ m. S.E. of Bridgwater; pop. 416. Map 74.

Otley, urb. dist., market town and par., W.R. Yorkshire, 6 m. E. of Ilkley; pop. 11,020. Map 32.

Otterburn, par. and vil., Northumberland, 8 m. N.E. of Bellingham; pop. 350. Map 17.

Ottershaw, eccl. par. and vil., Surrey, 2½ m. S.S.W. of Chertsey; pop. 783. Map 78.

Otterton, par. and vil., Devonshire, 3½ m. S.W. of Sidmouth; pop. 581. Map 89.

Ottery St Mary, urb. dist. and par., Devonshire, 12 m. N.E. of Exeter; pop. 3713. Map 85.

Ottringham, par. and vil., E.R. Yorks, 13 m. E. of Hull; pop. 516. Map 35.

Oughterard, market town, in co. and 17 m. N.W. of Galway; pop. 601. Map 94.

Oughtibridge, eccl. dist., N.W. suburb of Sheffield, W.R. Yorkshire; pop. 2328. Map 40.

Oulton, par. and vil., Cumberland, 2 m. N.W. of Wigton; pop. 307. Map 20.

Oulton, par. and vil., E. Suffolk, 1½ m. N.W. of Lowestoft; pop. 643. Map 53.

Oulton, vil. and par., W.R. Yorkshire, 5½ m. S.E. of Leeds; pop. 3752. Map 33.

Oundle, urb. dist. and par., Northamptonshire, 13¼ m. S.W. of Peterborough; pop. 2001. Map 50.

Outwell, par. and vil., Isle of Ely, Cambridgeshire, 5 m. S.E. of Wisbech; pop. 483. Map 51.

Over, par. and vil., in co. and 8½ m. N.W. of Cambridge; pop. 896. Map 61.

Overstrand, coast par. and vil., Norfolk, 2 m. S.E. of Cromer; pop. 633. Map 53.

Overton, par. and ry. sta., Flintshire, 4½ m. N.W. of Ellesmere; pop. 1131. Map 46.

Overton, par. and vil., N. Lancashire, 3½ m. S.W. of Lancaster; pop. 367. Map 30.

Overton, par. and vil., Hants, 7¾ m. S.W. of Basingstoke; pop. 1779. Map 76.

Oxenhope, urb. dist., W.R. Yorkshire, 5 m. S.W. of Keighley; pop. 2276. Map 31.

Oxford, city and co. bor., Oxon, 63 m. W.N.W. of London; pop. 80,540. Map 70.

Oxnam, par. and ham., Roxburghshire, 4½ m. S.E. of Jedburgh; pop. 550. Map 16.

Oxshott, eccl. par., Surrey, 4½ m. S.W. of Surbiton; pop. 1245. Map 78.

Oxted, par. and vil., Surrey, 11 m. S.E. of Croydon; pop. 3284. Map 80.

Oxton, vil. and ry. sta., Berwickshire, 5 m. N.W. of Lauder; pop. 188. Map 10.

Oxwich, par. and vil., Glamorganshire, 10 m. W.S.W. of Swansea; pop. 194. Map 65.

PADGATE STATION, eccl. dist. and vil., Lancashire, 2 m. N.E. of Warrington; pop. 2101. Map 39.

Padiham, urb. dist., mfr. town and par., N.E. Lancashire, 3 m. W. of Burnley; pop. 11,632. Map 31.

Padstow, urb. dist., par. and seaport, Cornwall, 11 m. N.W. of Bodmin; pop. 1929. Map 91.

Paignton, urb. dist. and par., Devonshire, 2 m. S. of Torquay; pop. 18,405. Map 89.

Pailton, par. and vil., Warwickshire, 5 m. N.N.W. of Rugby; pop. 450. Map 59.

Painscastle, vil., Radnorshire, 5 m. N.W. of Hay. Map 56.

Painswick, par. and town, in co. and 6 m. S.E. of Gloucester; pop. 2639. Map 68.

Paisley, mun. bur., par. and r. port, Renfrewshire, 7¼ m. W. of Glasgow; pop. 86,441. Map 8.

Pakenham, par. and vil., W. Suffolk, 5 m. N.E. of Bury St Edmunds; pop. 829. Map 62.

Palgrave, par. and vil., E. Suffolk, 4 m. N.W. of Eye; pop. 693. Map 63.

Palling, coast par. and vil., Norfolk, 4 m. E. of Stalham; pop. 399. Map 53.

Pangbourne, par. and vil., Berkshire, 5½ m. N.W. of Reading; pop. 1936. Map 70.

Panteg, urb. dist., Monmouthshire, 1½ m. S.E. of Pontypool; pop. 11,500. Map 67.

Parkgate, vil., Cheshire, on Dee estuary, 13 m. N.W. of Chester. Sea bathing resort. Map 38.

Parkmill, ham., Gower peninsula, Glamorganshire, 9 m. W.S.W. of Swansea. Map 65.

Parknasilla, vil., co. Kerry, on west side of Sneen Harbour. Map 94.

Parkstone, dist. and ry. sta., in bor. of Poole, Dorsetshire. Map 87.

Parrog, seaside resort, Pembrokeshire, ½ m. N.W. of Newport. Map 64.

Parsley Hay Sta., on W. border of Derbyshire, 9 m. S.E. of Buxton. Map 40.

Parton, small seaport and par., Cumberland, 1½ m. N. of Whitehaven; pop. 1552. Map 24.

Paston, coast par. and vil., Norfolk, 4 m. N.E. of N. Walsham; pop. 281. Map 53.

Patcham, par. and vil., E. Sussex, 3 m. N. of Brighton; pop. 1768. Map 81.

Pateley Bridge, market town, W.R. Yorkshire, 14 m. N.W. of Harrogate; pop. 2558. Map 27.

Pathhead, vil., Midlothian, 5 m. S.E. of Dalkeith; pop. 465. Map 10.

Patrick Brompton, par., vil. and seat, N.R. Yorkshire, 3½ m. N.W. of Bedale; pop. 132. Map 27.

Patrington, small town and par., E.R. Yorkshire, 4 m. S.W. of Withernsea; pop. 1137. Map 35

Patterdale, par. and vil., Westmorland, 8½ m. N. of Ambleside; pop. 961. Map 25.
Paul, urb. dist., Cornwall, 2½ m. S. of Penzance; pop. 5813. Map 90.
Paulerspury, par. and vil., Northamptonshire, 2½ m. S.E. of Towcester; pop. 804. Map 59.
Peacehaven, seaside garden city, E. Sussex, 6½ m. E. of Brighton. Map 81.
Peak Forest, par. and vil., Derbyshire, 5 m. N.E. of Buxton; pop. 420. Map 40.
Peak, The, Kinder Scout, Derbyshire, 4 m. S.E. of Glossop; alt. 2088 ft. highest summit. Map 40.
Pebworth, par. and vil., Worcestershire, 5 m. N.N.W. of Chipping Campden; pop. 542. Map 58.
Peebles, mun. bur. and par., Peeblesshire, 23 m. S. of Edinburgh; pop. 5853. Map 15.
Peel, coast town, lifeboat and coastguard sta., I. of Man, 11½ m. N.W. of Douglas; pop. 2690. Map 24.
Pegswood, par. and vil., Northumberland, 2 m. N.E. of Morpeth; pop. 2875. Map 17.
Pegwell, ham., Kent, 1 m. S.W. of Ramsgate. Map 83.
Pembrey, seaport and par., Carmarthenshire, 5 m. W. of Llanelly; pop. 5544. Map 65.
Pembridge, par. and vil., Herefordshire, 7 m. W. of Leominster; pop. 991. Map 56.
Pembroke, mun. bor. and spt., on Milford Haven, 9½ m. W. of Tenby, Pembrokeshire; pop. 12,008. Map 64.
Penarth, urb. dist. and seaport town, Glamorganshire, 3 m. S. of Cardiff; pop. 17,710. Map 74.
Penbryn, coast par., in co. and 8 m. N.E. of Cardigan; pop. 1100. Map 54.
Pencader, vil., in co. and 10 m. N.N.E. of Carmarthen. Map 65.
Pendlebury, par., S.E. Lancashire, containing part of Swinton and Pendlebury; pop. 10,130. Map 39.
Penge, urb. dist., Kent, 7 m. S. of London Bridge Sta.; pop. 27,762. Map 80.
Penicuik, police bur. and par., S. Midlothian, 10 m. S. of Edinburgh; pop. 2750. Map 10.
Penistone, urb. dist. and par., W.R. Yorkshire, on r. Don, 12½ m. N.W. of Sheffield; pop. 3264. Map 40.
Penkridge, small town and par., Staffordshire, 6 m. S. of Stafford; pop. 2570. Map 47.
Penmaenmawr, N. coast of Carnarvonshire, 4½ m. S.W. of Conway, watering place; pop. 4021, Map 37.
Penn, par. and vil., Buckinghamshire, 4 m. S.W. of Amersham; pop. 1604. Map 70.
Penrhiwceiber, vil., with ry. stas., Glamorganshire, 1¼ m. S.E. of Mountain Ash. Map 66.
Penrhos, ham., Carmarthenshire, 7 m. N.W. of Llanelly. Map 64.
Penrhyn Bay, par., N.E. Carnarvonshire, 2 m. E. of Llandudno; pop. 1252. Map 37.
Penrhyndeudraeth, par. and vil., Merionethshire, 3½ m. E. of Portmadoc; pop. 1949. Map 37.
Penrhyn Slate Quarries, Carnarvonshire, in S. vicinity of Bethesda. Map 36.
Penrice, par. and vil., Glamorganshire, 10 m. W.S.W. of Swansea; pop. 311. Map 65.
Penrith, urb. dist., market town and par., Cumberland, 17¾ m. S.E. of Carlisle; pop. 9065. Map 21.
Penruddock, vil. (alt. 857 ft.), Cumberland, 7½ m. S.W. of Penrith. Map 21.
Penryn, mun. bor. and par., Cornwall, 3½ m. N.W. of Falmouth; pop. 3414. Map 90.
Pensarn, locality, Anglesey, in Twrcelyn rural dist. Map 36.
Penshaw, par. and ry. sta., in co. and 8 m. N.E. of Durham; pop. 7265. Map 23.
Penshurst, par. and vil., Kent, 4 m. S.W. of Tonbridge; pop. 1531. Map 82.
Pentland Hills, extend through cos. of Midlothian, Peebles and Lanark. Map 12.
Pentraeth, par. and vil., Anglesey, 5 m. W. of Beaumaris; pop. 712. Map 36.
Pentre, ham., Flintshire, 2 m. E. of Hawarden. Map 38.
Pentyrch, par. and vil., Glamorganshire, 7 m. N.W. of Cardiff; pop. 2440. Map 67.
Penwortham, par. and vil., Lancashire, 2 m. S.W. of Preston; pop. 3999. Map 30.
Penybont, vil. and sta., Radnorshire, 4 m. N.E. of Llandrindod Wells. Map 56.
Pen-y-cae, par. and vil., Denbighshire, 2 m. W. of Ruabon; pop. 2037. Map 46.
Penzance, mun. bor., par. and seaport, Cornwall, 26 m. S.W. of Truro; pop. 11,342. Map 90.
Perranporth, vil., Cornwall, 7½ m. N.W. of Truro. Map 90.
Perranzabuloe, par. and vil., Cornwall, 5½ m. N.W. of Truro; pop. 2380. Map 90.
Perrott, South, par. and vil., Dorsetshire, 3 m. S.E. of Crewkerne; pop. 213. Map 86.
Perry Barr, dist. in N. of Birmingham. Map 48.
Pershore, market town, in co. and 8½ m. S.E. of Worcester; pop. 4035. Map 57.
Perth, city, bur., par., r. port and co. town, Perthshire, 21 m. W.S.W. of Dundee; pop. 34,807. Map 6.
Peterborough, city and mun. bor., in Soke of Peterborough, Northamptonshire, on r. Nen, 14½ m. W. of March; pop. 43,558. Map 51.
Peterchurch, par. and vil., Herefordshire, 11 m. W. of Hereford; pop. 528. Map 56.
Peterhead, mun. bur., spt.- tn. and par., Aberdeenshire, 44¼ m. N.E. of Aberdeen; pop. 12,545. Map 3.
Petersfield, urban dist. and par., Hants, 19 m. N.E. of Portsmouth; pop. 4386. Map 79.
Petersham, par. and vil., Surrey, 10 m. S.W. of London; pop. 592. Map 71.
Petham, par. and vil., Kent, 4 m. S.S.W. of Canterbury; pop. 562. Map 83.
Petherton, North, par. and vil., Somersetshire, 2 m. S. of Bridgwater; pop. 3179. Map 74.
Petherton, South, small town and par., Somersetshire, 4½ m. N. of Crewkerne; pop. 1971. Map 86.
Pettaugh, par. and vil., E. Suffolk, 10 m. N. of Ipswich; pop. 171. Map 63.
Pettinain, par. and vil., Lanarkshire, 3 m. S. of Carstairs Junction; pop. 301. Map 9.
Petworth, par. and town, Sussex, 55½ m. S.W. of London; pop. 2435. Map 79.
Pevensey, par. and vil., E. Sussex, 4 m. N.E. of Eastbourne; pop. 764. Map 81.
Pewsey, town and par., E. Wiltshire, 7 m. S. of Marlborough; pop. 1692. Map 76.
Philipstown, market town, E. Offaly, 8 m. E. of Tullamore; pop. 659. Map 93.
Philipstoun, vil., with ry. sta., West Lothian, 3½ m. E. of Linlithgow. Map 9.
Phillack, urb. dist., Cornwall, 1½ m. N.E. of Hayle; pop. 3232. Map 90.
Pickering, par. and urb. dist., N.R. Yorkshire, 11 m. N. of Malton; pop. 3668. Map 29.
Pickwell with Leesthorpe, par. and vil., Leicestershire, 6 m. S.E. of Melton Mowbray; pop. 170. Map 50.
Pickworth, par. and vil., Kesteven, Lincolnshire, 8 m. E.S.E. of Grantham; pop. 153. Map 50.
Piddletrenthide, par. and vil., Dorsetshire, 7 m. N. of Dorchester; pop. 504. Map 87.
Piercebridge, par. and vil., Durham, 5 m. W. of Darlington; pop. 204. Map 27.
Pilling, par. and vil., Lancashire, 5 m. W.N.W. of Garstang; pop. 1465. Map 30.
Pilsley, par. and vil., Derbyshire, 6 m. S.E. of Chesterfield; pop. 2885. Map 41.
Pilton, East, par. in mun. bor. of Barnstaple pop. 2276. Map 84.

Portobello, seaside resort, in city and 3 m. E. of G.P.O., Edinburgh. Map 10.

Port of Menteith, par. and ry. sta., Perthshire, 3 m. N.E. of Buchlyvie; pop. 1019. Map 8.

Portpatrick, par. and seaport, Wigtownshire, 7½ m. S.W. of Stranraer; pop. 1495. Map 18.

Portreath, seaport vil., Cornwall, 4 m. N.W. of Redruth. Map 90.

Portree, par. and spt. vil., I. of Skye, Inverness-shire, 60 m. S.E. of Stornoway; pop. 793. Map 2.

Portrush, urb. dist. and seaport town, Antrim, 67½ m. N.W. of Belfast; pop. 2107. Map 93.

Port St Mary, coast vil. and lifeboat sta., Isle of Man, 4¾ m. W. of Castletown. Map 24.

Portsea, dist. and ward, Hants, within co. bor. of Portsmouth; ward pop. 20,712. Map 77.

Portslade-by-Sea, urb. dist., E. Sussex, 4 m. W. of Brighton; pop. 9527. Map 81.

Portsmouth, co. bor., naval sta. and par., Hants, 27 m. S.E. of Southampton; pop. 249,288. Map 79.

Port Soderick, coast ham., Isle of Man, 3 m. S.W. of Douglas. Map 24.

Port Sonachan, ham., Argyllshire, 8½ m. S.W. of Dalmally. Map 12.

Portsoy, seaport town, police bur. and *q.s.* par., Banff-shire, 8½ m. W. of Banff; pop. 1651. Map 3.

Portstewart, vil., co. Londonderry, 4 m. N.W. of Coleraine; pop. 1459. Map 93.

Port Sunlight, vil. and soapworks of Lever Bros. Ltd., 3 m. S.S.E. of Birkenhead, Cheshire. Map 38.

Port Talbot, mun. bor. and port, Glamorganshire, 10¾ m. S.E. of Swansea; pop. 40,672. Map 66.

Portumna, market town, Galway, 14½ m. W. of Parsonstown; pop. 873. Map 94.

Port Victoria, ry. sta., Kent, at mouth of r. Medway, 2 m. S.W. of Sheerness. Map 73.

Potter Street, vil., Essex, 2 m. S. of Harlow. Map 72.

Potters Bar, eccl. par. and vil., Middlesex, 12¼ m. N. of London; pop. 1752. Map 71.

Potton, market town and par., Bedfordshire, 4 m. N.E. of Biggleswade; pop. 2087. Map 60.

Potton, island, Essex, in estuary of river Roach. Map 73.

Poulton, eccl. dist., in Morecambe mun. bor., N. Lancashire; pop. 6956. Map 26.

Poulton-le-Fylde, urb. dist., small mkt. tn. and par., N. Lancs, 6 m. S. of Fleetwood; pop. 3366. Map 30.

Powfoot, ham., Dumfriesshire, 4 m. S.W. of Annan. Map 20.

Powick, par. and vil., in co. and 3 m. W. of Worcester; pop. 2640. Map 52.

Poyntzpass, vil., cos. Armagh and Down, 10 m. S. of Portadown Junction; pop. 348. Map 93.

Prawle, fishing vil., S. Devonshire, 7 m. S.E. of Kingsbridge. Map 89.

Prees, par. and vil., Shropshire, 4¼ m. S.E. of Whitchurch; pop. 1987. Map 47.

Preesall, urb. dist. and par., N. Lancashire, on r. Wyre, opposite Fleetwood; pop. 2043. Map 30.

Prendergast, par., Pembrokeshire, in bor. of Haverfordwest; pop. 1179. Map 64.

Prengwyn, ham., Cardiganshire, 2½ m. N.N.E. of Llandyssul. Map 54.

Prescot, urb. dist., mfg. and mkt. tn. and par., S.W. Lancs, 7¼ m. E. of Liverpool; pop. 9396. Map 38.

Prestatyn, par., small mkt. tn. and urb. dist., Flintshire, 4 m. E. of Rhyl; pop. 4511. Map 37.

Presteigne, urb. dist., Radnorshire, 6½ m. N.E. of New Radnor; pop. 1102. Map 56.

Preston, bor., par. and port, N. Lancashire, 28 m. N.E. of Liverpool; pop. 118,839. Map 30.

Preston, par. and vil., Dorsetshire, 3 m. N.E. of Weymouth; pop. 886. Map 87.

Preston Candover, par. and vil., Hants, 6 m. N. of Alresford; pop. 379. Map 76.

Preston-on-Wye, par. and vil., Herefordshire, 6½ m. S. of **Weobley**; pop. 301. Map 56.

Prestonpans, coast tn., police bur. and par., E. Lothian, 9½ m. E. of Edinburgh; pop. 2426. Map 10.

Prestwich, urb. dist. and par., Lancashire, 4½ m. N.W. of Manchester; pop. 23,876. Map 39.

Prestwick, town, Ayrshire, 38¼ m. S.W. of Glasgow; pop. 8538. Map 12.

Princes Risborough, market town and par., Bucks, 7½ m. S.S.W. of Aylesbury; pop. 2438. Map 70.

Princetown, eccl. dist. and vil., Devonshire, 21¾ m. N.N.E. of Plymouth; pop. 2061. Map 88.

Priors Marston, par. and vil., Warwickshire, 5 m. S.E. of Southam; pop. 451. Map 59.

Prudhoe, urb. dist. and par., Northumberland, 11 m. W. of Newcastle; pop. 9260. Map 22.

Puckeridge, vil., Hertfordshire, 6 m. N.E. of Ware. Map 71.

Pucklechurch, par. and vil., Gloucestershire, 4 m. S.W. of Chipping Sodbury; pop. 1283. Map 68.

Puddletown, par. and vil., Dorsetshire, 5 m. N.E. of Dorchester; pop. 761. Map 87.

Pudsey, mun. bor. and par., W.R. Yorkshire, 3 m. E. of Bradford; pop. 14,762. Map 32.

Puffin Island, or **Priestholm,** off E. point of Anglesey; area 58 acres. Map 37.

Pulborough, par. and market town, W. Sussex, 3¼ m. S.E. of Petworth; pop. 2065. Map 79.

Pulham Market, vil. and ry. sta., Norfolk, 3½ m. N.W. of Harleston. Map 63.

Puncheston, par. and vil., Pembrokeshire, 11 m. S.E. of Fishguard; pop. 204. Map 64.

Purfleet, urb. dist., Essex, 7 m. N.W. of Tilbury sta.; pop. 8511. Map 72.

Purley, vil., Surrey, 2½ m. S.S.W. of Croydon. Map 80.

Pwllheli, mun. bor. and seaport town, in co. and 21 m. S.W. of Carnarvon; pop. 3599. Map 44.

QUAINTON, par. and vil., Buckinghamshire, 6½ m. N.W. of Aylesbury; pop. 928. Map 70.

Quarry Bank, urb. dist., Staffordshire, 1½ m. S.E. of Brierley Hill; pop. 8100. Map 57.

Queenborough, mun. bor., Isle of Sheppey, Kent, 2 m. S.S.W. of Sheerness; pop. 2941. Map 73.

Queensbury, urb. dist. and par., W.R. Yorkshire, 4 m. N. of Halifax; pop. 5763. Map 32.

Queensferry, vil. and ry. sta., on r. Dee, in co. and 5½ m. S.E. of Flint. Map 38.

Queensferry, North, vil., with ry. sta., Fifeshire, 2 m. S. of Inverkeithing; pop. 1647. Map 10.

Queensferry, South, *q.s.* par., mun. bur. and spt. tn., West Lothian, 9½ m. W. of Edinburgh; pop. 1798. Map 10.

Queenstown, now **Cobh,** seaport, in co. and 13 m. S.E. of Cork; pop. 8209. Map 94.

Quendon, par. and vil., Essex, 6 m. S.W. of Saffron Walden; pop. 124. Map 61.

Quorndon, urb. dist. and par., Leicestershire, 2½ m. S.E. of Loughborough; pop. 2603. Map 49.

RADCLIFFE, urb. dist. and par., S.E. Lancashire, 3 m. S.W. of Bury; pop. 24,674. Map 31.

Radcliffe-on-Trent, par. and vil., in co. and 4¾ m. E. of Nottingham; pop. 2849. Map 49.

Radlett, eccl. dist. and vil., Hertfordshire, 5 m. S. of St Albans; pop. 2431. Map 71.

Radstock, urb. dist. and par., Somersetshire, 16 m. S.E. of Bristol; pop. 3622. Map 75.

Raglan, par. and vil., in co. and 7 m. S.W. of Monmouth; pop. 676. Map 67.

Rainford, urb. dist. and par., Lancashire, 4 m. N.W. of St Helens; pop. 3494. Map 38.

Rainham, par. and vil., Essex, 5 m. S.E. of Barking; pop. 2196. Map 72.

Rainhill, par. and vil., Lancashire, 9 m. E. of Liverpool; pop. 2463. Map 38.

Ramelton, market town, co. Donegal, 7 m. N.N.E. of Letterkenny; pop. 932. Map 93.

Rampside, eccl. dist. and vil., Lancashire, Dalton-in-Furness par.; pop. 481. Map 25.
Ramsbottom, urb. dist. and par., S.E. Lancashire, 4 m. N. of Bury; pop. 14,926. Map 31.
Ramsbury, par. and vil., Wiltshire, 5 m. N.W. of Hungerford; pop. 1504. Map 69.
Ramsey, seaport town, Isle of Man, 13 m. N. of Douglas; pop. 4642. Map 24.
Ramsey, urb. dist. and par., in co. and 10 m. N.E. of Huntingdon; pop. 5180. Map 61.
Ramsgate, mun. bor. and wtg. place, I. of Thanet, Kent, 74 m. S.E. of London; pop. 33,597. Map 83.
Randalstown, market town, in co. and 5 m. N.W. of Antrim; pop. 986. Map 93.
Rannoch, dist., loch and ry. sta., Perthshire and Argyllshire. Map 3.
Raphoe, mkt. tn. and par., co. Donegal, 6½ m. N.W. of Strabane; town pop. 705. Map 93.
Rastrick, now part of Brighouse mun. bor., W.R. Yorks, 3½ m. N. of Huddersfield. Map 32.
Rathdrum, market town and par., in co. and 9 m. S.W. of Wicklow; town pop. 680. Map 95.
Rathfriland, or **Rathfryland,** market town, co. Down, 9 m. N.E. of Newry; pop. 1365. Map 93.
Rathkeale, market town and par., in co. and 18 m. S.W. of Limerick; pop. 1550. Map 94.
Rathlin Island, par., off N. coast of co. Antrim; pop. 351. Map 93.
Rathmullan, vil., co. Donegal, on Lough Swilly, 7 m. N.E. of Ramelton; pop. 485. Map 93.
Rattray, Perthshire. *See* Blairgowrie and Rattray.
Raunds, urb. dist. and par., Northamptonshire, 4 m. S. of Thrapston; pop. 3683. Map 60.
Ravenglass, seaport and market town, Cumberland, 5 m. N.W. of Bootle. Map 25.
Raveningham, par. and vil., Norfolk, 3½ m. S.E. of Loddon; pop. 289. Map 53.
Ravenscar, seaside resort, N.R. Yorkshire, 8 m. S.E. of Whitby; pop. 496. Map 29.
Ravenstonedale, par. and vil., Westmorland, 4½ m. S.W. of Kirkby Stephen; pop. 831. Map 26.
Ravensworth, par. and vil., N.R. Yorkshire, 5 m. N.W. of Richmond; pop. 259. Map 27.
Raventhorpe, par., W.R. Yorkshire, a western ward of Dewsbury; pop. 6719. Map 32.
Rawdon, urb. dist. and par., W.R. Yorkshire, 5 m. N.E. of Bradford; pop. 4574. Map 32.
Rawmarsh, urb. dist. and par., W.R. Yorkshire, 2 m. N.N.E. of Rotherham; pop. 18,570. Map 41.
Rawtenstall, mun. bor. and par., N.E. Lancashire, 8 m. N. of Bury; pop. 28,575. Map 31.
Rayleigh, par. and urban dist., Essex, 7 m. W.N.W. of Southend; pop. 6256. Map 72.
Read, par. and vil., N.E. Lancashire, 2 m. E.S.E. of Whalley; pop. 904. Map 31.
Reading, co. bor., Berkshire, on r. Kennet, 36 m. W. of Paddington sta., London; pop. 97,153. Map 78.
Reay, par. and vil., Caithness, 10½ m. W. of Thurso; pop. 1355. Map 3.
Redcar, mun. bor. and par., Yorkshire, 7¾ m. N.E. of Middlesbrough; pop. 20,159. Map 23.
Redditch, urb. dist. and par., Worcestershire, 15½ m. S. of Birmingham; pop. 19,280. Map 58.
Redgrave, par. and vil., E. Suffolk, 7 m. N.W. of Eye; pop. 447. Map 62.
Redhill, residential dist., forming Eastern part of bor. of Reigate, Surrey. Map 80.
Redmarley D'Abitot, par. and vil., Gloucestershire, 5 m. S.E. of Ledbury; pop. 722. Map 57.
Redmire, par. and vil., N.R. Yorkshire, 4½ m. W. of Leyburn; pop. 238. Map 27.
Redruth, urb. dist. and par., Cornwall, 9 m. S.W. of Truro; pop. 9904. Map 90.
Red Wharf, on N.E. coast of Anglesey, 5½ m. N.W. of Beaumaris. Map 36.
Reedham, par. and vil., Norfolk, 8 m. S.W. of Yarmouth; pop. 840. Map 53.
Reepham with Kerdiston, par. and vil., Norfolk, 6½ m. W.S.W. of Aylsham; pop. 372. Map 53.
Reeth, par. and moorland vil., N.R. Yorkshire, 9 m. W. of Richmond; pop. 709. Map 27.
Reigate, mun. bor., Surrey, 24¼ m. S. of London; pop. 30,830. Map 80.
Reighton, par. and vil., E.R. Yorkshire, 6 m. N.W. of Bridlington; pop. 202. Map 29.
Renfrew, mun. bor. and co. town of Renfrewshire, 5 m. W. of Glasgow; pop. 14,986. Map 8.
Renton, town and *q.s.* par., in co. and 2¼ m. N. of Dumbarton; pop. 4923. Map 8.
Renwick, par. and vil., Cumberland, 3 m. N.E. of Kirkoswald; pop. 174. Map 21.
Repton, par. and vil., Derbyshire, 4¾ m. N.E. of Burton-on-Trent; pop. 1929. Map 48.
Reston, vil. and ry. sta., Berwickshire, 6¾ m. N.E. of Duns. Map 11.
Rettendon, par. and vil., Essex, 6½ m. S.E. of Chelmsford; pop. 851. Map 72.
Reynalton, par., Pembrokeshire, 4 m. S.S.W. of Narberth; pop. 62. Map 64.
Reynoldston, par. and vil., Glamorganshire, 12 m. W.S.W. of Swansea; pop. 278. Map 65.
Rhayader, market town and par., Radnorshire, 14 m. S. of Llanidloes; pop. 910. Map 55.
Rheidol Falls, ry. sta., Cardiganshire, 2½ m. W.N.W. of Devil's Bridge. Map 55.
Rhondda, urb. dist., Glamorganshire, 7½ m. N.W. of Pontypridd; pop. 141,344. Map 66.
Rhos-Goch, Anglesey, 3 m. S.W. of Amlwch. Map 36.
Rhosllanerchrugog, par. and vil., Denbighshire, 4 m. S.W. of Wrexham; pop. 11,139. Map 38.
Rhosneigr, vil., lifeboat and coastguard sta., 1½ m. W. of Llanfaelog, W. Anglesey. Map 36.
Rhos-on-Sea, vil. and seaside resort, Denbighshire and Carnarvonshire. Map 37.
Rhossili, par. and vil., Glamorganshire, 12 m. S.W. of Loughor; pop. 304. Map 65.
Rhostyllen, ham. and ry. sta., S.E. Denbighshire, 1¾ m. S.W. of Wrexham. Map 38.
Rhuddlan, par., Flintshire, on r. Clwyd, 3 m. N.W. of St Asaph; pop. 1701. Map 37.
Rhydowen, ham., Cardiganshire, 3½ m. N.N.E. of Llandyssul. Map 55.
Rhyl, watering place, par. and urb. dist., Flintshire, 6 m. S.W. of St Asaph; pop. 13,489. Map 37.
Rhymney, urb. dist. and par., Monmouthshire, 2½ m. W. of Tredegar; pop. 10,505. Map 66.
Ribbleton, par. and seat, Lancashire, 2 m. N.E. of Preston; pop. 78. Map 30.
Ribchester, town and par., N.E. Lancashire, 5½ m. N.N.W. of Blackburn; pop. 1450. Map 30.
Riccall, par. and vil., E.R. Yorkshire, 4 m. N. of Selby; pop. 739. Map 34.
Richard's Castle, par. and vil., Salop, 3½ m. S.W. of Ludlow; pop. 393. Map 56.
Richborough, ham. and ancient seaport, Kent, 1½ m. N.W. of Sandwich. Map 83.
Richmond, mun. bor., Surrey, on r. Thames, 9¾ m. S.W. of London; pop. 37,791. Map 71.
Richmond, mun. bor., par. and mkt. tn., N.R. Yorkshire, 15 m. S.W. of Darlington; pop. 4769. Map 27.
Rickmansworth, urb. dist. and par., Hertfordshire, 3½ m. S.W. of Watford; pop. 10,810. Map 71.
Riding, par. and ry. sta. (**R. Mill**), Northumberland, 5½ m. S.E. of Hexham; pop. 318. Map 22.
Ridsdale, vil., Northumberland, 1 m. S.S.E. of Woodburn ry. sta. Map 17.
Rigg, vil. and ry. sta., Dumfriesshire, 6 m. E. of Annan. Map 21.
Rillington, par. and vil., E.R. Yorkshire, 4¼ m. N.E of Malton; pop. 684. Map 29.

Ringwood, market town and par., Hants, 8 m. N. of Christchurch; pop. 5131. Map 77.
Ripley, urb. dist. and par., Derbyshire, 10 m. N.E. of Derby; pop. 13,415. Map 41.
Ripley, eccl. par. and vil., Surrey, 5½ m. N.E. of Guildford; pop. 1557. Map 78.
Ripley, market vil. and par., W.R. Yorkshire, 3½ m. N.W. of Harrogate; pop. 231. Map 32.
Ripon, city, mun. bor. and par., W.R. Yorkshire, 13¾ m. S. of Northallerton; pop. 8576. Map 27.
Rippingale, par. and vil., Kesteven, Lincolnshire, 5½ m. N. of Bourne; pop. 435. Map 50.
Risca, urb. dist. and par., Monmouthshire, 6½ m. N.W. of Newport; pop. 16,605. Map 67.
Riseley, par. and vil., in co. and 9 m. N. of Bedford; pop. 600. Map 60.
Rishton, urb. dist. and par., N.E. Lancashire, 3 m. N.E. of Blackburn; pop. 6631. Map 31.
Rishworth, urb. dist., W.R. Yorkshire, 4½ m. S.S.W. of Sowerby Bridge; pop. 838. Map 31.
Riverhead, par. and vil., Kent, 1½ m. N.W. of Sevenoaks; pop. 943. Map 82.
Rivington, par. and vil., mid. Lancashire, 4 m. S.E. of Chorley; pop. 238. Map 30.
Roberton, par., Roxburghshire; Church 5 m. W. of Hawick; pop. 383. Map 16.
Robertsbridge, or **Rotherbridge,** town, E. Sussex, on r. Rother, 4¾ m. N. of Battle. Map 82.
Robin Hood's Bay, fishing town, N.R. Yorkshire, 5 m. S.E. of Whitby. Map 29.
Roby, par. and seat, S.W. Lancashire, 5½ m. E. of Liverpool; pop. of eccl. dist. 985. Map 38.
Rochdale, parl. and co. bor. and par., S.E. Lancashire, 10½ m. N.E. of Manchester; pop. 90,278. Map 31.
Rochester, mun. bor. and r. port, Kent, 30 m. S.E of London; pop. 31,196. Map 80.
Rochford, town and par., Essex, 3 m. N. of Southend; pop. 2077. Map 73.
Rock, par. and vil., Worcestershire, 4½ m. S.W. of Bewdley; pop. 1534. Map 57.
Rockbourne, par. and vil., Hants, 3½ m. N.W. of Fordingbridge; pop. 423. Map 77.
Rockcliffe, par. and vil., Cumberland, 4 m. N.W. of Carlisle; pop. 559. Map 21.
Rock Ferry, summer resort, Cheshire, on r. Mersey, in S. suburbs of Birkenhead. Map 38.
Rockingham, par. and vil., Northamptonshire, 10 m. N.E. of Market Harborough; pop. 163. Map 50.
Rodborough, par. and vil., Gloucestershire, ½ m. S.W. of Stroud; pop. 3824. Map 68.
Rodbourne Cheney, par. and vil., Wiltshire, 2 m. N.W. of Swindon; pop. 2115. Map 69.
Rodlington, par. and vil., Salop, 4½ m. N.W. of Wellington; pop. 483. Map 47.
Rodney Stoke, par. and vil., Somersetshire, 5 m. N.W. of Wells; pop. 608. Map 74.
Rogate, par. and vil., W. Sussex, 5 m. W. of Midhurst; pop. 1001. Map 79.
Rolleston, par. and vil., Staffordshire, 3 m. N.W. of Burton-on-Trent; pop. 764. Map 48.
Rolvenden, par. and vil., Kent, 3 m. W.S.W. of Tenterden; pop. 1194. Map 82.
Romaldkirk, par. and vil., N.R. Yorkshire, 5 m. N.W. of Barnard Castle; pop. 233. Map 27.
Romford, urb. dist. and market town, Essex, 6 m. S.W. of Brentwood; pop. 35,918. Map 72.
Romsey, mun. bor. and par., Hants, 10 m. S.W. of Southampton by rail; pop. 4863. Map 77.
Roos, par. and vil., E.R. Yorkshire, 7 m. E. of Hedon; pop. 455. Map 35.
Ropley, par. and vil., Hants, 4 m. E.S.E. of Alresford; pop. 1473. Map 79.
Ropsley, par. and vil., Kesteven, Lincolnshire, 5 m. E.S.E. of Grantham; pop. 519. Map 50.
Roscommon, par., market and co. town of Roscommon, 96 m. W.N.W. of Dublin; pop. 1830. Map 92.
Roscrea, market town, with ry. sta., Tipperary, 46¾ m. N.E. of Limerick by rail; pop. 2694. Map 95.
Rosehearty, vil. (police bur.), Aberdeenshire, 4½ m. W. of Fraserburgh; pop. 1079. Map 3.
Rosemarket, par. and vil., Pembrokeshire, 3½ m. N.E. of Milford; pop. 384. Map 64.
Roseneath, par. and vil., Dumbartonshire, 2½ m. W. of Helensburgh; pop. 2770. Map 8.
Roslin, *q.s.* par. and vil., Midlothian, 6½ m. S. of Edinburgh; pop. 1891. Map 10.
Rosliston, par. and vil., Derbyshire, 4½ m. S. of Burton-on-Trent; pop. 467. Map 48.
Ross, urb. dist. and par., Herefordshire, 18 m. N.W. of Gloucester by rail; pop. 4738. Map 68.
Rossington, par. and vil., W.R. Yorkshire, 4¾ m. S.E. of Doncaster; pop. 3029. Map 41.
Rosslare, par. and vil., in co. and 6 m. S.E. of Wexford; pop. 667. Map 95.
Rosyth, vil., Fifesh., 1¾ m. N.W. of Queensferry. Map 10.
Rothbury, urb. dist. and par., Northumberland, 11 m. S.W. of Alnwick; pop. 1255. Map 17.
Rotherfield, par. and vil., Sussex, 8½ m. S.W. of Tunbridge Wells; pop. 2178. Map 81.
Rotherham, co. bor., mkt. tn. and par., W.R. Yorkshire, 6 m. N.E. of Sheffield; pop. 69,689. Map 41.
Rothes, par. and police bur., Morayshire, 9¾ m. S.E. of Elgin; pop. 1292. Map 3.
Rothesay, mun. bur., co. tn. of Bute, Firth of Clyde, 19 m. S.W. of Greenock; pop. 9346. Map 12.
Rothley, par. and vil., Leicestershire, 1½ m. S. of Mountsorrel; pop. 2264. Map 49.
Rothwell, urb. dist. and par., Northamptonshire, 4 m. N.W. of Kettering; pop. 4516. Map 60.
Rothwell, par. and vil., Lindsey, Lincolnshire, 2½ m. S.E. of Caistor; pop. 198. Map 42.
Rothwell, urb. dist., W.R. Yorkshire, 4 m. S.E. of Leeds; pop. 15,639. Map 32.
Rottingdean, coast par. and vil., E. Sussex, 4 m. S.E. of Brighton; pop. 2769. Map 81.
Roughton, par. and vil., Norfolk, 3½ m. S. of Cromer; pop. 479. Map 53.
Row (Rhu), par. and vil., Dumbartonshire, 2 m. N.W. of Helensburgh; vil., pop. 1136. Map 8.
Rowhedge, vil., Essex, 3 m. S.E. of Colchester. Map 73.
Rowley Regis, urb. dist. and par., Staffordshire, 2½ m. S.E. of Dudley; pop. 41,238. Map 47.
Rowsley, Great, par. and vil., Derbyshire, 3½ m. S.E. of Bakewell; pop. 338. Map 40.
Roxburgh, par. and vil., Roxburghshire, vil., 3 m. S.W. of Kelso; pop. 742. Map 16.
Roxby-cum-Risby, urb. dist., Lincoln, 8 m. N.W. of Brigg; pop. 548. Map 34.
Roydon, par. and vil., W. Essex, 4½ m. W.S.W. of Harlow; pop. 1182. Map 71.
Royston, urb. dist., par. and vil., W.R. Yorkshire, 4 m. N.E. of Barnsley; pop. 7156. Map 33.
Royston, urb. dist. and par., Hertfordshire, 12½ m. N.E. of Hitchin; pop. 3831. Map 61.
Royton, urb. dist. and par., S.E. Lancashire, 3 m. N. of Oldham; pop. 16,687. Map 31.
Ruabon, town and par., Denbighshire, 4½ m. S.W. of Wrexham; pop. 3333. Map 38.
Ruddington, par. and vil., with ry. sta., in co. and 4½ m. S. of Nottingham; pop. 2877. Map 49.
Rudgwick, par. and vil., W. Sussex, 6 m. N.W. of Horsham; pop. 1175. Map 79.
Rudham, East and **West,** 2 pars., Norfolk, 6½ m. W. of Fakenham; pop. 639 and 346. Map 52.
Rudston, par. and vil., E.R. Yorkshire, 5 m. W. of Bridlington; pop. 492. Map 29.
Rugby, urb. dist. and par., in co. and 15¾ m. N.E. of Warwick; pop. 23,824. Map 59.
Rugeley, urb. dist. and par., in co. and 8½ m. S.E. of Stafford; pop. 5263. Map 48.

Ruislip, urb. dist., Middlesex, 3½ m. N.E. of Uxbridge ; pop. 16,038. Map 71.

Rum Island, Inner Hebrides, Inverness-shire, 15 m. N.W. of Ardnamurchan Point ; pop. 149. Map 2.

Rumbling Bridge, place, border of Kinross-shire and Perthshire, 4¼ m. N.E. of Dollar. Map 7.

Runcorn, urb. dist., seaport and par., Cheshire, 12½ m. S.E. of Liverpool by rail ; pop. 18,158. Map 38.

Rushall, par. and vil., Staffordshire, 1½ m. N.E. of Walsall ; pop. 3256. Map 48.

Rushden, urb. dist. and par., Northamptonshire, 1¼ m. S. of Higham Ferrers ; pop. 14,247. Map 60.

Rushyford, ham., Durham, 5 m. E.S.E. of Bishop Auckland. Map 23.

Ruskington, urb. dist. and par., Kesteven, Lincolnshire, 3½ m. N.N.E. of Sleaford ; pop. 1101. Map 42.

Ruswarp, par. and vil., N.R. Yorkshire, in urb. dist. of Whitby ; pop. 6195. Map 29.

Rutherglen, mun. bur. and par., Lanarkshire, 2 m. S.E. of Central sta., Glasgow ; pop. 25,157. Map 8.

Ruthin, mun. bor., mkt. tn. and par., Denbighshire, on r. Clwyd, 7¾ m. S.E. of Denbigh ; pop. 2912. Map 38.

Ruthwell, coast par. and vil., in co. and 9 m. S.E. of Dumfries ; pop. 727. Map 20.

Ryburgh, par. and vil., Norfolk, 3 m. S.E. of Fakenham ; pop. 550. Map 52.

Ryde, wtg. pl., mun. bor. and par., Isle of Wight, 20 m. from Southampton ; pop. 10,519. Map 77.

Rye, mun. bor., par. and Cinque port, Sussex, 11 m. N.E. of Hastings by rail ; pop. 3947. Map 82.

Ryhope, par. and vil., Durham, 3 m. S. of Sunderland ; pop. 11,650. Map 23.

Ryton, urb. dist. and par., Durham, 6 m. W. of Newcastle ; pop. 14,204. Map 22.

SABDEN, par. and vil., N.E. Lancashire, 5 m. N.W. of Burnley ; pop. 1645. Map 31.

Saddleworth, urb. dist., W.R. Yorkshire, 12 m. S.W. of Huddersfield ; pop. 12,577. Map 31.

Saffron Walden, mun. bor. and par., Essex, 43¾ m. N.E. of London ; pop. 5930. Map 61.

Saham Toney, par. and vil., Norfolk, 1½ m. N.W. of Watton ; pop. 882. Map 52.

St Abb's, vil., Berwickshire, 1½ m. N.E. of Coldingham ; pop. 403. Map 11.

St Agnes, seaport and par., Cornwall, 8½ m. N.W. of Truro ; pop. 3347. Map 90.

St Albans, mun. bor., city and par., Hertfordshire, 21½ m. N.W. of London by rail ; pop. 28,625. Map 71.

St Andrews, mun. bur., spt. and par., Fifeshire, 13½ m. S.E. of Dundee by rail ; bur. pop. 8269. Map 7.

St Anne's Chapel, ham., S. Devonshire, ½ m. N. of Bigbury. Map 89.

St Anne's-on-the-Sea. *See* Lytham.

St Asaph, city and par., Flintshire, 5¼ m. N. of Denbigh ; pop. 1830. Map 37.

St Athan, par. and vil., Glamorganshire, 4½ m. S.S.E. of Cowbridge ; pop. 444. Map 66.

St Austell, urb. dist. and par., Cornwall, 1½ m. W. of St Austell Bay ; pop. 8295. Map 91.

St Bees, coast town and par., Cumberland, 5 m. S. of Whitehaven ; pop. 1609. Map 24.

St Blazey, town and par., Cornwall, 4 m. E.N.E. of St Austell ; pop. 3146. Map 91.

St Breock, par. and vil., Cornwall, 7 m. N.W. of Bodmin ; pop. 713. Map 91.

St Briavals, par. and vil., Gloucestershire, 7¼ m. N.N.E. of Chepstow ; pop. 1210. Map 68.

St Brides Minor, par., Glamorganshire, 2½ m. N. of Bridgend ; pop. 1837. Map 66.

St Budeaux, par. and vil., Devonshire, 4 m. N.W. of Plymouth ; pop. 1803. Map 88.

St Buryan, par. and vil., Cornwall, 5½ m. S.W. of Penzance ; pop. 1132. Map 90.

St Clears, par., town and r. port, in co. and 8 m. S.W. of Carmarthen ; pop. 931. Map 65.

St Columb Major, market town and par., Cornwall, 9 m. N.W. of St. Austell ; pop. 2880. Map 91.

St Cyrus, par. and vil., Kincardineshire, 5¼ m. N.N.E. of Montrose ; pop. 1306. Map 3.

St David's, city and par., Pembrokeshire, 14 m. N.W. of Haverfordwest ; pop. 1543. Map 64.

St Dennis, par. and vil., Cornwall, 4 m. N.W. of St Austell ; pop. 2158. Map 91.

St Dogmells, par., partly within the bor. of Cardigan ; pop. 844. Map 54.

St Dogwells, par., Pembrokeshire, 6 m. S. of Fishguard ; pop. 309. Map 64.

St Endellion, par. and vil., Cornwall, 9 m. N.W. of Bodmin ; pop. 1047. Map 91.

St Ewe, par. and vil., Cornwall, 5 m. S.S.W. of St Austell ; pop. 889. Map 91.

Saintfield, market town and par., co. Down, 15¼ m. S.E. of Belfast ; pop. (town) 533. Map 93.

St Fillans, vil., with ry. sta., Perthshire, 11½ m. W. of Crieff ; pop. 300. Map 5.

St Germans, market town and par., Cornwall, 9½ m. W.N.W. of Plymouth ; pop. 1986. Map 88.

St Helens, par. and co. bor., Lancashire, 10 m. E.N.E. of Liverpool ; pop. 106,793. Map 38.

St Helens, urb. dist. and par., Isle of Wight, 4 m. S.E. of Ryde ; pop. 5478. Map 77.

St Ives, mun. bor., par. and seaport, Cornwall, 8 m. N.E. of Penzance ; pop. 6687. Map 90.

St Ives, mun. bor. and par., in co. and 5¼ m. E. of Huntingdon ; pop. 2664. Map 61.

St Johns, ham., Isle of Man, on r. Neb, 3 m. S.E. of Peel. Map 24.

St John's Chapel, ry. sta., Durham, 7 m. W. of Stanhope. Map 22.

St Just, urb. dist. and par., Cornwall, 7 m. W. of Penzance ; pop. 4356. Map 90.

St Keverne, coast par. and vil., Cornwall, 8 m. S. of Falmouth ; pop. 1745. Map 90.

St Leonards, western suburb of Hastings, Sussex. Map 81.

St Margaret at Cliffe, par. and vil., Kent, 3½ m. N.E. of Dover ; pop. 1280. Map 83.

St Martin's, par. and vil., Salop, 5 m. N.E. of Oswestry ; pop. 1459. Map 46.

St Mary Bourne, par. and vil., Hants, 3 m. N.W. of Whitchurch ; pop. 1151. Map 76.

St Mary Cray, par. and vil., Kent, 4½ m. E.S.E. of Bromley ; pop. 2178. Map 80.

St Mawes, market town, Cornwall, 3 m. E. of Falmouth. Map 91.

St Mellons, par. and vil., Monmouthshire, 4 m. N.E. of Cardiff ; pop. 709. Map 67.

St Michaels-on-Wyre, eccl. dist. and vil., N. Lancashire, 3½ m. S.W. of Garstang ; pop. 548. Map 30.

St Monans, par. and vil., Fifeshire, 3 m. S.W. of Anstruther ; pop. 1796. Map 7.

St Neots, par. and vil., Cornwall, 4½ m. N.W. of Liskeard ; pop. 1086. Map 88.

St Neots, urb. dist. and par., in co. and 8 m. S.W. of Huntingdon ; pop. 4314. Map 61.

St Nicholas at Wade, par. and vil., Kent, 6½ m. S.W. of Margate ; pop. 538. Map 83.

St Osyth, par. and vil., Essex, 10 m. S.E. of Colchester ; pop. 1286. Map 73.

St Stephen, par. and vil., Hertfordshire, 2 m. S. of St Albans ; pop. 1960. Map 71.

Salcombe, urb. dist., Devonshire, 3¼ m. S. of Kingsbridge ; pop. 2383. Map 89.

Sale, urb. dist. and par., Chester, on r. Mersey, 5 m. S.W. of Manchester ; pop. 28,063. Map 39.

Salehurst, par. and vil., E. Sussex, 5 m. N. of Battle ; pop. 1978. Map 81.

Salford, city, parl. and co. bor. and par., S.E. Lancashire ; pop. 223,442. Map 39.

Saline, par. and vil., Fifeshire, 5½ m. N.W. of Dunfermline ; pop. 1379. Map 9.

Salisbury, mun. bor. and co. town of Wiltshire, 23 m. W. of Winchester ; pop. 26,456. Map 76.

Salkeld, Great, par. and vil., Cumberland, 4½ m. N.E. of Penrith ; pop. 394. Map 21.

Saltash, mun. bor. and par., Cornwall, 4 m. N.W. of Devonport ; pop. 3603. Map 88.

Saltburn-by-the-Sea, urb. dist. and par., N.R. Yorkshire, 4½ m. S.E. of Redcar ; pop. 3911. Map 28.

Saltcoats, police bur. and seaport, Ayrshire, 29½ m. S.W. of Glasgow by rail ; pop. 10,173. Map 12.

Salterforth, par. and vil., W.R. Yorkshire, 8 m. S.W. of Skipton ; pop. 643. Map 31.

Saltwood, par. and vil., Kent, ¾ m. N. of Hythe ; pop. 861. Map 83.

Samlesbury, par. and vil., N.E. Lancashire, 3½ m. E. of Preston ; pop. 835. Map 30.

Sampford Courtenay, par. and vil., Devonshire, 3¾ m. N.E. of Okehampton : pop. 731. Map 84.

Sandbach, urb. dist., market town and par., Cheshire, 4½ m. N.E. of Crewe ; pop. 6411. Map 39.

Sandbank, q.s. par. and vil., Argyllshire, 2¾ m. N.W. of Dunoon ; pop. 1257. Map 12.

Sanderstead, par. and vil., Surrey, 3 m. S.E. of Croydon ; pop. 3351. Map 80.

Sandford, par. and vil., Devonshire, 2 m. N.W. of Crediton ; pop. 961. Map 85.

Sandgate, urb. dist. and par., Kent, 1½ m. W.S.W. of Folkestone ; pop. 2596. Map 83.

Sandhurst, par. and vil., S.E. Berkshire, 4½ m. S.E. of Wokingham ; pop. 3802. Map 78.

Sandhurst, par. and vil., Kent, 6 m. S. of Cranbrook ; pop. 898. Map 82.

Sandon, par. and vil., in co. and 5 m. N.E. of Stafford ; pop. 477. Map 47.

Sandown, urb. dist. and par., Isle of Wight, 6½ m. S. of Ryde ; pop. 6167. Map 77.

Sandringham, par. and royal seat, Norfolk, 6 m. N.E. of King's Lynn ; pop. 96. Map 52.

Sandwich, mun. bor. and Cinque port, Kent, 5 m. S.W. of Ramsgate by rail ; pop. 3287. Map 83.

Sandy, urb. dist., Bedfordshire, 3 m. N.W. of Biggleswade ; pop. 3140. Map 60.

Sandygate, vil., Isle of Man, 2½ m. N.N.W. of Sulby. Map 24.

Sandylands, rising watering place, N.W. Lancashire, on S. side of Morecambe ; pop. 3553. Map 30.

Sanquhar, mun. bur. and par., in co. and 26¼ m. N.W. of Dumfries by rail ; pop. 1753. Map 14.

Sarnau, ham., in co. and 9 m. N.E. of Cardigan. Map 54.

Sarre, par. and vil., Kent, 7 m. S.W. of Margate ; pop. 147. Map 83.

Saundersfoot, seaport vil., Pembrokeshire, 2½ m. N. of Tenby. Map 64.

Sawbridgeworth, urb. dist. and par., Hertfordshire, 4 m. S. of Bishop's Stortford ; pop. 2604. Map 72.

Sawley, par. and vil., W.R. Yorkshire, 5 m. S.W. of Ripon ; pop. 312. Map 27.

Sawtry, vil., in co. and 8½ m. N.W. of Huntingdon. Map 60.

Saxmundham, urb. dist. and par., E. Suffolk, 23 m. N.E. of Ipswich ; pop. 1259. Map 63.

Saxthorpe, par. and vil., Norfolk, 5 m. N.W. of Aylsham ; pop. 276. Map 53.

Sca Fell and Pike, mts., Cumberland, 10½ and 10 m. S.W. of Keswick ; alt. 3162 and 3210 ft. Map 25.

Scalby, urb. dist. and par., N.R. Yorkshire, 2½ m. N.W. of Scarborough ; pop. 2771. Map 29.

Scaleby, par. and vil., Cumberland, 5 m. N.E. of Carlisle ; pop. 358. Map 21.

Scales, vil., Lancashire, 4 m. N.W. of Ulverston. Map 25.

Scalford, par. and vil., Leicestershire, 3½ m. N. of Melton Mowbray ; pop. 581. Map 49.

Scammonden, urb. dist., W.R. Yorkshire, 6 m. W. of Huddersfield ; pop. 394. Map 31.

Scampston, par., E.R. Yorkshire, 5 m. N.E. of Malton ; pop. 198. Map 29.

Scarborough, mun. bor., par., spt. and wtg. pl., N.R. Yorks, 42 m. N.E. of York ; pop. 41,791. Map 29.

Scarcliffe, par. and vil., Derbyshire, 8 m. E.S.E. of Chesterfield ; pop. 3442. Map 41.

Scartho, par. and vil., Lindsey, Lincolnshire, 2½ m. S.S.W. of Grimsby ; pop. 744. Map 35.

Scole, par. and vil., Norfolk, 1½ m. E. of Diss ; pop. 566. Map 63.

Scone, Old and **New,** par. and vil., Perthshire, 2 m. N.E. of Perth ; pop. 2935. **S. Palace.** Map 6.

Scopwick, par. and vil., Kesteven, Lincolnshire, 8 m. N. of Sleaford ; pop. 423. Map 42.

Scotby, eccl. dist. and vil., Cumberland, 2½ m. E. of Carlisle ; pop. 769. Map 21.

Scotch Corner, N.R. Yorkshire, 4 m. N. of Catterick Bridge. Map 27.

Scotforth, par., Lancashire, forming a S. suburb of Lancaster ; pop. 301. Map 30.

Scotlandwell, vil., Kinross-shire, 5 m. W. of Leslie. Map 6.

Scots Gap, ry. sta., Northumberland, 11 m. W. of Morpeth. Map 17.

Scotter, par. and vil., Lindsey, Lincolnshire, 3½ m. N.W. of Kirton-in-Lindsey ; pop. 1043. Map 42.

Scourie, vil., Sutherlandshire, 43½ m. N.W. of Lairg ; pop. 77. Map 2.

Scunthorpe, urb. dist. and par., Lincolnshire, 8 m. E. of Crowle ; pop. 33,761. Map 34.

Seaford, urb. dist. and Cinque port, E. Sussex, 2¾ m. S.E. of Newhaven ; pop. 6570. Map 81.

Seaham, coast par. and ry. sta., Durham, 5 m. S. of Sunderland ; pop. 6488. Map 23.

Seaham Harbour, urb. dist. and spt., Durham, 5½ m. S. of Sunderland ; pop. 19,394. Map 23.

Sea Houses, vil. and harbour, Northumberland, 4 m. N.E. of Chathill by rail. Map 17.

Seal, par. and vil., Kent, 1½ m. N.E. of Sevenoaks ; pop. 1627. Map 82.

Seamer, par. and vil., N.R. Yorkshire, 3 m. S.W. of Scarborough ; pop. 640. Map 29.

Seaton, urb. dist. and par., Devonshire, 7½ m. S.W. of Axminster ; pop. 2351. Map 86.

Seaton Carew, eccl. dist. and ry. sta., Durham, in W. Hartlepool co. bor. ; pop. 2170. Map 23.

Seaton Delaval, urb. dist. and par., Northumberland, 3 m. S.W. of Blyth ; pop. 7377. Map 23.

Seaton Sluice, seaport, Northumberland, 3 m. S.E. of Blyth. Map 23.

Sedbergh, market town and par., W.R. Yorkshire, 14½ m. N.W. of Ingleton ; pop. 2586. Map 26.

Sedgeberrow, par. and vil., Worcestershire, 3½ m. S.S.W. of Evesham ; pop. 332. Map 58.

Sedgefield, market town and par., Durham, 8½ m. N.W. of Stockton ; pop. 3111. Map 23.

Sedgemoor, marshy tract, Somersetshire, 8 m. S.E. of Bridgwater. Map 86.

Sedgley, urb. dist. and par., Staffordshire, 3 m. S. of Wolverhampton ; pop. 19,261. Map 47.

Sedgwick, par. and seat, Westmorland, 3½ m. S. of Kendal ; pop. 200. Map 26.

Sedlescombe, par. and vil., E. Sussex, 2½ m. N.E. of Battle ; pop. 546. Map 81.

Seend, par. and vil., Wiltshire, 4 m. W. of Devizes ; pop. 934. Map 75.

Sefton, par. and vil., Lancashire, 6 m. N. of Liverpool ; pop. 296. Map 38.

Seghill, urb. dist. and par., Northumberland, 7 m. N.E. of Newcastle ; pop. 2582. Map 23.

Selborne, par. and vil., Hampshire, 4 m. S.E. of Alton ; pop. 2004. Map 79.

Selby, urb. dist., market town and par., W.R. Yorkshire, 14 m. S. of York; pop. 10,064. Map 33.
Selkirk, mun. bur. and co. town of Selkirkshire, 40 m. S.E. of Edinburgh; pop. 5667. Map 16.
Selling, par. and vil., Kent, 3½ m. S.E. of Faversham; pop. 722. Map 83.
Sellinge, par. and vil., Kent, 5 m. N.W. of Hythe; pop. 793. Map 83.
Selly Oak, a ward in the S.W. of Birmingham. Map 58.
Selsey, par. and vil., W. Sussex, 7 m. S. of Chichester; pop. 2307. Map 79.
Selston, par. and vil., Nottinghamshire, 7 m. S.W. of Mansfield; pop. 9285. Map 41.
Senghennydd, vil. and ry. sta., Glamorganshire, 11 m. N.N.W. of Cardiff. Map 67.
Senny, par., in co. and 8 m. S.W. of Brecknock; pop. 187. Map 66.
Settle, market town and par., W.R. Yorkshire, 15½ m. N.W. of Skipton; pop. 2389. Map 26.
Settrington, par. and vil., E.R. Yorkshire, 3 m. E. of Malton; pop. 448. Map 29.
Sevenoaks, urb. dist. and market town, Kent, 22 m. S.E. of London; pop. 10,482. Map 82.
Severn Stoke, par. and vil., Worcestershire, 2½ m. N.N.E. of Upton; pop. 555. Map 57.
Shadforth, par. and vil., in co. and 5 m. E.S.E. of Durham; pop. 2217. Map 23.
Shaftesbury, mun. bor., N. Dorsetshire, 3½ m. S.W. of Semley; pop. 2366. Map 87.
Shafton, par. and vil., W.R. Yorkshire, 4 m. N.E. of Barnsley; pop. 1290. Map 32.
Shakespeare's Cliff, on coast, Kent, 1 m. S. of Dover; alt. 350 ft. Map 83.
Shaldon, vil., Devonshire, at mouth of r. Teign. Map 89.
Shalfleet, par. and vil., Isle of Wight, 3½ m. E. of Yarmouth; pop. 835. Map 77.
Shalford, par. and vil., Essex, 4½ m. N.W. of Braintree; pop. 515. Map 72.
Shalford, par. and vil., Surrey, 1 m. S. of Guildford; pop. 3077. Map 78.
Shanagolden, par. and vil., in co. and 21 m. W.S.W. of Limerick; pop. 771. Map 94.
Shandon, vil., Dumbartonshire, on E. shore of Gare Loch, 5 m. N.W. of Helensburgh. Map 8.
Shankill, vil. and ry. sta., in co. and 9½ m. S.E. of Dublin. Map 95.
Shanklin, urb. dist. and par., Isle of Wight, 3 m. N.E. of Ventnor; pop. 5071. Map 77.
Shap, urb. dist. and par., Westmorland, 12 m. S.E. of Penrith; pop. 1227. Map 26.
Sharlston, par. and vil., W.R. Yorkshire, 4 m. S.E. of Wakefield; pop. 2776. Map 33.
Sharnbrook, par. and vil., in co. and 7 m. N.N.W. of Bedford; pop. 772. Map 60.
Shaw, eccl. dist. and vil., S.E. Lancashire, 3½ m. N. of Oldham; pop. 5121. Map 31.
Sheerness, urb. dist., spt. and dockyard, Kent, 51¾ m. E. of London; pop. 16,721. Map 73.
Sheffield, co. bor., mfg. tn. and par., W.R. Yorkshire, 53 m. S.W. of York; pop. 511,742. Map 41.
Shefford, market town and par., in co. and 10 m. S.E. of Bedford; pop. 849. Map 60.
Shelf, urb. dist., W.R. Yorkshire, 3 m. N.E. of Halifax; pop. 2600. Map 32.
Shelfield, vil., Staffs., 2½ m. N.E. of Walsall. Map 48.
Shelford, Great, par. and vil., in co. and 3 m. S. of Cambridge; pop. 1534. Map 61.
Shelley, urb. dist. and par., W.R. Yorkshire, 6 m. S.E. of Huddersfield; pop. 1566. Map 32.
Shelsley Beauchamp, par., Worcestershire, 7½ m. S.W. of Stourport; pop. 197. Map 57.
Shenfield, par. and vil., Essex, 1 m. N.E. of Brentwood; pop. 2604. Map 72.
Shenley, par. and vil., Hertfordshire, 5 m. N.W. of Barnet; pop. 1729. Map 71.
Shenstone, par. and vil., Staffordshire, 3 m. S. of Lichfield; pop. 2411. Map 48.
Shepley, urb. dist., W.R. Yorkshire, 7 m. S.E. of Huddersfield; pop. 1668. Map 32.
Shepperton, par. and vil., Middlesex, 2 m. E. of Chertsey; pop. 2858. Map 78.
Sheppey, Isle of, off N. coast of Kent, at mouth of the Thames. Map 83.
Shepshed, urb. dist., Leicestershire, 4 m. W. of Loughborough; pop. 5759. Map 49.
Shepton Mallet, market town and par., Somersetshire, 5 m. E.S.E. of Wells; pop. 4105. Map 75.
Sherborne, urb. dist. and par., Dorsetshire, 18 m. N. of Dorchester; pop. 6542. Map 87.
Sherborne St John, par. and vil., Hants, 2½ m. N.W. of Basingstoke; pop. 736. Map 76.
Sherburn, par. and vil., E.R. Yorkshire, 3½ m. S. of Brompton; pop. 581. Map 29.
Sherburn-in-Elmet, small market town and par., W.R. Yorks, 6¾ m. N. of Knottingley; pop. 1731. Map 33.
Shere, par. and vil., Surrey, 5 m. S.E. of Guildford; pop. 2596. Map 78.
Sheriff Hutton, vil., N.R. Yorkshire, 2½ m. N.W. of Flaxton sta. Map 28.
Sheringham, urb. dist. and par., Norfolk, 4 m. W.N.W. of Cromer; pop. 4141. Map 53.
Sherston, par. and vil., Wiltshire, 5½ m. S.W. of Malmesbury; pop. 1070. Map 68.
Shifnal, market town and par., Salop, 17 m. E.S.E. of Shrewsbury; pop. 3303. Map 47.
Shilbottle, par. and vil., Northumberland, 3 m. S. of Alnwick; pop. 799. Map 17.
Shildon and East Thickley, urb. dist., Durham, 3 m. S.E. of Bishop Auckland; pop. 12,690. Map 23.
Shillelagh, vil. and ry. sta., co. Wicklow, 5 m. S.W. of Tinahely. Map 95.
Shimpling, par. and vil., W. Suffolk, 4 m. N.W. of Lavenham; pop. 381. Map 62.
Shipdham, par. and vil., Norfolk, 4½ m. S.W. of E. Dereham; pop. 1272. Map 52.
Shipley, urb. dist. and par., W.R. Yorkshire, 3 m. N.W. of Bradford; pop. 30,243. Map 32.
Shipston-on-Stour, mkt. tn. and par., Warwickshire, 6½ m. E.N.E. of Chipping Campden; pop. 1365. Map 58.
Shipton-under-Wychwood, par. and vil., Oxon, 6 m. S.S.W. of Chipping Norton; pop. 667. Map 69.
Shirebrook, par. and vil., Derbyshire, 2¼ m. N.E. of Pleasley; pop. 11,309. Map 41.
Shirehampton, eccl. par., on r. Avon, in N.W. of Bristol; pop. 4009. Map 74.
Shirley, eccl. par. and vil., Warwickshire, 6¾ m. S.E. of Birmingham; pop. 3073. Map 58.
Shobdon, par. and vil., Herefordshire, 6½ m. W.N.W. of Leominster; pop. 298. Map 56.
Shoeburyness, urb. dist. and garrison town, Essex, 3 m. S.E. of Southend; pop. 6717. Map 73.
Sholing, eccl. dist. and ry. sta., Hants, in bor. of Southampton; pop. 7527. Map 77.
Shoreham, par. and vil., Kent, 4½ m. N. of Sevenoaks; pop. 1509. Map 80.
Shoreham-by-Sea, urb. dist., par. and spt., W. Sussex, 6 m. W. of Brighton; pop. 8757. Map 79.
Shorncliffe Camp, with ry. sta., Kent, 2 m. W. of Folkestone. Map 83.
Short Heath, Staffordshire, within parl. limits of Wolverhampton; pop. 5048. Map 47.
Shotley Bridge, vil., with ry. sta., Durham, in Benfieldside urb. dist. Map 22.
Shottery, vil., Warwickshire, on W. side of Stratford-on-Avon. Map 58.
Shouldham, par. and vil., Norfolk, 6 m. N.E. of Downham Market; pop. 447. Map 52.
Shrewsbury, mun. bor. and co. town, Salop, 42 m. N.W. of Birmingham; pop. 32,370. Map 47.

Shrewton, par. and vil., Wiltshire, 6 m. N.W. of Amesbury; pop. 634. Map 76.
Shrivenham, par. and vil., Berkshire, 6 m. N.E. of Swindon; pop. 592. Map 69.
Sible Hedingham, par. and vil., Essex, $3\frac{1}{2}$ m. N.W. of Halstead; pop. 1762. Map 62.
Sibsey, par. and vil., Lindsey, Lincolnshire, $4\frac{1}{2}$ m. N.E. of Boston; pop. 1063. Map 43.
Sidcup, urb. dist., Kent, 12 m. S.E. of Charing Cross sta., London; pop. 12,360. Map 80.
Sidestrand, coast par. and vil., Norfolk, 3 m. E.S.E. of Cromer; pop. 103. Map 53.
Sidlesham, par. and vil., W. Sussex, 4 m. S. of Chichester; pop. 801. Map 79.
Sidmouth, urb. dist. and par., Devonshire, 16 m. S.E. of Exeter; pop. 6126. Map 86.
Silchester, par. and vil., Hants, 7 m. N. of Basingstoke; pop. 390. Map 78.
Silecroft, vil., Cumberland, 10 m. S.E. of Ravenglass. Map 25.
Silloth, seaport town, Cumberland, $22\frac{1}{2}$ m. W.S.W. of Carlisle. Map 20.
Silsden, urb. dist. and par., W.R. Yorkshire, 4 m. N.W. of Keighley; pop. 4881. Map 31.
Silverdale, par. and vil., Lancashire, $3\frac{1}{2}$ m. N.W. of Carnforth; pop. 895. Map 25.
Silverstone, par. and vil., Northamptonshire, 4 m. S.S.W. of Towcester; pop. 862. Map 59.
Singleton, Great, par., N. Lancashire, 5 m. E.N.E. of Blackpool; pop. 453. Map 30.
Sittingbourne, urb. dist., par. and seaport, Kent, 16 m. N.W. of Canterbury; pop. 20,175. Map 82.
Sizewell, coast ham., E. Suffolk, 6 m. E. of Saxmundham. Map 63.
Skateraw, vil., Kincardineshire, 6 m. N.E. of Stonehaven. Map 3.
Skegly, par. and vil., Nottinghamshire, 3 m. W. of Mansfield; pop. 6230. Map 41.
Skegness, urb. dist. and par., Lindsey, Lincolnshire, 5 m. N.E. of Wainfleet; pop. 9121. Map 43.
Skelmanthorpe, urb. dist. and par., W.R. Yorkshire, 6 m. S.E. of Huddersfield; pop. 3711. Map 32.
Skelmersdale, urb. dist. and par., S.W. Lancashire, $3\frac{1}{2}$ m. E.S.E. of Ormskirk; pop. 6177. Map 30.
Skelmorlie, coast vil., Ayrshire, $4\frac{1}{2}$ m. N.W. of Largs; par. pop. 1878. Map 12.
Skelton, par. and vil., N.R. Yorkshire, 4 m. N.W. of York; pop. 405. Map 33.
Skelton, par. and vil., Cumberland, $6\frac{1}{2}$ m. N.W. of Penrith; pop. 591. Map 21.
Skelton, urb. dist. and par., N.R. Yorkshire, 3 m. N.E. of Guisborough; pop. 13,654. Map 28.
Skene, par. and ham., in co. and $8\frac{3}{4}$ m. W. of Aberdeen; pop. 1405. Map 3.
Skerries, seaport and watering place, in co. and 18 m. N. of Dublin; pop. 1770. Map 93.
Skerries, The, group of rocky isles off N.W. coast of Anglesey; lighthouse 75 ft. high. Map 36.
Skewen, dist. and ry. sta., Glamorganshire, on N. side of Neath. Map 66.
Skibbereen, urb. dist. and seaport, in co. and 54 m. S.W. of Cork; pop. 2620. Map 94.
Skidby, par. and vil., E.R. Yorkshire, 4 m. S.W. of Beverley; pop. 291. Map 35.
Skinburness, vil., Cumberland, 2 m. N.E. of Silloth. Map 20.
Skipsea, coast par. and vil., E.R. Yorkshire; pop. 286. Ruins of Saxon castle in vicinity. Map 35.
Skipton, urb. dist., market town and par., W.R. Yorks, 9 m. N.W. of Keighley; pop. 12,434. Map 32.
Skipwith, par. and vil., E.R. Yorkshire, $12\frac{3}{4}$ m. S.E. of York; pop. 226. Map 34.
Skirling, par. and vil., Peeblesshire, $2\frac{1}{2}$ m. N.E. of Biggar; pop. 222. Map 15.
Skirwith, par. and vil., Cumberland, $6\frac{1}{2}$ m. E.N.E. of Penrith; pop. 238. Map 21.
Skye, Isle of, Inverness-shire; pop. 11,031. Map 2.
Slaithwaite, urb. dist., par. and mkt. tn., W.R. Yorks. 4 m. S.W. of Huddersfield; pop. 5181. Map 31.
Slaley, par. and vil., Northumberland, $4\frac{1}{2}$ m. S.E. of Hexham; pop. 585. Map 22.
Slamannan, par. and vil., Stirlingshire, $5\frac{1}{2}$ m. S.W. o Falkirk; pop. 1610. Map 9.
Slane, par. and vil., Meath, 8 m. W. of Drogheda pop. 992. Map 93.
Sleaford, urb. dist., Kesteven, in co. and $21\frac{1}{2}$ m. S.E. of Lincoln; pop. 7024. Map 42.
Sledmere, par. and vil., E.R. Yorkshire, 8 m. N.W. of Driffield; pop. 491. Map 29.
Sleights, vil., N.R. Yorkshire, $3\frac{1}{2}$ m. S.W. of Whitby. Map 29.
Sligachan, place, Isle of Skye, 9 m. S. of Portree. Map 2.
Sligo, mun. bor., spt. and co. tn. of Sligo, 134 m. N.W. of Dublin by rail; pop. 11,439. Map 92.
Slinfold, par. and vil., W. Sussex, 4 m. W. of Horsham; pop. 979. Map 79.
Slingsby, par. and vil., N.R. Yorkshire, 6 m. W.N.W. of Malton; pop. 440. Map 28.
Slough, urb. dist. and market town, Buckinghamshire, 2 m. N.E. of Windsor; pop. 33,530. Map 71.
Slyne, par. and vil., N. Lancashire, 3 m. N. of Lancaster; pop. 695. Map 25.
Sma' Glen, Perthshire, $8\frac{3}{4}$ m. N. of Crieff. Map 6.
Smailholm, par. and vil., Roxburghshire, 6 m. N.W. of Kelso; pop. 261. Map 16.
Smallburgh, par. and vil., Norfolk, 12 m. N.E. of Norwich; pop. 346. Map 53.
Smallthorne, urb. dist., now in Stoke-on-Trent, $1\frac{1}{2}$ m. E.N.E. of Burslem; pop. 14,013. Map 39.
Smarden, par. and vil., Kent, 8 m. W. of Ashford; pop. 992. Map 82.
Smeeth Road, ry. sta., Norfolk, $3\frac{3}{4}$ m. E. of Wisbech. Map 51.
Smethwick, co. and parl. bor., Staffordshire, $3\frac{1}{2}$ m. N.W. of Birmingham; pop. 84,354. Map 48.
Smithfield, vil., N.W. Cumberland, $4\frac{1}{4}$ m. S.E. of Longtown. Map 21.
Snainton, par. and vil., N.R. Yorkshire, 9 m. S.W. of Scarborough; pop. 685. Map 29.
Snaith, market town and par., W.R. Yorkshire, 7 m. W. of Goole; pop. 1560. Map 34.
Snettisham, par. and vil., Norfolk, 4 m. S. of Hunstanton; pop. 1443. Map 52.
Snitterfield, par. and vil., Warwickshire, $3\frac{1}{2}$ m. N.N.E. of Stratford-on-Avon; pop. 691. Map 58.
Snodland, par. and vil., Kent, 6 m. S.S.W. of Rochester by rail; pop. 4481. Map 80.
Snowdon, Mt., in co. and 9 m. S.E. of Carnarvon; alt. 3560 ft. Map 36.
Soham, market town and par., Cambridgeshire, 5 m. S.E. of Ely; pop. 4737. Map 61.
Solihull, market town and par., Warwickshire, $6\frac{1}{2}$ m. S.E. of Birmingham; pop. 11,552. Map 58.
Solva, seaport vil., Pembrokeshire, 3 m. E. of St David's. Map 64.
Somerby, par. and vil., Leicestershire, 5 m. W. of Oakham; pop. 480. Map 50.
Somerby, Old, par. and vil., Kesteven, Lincolnshire, 3 m. S.E. of Grantham; pop. 185. Map 50.
Somerford, Great, par. and vil., Wiltshire, 4 m. S.E. of Malmesbury; pop. 421. Map 68.
Somerton, market town and par., Somersetshire, $4\frac{1}{2}$ m. E.N.E. of Langport; pop. 1776. Map 86.
Sopley, par. and vil., Hants, $2\frac{1}{2}$ m. N. of Christchurch; pop. 793. Map 77.
Soulby, par. and vil., Westmorland, 2 m. N.W. of Kirkby Stephen; pop. 200. Map 26.
Southall, urb. dist. and market town, Middlesex, $3\frac{1}{2}$ m. N.W. of Brentford; pop. 38,932. Map 71.
Southam, market town and par., in co. and 9 m. S.E. of Warwick; pop. 1744. Map 59.

Southampton, co. bor., par., spt. and co. town of Hampshire, 79 m. S.W. of London by rail; co. bor. pop. 176,025. Map 77.

Southborough, urb. dist. and par., Kent, 1½ m. N. of Tunbridge Wells; pop. 7352. Map 82.

South Brent, par. and vil., S. Devonshire, 7 m. W. of Totnes; pop. 1601. Map 89.

South Crosland, urb. dist., W.R. Yorkshire, 3 m. S.W. of Huddersfield; pop. 2993. Map 32.

South Darley, urb. dist., Derbyshire, adjoining North Darley; pop. 731. Map 40.

Southend-on-Sea, co. bor. and spt., Essex, 3 m. W. of Shoeburyness; pop. 120,093. Map 72.

Southerness, vil., Kirkcudbrightshire, 10 m. S.E. of Dalbeattie. Map 20.

Southfleet, par. and vil., Kent, 3 m. S.W. of Gravesend; pop. 1311. Map 80.

Southgate, urb. dist., Middlesex, 2½ m. S.W. of Enfield station; pop. 55,570. Map 71.

South Harting, locality, W. Sussex, in Midhurst rural district. Map 79.

South Milford, par. and vil., W.R. Yorkshire, 12 m. E. of Leeds; pop. 1122. Map 33.

Southminster, par. and vil., Essex, 8 m. S.E. of Maldon; pop. 1592. Map 73.

South Molton, mun. bor. and par., Devonshire, 10½ m. S.E. of Barnstaple; pop. 2818. Map 85.

South Newton, par. and vil., Wiltshire, 2 m. N. of Wilton; pop. 407. Map 76.

South Ockendon, par. and vil., Essex, 5½ m. S.E. of Romford; pop. 1432. Map 72.

South Otterington, par. and vil., N.R. Yorkshire, 4 m. S. of Northallerton; pop. 292. Map 28.

Southowram, urb. dist., W.R. Yorkshire, adjoining Halifax; pop. 2570. Map 32.

Southport, wtg. pl., parl. and co. bor. and par., S.W. Lancs, 18½ m. N. of Liverpool; pop. 78,927. Map 30.

Southrepps, par. and vil., Norfolk, 4½ m. S.E. of Cromer; pop. 755. Map 53.

Southsea, residential dist. and watering place, Hants, on S. side of Portsmouth. Map 79.

South Shields, parl. and co. bor., Durham, 8 m. E. of Newcastle-on-Tyne; pop. 113,452. Map 23.

Southwell, market town, see of a bishop and par., Notts, 6 m. W. of Newark; pop. 3085. Map 41.

Southwick, par., Wiltshire, 2 m. S.W. of Trowbridge; pop. 754. Map 75.

Southwick, urb. dist., Sussex, 4 m. W. of Brighton; pop. 6138. Map 81.

South Wingfield, par. and vil., Derbyshire, 2 m. W. of Alfreton; pop. 1605. Map 41.

Southwold, mun. bor. and seaport, E. Suffolk, 11 m. S. of Lowestoft; pop. 2753. Map 63.

Sowerby, urb. dist. and par., W.R. Yorkshire, 4 m. S.W. of Halifax; pop. 14,679. Map 32.

Sowerby Bridge, dist., 2½ m. S.W. of Halifax. Map 32.

Soyland, urb. dist., W.R. Yorkshire, 4½ m. S.W. of Halifax; pop. 3057. Map 32.

Spalding, urb. dist., Holland, Lincolnshire, 14 m. S.W. of Boston; pop. 12,592. Map 51.

Spaldington, par. and vil., E.R. Yorkshire, 4 m. N. of Howden; pop. 547. Map 34.

Sparsholt, par. and vil., Hants, 2½ m. N.W. of Winchester; pop. 376. Map 76.

Sparsholt, par. and vil., Berkshire, 3½ m. W. of Wantage; pop. 286. Map 69.

Spean Bridge, ham. and ry. sta., Inverness-shire, 9½ m. N.E. of Fort William. Map 2.

Speen, par. and vil., Berkshire, 1½ m. N.W. of Newbury; pop. 1090. Map 70.

Spenborough, urb. dist., W.R. Yorkshire, 6 m. S.E. of Bradford; pop. 30,962. Map 32.

Spennymoor, urb. dist. and par., Durham, 4 m. N.E. of Bishop Auckland; pop. 16,361. Map 23.

Spettisbury, par. and vil., Dorsetshire, 3 m. S.E. of Blandford; pop. 426. Map 87.

Spilsby, town and par., Lindsey, Lincolnshire, 7 m. S.W. of Alford; pop. 1400. Map 43.

Spittal, coast town and watering place, Northumberland, near Berwick-on-Tweed; pop. 2268. Map 11.

Spittal, place, Roxburghshire, on Rule Water, 1½ m. E. of Denholm. Map 16.

Spofforth, par. and vil., W.R. Yorkshire, 3½ m. N.W. of Wetherby; pop. 799. Map 33.

Spondon, par. and vil., Derbyshire, 3 m. E. of Derby; pop. 3132. Map 49.

Spreyton, par. and vil., Devonshire, 7 m. E. of Okehampton; pop. 338. Map 85.

Springfield, vil. and ry. sta., Fifeshire, 3 m. S.W. of Cupar. Map 7.

Springhead, urb. dist., W.R. Yorkshire, on E. side of Oldham; pop. 4833. Map 40.

Sproatley, par. and vil., E.R. Yorkshire, 4 m. N. of Hedon; pop. 274. Map 35.

Sprouston, par. and vil., Roxburghshire, 2 m. N.E. of Kelso; pop. 776. Map 16.

Stackpole, coast par. and ham., in co. and 3 m. S. of Pembroke; pop. 225. Map 64.

Stacksteads, vil., S.E. Lancashire, 1½ m. S.W. of Bacup. Map 31.

Staffa, isl., Inner Hebrides, Argyllshire. Map 12.

Stafford, mun. bor., par. and co. tn., Staffordshire, 27 m. N.N.W. of Birmingham; pop. 29,485. Map 47.

Staindrop, par. and vil., Durham, 8 m. S.W. of Bishop Auckland; pop. 1347. Map 27.

Staines, urb. dist. and market town, S.W. Middlesex, 6 m. S.E. of Windsor; pop. 21,209. Map 71.

Stainforth, par. and vil., W.R. Yorkshire, 3 m. N. of Settle; pop. 198. Map 26.

Stainforth and Hatfield, par. and vil., W.R. Yorks, on r. Don, 9 m. N.E. of Doncaster; pop. 2217. Map 33.

Stainland, urb. dist. and par., W.R. Yorkshire, 3½ m. S.W. of Halifax; pop. 4246. Map 31.

Stainton, par., Durham, 2½ m. N.E. of Barnard Castle; pop. 302. Map 27.

Staintondale, coast par. and ry. sta., N.R. Yorkshire, 7 m. N.W. of Scarborough; pop. 355. Map 29.

Staithes, vil. and ry. sta., N.R. Yorkshire, 9 m. N.W. of Whitby. Map 29.

Stalbridge, town and par., Dorsetshire, 7 m. E. of Sherborne; pop. 1222. Map 87.

Stalham, par. and vil., Norfolk, 6 m. S.E. of N. Walsham; pop. 937. Map 53.

Stallingborough, par. and vil., Lincolnshire, 5 m. N.W. of Grimsby; pop. 508. Map 35.

Stalybridge, mun. bor. and par., Cheshire, on r. Tame, 7½ m. E. of Manchester; pop. 2483. Map 40.

Stambourne, par. and vil., Essex, 8 m. N.W. of Halstead; pop. 299. Map 62.

Stamford, mun. bor., Kesteven, Lincolnshire, 16½ m. N.W. of Peterborough; pop. 9946. Map 50.

Standish with Langtree, urb. dist., Lancashire, 3½ m. N.W. of Wigan; pop. 7262. Map 30.

Standlake, par. and vil., Oxon, 5 m. S.E. of Witney; pop. 510. Map 69.

Standon, par. and vil., Hertfordshire, 8 m. N.E. of Hertford; pop. 2485. Map 71.

Stanford Bridge, ham., Worcestershire, 7 m. S.W. of Stourport. Map 57.

Stanford-in-the-Vale, par. and vil., Berkshire, 4 m. S.E. of Faringdon; pop. 764. Map 69.

Stanford-le-Hope, par. and vil., Essex, 5 m. S.W. of Pitsea; pop. 3379. Map 72.

Stanhope, urb. dist. and par., Durham, 6 m. N.W. of Wolsingham; pop. 1746. Map 22.

Stanley, urb. dist., par. and vil., Durham, 4 m. N.E. of Lanchester; pop. 24,458. Map 23.

Stanley, urb. dist., W.R. Yorkshire, 2 m. N.E. of Wakefield; pop. 14,570. Map 33.

Stanley, vil. and *q.s.* par., Perthshire, 7 m. N. of Perth ; pop. 1240.   Map 6.

Stanmore, Great, par. and vil., N. Middlesex, 2 m. N.E. of Harrow ; pop. 1849.   Map 71.

Stanningfield, par. and vil., W. Suffolk, 5½ m. S. of Bury St Edmunds ; pop. 211.   Map 62.

Stannington, par. and vil., Northumberland, 4 m. S. of Morpeth ; pop. 1664.   Map 23.

Stanstead Abbots, par. and vil., Hertfordshire, 4 m. E. of Hertford ; pop. 1362.   Map 71.

Stanton Harcourt, par. and vil., Oxon, 4½ m. S.E. of Witney ; pop. 451.   Map 61.

Stansted, par. and vil., Kent, 7 m. N.E. of Sevenoaks ; pop. 426.   Map 82.

Stanwell, par. and vil., Middlesex, 2 m. N.E. of Staines ; pop. 2306.   Map 71.

Stanwix, par., Cumberland, on N. side of Carlisle ; pop. 681.   Map 21.

Stapleford, par. and vil., in co. and 4 m. S.E. of Cambridge ; pop. 514.   Map 61.

Stapleford, par., Leicestershire, 4 m. E. of Melton Mowbray ; pop. 133.   Map 50.

Stapleford-Abbots, par., Essex, 5 m. N. of Romford ; pop. 391.   Map 72.

Staplehurst, par. and vil., Kent, 8 m. S.S.E. of Maidstone ; pop. 1897.   Map 82.

Star, vil., Fifeshire, 1¾ m. N.E. of Markinch.   Map 7.

Staughton, Great, par. and vil., Huntingdonshire, 2½ m. S.E. of Kimbolton ; pop. 685.   Map 60.

Staunton, par. and vil., in co. and 7½ m. N.N.W. of Gloucester.   Map 57.

Staunton-on-Arrow, par., Herefordshire, 5 m. N.E. of Kington ; pop. 237.   Map 56.

Staunton-on-Wye, par. and vil., in co. and 9 m. W.N.W. of Hereford ; pop. 446.   Map 56.

Staveley, par., Derbyshire, 4 m. N.E. of Chesterfield ; pop. 12,646.   Map 41.

Staveley, par. and ham., N. Lancashire, 5 m. N. of Cartmel ; pop. 384.   Map 25.

Steeple Ashton, par. and vil., Wiltshire, 3 m. E. of Trowbridge ; pop. 667.   Map 75.

Stenhousemuir, town, Stirlingshire, 3 m. N.W. of Falkirk ; pop. 4601.   Map 9.

Stenton, par. and vil., East Lothian, 4 m. S.E. of East Linton ; pop. of vil. 113.   Map 11.

Steps, residential dist., Lanarkshire, 4½ m. N.E. of Glasgow ; pop. 2823.   Map 8.

Sterridge, vil., N. Devon, 3 m. S.E. of Ilfracombe. Map 84.

Stetchworth, par. and vil., Cambridgeshire, 3 m. S. of Newmarket ; pop. 659.   Map 61.

Stevenage, urb. dist. and par., Hertfordshire, 4 m. S.E. of Hitchin ; pop. 5476.   Map 71.

Stevenston, town and par., Ayrshire, 28 m. S.W. of Glasgow ; pop. 8224.   Map 12.

Stewarton, town, police bur. and par., Ayrshire, 18 m. S.W. of Glasgow ; pop. 2749.   Map 8.

Stewartstown, market town, with ry. sta., Tyrone, 8½ m. N.E. of Dungannon ; pop. 623.   Map 93.

Stewkley, par. and vil., Buckinghamshire, 4 m. N.W. of Leighton Buzzard ; pop. 1018.   Map 60.

Steyning, par. and market town, W. Sussex, 5 m. N.W. of Shoreham ; pop. 1875.   Map 79.

Steynton, par. and ham., Pembrokeshire, 1½ m. N.N.E. of Milford ; pop. 1408.   Map 64.

Stichill, par., Roxburghshire and Berwickshire, 3½ m. N. of Kelso ; pop. 523.   Map 16.

Stickford, par. and vil., Lindsey, Lincolnshire, 5 m. S.W. of Spilsby ; pop. 404.   Map 43.

Sticklepath, vil., Devonshire, 3½ m. E.S.E. of Okehampton.   Map 84.

Stiffkey, par. and vil., Norfolk, 3½ m. E. of Wells ; pop. 521.   Map 52.

Stillingfleet, par. and vil., E.R. Yorkshire, 7 m. S. of York ; pop. 317.   Map 34.

Stillington, par. and vil., N.R. Yorkshire, 4 m. S.E. of Easingwold ; pop. 510.   Map 28.

Stilton, par. and vil., Huntingdonshire, 2 m. N.W. of Holme ; pop. 455.   Map 50.

Stirling, par., bur. and co. town of Stirlingshire, 20½ m. N.E. of Glasgow ; pop. 22,593.   Map 9.

Stithians, par. and vil., Cornwall, 4 m. S.E. of Redruth ; pop. 1522.   Map 90.

Stockbridge, par. and vil., Hants, 6½ m. S. of Andover ; pop. 862.   Map 76.

Stockbury, par. and vil., Kent, 4 m. S.W. of Sittingbourne ; pop. 481.   Map 82.

Stockcross, eccl. dist. and vil., Berkshire, 2 m. N.W. of Newbury ; pop. 514.   Map 76.

Stockingford, eccl. dist. and vil., Warwickshire, 1½ m. W. of Nuneaton ; pop. 10,598.   Map 48.

Stockland, par. and vil., Devonshire, 5 m. N.W. of Axminster ; pop. 731.   Map 86.

Stockport, co. bor. and par., Cheshire and Lancashire, 5½ m. S.E. of Manchester ; pop. 125,505.   Map 39.

Stocksbridge, urb. dist., W.R. Yorkshire, 7½ m. N.W. of Sheffield ; pop. 9253.   Map 40.

Stockton Heath, par. and vil., Cheshire, 1½ m. S. of Warrington sta.   Map 39.

Stockton-on-Tees, parl. and mun. bor., Durham, 4 m. S.W. of Middlesbrough ; pop. 67,724.   Map 28.

Stockton-on-Teme, par. and vil., Worcestershire, 6½ m. S.W. of Bewdley ; pop. 115.   Map 57.

Stockton-on-the-Forest, par. and vil., N.R. Yorkshire, 4½ m. N.E. of York ; pop. 393.   Map 34.

Stockwith, East, par. and vil., Lindsey, Lincolnshire, 3½ m. N.E. of Gainsborough ; pop. 314.   Map 42.

Stogumber, par. and vil., Somersetshire, 5 m. S.E. of Watchet ; pop. 722.   Map 85.

Stogursey, par. and vil., Somersetshire, 7½ m. N.W. of Bridgwater ; pop. 886.   Map 74.

Stoke, par. and vil., Kent, 7 m. N.E. of Rochester ; pop. 686.   Map 72.

Stoke-by-Clare, par. and vil., W. Suffolk, 2 m. S.W. of Clare ; pop. 427.   Map 62.

Stoke Canon, par. and vil., Devonshire, 3½ m. N.E. of Exeter ; pop. 360.   Map 85.

Stoke Climsland, par., Cornwall, 7½ m. W. of Tavistock ; pop. 1578.   Map 88.

Stoke Ferry, par. and vil., Norfolk, 6 m. S.E. of Downham Market ; pop. 589.   Map 52.

Stoke Fleming, coast par. and vil., Devonshire, 2½ m. S.W. of Dartmouth ; pop. 602.   Map 89.

Stoke-in-Teignhead, coast par. and vil., Devonshire, 2 m. S.W. of Teignmouth ; pop. 469.   Map 89.

Stoke-on-Trent, city, co. bor. and par., Staffordshire, 16 m. N. of Stafford ; pop. 276,619.   Map 39.

Stoke Poges, vil., Buckinghamshire, 2 m. N. of Slough. Map 71.

Stokesley, market town and par., N.R. Yorkshire, 8½ m. S.E. of Stockton ; pop. 1641.   Map 28.

Stone, urb. dist. and par., in co. and 7 m. N. of Stafford ; pop. 5952.   Map 47.

Stonegrave, par. and vil., N.R. Yorkshire, 5 m. S.E. of Helmsley ; pop. 98.   Map 28.

Stonehaven, bur. spt. and co. town of Kincardineshire, 16 m. S.W. of Aberdeen ; pop. 4185. Map 3.

Stonehenge, group of large standing stones, Salisbury Plain, Wiltshire, 2 m. W. of Amesbury.   Map 76.

Stonehouse, town and par., Lanarkshire, 7 m. S.E. of Hamilton ; pop. 3555.   Map 9.

Stonehouse, par. and vil., Gloucestershire, 3 m. W. of Stroud ; pop. 2393.   Map 68.

Stonehouse, par., Devonshire, in co. bor. of Plymouth ; pop. 13,857.   Map 88.

Stoney Middleton, par. and vil., Oxon, 3 m. W.N.W. of Bicester ; pop. 256.   Map 70.

Stony Stratford, market town, in co. and 8 m. N.E. of Buckingham ; pop. 1992.   Map 60.

Storeton, par. and vil., Cheshire, 3 m. S.W. of Birkenhead ; pop. 279.   Map 38.

Stornoway, bur., seaport and par., Lewis, Isl., Outer Hebrides ; town pop. 3771. Map 2.

Storrington, par. and vil., W. Sussex, 6½ m. N.E. of Arundel ; pop. 1388. Map 79.

Stoughton, par., W. Sussex, 6 m. N.W. of Chichester ; pop. 615. Map 79.

Stoughton, eccl. dist. and ham., Surrey, 1½ m. N.N.W. of Guildford. Map 78.

Stourbridge, mun. bor., Worcestershire, 11½ m. W. of Birmingham ; pop. 19,903. Map 57.

Stourport, urb. dist., Worcestershire, 4 m. W. of Kidderminster ; pop. 5949. Map 57.

Stourton, par. and vil., Wiltshire, 3 m. N.W. of Mere ; pop. 418. Map 75.

Stourton Caundle, par. and vil., Dorsetshire, 4½ m. N.W. of Sturminster Newton ; pop. 254. Map 87.

Stow, par. and vil., Midlothian, 6¼ m. N. of Galashiels ; pop. 493. Map 10.

Stow Bardolf, par. and vil. (**Stowbridge**), Norfolk, 2½ m. N.N.E. of Downham Market ; pop. 1275. Map 52.

Stowmarket, urb. dist. and par., E. Suffolk, 12½ m. N.W. of Ipswich ; pop. 4296. Map 62.

Stow-on-the-Wold, urb. dist. and par., Glos., 4 m. S.S.W. of Moreton-in-the-Marsh ; pop. 1266. Map 58.

Strabane, urb. dist., co. Tyrone, 14 m. S.W. of Londonderry ; pop. 5107. Map 93.

Strachur, par. and vil., Argyllshire, on E. side of Loch Fyne ; pop. 548. Map 12.

Stradbally, market town and par., Leix co., 6 m. E.S.E. of Maryborough ; pop. 1092. Map 95.

Stradbally, coast par. and vil., Waterford, 8 m. N.E. of Dungarvan ; pop. 1251. Map 95.

Stradbroke, par. and town, E. Suffolk, 5½ m. E. of Eye ; pop. 927. Map 63.

Stradishall, par. and vil., W. Suffolk, 5 m. N. of Clare ; pop. 263. Map 62.

Straiton, par. and vil., Ayrshire, 7 m. S.E. of Maybole ; pop. 1166. Map 12.

Straits, vil., Lancashire, 4½ m. S. of Preston. Map 30.

Stranraer, mun. bur., spt. and par., Wigtownshire, at head of Loch Ryan ; pop. 6490. Map 18.

Strata Florida, par. and ham., Cardiganshire, 5 m. N.N.E. of Tregaron ; pop. 440. Map 55.

Stratford, populous dist. in mun. bor. of West Ham, Essex, 3½ m. N.E. of London. Map 71.

Stratford-on-Avon, mun. bor., in co. and 8 m. S.W. of Warwick ; pop. 11,616. Map 58.

Stratford Tony, par., Wiltshire, 4 m. S.W. of Salisbury; pop. 86. Map 76.

Strathallan, valley of r. Allan, Perthshire and Stirlingshire. Map 6.

Strathaven, town, Lanarkshire, 7 m. S. of Hamilton ; pop. 4207. Map 14.

Strathblane, par. and vil., Stirlingshire, 11 m. N. of Glasgow ; pop. 1275. Map 8.

Strathearn, valley of r. Earn, Perthshire, 32 m. in length. Map 6.

Strathkinnes, q.s. par. and vil., Fifeshire, 3 m. W. of St Andrews ; pop. 851. Map 7.

Strathmiglo, par. and vil., Fifeshire, 6½ m. W. of Ladybank Junction ; pop. 1609. Map 6.

Strathpeffer, vil., Ross and Cromarty, 5 m. W. of Dingwall ; pop. 875. Map 3.

Strathyre, vil. and ry. sta., Perthshire, 8 m. N.W. of Callander. Map 5.

Stratton and Bude, urb. dist., Cornwall, 16 m. N.W. of Launceston ; pop. 3836. Map 84.

Stratton-on-the-Fosse, par. and vil., Somersetshire, 7½ m. W.N.W. of Frome ; pop. 412. Map 75.

Streatley, par. and vil., Berkshire, 6 m. S. of Wallingford ; pop. 793. Map 70.

Street, urb. dist. and par., Somersetshire, 2 m. S.W. of Glastonbury ; pop. 4453. Map 74.

Street Cobham, ham., N. Surrey, ½ m. N.W. of Cobham. Map 78.

Strensall, par. and vil., N.R. Yorkshire, 6 m. N.N.E. of York ; pop. 738. Map 34.

Stretford, urb. dist., Lancashire, 4 m. S.W. of Manchester ; pop. 56,795. Map 39.

Stretton, par. and vil., Cheshire, 3½ m. S. of Warrington ; pop. 352. Map 39.

Stretton-on-Dunsmore, par. and vil., Warwickshire, 7 m. S.E. of Coventry ; pop. 612. Map 59.

Strichen, par. and vil., Aberdeenshire, 10 m. S.W. of Fraserburgh ; pop. 2243. Map 3.

Strokestown, market town, in co. and 12 m. N.E. of Roscommon ; pop. 801. Map 92.

Strome Ferry, vil., Ross and Cromarty, on Loch Carron, 53 m. S.W. of Dingwall. Map 2.

Strone, watering place, Argyllshire, 6 m. N.W. of Greenock by water. Map 12.

Strood Intra, par. and town, Kent, on left bank of r. Medway ; pop. 10,283. Map 82.

Stroud, urb. dist. and par., in co. and 12 m. S. of Gloucester ; pop. 8360. Map 68.

Studland, par. and vil., Isle of Purbeck, Dorsetshire, 5 m. E. of Corfe Castle ; pop. 691. Map 87.

Sturminster Newton, market town and par., Dorsetshire, 9 m. N.W. of Blandford ; pop. 1619. Map 87.

Sturry, par. and vil., Kent, 2½ m. N.E. of Canterbury ; pop. 1386. Map 83.

Sturton, par. and vil., Lindsey, Lincolnshire, 6 m. S.E. of Gainsborough ; pop. 539. Map 42.

Sudbourne, par. and vil., E. Suffolk, 4 m. S.W. of Aldeburgh ; pop. 462. Map 63.

Sudbury, vil., Middlesex, 3 m. S.E. of Harrow. Map 71.

Sudbury, mun. bor. and par., W. Suffolk, 21 m. W. of Ipswich ; pop. 7007. Map 62.

Sulby, vil., Isle of Man, 4 m. W. of Ramsey, on r. Sulby. Map 24.

Sully, coast par. and ry. sta., Glamorganshire, 6 m. S.W. of Cardiff ; pop. 576. Map 67.

Sunbury-on-Thames, urb. dist. and par., Middlesex, 4½ m. W. of Kingston ; pop. 13,329. Map 78.

Sunderland, co. bor., spt. and par., Durham, 12 m. S.E. of Newcastle ; pop. 185,870. Map 23.

Sunderland, North, par. and vil., Northumberland, 7 m. S.E. of Belford ; pop. 1449. Map 17.

Sundridge, par. and vil., Kent, 3 m. W. of Sevenoaks ; pop. 1814. Map 80.

Sunningdale, par. and vil., Berkshire, 8 m. S.W. of Staines ; pop. 1657. Map 78.

Sunninghill, par. and vil., Berkshire, 5 m. S.W. of Windsor ; pop. 5839. Map 78.

Surbiton, urb. dist., Surrey, 12 m. S.W. of Waterloo sta., London ; pop. 29,396. Map 78.

Sutton, par. and vil., Kent, 3½ m. S.W. of Deal ; pop. 144. Map 83.

Sutton, par., in co. and 4 m. N.E. of Hereford ; pop. 351. Map 57.

Sutton and Cheam, urb. dist., Surrey, 4½ m. S.W. of Croydon ; pop. 46,488. Map 80.

Sutton at Hone, par. and vil., Kent, 7 m. S.W. of Gravesend ; pop. 5804. Map 80.

Sutton Benger, par. and vil., Wiltshire, 4 m. N.E. of Chippenham ; pop. 327. Map 75.

Sutton Bridge, urb. dist., Holland, Lincolnshire, 7 m. N. of Wisbech ; pop. 2837. Map 51.

Sutton Coldfield, mun. bor. and par., Warwickshire, 7 m. N.E. of Birmingham ; pop. 29,924. Map 48.

Sutton-in-Ashfield, urb. dist., mfg. mkt. tn. and par., Notts, 3 m. S.W. of Mansfield ; pop. 25,151. Map 41.

Sutton St Edmund, par. and vil., Holland, Lincolnshire, 6½ m. N.W. of Wisbech ; pop. 677. Map 51.

Sutton St James, par. and vil., Holland, Lincolnshire, 3½ m. S.W. of Long Sutton sta. ; pop. 676. Map 51.

Sutton Valence, par. and vil., Kent, 4 m. N.E. of Staplehurst; pop. 1174. Map 82.

Swadlincote, urb. dist. and par., Derbyshire, 5 m. S.E. of Burton-on-Trent; pop. 20,305. Map 48.

Swaffham, urb. dist. and par., Norfolk, 15 m. S.E. of King's Lynn; pop. 2783. Map 52.

Swaffham Bulbeck, par. and vil., in co. and 7 m. E.N.E. of Cambridge; pop. 639. Map 61.

Swaffham Prior, par. and vil., in co. and 8 m. N.E. of Cambridge; pop. 892. Map 61.

Swafield, par. and vil., Norfolk, 2 m. N. of North Walsham; pop. 148. Map 53.

Swainswick, par. and vil., Somersetshire, 2½ m. N.E. of Bath; pop. 502. Map 75.

Swallowcliffe, par. and vil., Wiltshire, 1½ m. S.E. of Tisbury; pop. 236. Map 87.

Swallowfield, par. and vil., S. Berkshire, 6 m. S. of Reading; pop. 1587. Map 78.

Swanage, urb. dist. and par., Dorsetshire, 9 m. S.E. of Wareham; pop. 6276. Map 87.

Swanbach, vil., Cheshire, 6 m. S. of Nantwich. Map 47.

Swanley Junction, vil. and ry. stn., Kent, 4 m. S.E. of Sidcup. Map 80.

Swanscombe, urban dist. and par., Kent, on r. Thames, W. of Northfleet; pop. 8541. Map 72.

Swansea, parl. and co. bor., spt. and par., Glamorganshire, 32½ m. S.W. of Merthyr Tydfil, and 192¾ m. W. of London by rail; pop. 164,825. Map 66.

Swanton Abbot, par. and vil., Norfolk, 3 m. S.W. of North Walsham; pop. 443. Map 53.

Swanton Morley, par. and vil., Norfolk, 3½ m. N.E. of East Dereham; pop. 546. Map 52.

Swanton Novers, par., Norfolk, 6 m. E.N.E. of Fakenham; pop. 270. Map 52.

Swanwick, eccl. dist. and vil., Derbyshire, in par. of and 2½ m. S.W. of Alfreton; pop. 2034. Map 41.

Swarkeston, par. and vil., Derbyshire, 5 m. S. of Derby; pop. 155. Map 49.

Swavesey, par. and vil., Cambridgeshire, 3½ m. S.E. of St Ives; pop. 830. Map 61.

Swefling, par. and vil., E. Suffolk, 2½ m. W. of Saxmundham; pop. 236. Map 63.

Swepstone, par. and vil., Leicestershire, 5 m. N.W. of Bosworth; pop. 630. Map 49.

Swinbrook, par. and vil., Oxon, 2 m. E. of Burford; pop. 167. Map 69.

Swindon, mun. bor. and par., Wiltshire, 10½ m. N. of Marlborough; pop. 62,407. Map 69.

Swinefleet, par. and vil., W.R. Yorkshire, 2½ m. S.E. of Goole; pop. 1126. Map 34.

Swineford, market town, co. Mayo, 22 m. S.W. of Ballymote; pop. 1302. Map 92.

Swineshead, par. and vil., Bedfordshire, 3 m. S.W. of Kimbolton; pop. 129. Map 60.

Swineshead, town and par., Lincolnshire, 6 m. S.W. of Boston; pop. 1895. Map 51.

Swinton, urb. dist. and par., W.R. Yorkshire, 10½ m. N.E. of Sheffield; pop. 13,820. Map 41.

Swinton, par. and vil., Berwickshire, 5½ m. S.E. of Duns; pop. 689. Map 11.

Swinton and Pendlebury, urb. dist., Lancashire, 4 m. N.W. of Manchester; pop. 32,761. Map 39.

Swords, town and par., in co. and 8 m. N. of Dublin; pop. of town 907. Map 93.

Swyre, par. and vil., Dorsetshire, 5 m. S.E. of Bridport; pop. 111. Map 86.

Syderstone, par. and vil., Norfolk, 4½ m. W.N.W. of Fakenham; pop. 429. Map 52.

Sydling St. Nicholas, par. and vil., Dorsetshire, 8 m. N.N.W. of Dorchester; pop. 346. Map 87.

Sykehouse, par. and vil., W.R. Yorkshire, 4 m. S.S.W. of Snaith; pop. 453. Map 33.

Synod, ham., Cardiganshire, 3¾ m. S.S.E. of New Quay. Map 54.

Syston, par. and vil., Kesteven, Lincolnshire, 3 m. N. of Grantham; pop. 172. Map 50.

Syston, par. and vil., in co. and 5 m. N.N.E. of Leicester; pop. 3214. Map 49.

TADCASTER, market town, W.R. Yorkshire, 14 m. S.E. of Harrogate; pop. 4005. Map 34.

Taddington, par. and mining vil., Derbyshire, 5½ m. N.W. of Bakewell; pop. 384. Alt. 1050 ft.; claims to be highest vil. in England. Map 40.

Tadley, par. and vil., Hants, 6½ m. N.N.W. of Basingstoke; pop. 1269. Map 78.

Tain, bur., seaport and par., Ross and Cromarty, 25½ m. N.E. of Dingwall; pop. 1383. Map 3.

Talaton, par. and vil., Devonshire, 3 m. N.W. of Ottery St Mary; pop. 397. Map 85.

Talgarth, market town, Breconshire, 12 m. S.W. of Hay; pop. 1881. Map 56.

Taliesin (Tre Taliesin), ham., Cardiganshire, 1½ m. N. of Talybont. Map 45.

Talkin, vil., N. Cumberland, 1½ m. S. of Brampton (**T. Tarn,** alt. 419 ft.). Map 21.

Tallentire, par. and vil., Cumberland, 3 m. N.W. of Cockermouth; pop. 202. Map 20.

Talsarn, ham., Cardiganshire, 5½ m. N.N.W. of Lampeter. Map 54.

Talybont, ham., Cardiganshire, 6½ m. N.E. of Aberystwyth. Map 45.

Tamworth, mun. bor. and par., in co. and 22 m. S.E. of Stafford; pop. 7510. Map 48.

Tanfield, urb. dist. and par., Durham, 7 m. S.W. of Gateshead; pop. 9236. Map 23.

Tanworth, par. and vil., Warwickshire, 4 m. N.W. of Henley-in-Arden; pop. 2839. Map 58.

Taplow, par. and vil., Buckinghamshire, on r. Thames, 1½ m. E. of Maidenhead; pop. 1502. Map 70.

Tarbert, *q.s.* par. and seaport, Argyllshire, 13½ m. S. of Lochgilphead; pop. 1983. Map 12.

Tarbert, seaport town, co. Kerry, 10 m. N.E. of Listowel; pop. 354. Map 94.

Tarbet, ham. and ry. sta., on W. shore of Loch Lomond, Dumbartonshire. Map 12.

Tarleton, par. and vil., S.W. Lancashire, 8 m. S.W. of Preston; pop. 2115. Map 30.

Tarporley, urb. dist., Cheshire, 10 m. E.S.E. of Chester; pop. 2152. Map 39.

Tarrington, par. and vil., in co. and 7 m. E. of Hereford; pop. 410. Map 57.

Tattenhall, market town and par., in co. and 7½ m. S.E. of Chester; pop. 1055. Map 38.

Tattershall, par. and vil., Lindsey, Lincolnshire, 11 m. N.W. of Boston; pop. 424. Map 43.

Taunton, mun. bor. and co. town of Somersetshire, 44¾ m. S.W. of Bristol; pop. 25,177. Map 86.

Tavistock, urb. dist. and par., Devonshire, 14½ m. N. of Plymouth; pop. 4453. Map 88.

Tawton, North, par. and town, Devonshire, 6½ m. N.E. of Okehampton; pop. 1408. Map 85.

Tay, largest r. of Scotland, flows from Loch Tay and expands into the Firth of Tay. Map 5.

Taynton, par. and vil., Oxon, 1½ m. N.W. of Burford; pop. 215. Map 69.

Taynuilt, vil. and ry. sta., Argyllshire, 13 m. E. of Oban. Map 12.

Tayport, bur. and par., Fifeshire, on Firth of Tay, opposite Dundee; pop. 3164. Map 7.

Tebay, par. and vil., Westmorland, 7½ m. S.E. of Shap; pop. 1030. Map 26.

Tedburn St Mary, par. and vil., Devonshire, 4 m. S.W. of Crediton; pop. 449. Map 85.

Teddington, urb. dist., Middlesex, on r. Thames, 1½ m. N.W. of Kingston; pop. 23,362. Map 71.

Tees, River, flows 70 m. to North Sea between Hartlepool and Redcar. Map 23.

Teignmouth, urb. dist., par. and seaport, Devonshire, 15 m. S. of Exeter; pop. 10,019. Map 89.

Temple Ewell, par. and vil., Kent, 2½ m. N.W. of Dover; pop. 1034. Map 83.

Temple Grafton, par., Warwickshire, 5 m. W. of Stratford-on-Avon; pop. 314. Map 58.

Templemore, urb. dist. and par., Tipperary, 79 m. S.W. of Dublin; pop. 2230. Map 95.

Templenewsam, par. and seat, W.R. Yorkshire, 4 m. E. of Leeds; pop. 3370. Map 33.

Templepatrick, par. and vil., co. Antrim, 9 m. N.W. of Belfast; pop. 2673. Map 96.

Templeton, vil., Pembrokeshire, in par. and 2 m. S. of Narberth. Map 64.

Tempsford, par., vil. and seat, Bedfordshire, 5½ m. N.N.W. of Biggleswade; pop. 468. Map 60.

Tenbury, market town, Worcestershire, 5 m. E. of Woofferton Junction; pop. 1922. Map 57.

Tenby, mun. bor. and seaport, in co. and 9½ m. E. of Pembroke; pop. 4108. Map 64.

Tendring, par. and vil., Essex, 9 m. E. of Colchester; pop. 791. Map 73.

Tenterden, mun. bor. and par., Kent, 7 m. E.S.E. of Cranbrook; pop. 3473. Map 82.

Terenure, vil., in co. and 3 m. S. of Dublin; pop. 4697. Map 95.

Ternhill, ham. with ry. sta., Salop, 3 m. S.W. of Market Drayton. Map 47.

Terregles, par., E. Kirkcudbrightshire, 2 m. W. of Dumfries; pop. 428. Map 20.

Terrington St Clement and **St John**, 2 pars., Norfolk, 4 m. W. of King's Lynn; pop. 2689 and 818. Map 51.

Tetbury, urb. dist. and par., Gloucestershire, 8 m. S.E. of Stroud; pop. 2237. Map 68.

Tetford, par. and vil., Lincolnshire, 6 m. N.E. of Horncastle; pop. 367. Map 43.

Tettenhall, urb. dist., Staffordshire, 2 m. N.W. of Wolverhampton; pop. 5767. Map 47.

Teviotdale, the vale of the Teviot, Roxburghshire. Map 16.

Teviot, River, Roxburghshire, flows 37 m. N.E. to the Tweed at Kelso. Map 16.

Tewkesbury, mun. bor. and par., Gloucestershire, 8 m. N.W. of Cheltenham; pop. 4352. Map 57.

Teynham, par. and vil., Kent, 3½ m. N.W. of Faversham; pop. 1734. Map 83.

Thame, urb. dist. and par., Oxon, 48 m. N.W. of London; pop. 3019. Map 70.

Thames Ditton, par. and vil., Surrey, on r. Thames, opposite Hampton Court Palace; pop. 8450. Map 78.

Thanet, Isle of, in N.E. extremity of Kent, contains wtg. pls., Margate, Ramsgate and Broadstairs. Map 83.

Thankerton, vil., Lanarkshire, on r. Clyde, 5 m. S. of Carstairs; pop. 290. Map 14.

Thatcham, par. and vil., Berkshire, 3 m. E. of Newbury; pop. 2459. Map 76.

Thaxted, small town and par., Essex, 7 m. N. of Dunmow; pop. 1596. Map 72.

Theale, par. and vil., Berkshire, 5 m. S.W. of Reading; pop. 1021. Map 78.

Theberton, par. and vil., E. Suffolk, 4 m. N.E. of Saxmundham; pop. 477. Map 63.

Theddingworth, par. and ry. sta., Leicestershire, 5½ m. S.W. of Market Harborough; pop. 193. Map 59.

Thetford, mun. bor., Norfolk, 14 m. N. of Bury St Edmunds; pop. 4097. Map 62.

Thirsk, par. and market town, N.R. Yorkshire, 22½ m. N.W. of York; pop. 2755. Map 28.

Thomastown, market town and par., in co. and 11 m. S.S.E. of Kilkenny; town pop. 959. Map 95.

Thormanby, par., N.R. Yorkshire, 4 m. N.W. of Easingwold; pop. 102. Map 28.

Thornaby-on-Tees, mun. bor. and par., N.R. Yorkshire, opposite Stockton; pop. 21,233. Map 28.

Thornbury, par. and market town, Gloucestershire, 12 m. N. of Bristol; pop. 2493. Map 68.

Thornby, par. and vil., in co. and 11 m. N.N.W. of Northampton; pop. 214. Map 59.

Thorndon, par. and vil., E. Suffolk, 3 m. S. of Eye; pop. 553. Map 63.

Thorne, market town and par., W.R. Yorkshire, on r. Don, 9 m. N.E. of Doncaster; pop. 6076. Map 34.

Thorner, par. and vil., W.R. Yorkshire, 6 m. N.E. of Leeds; pop. 1017. Map 33.

Thorney, par., Isle of Ely, Cambridgeshire, 7 m. N.E. of Peterborough; pop. 2165. Map 51.

Thornham, par. and vil., Kent, 3½ m. E. of Maidstone; pop. 716. Map 82.

Thornhill, vil. with ry. sta., in co. and 14 m. N.W. of Dumfries; pop. 1577. Map 14.

Thornhill, vil., Perthshire, 9¼ m. N.W. of Stirling. Map 8.

Thornton, vil. with ry. sta., Fifeshire, 3 m. S. of Markinch; pop. 1960. Map 10.

Thornton Cleveleys, urb. dist., Lancashire, 4 m. S.S.W. of Fleetwood; pop. 10,144. Map 30.

Thornton Dale, par. and vil., N.R. Yorkshire, 3 m. E. of Pickering; pop. 1186. Map 29.

Thornton Steward, par., N.R. Yorkshire, 5 m. S.E. of Leyburn; pop. 222. Map 27.

Thorpe, par. and vil., Derbyshire, on r. Dove, 3 m. N.W. of Ashbourne; pop. 196. Map 40.

Thorpe-le-Soken, small town and par., Essex, 4½ m. W. of Walton-on-the-Naze; pop. 1130. Map 73.

Thorpe Market, par. and vil., Norfolk, 4 m. N.W. of N. Walsham; pop. 231. Map 53.

Thorpeness, fishing and garden vil., E. Suffolk, 2 m. N.N.E. of Aldeburgh. Map 63.

Thorpe Thewles, vil. with ry. sta., Durham, 4 m. N.W. of Stockton. Map 23.

Thorrington, par., Essex, 7 m. S.E. of Colchester; pop. 397. Map 73.

Thorverton, par. and vil., Devonshire, 7 m. N. of Exeter; pop. 737. Map 85.

Thrapston, market town and par., Northamptonshire, 8½ m. S.W. of Oundle; pop. 1662. Map 60.

Threapwood, par. and vil., Cheshire, 3 m. S.W. of Malpas; pop. 294. Map 38.

Three Bridges, vil. and ry. sta., Sussex, 8¼ m. S. of Redhill Junction. Map 81.

Three Cocks Junction, ry. sta., Breconshire, 5 m. S.W. of Hay. Map 56.

Threlkeld, par. and vil., Cumberland, 3½ m. N.E. of Keswick; pop. 559. Map 21.

Threshfield, par. and vil., W.R. Yorkshire, 8 m. N. of Skipton; pop. 403. Map 31.

Thriplow, par. and vil., in co. and 7 m. S. of Cambridge; pop. 381. Map 61.

Thringstone, par., Leicestershire, 4 m. E. of Ashby-de-la-Zouch; pop. 1447. Map 49.

Thropton, par. and vil., Northumberland, 2 m. W. of Rothbury; pop. 233. Map 17.

Throston, par., Durham, within mun. bor. of Hartlepool; pop. 8569. Map 23.

Thurlby, par. and vil., Kesteven, Lincolnshire, 2 m. S. of Bourne; pop. 762. Map 50.

Thurles, urb. dist. and par., Tipperary, 29 m. N. of Clonmel; pop. 4796. Map 95.

Thurlston, urb. dist., W.R. Yorkshire, 1½ m. N.W. of Penistone; pop. 2640. Map 32.

Thurlton, par. and vil., Norfolk, 3½ m. E. of Loddon; pop. 320. Map 53.

Thurmaston, urb. dist. and par., in co. and 3½ m. N.E. of Leicester; pop. 3723. Map 49.

Thurnscoe, urb. dist., W.R. Yorkshire, 2 m. N.E. of Darfield; pop. 10,540. Map 41.

Thurso, spt., police bur. and par., Caithness-shire, 20¾ m. N.W. of Wick by rail; pop. 2946. Map 3.

Thurstonland and **Farnley Tyas**, urb. dist., W.R. Yorkshire, 4½ m. S.E. of Huddersfield; pop. 3980. Map 32.

Thurton, par. and vil., Norfolk, 2½ m. N.W. of Loddon; pop. 221. Map 53.

Thwing, par. and vil., E.R. Yorkshire, 6 m. N.W. of Hunmanby; pop. 307. Map 29.

Tibenham, par. and vil., Norfolk, 2 m. N.W. of Tivetshall; pop. 476. Map 63.
Tibshelf, par. and vil., Derbyshire, 4 m. N.E. of Alfreton; pop. 4053. Map 41.
Tichborne, par. and vil., Hants, 2 m. S.W. of Alresford; pop. 263. Map 76.
Tickhill and Wadworth, urb. dist. and par., W.R. Yorkshire, 4 m. W. of Bawtry; pop. 2297. Map 41.
Ticklerton, ham., S. Salop, $2\frac{3}{4}$ m. S.E. of Church Stretton. Map 46.
Tideswell, par. and small town, Derbyshire, $6\frac{1}{2}$ m. E.N.E. of Buxton; pop. 1972. Map 40.
Tidworth, North, par. and vil., Wiltshire, 2 m. S.W. of Ludgershall; pop. 1253. Map 76.
Tilbury, urb. dist., Essex, on r. Thames, 22 m. E. of London; pop. 16,826. Map 80.
Tillicoultry, town, police bur. and par., Clackmannanshire, 3 m. S.W. of Dollar; pop. 2953. Map 9.
Tilshead, par. and vil., Wiltshire, on Salisbury Plain, 9 m. S. of Devizes; pop. 395. Map 75.
Timperley, par. and vil., Cheshire, $1\frac{1}{2}$ m. N.E. of Altrincham; pop. 4263. Map 39.
Tinahely, vil, with ry. sta., Wicklow, 14 m. W. of Arklow; pop. 392. Map 95.
Tinsley, par., W.R. Yorkshire, in bor. and $3\frac{1}{2}$ m. N.E. of Sheffield; pop. 7365. Map 41.
Tintagel Head, par., Cornwall, 5 m. N.W. of Camelford; pop. 1307. Map 91.
Tintern Abbey, ruin, on r. Wye, Monmouthshire, 4 m. N. of Chepstow. Map 68.
Tintinhull, par. and vil., Somersetshire, $4\frac{1}{2}$ m. N.W. of Yeovil; pop. 488. Map 86.
Tintwistle, par. and vil., Cheshire, on r. Etherew, $3\frac{1}{2}$ m. E. of Stalybridge; pop. 1530. Map 40.
Tipperary, urb. dist. and par., Tipperary, 25 m. S.E. of Limerick; pop. 5554. Map 95.
Tipton, urb. dist. and par., Staffordshire, $8\frac{1}{2}$ m. N.W. of Birmingham; pop. 35,792. Map 47.
Tiptree, railway station, Essex, $3\frac{1}{2}$ m. S.E. of Kelvedon. Map 73.
Tisbury, town and 2 pars. (**E.** and **W.**), Wiltshire, $12\frac{3}{4}$ m. W. of Salisbury; pop. **E. T.** 729, **W. T.** 691. Map 87.
Titchfield, par. and vil., Hants, 2 m. W. of Fareham; pop. 1915. Map 77.
Titchmarsh, par. and vil., Northamptonshire, 2 m. N.E. of Thrapston; pop. 620. Map 60.
Titterstone Clee Hill, Salop, 6 m. N.E. of Ludlow; altitude 1749 ft. Map 57.
Tiverton, par. and vil., Cheshire, $1\frac{1}{2}$ m. S.E. of Tarporley; pop. 565. Map 39.
Tiverton, mun. bor. and par., Devonshire, 12 m. N. of Exeter; pop. 9611. Map 85.
Tobercurry, market town, in co. and $21\frac{3}{4}$ m. S.W. of Sligo; pop. 829. Map 92.
Tobermore, vil., S.E. co. Londonderry, 5 m. N.W. of Magherafelt; pop. 342. Map 93.
Tobermory, spt. and police bur., Mull Island, Argyllshire, 28 m. N.W. of Oban; pop. 771. Map 12.
Toddington, town and par., Bedfordshire ,$4\frac{1}{2}$ m. N. of Dunstable; pop. 2001. Map 71.
Todmorden, par., mun. bor., mfg. mkt. town, W.R. Yorks, $8\frac{3}{4}$ m. S.E. of Burnley; pop. 22,223. Map 31.
Toft Monks, par. and vil., Norfolk, 3 m. N.E. of Beccles; pop. 344. Map 53.
Tollesbury, par. and vil., Essex, 7 m. E.N.E. of Maldon; pop. 1721. Map 73.
Tolleshunt d'Arcy, par. and vil., Essex, 2 m. N.W. of Tollesbury; pop. 861. Map 73.
Tolworth, par. and vil., Surrey, 2 m. S. of Kingston-on-Thames; pop. 5387. Map 78.
Tomintoul, *q.s.* par. and vil., Banffshire, $14\frac{1}{2}$ m. S. of Ballindalloch; pop. 596. Map 3.
Tonbridge, urb. dist. and market town, Kent, $29\frac{1}{2}$ m. S.E. of London; pop. 16,332. Map 82.
Tongue, par. and vil., on N. coast of Sutherlandshire; pop. 1350. Map 3.
Ton-gwynlais, place, Glamorganshire, 3 m. N.W. of Llandaff. Map 67.
Ton-yr-efail, place, with ry. sta., Glamorganshire, 5 m. N.W. of Llantrisant sta. Map 66.
Topcliffe, par. and vil., N.R. Yorkshire, $4\frac{1}{2}$ m. S.W. of Thirsk; pop. 490. Map 28.
Toppesfield, par. and vil., Essex, $6\frac{1}{2}$ m. N.W. of Halstead; pop. 535. Map 62.
Topsham, town and par., Devonshire, $5\frac{1}{4}$ m. N.W. of Exmouth; pop. 3255. Map 89.
Torbryan, par. and vil., Devonshire, $4\frac{1}{2}$ m. S.W. of Newton Abbot; pop. 443. Map 89.
Torksey, par. and vil., in co. and $9\frac{3}{4}$ m. N.W. of Lincoln; pop. 191. Map 42.
Tormaston, par. and vil., Gloucestershire, 4 m. S.E. of Chipping Sodbury; pop. 311. Map 75.
Torpenhow, par., Cumberland, 7 m. N.E. of Cockermouth; pop. 281. Map 20.
Torphichen, par. and vil., West Lothian, $2\frac{1}{2}$ m. N. of Bathgate; pop. 4486. Map 9.
Torpoint, urb. dist. and par., Cornwall, opposite Devonport; pop. 3975. Map 88.
Torquay, mun. bor., watering place and seaport, Devonshire, 23 m. S. of Exeter; pop. 46,165. Map 89.
Torrington, par. and vil., Devonshire, $4\frac{1}{2}$ m. W.N.W. of Hatherleigh; pop. 581. Map 84.
Torryburn, par. and vil., Fifeshire, $2\frac{1}{2}$ m. E. of Culross; pop. 2224. Map 9.
Torthorwald, par. and vil., Dumfriesshire, 4 m. N.E. of Dumfries; pop. 801. Map 20.
Totland, par., Isle of Wight, 3 m. S.W. of Yarmouth; pop. 1689. Map 77.
Totley, par. and vil., Derbyshire, 6 m. S.W. of Sheffield; pop. 1341. Map 40.
Totnes, mun. bor. and par., Devonshire, 22 m. S.W. of Exeter; pop. 4525. Map 89.
Tottenham, urb. dist. and par., Middlesex, in N. suburbs of London; pop. 157,748. Map 71.
Totternhoe, par. and vil., Bedfordshire, 2 m. W. of Dunstable; pop. 449. Map 71.
Tottington, urb. dist. and par., S.E. Lancashire, $2\frac{1}{2}$ m. N.W. of Bury; pop. 6532. Map 31.
Totton, vil., with ry. sta., Hants, 4 m. W. of Southampton. Map 77.
Towcester, market town and par., in co. and $8\frac{1}{2}$ m. S.W. of Northampton; pop. 2383. Map 59.
Tow Law, urb. dist. and par., Durham, 8 m. N.W. of Bishop Auckland; pop. 3556. Map 22.
Towyn, wtg. pl. and urb. dist., Merionethshire, 3 m. N.W. of Aberdovey; pop. 3,803. Map 44.
Towyn, dist., Abergele par., Denbighshire. Map 37.
Tralee, spt., urb. dist. and par., Kerry, $31\frac{1}{2}$ m. N.E. of Dingle by rail; pop. 10,536. Map 94.
Tramore, market town and watering pl., in co. and $7\frac{1}{4}$ m. S. of Waterford; pop. 1812. Map 95.
Tranent, police bur., E. Lothian, $9\frac{1}{2}$ m. E. of Edinburgh; pop. 4526. Map 10.
Traquair, par. and vil., Peeblesshire, $1\frac{1}{2}$ m. S. of Innerleithen; pop. 556. Map 15.
Trawden, urb. dist., Lancashire, 2 m. S.E. of Colne; pop. 2548. Map 31.
Trearddwr, seaside resort, Anglesey, 12 m. S. of Holyhead. Map 36.
Tredegar, urb. dist. and par., Monmouthshire, 7 m. E.N.E. of Merthyr Tydfil; pop. 23,195. Map 67.
Treeton, par., W.R. Yorkshire, $3\frac{1}{2}$ m. S. of Rotherham; pop. 1903. Map 41.
Treffgarne, par. and ham., Pembrokeshire, 5 m. N. of Haverfordwest; pop. 79. Map 64.
Treforest, ham., with ry. stas., Glamorganshire, $11\frac{3}{4}$ m. N.W. of Cardiff. Map 66.
Tregaron (Caron-is-Clawdd), par., Cardiganshire, $9\frac{1}{2}$ m. N.E. of Lampeter; pop. 1364. Map 55.

Treharris, vil. and ry. sta., Glamorganshire, 5 m. N.E. of Pontypridd. Map 67.
Treig, Loch, Inverness-shire, extends 5 m. N. and S. r. Treig flows into Spean 6 m. E. Br. of Roy. Map 2.
Tremadoc, small town, Carnarvonshire, 4½ m. N.E. of Criccieth. Map 36.
Trentham, par. and vil., Staffordshire, 3 m. S. of Stoke-upon-Trent ; pop. 3141. Map 47.
Treorky, vil., with ry. sta., Glamorganshire, 8¾ m. N.W. of Pontypridd. Map 66.
Trevalga, coast par. and vil., Cornwall, 4 m. N.W. of Camelford ; pop. 105. Map 91.
Trim, urb. dist. and par., Meath, 29 m. N.W. of Dublin ; pop. 1488. Map 93.
Trimdon, par. and vil., Durham, 8 m. S.E. of Durham ; pop. 5410. Map 23.
Trimingham, coast par. and vil., Norfolk, 5 m. S.E. of Cromer ; pop. 259. Map 53.
Trimsuran, ham., Carmarthenshire, 3 m. S.E. of Kidwelly. Map 65.
Tring, urb. dist. and par., Hertfordshire, 5 m. N.W. of Berkhampstead by rail ; pop. 4364. Map 71.
Troon, police bur. and *q.s.* par., Ayrshire, 6½ m. N. of Ayr ; pop. 8544. Map 12.
Trossachs, mountain defile, Perthshire, 8 m. W. of Callander. Map 5.
Troutbeck, par. and vil., Westmorland, 3 m. S.E. of Ambleside ; pop. 486. Map 25.
Trowbridge, urb. dist. and market town, Wiltshire, 11¾ m. S.S.W. of Chippenham ; pop. 12,011. Map 75.
Trull, par. and vil., Somersetshire, 2 m. S.S.W. of Taunton ; pop. 9855. Map 86.
Trumpington, par. and vil., in co. and 2 m. S. of Cambridge ; pop. 820. Map 61.
Trunch, par. and vil., Norfolk, 3 m. N. of N. Walsham ; pop. 377. Map 53.
Truro, mun. bor., seaport and par., Cornwall, 11¾ m. N. of Falmouth by rail ; pop. 11,074. Map 90.
Tuam, town and par., Galway, 15½ m. N.N.W. of Athenry ; pop. 3288. Map 94.
Tuddenham, par. and vil., E. Suffolk, 3 m. N.E. of Ipswich ; pop. 337. Map 63.
Tulla, market town and par., Clare, 10 m. E.N.E. of Ennis ; pop. 2660. Map 94.
Tullamore, assize town and urb. dist., Offaly, 58 m. W. of Dublin ; pop. 4924. Map 93.
Tulliallan, par., containing Kincardine, Fifeshire, on r. Forth ; pop. 2298. Map 9.
Tullibody, vil., Clackmannanshire, 2¼ m. N.W. of Alloa ; pop. 879. Map 9.
Tullow, market town, in co. and 9 m. S.E. of Carlow ; pop. 1894. Map 95.
Tumble, vil., in co. and 10 m. S.E. of Carmarthen. Map 65.
Tumley, par. and vil., Lindsey, Lincolnshire, 6 m. S. of Horncastle ; pop. 264. Map 43.
Tunbridge Wells, mun. bor. and par., Kent, 34½ m. S.E. of London ; pop. 35,367. Map 82.
Tunstall, par. and vil., N. Lancashire, 3 m. S. of Kirkby Lonsdale ; pop. 96. Map 26.
Tunstall, par., Staffordshire, 2¼ m. N.E. of Newcastle-under-Lyme ; pop. 22,740. Map 39.
Tunstall, par. and vil., Kent, 1½ m. S.W. of Sittingbourne ; pop. 265. Map 82.
Tupton, par. and seat, Derbyshire, 3 m. S. of Chesterfield ; pop. 2034. Map 41.
Turkdean, par. and vil., Gloucestershire, 2 m. N. of Northleach ; pop. 133. Map 69.
Turnershill, eccl. dist. and ham., E. Sussex, 3½ m. S.W. of East Grinstead ; pop. 820. Map 81.
Turriff, police bur. and par., Aberdeenshire, 12 m. S. of Macduff ; pop. 2298. Map 3.
Turton, urb. dist., Lancashire, 5 m. N. of Bolton ; pop. 11,847. Map 31.
Turvey, par. and vil., in co. and 7 m. N.W. of Bedford ; pop. 849. Map 60.
Tutbury, town and par., Staffordshire, 4½ m. N.E. of Burton-on-Trent ; pop. 2062. Map 48.
Tuxford, small market town and par., Nottinghamshire, 6¾ m. S. of Retford ; pop. 1191. Map 41.
Tweedmouth, par. and seaport, Northumberland, at mouth of r. Tweed ; pop. 5151. Map 11.
Twickenham, urb. disr., Middlesex, on r. Thames, 11¼ m. S.W. of London ; pop. 39,909. Map 78.
Twizell, par. and vil., Northumberland, 3 m. N.E. of Cornhill ; pop. 223. Map 17.
Two Bridges, place, with inn, Devonshire, 8 m. E. of Tavistock. Map 88.
Twyford, par. and vil., Hants, 3 m. S. of Winchester ; pop. 2214. Map 76.
Twyford, par. and vil., Berkshire, 4½ m. N.E. of Reading ; pop. 1269. Map 70.
Twyford, par. and vil., Leicestershire, 6 m. S.S.W. of Melton Mowbray ; pop. 333. Map 49.
Tydd, ry. sta., Holland, Lincolnshire, 5 m. S. of Wisbech. Map 51.
Tyldesley (with Shakerley), urb. dist. and par., S.W. Lancashire, 5 m. S. of Bolton ; pop. 14,848. Map 39.
Tylorstown, ry. sta., Glamorganshire, between Porth sta. and Ferndale sta. Map 66.
Tyndrum, vil., with ry. stas., Perthshire, 34¼ m. N.W. of Callander. Map 4.
Tyne, River, flows through Northumberland and Durham, and is 30 m. in length. Map 22.
Tynemouth, parl. and co. bor. and par., Northumberland, 8 m. N.E. of Newcastle ; pop. 64,913. Map 23.
Tywardreath, par. and vil., Cornwall, 5 m. N.E. of St Austell ; pop. 2512. Map 91.
UCKFIELD, urb. dist. and par., Sussex, 50 m. S. of London ; pop. 3557. Map 81.
Uddingston, town and *q.s.* par., Lanarkshire, 7 m. S.E. of Glasgow ; pop. 8414. Map 9.
Uffculme, par. and vil., Devonshire, 7¼ m. E. of Tiverton ; pop. 1551. Map 85.
Uffington, par. and vil., Berkshire, 4 m. S.E. of Faringdon ; pop. 480. Map 69.
Ufford, par. and vil., E. Suffolk, 3 m. N.E. of Woodbridge ; pop. 432. Map 63.
Uist, North, isl. and par., Outer Hebrides, Inverness-shire ; pop. 2579. Map 2.
Uist, South, isl. and par., Outer Hebrides, Inverness-shire ; pop. 3235. Map 2.
Ulceby, par. and vil., Lindsey, Lincolnshire, 6 m. S. of New Holland ; pop. 924. Map 35.
Uldale, par. and vil., Cumberland, 7½ m. S. of Wigton ; pop. 228. Map 20.
Uley, par. and vil., Gloucestershire, 6 m. S.W. of Stroud ; pop. 967. Map 68.
Ulgham, par. and vil., Northumberland, 4½ m. N.E. of Morpeth ; pop. 1125. Map 17.
Ullapool, *q.s.* par. and vil., Ross and Cromarty, 32 m. N.W. of Garve ry. sta. ; pop. 598. Map 2.
Ullswater, lake, 7½ m. long, Cumberland and Westmorland, 5 m. S.W. of Penrith. Map 25.
Ulverston, urb. dist., spt. and par., N. Lancashire, 8 m. N.E. of Barrow-in-Furness ; pop. 9235. Map 25.
Upavon, par. and vil., Wiltshire, 4 m. S.W. of Pewsey ; pop. 767. Map 76.
Upchurch, par. and vil., Kent, 5 m. E. of Chatham ; pop. 1312. Map 82.
Uphall, par. and vil., West Lothian, 13½ m. W.S.W. of Edinburgh ; pop. 3441. Map 9.
Upholland, urb. dist., Lancashire, 4 m. W. of Wigan ; pop. 5480. Map 39.
Upminster, par. and vil., Essex, 3 m. S.E. of Romford ; pop. 3559. Map 72.
Upper Clatford, par., Hampshire, 1 m. S. of Andover ; pop. 688. Map 76.
Upper Tean, eccl. dist. and vil., Staffordshire, 2½ m. S. of Cheadle ; pop. 1314. Map 48.

Uppingham, market town, Rutlandshire, 6 m. S. of Oakham; pop. 2453. Map 50.
Upton-on-Severn, market town, Worcestershire, 6 m. S.E. of Malvern; pop. 2004. Map 57.
Upwell, par. and vil., Cambridgeshire, 5 m. S.E. of Wisbech; pop. 1583. Map 51.
Urmston, urb. dist. and par., S.E. Lancashire, 5 m. S.W. of Central sta., Manchester; pop. 9284. Map 39.
Usk, par. and urb. dist., in co. and 12 m. S.W. of Monmouth; pop. 1315. Map 67.
Uttoxeter, urb. dist. and par., in co. and 13 m. N.E. of Stafford; pop. 5907. Map 48.
Uxbridge, urb. dist. and par., Middlesex, 16 m. N.W. of London; pop. 31,866. Map 71.
VALENTIA ISLAND, isl. and par., S.W. co. Kerry, 4 m. S.W. of Cahirciveen; pop. 1625. Map 94.
Velindre, ham., E. Breconshire, 4½ m. S.W. of Hay. Map 56.
Velindre-farchog, ham., Pembrokeshire, 2½ m. E. of Newport. Map 64.
Vennacher, Loch, Perthshire, 2¼ m. S.W. of Callander; is 3¾ m. in length. Map 5.
Ventnor, urb. dist. and par., Isle of Wight, 11 m. S. of Ryde; pop. 5112. Map 77.
Vernhams Dean, par. and vil., Hampshire, 7 m. N. of Andover; pop. 449. Map 76.
Verwood, par., vil. and ry. sta., Dorsetshire, 3½ m. S.E. of Cramborne; pop. 1217. Map 77.
Voil, Loch, Perthshire, 3 m. W. of Balquhidder; is 3½ m. in length. Map 5.
Vowchurch, par. and vil., in co. and 10 m. W.S.W. of Hereford; pop. 281. Map 56.
Vyrnwy, lake and river, Montgomeryshire, forming Liverpool's chief water supply. Map 45.
WADDESDON, par. and vil., Buckinghamshire, 5½ m. N.W. of Aylesbury; pop. 1439. Map 70.
Wadebridge, urb. dist. and par., Cornwall, 7 m. N.W. of Bodmin; pop. 2460. Map 91.
Wadhurst, par. and vil., Sussex, 6 m. S.E. of Tunbridge Wells; pop. 3674. Map 82.
Wadworth, par., vil. and seat, W.R. Yorkshire, 4 m. S. of Doncaster; pop. 710. Map 41.
Wainfleet, market town and par., Lindsey, Lincolnshire, 8½ m. S.E. of Spilsby; pop. 1375. Map 43.
Wakefield, city, parl. and co. bor. and par., W.R. Yorkshire, 9 m. S. of Leeds; pop. 59,115. Map 33.
Wakering, Great, par. and vil., Essex, 4½ m. E.N.E. of Southend; pop. 1826. Map 73.
Walkerburn, vil. and *q.s.* par., Peeblesshire, 1¾ m. E. of Innerleithen; pop. 1110. Map 15.
Walkeringham, par. and vil., Nottinghamshire, 4 m. N.W. of Gainsborough; pop. 973. Map 42.
Walkern, par. and vil., Hertfordshire, 3 m. E. of Stevenage; pop. 700. Map 71.
Walkington, par. and vil., E.R. Yorkshire, 3 m. S.W. of Beverley; pop. 1199. Map 35.
Wall, par. and vil., Northumberland, 3¼ m. N.W. of Hexham; pop. 381. Map 22.
Wallasey, co. bor. and par., Cheshire, in Wirral Peninsula, 3 m. N.W. of Birkenhead; pop. 97,465. Map 38.
Wallbottle, par. and vil., Northumberland, 5 m. W. of Newcastle-on-Tyne; pop. 3080. Map 23.
Wall Grange, sta., Staffordshire, between Leek and Endon. Map 40.
Wallingford, mun. bor., Berkshire, 14½ m. N.W. of Reading; pop. 2840. Map 70.
Wallington, par. and vil., Surrey, 2½ m. S.W. of West Croydon; pop. 9223. Map 80.
Wallsend, mun. bor. and par., Northumberland, 4 m. E.N.E. of Newcastle; pop. 44,582. Map 23.
Walmer, urb. dist., Kent, 1¼ m. S.S.W. of Deal; pop. 5324. Map 83.
Walney Island, eccl. dist., N. Lancashire, in Dalton-in-Furness par.; pop. 8013. Map 25.
Walpole, ry. sta., Norfolk, 8½ m. W. of King's Lynn. Map 51.
Walpole, par. and vil., E. Suffolk, 2½ m. S.W. of Halesworth; pop. 325. Map 63.
Walsall, parl. and co. bor. and par., Staffordshire, 8 m. N.W. of Birmingham; pop. 103,102. Map 48.
Walsden, eccl. dist., W.R. Yorkshire, 7 m. N.E. of Rochdale; pop. 4292. Map 31.
Walsgrave-on-Sowe, par. and vil., Warwickshire, 3½ m. N.E. of Coventry; pop. 2060. Map 59.
Walsham, North, urb. dist. and par., Norfolk, 16 m. N. of Norwich; pop. 4137. Map 53.
Walsham, South, par. and vil., Norfolk, 9 m. E.N.E. of Norwich; pop. 509. Map 53.
Walsingham, Great, par., Norfolk, 3½ m. S.S.E. of Wells; pop. 295. Map 52.
Walsingham, Little, par. and town, Norfolk, 4½ m. S. of Wells; pop. 788. Map 52.
Walsoken, urb. dist., Norfolk, 1 m. N.E. of Wisbech; pop. 4058. Map 51.
Waltham, market town and par., Lindsey, Lincolnshire, 4½ m. S. of Grimsby; pop. 978. Map 43.
Waltham Cross, eccl. par. and vil., Hertfordshire, on S. side of Cheshunt. Map 71.
Waltham, Great, par. and vil., Essex, 4 m. N. of Chelmsford; pop. 2029. Map 72.
Waltham (W. Holy Cross) (Abbey), urb. dist. and par., Essex, 15 m. N. of London; pop. 7116. Map 71.
Waltham-on-the-Wold, par. and vil., Leicestershire, 5 m. N.E. of Melton Mowbray; pop. 484. Map 50.
Waltham St Lawrence, par. and vil., Berkshire, 2½ m. N.E. of Twyford; pop. 960. Map 70.
Walthamstow, municipal bor., S.W. Essex, 6 m. N.E. of Liverpool St. sta., London; pop. 132,965. Map 71.
Walton, vil., Staffordshire, ½ m. S. of Stone. Map 47.
Walton, par. and vil., Cumberland, 2½ m. N. of Brampton; pop. 286. Map 21.
Walton-in-Gordano, coast par. and vil., Somersetshire, 1½ m. N.E. of Clevedon; pop. 732. Map 74.
Walton-le-dale, urb. dist. and par., Lancashire, 2 m. S.E. of Preston; pop. 12,718. Map 30.
Walton-on-Thames, urb. dist., Surrey, 17 m. S.W. of London; pop. 17,953. Map 78.
Walton-on-the-Naze, urb. dist. and par., Essex, 7 m. S. of Harwich; pop. 3066. Map 73.
Wanborough, par., ham. and ry. sta., Surrey, 3½ m. W. of Guildford; pop. 303. Map 78.
Wanstead, urb. dist., Essex, 7 m. N.E. of London; pop. 19,183. Map 71.
Wanstrow, par. and vil., Somersetshire, 6½ m. E.N.E. of Shepton Mallet; pop. 305. Map 75.
Wantage, urb. dist. and par., Berkshire, 9 m. S.W. of Abingdon; pop. 3424. Map 69.
Warblington, urb. dist. and par., Hants, 1 m. S.E. of Havant; pop. 4320. Map 79.
Warboys, par. and vil., Huntingdonshire, 3½ m. S.S.E of Ramsey; pop. 1720. Map 61.
Warcop, par. and vil., Westmorland, 5 m. S.E. of Appleby; pop. 577. Map 26.
Warden, par. and vil., Northumberland, 3 m. N.W. of Hexham; pop. 828. Map 22.
Wardington, par. and vil., Oxon, 4 m. N.E. of Banbury; pop. 594. Map 59.
Wardle, urb. dist. and par., S.E. Lancashire, on N.E. side of Rochdale; pop. 4793. Map 31.
Wardlow, par. and vil., Derbyshire, 2 m. S.E. of Tideswell; pop. 124. Map 40.
Ware, urb. dist. and par., Hertfordshire, 22½ m. N. of London by rail; pop. 6171. Map 71.
Wareham, mun. bor., Dorsetshire, 15 m. E. of Dorchester; pop. 2057. Map 87.
Warfield, par. and vil., Berkshire, 5 m. N.E. of Wokingham; pop. 2499. Map 70.

Wargrave, par. and vil., E. Berkshire, 3 m. S.E. of Henley-on-Thames ; pop. 2383. Map 70.

Wark, par. and vil., Northumberland, 9 m. N.W. of Hexham ; pop. 738. Map 22.

Warkworth, par. and seaport, Northumberland, 7 m. S.E. of Alnwick ; pop. 1042. Map 17.

Warley, Great, par. and vil., Essex, 3½ m. S. of Brentwood ; pop. 2088. Map 72.

Warley Street, ham., 1½ m. N.N.W. of Great Warley, Essex. Map 72.

Warlingham, par. and vil., Surrey, 5 m. S.E. of Croydon ; pop. 3897. Map 80.

Warmfield, par. and vil., W.R. Yorkshire, 3 m. E. of Wakefield ; pop. 1094. Map 33.

Warmington, par. and vil., Warwickshire, 5½ m. N.W. of Banbury ; pop. 245. Map 59.

Warminster, urb. dist. and market town, Wiltshire, 9 m. S. of Trowbridge ; pop. 5176. Map 75.

Warmley, eccl. dist. and vil., Gloucestershire, 5 m. E. of Bristol ; pop. 2830. Map 75.

Warnborough, South, par. and vil., Hants, 2½ m. S.W. of Odiham ; pop. 279. Map 78.

Warnham, par. and vil., Sussex, 2 m. N.W. of Horsham ; pop. 1227. Map 79.

Warren Point, spt., urb. dist. and par., co. Down, 6 m. S.E. of Newry ; pop. 1938. Map 93.

Warrington, co. bor. and par., S.W. Lancashire, midway between Liverpool and Manchester ; pop. 79,322. Map 39.

Warsop, urb. dist., Nottinghamshire, 5½ m. N.E. of Mansfield ; pop. 10,748. Map 41.

Warter, par. and vil., E.R. Yorkshire, 4 m. E. of Pocklington ; pop. 436. Map 34.

Warton, par., vil. and seat, W. Lancashire, 3 m. S.S.W. of Kirkham ; pop. 684. Map 30.

Warton, par. and vil., N. Lancashire, 6½ m. N. of Lancaster ; pop. 1678. Map 26.

Warwick, mun. bor. and co. town of Warwickshire, 108 m. N.W. of London ; pop. 13,459. Map 58.

Warwick, par. and vil., Cumberland, on r. Eden, 4 m. E. of Carlisle ; pop. 262. Map 21.

Washington, urb. dist. and par., Durham, 6 m. W. of Sunderland ; pop. 16,989. Map 23.

Wash, River, rises Leicestershire and flows 20 m. E to the Welland, near Stamford. Map 50.

Wash, The, estuary of rivers Ouse, Welland, Nene and Witham, Lincolnshire and Norfolk. Map 51.

Wast Water, lake, Cumberland, 14 m. S.W. of Keswick. Map 25.

Watchet, urb. dist., Somersetshire, 16¾ m. N.W. of Taunton ; pop. 1936. Map 85.

Waterbeach, par. and vil., Cambridgeshire, 5 m. N.E. of Cambridge ; pop. 1363. Map 61.

Waterbeck, vil., Dumfriesshire, 7 m. S.E. of Lockerbie. Map 20.

Waterfoot, eccl. dist. and vil., Lancashire ; pop. 2873. Map 31.

Waterford, co. bor. and seaport, Waterford, 77 m. S.E. of Limerick ; pop. 26,646. Map 95.

Waterhouses, vil., Staffordsh., 7½ m. S.E. of Leek. Map 40.

Waterhouses, eccl. dist. and vil., in co. and 5½ m. W. of Durham. Map 23.

Waterlooville, par. and vil., Hants, 3½ m. N.N.W. of Havant ; pop. 1033. Map 79.

Waterloo with Seaforth, urb. dist. and town, Lancs, 4 m. N. of Liverpool ; pop. of urb. dist. 31,180. Map 38.

Watford, mun. bor. and market town, S.W. Hertfordshire, 8 m. S.W. of St Albans ; pop. 56,799. Map 71.

Watford, par. and vil., Northamptonshire, 4½ m. N.E. of Daventry ; pop. 336. Map 59.

Wath, place, Cumberland, 1 m. from Cleator Moor. Map 24.

Wath, par. and vil., N.R. Yorkshire, 4 m. N. of Ripon ; pop. 192. Map 27.

Wath-upon-Dearne, urb. dist. and par., W.R. Yorks 8 m. S.E. of Barnsley ; pop. 13,653. Map 41.

Watling Street, Roman military road, which extended from E. coast of Kent into North Wales. Map 83.

Watlington par. and town, Oxon, 8 m. N.E. of Wallingford ; pop. 1386. Map 70.

Watlington, par. and vil., Norfolk, 6 m. S. of King's Lynn ; pop. 590. Map 52.

Watten, par. and vil., Caithness-shire, 7½ m. N.W. of Wick ; pop. 934. Map 3.

Watton, market town and par., Norfolk, 13¼ m. N.N.E. of Thetford ; pop. 1331. Map 52.

Wavendon, par. and vil., Buckinghamshire, 5 m. S.E. of Newport Pagnell ; pop. 465. Map 60.

Weald, par. and vil., W. Kent, 2½ m. S. of Sevenoaks ; pop. 912. Map 82.

Weald, South, par. and vil., Essex, 1½ m. W. of Brent wood ; pop. 5682. Map 72.

Weald Basset, North, par. and vil., Essex, 2¾ m. N.E. of Epping ; pop. 1239. Map 72.

Wealdstone, urb. dist. and par., Middlesex, 1 m. N.E. of Harrow ; pop. 27,001. Map 71.

Wear Head, vil. and ry. sta., W. Durham, 8½ m. W. of Stanhope. Map 22.

Weaverham, par. and vil., Cheshire, 3 m. W.N.W. of Northwich ; pop. 2111. Map 39.

Weaverthorpe, ry. sta., E.R. Yorkshire, 1 m. N. of Sherburn. Map 29.

Wedmore, par. and vil., Somersetshire, 4½ m. S. of Axbridge ; pop. 2385. Map 74.

Wednesbury, mun. bor. and par., Staffordshire, 8 m. N. of Birmingham by rail ; pop. 31,534. Map 48.

Wednesfield, urb. dist., Staffordshire, in parl. bor. of Wolverhampton ; pop. 9333. Map 47.

Weedon, par. and vil., Buckinghamshire, 3 m. N. of Aylesbury ; pop. 325. Map 70.

Weedon Beck, par. and vil., Northamptonshire, 4 m. S.E. of Daventry ; pop. 2020. Map 59.

Weeford, par. and vil., Staffordshire, 3¾ m. S.E. of Lichfield ; pop. 245. Map 48.

Weekley, par. and vil., Northamptonshire, 1¼ m. N.E. of Kettering ; pop. 223. Map 60.

Week St Mary, par. and vil., Cornwall, 11 m. N.W. of Launceston ; pop. 452. Map 88.

Weeley, par., vil. and ry. sta., Essex, 6½ m. W. of Walton-on-the-Naze ; pop. 648. Map 73.

Weem, par. and vil., Perthshire, 1 m. N.W. of Aberfeldy ; pop. 429. Map 6.

Weeting with Bromehill, par. and vil., Norfolk, 1½ m. N. of Brandon ; pop. 312. Map 62.

Weeton, par. and vil., N. Lancashire, 3 m. N.W. of Kirkham ; pop. 361. Map 30.

Weetslade, urb. dist., Northumberland, 3 m. N.W. of Longbenton ; pop. 7736. Map 23.

Welbeck, par. and ry. sta., Nottinghamshire, 3½ m. S.W. of Worksop ; pop. 77. Map 41.

Welbourn, par. and vil., Kesteven, in co. and 12 m. S. of Lincoln ; pop. 524. Map 42.

Welby, par. and vil., Kesteven, Lincolnshire, 4 m. N.E. of Grantham ; pop. 312. Map 50.

Wellingborough, urb. dist. and par., in co. and 10¼ m. N.E. of Northampton ; pop. 21,221. Map 60.

Wellington, par. and vil., in co. and 5 m. N. of Hereford ; pop. 625. Map 56.

Wellington, urb. dist. and par., Salop, 10 m. E. of Shrewsbury by rail ; pop. 8185. Map 47.

Wellington, urb. dist. and par., Somersetshire, 7 m. S.W. of Taunton by rail ; pop. 7128. Map 86.

Wellington Heath, par. and vil., Herefordshire, 2 m. N. of Ledbury ; pop. 421. Map 57.

Wells, urb. dist., par. and seaport, Norfolk, 31 m. N.E. of King's Lynn ; pop. 2505. Map 52.

Wells, mun. bor. and ancient city, Somersetshire, 19 m. S.W. of Bath ; pop. 4833. Map 74.

Welnetham, Little, par., Suffolk, 3½ m. S.E. of Bury St Edmunds ; pop. 123. Map 62.

Welney, par. and vil., Norfolk, 8 m. S.W. of Downham Market; pop. 366. Map 51.

Welshampton, par. and vil., Salop, $2\frac{3}{4}$ m. E. of Ellesmere; pop. 432. Map 46.

Welsh Newton, par., S. Herefordshire, $3\frac{1}{2}$ m. N. of Monmouth; pop. 202. Map 67.

Welshpool, mun. bor., Montgomeryshire, $19\frac{3}{4}$ m. S.W. of Shrewsbury; pop. 5637. Map 46.

Welton, par. and vil., Northamptonshire, 2 m. N.E. of Daventry; pop. 339. Map 59.

Welton, par. and vil., E.R. Yorkshire, $9\frac{1}{2}$ m. W. of Hull; pop. 696. Map 35.

Welton, par. and vil., in co. and 6 m. N.N.E. of Lincoln; pop. 637. Map 42.

Welton-le-Marsh, par. and vil., Lindsey, Lincolnshire, 5 m. N.E. of Spilsby; pop. 289. Map 43.

Welwyn, par. and urb. dist., Hertfordshire, 4 m. N. of Hatfield; pop. 8585. Map 71.

Wem, urb. dist. and par., Salop, $10\frac{1}{2}$ m. N. of Shrews bury; pop. 2157. Map 46.

Wembley, urb. dist., Middlesex, $2\frac{1}{2}$ m. S.E. of Harrow; pop. 48,546. Map 71.

Wembury, par. and vil., Devonshire, 6 m. S.E. of Plymouth; pop. 501. Map 88.

Wemyss Bay, watering place, Renfrewshire, 8 m. S.W. of Greenock. Map 12.

Wendling, par. and vil., Norfolk, 4 m. W. of East Dereham; pop. 302. Map 52.

Wendover, market town and par., Buckinghamshire, 5 m. S.E. of Aylesbury; pop. 2366. Map 70.

Wendron, par. and vil., Cornwall, $2\frac{1}{2}$ m. N.E. of Helston; pop. 3281. Map 90.

Wenlock, mun. bor., Staffordshire, 14 m. S.E. of Shrewsbury; pop. 14,152. Map 47.

Wennington, par., N. Lancashire, 11 m. N.E. of Lancaster; pop. 120. Map 26.

Wennington, par. and vil., Essex, 5 m. S.E. of Romford; pop. 432. Map 72.

Wensley, par. and vil., N.R. Yorkshire, $1\frac{1}{2}$ m. S.W. of Leyburn; pop. 202. Map 27.

Wentnor, par. and vil., Salop, 5 m. N.E. of Bishop's Castle; pop. 432. Map 46.

Wenvoe, par. and vil., Glamorganshire, 5 m. S.W. of Cardiff; pop. 495. Map 67.

Weobley, town, Herefordshire, $7\frac{1}{2}$ m. S.W. of Leominster; pop. 601. Map 56.

Wereham, par. and vil., Norfolk, 6 m. S.E. of Downham; pop. 467. Map 52.

West Acre, par. and vil., Norfolk, 5 m. W. of Swaffham; pop. 339. Map 52.

West Allen Dale, valley of the West Allen r., Northumberland, $3\frac{1}{2}$ m. S.W. of Staward ry. sta. Map 22.

Westbourne, par. and vil., W. Sussex, 3 m. N.E. of Havant; pop. 3562. Map 79.

West Bridgford, par. and urb. dist., in co. and 2 m. S.E. of Nottingham; pop. 17,821. Map 49.

West Bromwich, parl. and co. bor., Staffordshire, $4\frac{1}{4}$ m. N.W. of Birmingham; pop. 81,281. Map 48.

Westbury, par. and vil., Salop, 9 m. W.S.W. of Shrewsbury; pop. 1064. Map 46.

Westbury, par. and vil., Somersetshire, 4 m. N.W. of Wells; pop. 532. Map 74.

Westbury, urb. dist. and market town, Wiltshire, $4\frac{1}{2}$ m. S. of Trowbridge; pop. 4044. Map 75.

Westbury Leigh, place, on S. side of Westbury, Wiltshire. Map 75.

Westbury-on-Severn, urb. dist., par. and vil., Glos., 8 m. S.W. of Gloucester; pop. 1746. Map 68.

Westbury-on-Trym, 2 eccl. pars. in N.W. of Bristol; pop. 8971 and 3626. Map 68.

West Butterwick, par. and vil., Lindsey, Lincolnshire, $5\frac{1}{2}$ m. N.E. of Epworth; pop. 624. Map 34.

West Calder, par. and market town, Midlothian, $15\frac{3}{4}$ m. S.W. of Edinburgh; pop. (town) 3350. Map 9.

West Cornforth, mining vil., with ry. sta., Durham, $4\frac{1}{2}$ m. N.W. of Sedgefield. Map 23.

Westcot Barton, par. and seat, Oxon, 6 m. N. of Woodstock; pop. 132. Map 69.

Westcott, par. and vil., Buckinghamshire, 7 m. N.W. of Aylesbury; pop. 270. Map 70.

Westdean, par. and vil., W. Sussex, $4\frac{1}{2}$ m. N. of Chichester; pop. 681. Map 79.

Westerham, par. and market town, Kent, 6 m. W. of Sevenoaks; pop. 3162. Map 80.

Westgate, eccl. dist. and vil., Durham, $5\frac{1}{2}$ m. W. of Stanhope; pop. 693. Map 22.

Westgate-on-Sea, watering place and par., Kent, 2 m. W.S.W. of Margate; pop. 5096. Map 83.

West Gordon, vil., Berwickshire, 4 m. S.W. of Greenlaw; pop. 322. Map 11.

West Grinstead, par. and vil., Sussex, $6\frac{3}{4}$ m. S. of Horsham; pop. 1515. Map 79.

West Ham, co. bor., Essex, in E. of London, opposite Greenwich; pop. 294,086. Map 71.

Westham, par. and vil., E. Sussex, $\frac{1}{2}$ m. W.S.W. of Pevensey sta.; pop. 1439. Map 81.

West Heslerton, par., E.R. Yorkshire, $8\frac{1}{2}$ m. N.E. of Malton; pop. 288. Map 29.

Westhoughton, urb. dist. and par., S.E. Lancs, 5 m. E. of Wigan by rail; pop. 16,018. Map 30.

West Kilbride, small town and par., Ayrshire, $4\frac{1}{4}$ m. N.W. of Ardrossan; pop. 3588. Map 12.

West Kirby, part of Hoylake and West Kirby urb. dist., Cheshire. Map 38.

West Linton, par. and vil., Peeblesshire, 15 m. S.W. of Edinburgh; pop. 1292. Map 10.

West Melton, par. and vil., W.R. Yorkshire, $5\frac{1}{2}$ m. N. of Rotherham; pop. 4745. Map 41.

West Meon, par. and vil., Hants, $12\frac{1}{2}$ m. S.W. of Alton; pop. 751. Map 79.

Westminster, city. and met. bor., London; pop. 129,535. Map 71.

Westnewton, par. and vil., Cumberland, 2 m. N.W. of Aspatria; pop. 323. Map 20.

Weston, par. and vil., Cheshire, $1\frac{1}{2}$ m. S.W. of Runcorn; pop. 2246. Map 38.

Weston, par. and vil., Somersetshire, 2 m. N.W. of Bath; pop. 1549. Map 75.

Weston-super-Mare, urb. dist. and wtg. pl., Somersetshire, 19 m. S.W. of Bristol; pop. 28,555. Map 74.

Weston Zoyland, par. and vil., Somersetshire, $3\frac{1}{2}$ m. S.E. of Bridgwater; pop. 611. Map 74.

Westow, par. and vil., E.R. Yorkshire, 5 m. S.W. of Malton; pop. 248. Map 28.

Westport, urb. dist. and seaport town, Mayo, 160 m. N.W. of Dublin; pop. 3490. Map 92.

Westruther, par. and vil., Berwickshire, $7\frac{1}{2}$ m. N.E. of Lauder; pop. 448. Map 11.

Westward Ho, coast vil. and watering place, Devonshire, 3 m. N.W. of Bideford. Map 84.

Westwell, par. and vil., Kent, 3 m. N.N.W. of Ashford; pop. 849. Map 83.

West Wemyss, vil. and *q.s.* par., Fifeshire, 2 m. N.E. of Dysart; pop. (par.) 2497. Map 10.

Wetheral, par. and vil., Cumberland, 4 m. S.E. of Carlisle; pop. 3418. Map 21.

Wetherby, par. and market town, W.R. Yorkshire, 8 m. S.E. of Harrogate; pop. 2126. Map 33.

Wetherden, par. and vil., E. Suffolk, 4 m. N.W. of Stowmarket; pop. 471. Map 62.

Wethersfield, par. and vil., Essex, 6 m. N.W. of Braintree; pop. 986. Map 72.

Wetwang, par. and vil., E.R. Yorkshire, $6\frac{1}{2}$ m. W. of Driffield; pop. 484. Map 34.

Wexford, mun. bor., spt. and cap., Wexford, $92\frac{3}{4}$ m. S. of Dublin; pop. 11,870. Map 95.

Weybourne, par. and vil., Norfolk, 3 m. N.E. of Holt; pop. 362. Map 53.

Weybridge, urb. dist. and par., Surrey, $2\frac{1}{2}$ m. S.E. of Chertsey; pop. 7359. Map 78.

Weyhill, vil., Hants, 4 m. W. of Andover. Map 76.

Weymouth and Melcombe Regis, mun. bor., par. and seaport, Dorsetshire, 7½ m. S. of Dorchester; pop. 21,982. Map 87.

Whaddon, par. and vil., Cambridgeshire, 4 m. N. of Royston; pop. 226. Map 61.

Whaddon, par. and vil., Buckinghamshire, 4½ m. S.E. of Stony Stratford; pop. 273. Map 60.

Whaley Bridge, vil., Cheshire, on r. Goyt, 10¼ m. S.E. of Stockport. Map 40.

Whalley, par. and vil., N.E. Lancashire, 3½ m. S. of Clitheroe; pop. 1379. Map 31.

Whalton, par. and vil., Northumberland, 5 m. S.W. of Morpeth; pop. 312. Map 17.

Whaplode, par. and vil., Holland, Lincolnshire, 2¼ m. W. of Holbeach; pop. 2357. Map 51.

Wharram-le-Street, par., E.R. Yorkshire, 7 m. S.E. of Malton; pop. 121. Map 29.

Whatfield, par. and vil., W. Suffolk, 3 m. N. of Hadleigh; pop. 274. Map 62.

Whatlington, par. and vil., E. Sussex, 2 m. N. of Battle; pop. 281. Map 82.

Wheathampstead, par. and vil., Hertfordshire, 5 m. N.E. of St Albans; pop. 2870. Map 71.

Wheatley, urb. dist. and par., Oxon, 5 m. E. of Oxford; pop. 1269. Map 70.

Wheatley, North, par. and vil., Nottinghamshire, 5 m. N.E. of Retford; pop. 357. Map 41.

Whetstone, eccl. par. and vil., N.E. Middlesex, 2 m. S.E. of Barnet; pop. 3627. Map 71.

Whetstone, par. and vil., Leicestershire, 5½ m. S.W. of Leicester; pop. 1388. Map 49.

Whickham, urb. dist. and par., Durham, 3½ m. W.S.W. of Gateshead; pop. 20,782. Map 23.

Whimple, par. and vil., Devonshire, 8½ m. N.E. of Exeter; pop. 744. Map 85.

Whippingham, par. and vil., Isle of Wight, 2½ m. N.E. of Newport; pop. 2033. Map 77.

Whipsnade, par., Bedfordshire, 3m. S. of Dunstable. Map 71.

Whissendine, par. and vil., Rutlandshire, 5 m. N.W. of Oakham; pop. 566. Map 50.

Whitburn, par. and vil., Durham, 3½ m. N. of Sunderland; pop. 5291. Map 23.

Whitburn, par. and town, West Lothian, 2½ m. S.W. of Bathgate; pop. (town) 2440. Map 9.

Whitby, urb. dist., par., spt. and mkt. tn., N.R. Yorks, 20 m. N.W. of Scarborough; pop. 11,441. Map 29.

Whitchurch, par. and vil., Buckinghamshire, 4 m. N. of Aylesbury; pop. 635. Map 70.

Whitchurch, urb. dist. and par., Salop, 18¾ m. N. of Shrewsbury; pop. 6016. Map 46.

Whitchurch, par. and vil., Herefordshire, 4½ m. N.E. of Monmouth; pop. 764. Map 67.

Whitchurch, par. and vil., Devonshire, 1½ m. S.E. of Tavistock; pop. 1477. Map 88.

Whitchurch, town and par., Hants, 7 m. N.E. of Andover; pop. 2461. Map 76.

Whitchurch, par. and vil., Glamorganshire, 1 m. N.W. of Llandaff; pop. 11,287. Map 74.

Whitechurch, par., Pembrokeshire, 6½ m. S. of Cardigan; pop. 241. Map 64.

White Colne, par. and vil., Essex, 4 m. E.S.E. of Halstead; pop. 348. Map 73.

Whitefield, urb. dist. and par., S.E. Lancashire, 6 m. N.N.W. of Manchester; pop. 9107. Map 31.

Whitehaven, mun. bor., spt. and par., Cumberland, 38 m. S.W. of Carlisle; pop. 21,142. Map 24.

Whiteparish, par. and vil., Wiltshire, 8 m. S.E. of Salisbury; pop. 839. Map 76.

Whiteshill, par. and vil., Gloucestershire, 1½ m. N.W. of Stroud; pop. 1364. Map 68.

Whitford, par. and vil., Flintshire, 3 m. N.W. of Holywell; pop. 3295. Map 38.

Whithorn, mun. bur. and par., Wigtownshire, 12¼ m. S. of Wigtown; pop. (bur.) 951. Map 19.

Whiting Bay, *q.s.* par., vil. and bay, Arran Island, 4 m. S.E. of Lamlash; pop. 2034. Map 12.

Whitkirk, eccl. dist. and vil., W.R. Yorkshire, 4 m. E. of Leeds; pop. 3525. Map 33.

Whitland, vil. and ry. sta., Carmarthenshire, 6 m. E.N.E. of Narberth. Map 65.

Whitley and Monkseaton, urb. dist., Northumberland; pop. 24,210 (contains **Whitley Bay**). Map 23.

Whitley Bay, watering place, Northumberland, 2½ m. N. of North Shields. Map 23.

Whitley, Upper, urb. dist. and par., W.R. Yorkshire, 6 m. E. of Huddersfield; pop. 932. Map 32.

Whitney, par. and vil., Herefordshire, 4 m. N.E. of Hay; pop. 197. Map 56.

Whitrigg, ham., Cumberland, 1 m. S. of Torpenhow. Map 20.

Whitstable, urb. dist. and par., Kent, 6 m. N.W. of Canterbury; pop. 11,201. Map 83.

Whittingham, par. and vil., Northumberland, 8½ m. W. of Alnwick; pop. 437. Map 17.

Whittingham, par. and vil., Lancashire, 5 m. N.E. of Preston; pop. 4032. Map 30.

Whittington, par. and vil., N. Lancashire, 2 m. S.W. of Kirkby Lonsdale; pop. 306. Map 26.

Whittington, par. and vil., Salop, 2½ m. E.N.E. of Oswestry; pop. 2729. Map 46.

Whittington, par. and vil., Staffordshire, 2½ m. S.E. of Lichfield; pop. 2525. Map 48.

Whittlesey, urb. dist., Isle of Ely, Cambridgeshire, 5¼ m. E. of Peterborough; pop. 8299. Map 51.

Whitton, par. and vil., Lincs, on r. Humber, 8 m. W.N.W. of Barton-upon-Humber; pop. 183. Map 34.

Whittonstall, par. and vil., Northumberland, 3 m. N.W. of Shotley Bridge; pop. 162. Map 22.

Whitwood, urb. dist., W.R. Yorkshire, 4½ m. N.W. of Pontefract; pop. 6196. Map 33.

Whitworth, urb. dist. and par., S.E. Lancashire, 3 m. N. of Rochdale; pop. 8360. Map 31.

Wibsey, eccl. dist., W.R. Yorkshire, in S.W. of co. bor. of Bradford; pop. 4647. Map 32.

Wick, mun. bur., spt., par. and co. town, Caithness-shire, 161½ m. N.E. of Inverness; bur. pop. 7548. Map 3.

Wickford, par. and vil., S. Essex, 8 m. S.S.E. of Chelmsford; pop. 1475. Map 72.

Wickham, par. and vil., Hants, 4 m. N. of Fareham; pop. 1146. Map 77.

Wickham Bishops, par. and vil., Essex, 2½ m. S. of Witham; pop. 498. Map 72.

Wickham Market, par. and town, E. Suffolk, 5 m. N.N.E. of Woodbridge; pop. 1259. Map 63.

Wicklow, assize and spt. tn. and cap. of Wicklow, 28¼ m. S. of Dublin; pop. 3027. Map 95.

Wickwar, par. and small town, Gloucestershire, 4 m. N. of Chipping Sodbury; pop. 769. Map 75.

Widdrington, par. and vil., Northumberland, 7 m. N.E. of Morpeth; pop. 802. Map 17.

Widnes, mun. bor. and par., S.W. Lancashire, 12¼ m. S.E. of Liverpool; pop. 40,608. Map 39.

Wield, par., Hants, 7 m. W. of Alton; pop. 241. Map 79.

Wigan, parl. and co. bor., mfg. tn. and par., S.W. Lancs, 15 m. S. of Preston; pop. 85,357. Map 30.

Wiggenhall St Mary Magdalen, par. and vil., Norfolk, 6 m. S.W. of King's Lynn; pop. 728. Map 51.

Wigginton, par. and vil., Hertfordshire, 1½ m. S.E. of Tring; pop. 696. Map 71.

Wigginton, par. and vil., Staffordshire, 1½ m. N. of Tamworth; pop. 1523. Map 48.

Wiggonby, vil., Cumberland, 4 m. N.E. of Wigton. Map 20.

Wighton, par. and vil., Norfolk, 2 m. N. of Walsingham; pop. 412. Map 52.

Wigley, ham., Hants, 5 m. N.W. of Southampton. Map 77.

Wigmore, par. and vil., Herefordshire, 8½ m. N.W. of Leominster; pop. 345. Map 56.

Wigston Magna, urb. dist. and par., in co. and 6 m. S.E. of Leicester; pop. 11,393. Map 49.
Wigtoft, par. and vil., Holland, Lincolnshire, 6½ m. S.W. of Boston; pop. 712. Map 51.
Wigton, urb. dist. and par., Cumberland, 11¾ m. S.W. of Carlisle; pop. 3521. Map 20.
Wigtown, mun. bor., spt., par. and co. tn., Wigtownshire, 7¼ m. S. of Newton Stewart; pop. 1261. Map 19.
Wilbarston, par. and vil., Northamptonshire, 6 m. E. of Market Harborough; pop. 468. Map 50.
Wilbraham, Great and **Little,** 2 pars., in co. and 6 m. E. of Cambridge; pop. 444 and 348. Map 61.
Wilburton, par. and vil., Isle of Ely, Cambridgeshire, 5¼ m. S.W. of Ely; pop. 497. Map 61.
Wilby, par. and vil., Northamptonshire, 2 m. S.W. of Wellingborough; pop. 418. Map 60.
Wilcot, par. and vil., Wiltshire, 1½ m. W.N.W. of Pewsey; pop. 531. Map 76.
Wilkieston, vil., Midlothian, 3 m. E. of Mid-Calder; pop. 425. Map 9.
Willaston, par. and vil., Cheshire, 2½ m. S.W. of Crewe; pop. 2764. Map 39.
Willenhall, urb. dist. and par., Staffordshire, 3 m. E. of Wolverhampton; pop. 21,147. Map 48.
Willerby, par., E.R. Yorkshire, 5 m. N.W. of Hull; pop. 1319. Map 35.
Willesborough, par. and vil., Kent, 2½ m. S.E. of Ashford; pop. 4748. Map 83.
Willesden, urb. dist., Middlesex, 7 m. N.W. of St Paul's, London; pop. 184,410. Map 71.
Willingdon, par. and vil., E. Sussex, 2½ m. N.N.W. of Eastbourne; pop. 884. Map 81.
Willingham, par. and vil., Cambridgeshire, 5½ m. E. of St Ives; pop. 1657. Map 61.
Willington, par. and vil., Derbyshire, 4½ m. N.E. of Burton-on-Trent; pop. 631. Map 48.
Willington, urb. dist. and par., Durham, 5 m. N. of Bishop Auckland; pop. 8960. Map 23.
Williton, par. and market town, N. Somersetshire, 14 m. N.W. of Taunton; pop. 1131. Map 85.
Willoughby, par. and vil., Warwickshire, 5 m. S. of Rugby; pop. 306. Map 59.
Willoughby Waterless, par. and vil., Leicestershire, 6 m. N.E. of Lutterworth; pop. 210. Map 49.
Wilmslow, urb. dist. and par., Cheshire, 6 m. S.W. of Stockport; pop. 9760. Map 39.
Wilsontown, mining vil., Lanarkshire, 9¼ m. N.W. of Carstairs. Map 9.
Wilton, mun. bor., Wiltshire, 2½ m. N.W. of Salisbury; pop. 2193. Map 76.
Wilton, *q.s.* par., Roxburghshire, within bur. of Hawick; pop. 3436. Map 16.
Wimbledon, mun. bor., Surrey, 7½ m. S.W. of Waterloo sta., London; pop. 59,520. Map 71.
Wimborne Minster, urb. dist. and par., Dorsetshire, 7 m. N. of Poole; pop. 3895. Map 77.
Wincanton, market town and par., Somersetshire, 19½ m. S.E. of Glastonbury; pop. 1711. Map 87.
Winchburgh, *q.s.* par. and vil., West Lothian, 12 m. W. of Edinburgh; pop. 1742. Map 9.
Winchcomb, par. and market town, Gloucestershire, 6 m. N.E. of Cheltenham; pop. 2741. Map 58.
Winchelsea, par. and ancient town, E. Sussex, 8 m. N.E. of Hastings; pop. 152. Map 82.
Winchester, mun. bor. and co. tn. of Hants, on r. Itchen, 12 m. S.E. of Southampton; pop. 22,969. Map 76.
Winchfield, par. and vil., Hants, 4 m. W. of Farnborough; pop. 445. Map 78.
Windermere and **Lake,** Westmorland and Lancashire, pop. 5701. Lake 10½ m. long. Map 25.
Windlesham, par. and urb. dist., Surrey, 1½ m. N.E. of Bagshot; pop. 5254. Map 78.
Windsor, New, mun. bor., Berkshire, on r. Thames, 21¼ m. W. of London; pop. 20,284. Map 78.
Windygates, vil., Fifeshire, 3½ m. N.E. of Thornton Junction; pop. 1639. Map 7.
Winford, par. and vil., Somersetshire, 6 m. S.W. of Bristol; pop. 791. Map 74.
Winforton, par. and vil., Herefordshire, 5½ m. N.E. of Hay; pop. 120. Map 56.
Wing, par. and vil., Buckinghamshire, 2½ m. S.W. of Leighton Buzzard; pop. 1498. Map 70.
Wingate, par. and vil., Durham, 8 m. W.N.W. of Hartlepool; pop. 11,424. Map 23.
Wingfield, North, par. and vil., Derbyshire, 4½ m. S. of Chesterfield; pop. 5169. Map 41.
Wingfield, South, par. and vil., Derbyshire, 2 m. W. of Alfreton; pop. 1605. Map 41.
Wingham, par. and vil., Kent, 6 m. E. of Canterbury; pop. 1240. Map 83.
Winsford, urb. dist., Cheshire, 5 m. S. of Northwich; pop. 10,997. Map 39.
Winsham, par. and vil., Somersetshire, 4 m. S.E. of Chard; pop. 690. Map 86.
Winslow, market town and par., in co. and 6½ m. S.E. of Buckingham; pop. 1532. Map 59.
Winster, par. and small town, Derbyshire, 4 m. W. of Matlock; pop. 684. Map 40.
Winterbourne, par. and vil., Gloucestershire, 6½ m. N.E. of Bristol; pop. 3368. Map 68.
Winterbourne Earls, par., Wiltshire, 3½ m. N.E. of Salisbury; pop. 250. Map 76.
Winterbourne St Martin, par. and seat, Dorsetshire, 3 m. S.W. of Dorchester; pop. 422. Map 87.
Winteringham, par. and vil., Lincolnshire, 6½ m. W. of Barton-upon-Humber; pop. 747. Map 34.
Winterslow, par. and vil., Wiltshire, 6 m. N.E. of Salisbury; pop. 788. Map 76.
Winterton, urb. dist., mkt. tn. and par., Lincolnshire, 5 m. N. of Scunthorpe; pop. 1958. Map 34.
Winterton, coast par. and vil., Norfolk, 8 m. N. of Yarmouth; pop. 967. Map 53.
Wintringham, par. and vil., E.R. Yorkshire, 6 m. E.N.E. of Malton; pop. 280. Map 29.
Winwick, par. and vil., S.W. Lancashire, 2½ m. N. of Warrington; pop. 1869. Map 39.
Wirksworth, urb. dist., par. and market town, Derbyshire, 13¾ m. N.W. of Derby; pop. 3911. Map 40.
Wisbech, mun. bor., Isle of Ely, Cambridgeshire, 22 m. N.E. of Peterborough; pop. 12,005. Map 51.
Wisborough Green, par. and vil., W. Sussex, 5 m. N.E. of Petworth; pop. 1572. Map 79.
Wishaw. *See* Motherwell and Wishaw.
Wisley, par. and ham., Surrey, 3½ m. S.S.W. of Weybridge; pop. 273. Map 78.
Wistanstow, par. and vil., Salop, 5½ m. S. of Church Stretton; pop. 885. Map 46.
Witchampton, par. and vil., Dorsetshire, 4 m. N.W. of Wimborne; pop. 435. Map 87.
Witham, urb. dist. and par., Essex, 9 m. N.E. of Chelmsford; pop. 4367. Map 72.
Witheridge, par. and vil., Devonshire, 8 m. E. of Chulmleigh; pop. 759. Map 85.
Withernsea, urb. dist. and par., E.R. Yorkshire, 4 m. N.E. of Patrington; pop. 4251. Map 35.
Withersfield, par. and vil., W. Suffolk, 2 m. N.W. of Haverhill; pop. 485. Map 61.
Witherslack, par. and vil., Westmorland, 7 m. S.W. of Kendal; pop. 401. Map 25.
Withiel, par. and vil., Cornwall, 5 m. W.N.W. of Bodmin; pop. 329. Map 91.
Withington, par. and vil., in co. and 4½ m. N.E. of Hereford; pop. 756. Map 57.
Withington, par. and vil., Gloucestershire, 7½ m. S.E. of Cheltenham; pop. 555. Map 69.
Withnell, urb. dist. and par., N. Lancashire, 5 m. S.W. of Blackburn; pop. 3040. Map 30.
Witley, par. and vil., Surrey, 3 m. S.S.W. of Godalming; pop. 4289. Map 79.
Witnesham, par. and vil., E. Suffolk, 4½ m. N.N.E. of Ipswich; pop. 511. Map 63.

Witney, urb. dist. and par., Oxon, 5 m. N.E. of Bampton; pop. 3409. Map 69.

Wittering, par., Soke of Peterborough, Northamptonshire, 3½ m. S.E. of Stamford; pop. 192. Map 50.

Wittersham, par. and vil., Kent, 4½ m. N.N.W. of Rye; pop. 643. Map 82.

Witton-le-Wear, par. and vil., Durham, 4½ m. W.N.W. of Bishop Auckland; pop. 2432. Map 23.

Wiveliscombe, urb. dist. and mkt. tn., Somersetshire, 9½ m. W.N.W. of Taunton; pop. 1262. Map 85.

Wivelsfield, par. and vil., E. Sussex, 2 m. S.S.E. of Hayward's Heath; pop. 2233. Map 81.

Wivenhoe, urb. dist., r. port and par., Essex, 4 m. S.E. of Colchester; pop. 2193. Map 73.

Woburn, town and par., Buckinghamshire, 4 m. S.E. of Wycombe; pop. 4648. Map 70.

Woburn, market town and par., Bedfordshire, 6 m. N.E. of Leighton Buzzard; pop. 1062. Map 60.

Woburn Sands, par. and vil., Buckinghamshire, 3 m. N.E. of Fenny Stratford; pop. 1131. Map 60.

Woking, town and par., Surrey, on r. Wey, 6 m. N. of Guildford; pop. 29,927. Map 78.

Wokingham, mun. bor., S.E. Berkshire, 7 m. S.E. of Reading; pop. 7294. Map 78.

Woldingham, par. and ham., Surrey, 2 m. E. of Caterham; pop. 646. Map 80.

Wollaston, par. and vil., Northamptonshire, 3½ m. S.S.E. of Wellingborough; pop. 2339. Map 60.

Wollaton, par. and vil., Nottinghamshire, 3 m. W. of Nottingham; pop. 551. Map 49.

Wolsingham, town and par., Durham, 10 m. N.W. of Bishop Auckland; pop. 3535. Map 22.

Wolstanton, United, urb. dist. and par., Staffordshire, 2 m. N.E. of Newcastle-under-Lyme; pop. 30,528. Map 39.

Wolston, par. and vil., Warwickshire, 6 m. W. of Rugby; pop. 962. Map 59.

Wolverhampton, parl. and co. bor., Staffs, 12¾ m. N.W. of Birmingham; co. bor. pop. 133,190. Map 47.

Wolverley, par. and vil., Worcestershire, 2 m. N. of Kidderminster; pop. 2217. Map 57.

Wolverton, urb. dist. and par., Buckinghamshire, 2 m. N.E. of Stony Stratford; pop. 12,870. Map 60.

Wolvey, par. and vil., Warwickshire, 5 m. S.E. of Nuneaton; pop. 686. Map 49.

Wolviston, par. and vil., Durham, 4½ m. N. of Stockton; pop. 642. Map 23.

Wombourn, par. and vil., Staffordshire, 4½ m. S.W. of Wolverhampton; pop. 1670. Map 47.

Wombwell, urb. dist., W.R. Yorkshire, 4½ m. S.E. of Barnsley; pop. 18,365. Map 41.

Wonersh, par. and vil., Surrey, 3 m. S.E. of Guildford; pop. 2023. Map 78.

Wonston, par. and vil., Hants, 6 m. N. of Winchester; pop. 910. Map 76.

Woodborough, par. and vil., in co. and 7½ m. N.E. of Nottingham; pop. 682. Map 41.

Woodbridge, urb. dist. and par., E. Suffolk, 8 m. N.E. of Ipswich; pop. 4734. Map 63.

Woodburn, West, vil., Northumberland, 4 m. N.E. of Bellingham. Map 17.

Woodbury, par. and vil., Devonshire, 7 m. S.E. of Exeter; pop. 1533. Map 89.

Woodchester, par. and vil., Gloucestershire, 2½ m. S.W. of Stroud; pop. 856. Map 68.

Woodchurch, par. and vil., Kent, 4 m. E.N.E. of Tenterden; pop. 1044. Map 83.

Woodford, urb. dist. and par., Essex, 4½ m. N.E. of Stratford; pop. 23,946. Map 72.

Wood Green, urb. dist. and par., Middlesex, 5 m. N. of London; pop. 54,190. Map 71.

Woodhall Spa, urb. dist. and par., Lindsey, Lincolnshire, 6½ m. S.W. of Horncastle; pop. 1372. Map 43.

Woodham Ferrers, par. and vil., Essex, 6 m. S.W. of Maldon; pop. 1168. Map 72.

Woodhay, East, par. and vil., Hants, 4½ m. S.W. of Newbury; pop. 1672. Map 76.

Woodstock, mun. bor. and par., in co. and 8 m. N.W. of Oxford; pop. 1484. Map 69.

Woodville, par. and vil., Derbyshire, 3½ m. N.W. of Ashby-de-la-Zouch; pop. 3146. Map 48.

Wofferton, vil. and ry. junction, Salop, 4 m. S. of Ludlow. Map 57.

Woolavington, par. and vil., Somersetshire, 4½ m. N.E. of Bridgwater; pop. 328. Map 74.

Wooler, par. and town, Northumberland, 15 m. S. of Berwick; pop. 1577. Map 17.

Woolhampton, par. and vil., Berkshire, 7 m. E. of Newbury; pop. 609. Map 76.

Woolhope, par. and vil., in co. and 7 m. S.E. of Hereford; pop. 536. Map 57.

Woolley, par. and vil., W.R. Yorkshire, 5½ m. S. of Wakefield; pop. 974. Map 33.

Woolpit, par. and vil., W. Suffolk, 5 m. N.W. of Stowmarket; pop. 734. Map 62.

Woolwich, met. bor. in E. of co. of London, on r. Thames; pop. 146,944. Map 72.

Wootton, North, par. and vil., Norfolk, 3 m. N. of King's Lynn; pop. 331. Map 52.

Wootton Basset, market town and par., Wiltshire, 6 m. W.S.W. of Swindon; pop. 2112. Map 69.

Wootton Wawen, par. and vil., Warwickshire, 7 m. N.W. of Stratford-on-Avon; pop. 1985. Map 58.

Woore, par. and vil., Salop, 7 m. N.E. of Market Drayton; pop. 877. Map 47.

Worcester, parl. and co. bor., city and co. town of Worcestershire, 22 m. S.W. of Birmingham; pop. 50,497. Map 57.

Worcestershire Beacon, on border of cos. Worcester and Hereford; alt. 1395 ft. Map 57.

Worfield, par. and vil., Salop, 3 m. N.E. of Bridgnorth; pop. 1475. Map 47.

Workington, mun. bor., spt. and par., Cumberland, 6½ m. N. of Whitehaven; pop. 24,691. Map 20.

Worksop, municipal bor. and par., Notts, on r. Ryton, nr. N. extremity of Sherwood Forest, 26 m. N. of Nottingham; pop. 26,286. Map 41.

Worle, par. and vil., Somersetshire, 2½ m. N.E. of Weston-super-Mare; pop. 1490. Map 74.

Worleston, par. and vil., Cheshire, 1¼ m. N. of Nantwich; pop. 463. Map 39.

Worlingworth, par. and vil., E. Suffolk, 5 m. N.W. of Framlingham; pop. 504. Map 63.

Wormit, q.s. par. and bay, Fifeshire, on Firth of Tay and 2 m. W. of Newport; pop. 1056. Map 7.

Worplesdon, par. and vil., Surrey, 3 m. N.W. of Guildford; pop. 2593. Map 78.

Worsborough, urb. dist., W.R. Yorkshire, 2½ m. S. of Barnsley; pop. 12,397. Map 33.

Worsley, urb. dist., Lancashire, 6 m. S. of Manchester; pop. 14,503. Map 39.

Worthing, mun. bor. and par., W. Sussex, 10½ m. W. of Brighton; pop. 46,230 (estimated,1935) 53,840. Map 79.

Wortley, par. and vil., W.R. Yorkshire, 6 m. S.W. of Barnsley; pop. 885. Map 40.

Wotton-under-Edge, par. and town, Gloucestershire, 9½ m. S.W. of Stroud; pop. 3010. Map 68.

Wouldham, par. and vil., Kent, 3 m. S.W. of Rochester; pop. 1077. Map 80.

Wragby, small town and par., Lindsey, Lincolnshire, 7 m. S.S.E. of Market Rasen; pop. 463. Map 42.

Wrangle, coast par. and vil., Holland, Lincolnshire, 8 m. N.E. of Boston; pop. 1142. Map 43.

Wrawby, par. and vil., Lindsey, Lincolnshire, 1½ m. N.E. of Brigg; pop. 847. Map 35.

Wraxall, par. and vil., Somersetshire, 6 m. W. of Bristol; pop. 813. Map 74.

Wreay, par. and vil., Cumberland, 5 m. S.E. of Carlisle ; pop. 140. Map 21.

Wrecclesham, eccl. par. and vil., Surrey, 1¼ m. S.W of Farnham ; pop. 1857. Map 78.

Wrentham, par. and vil., E. Suffolk, 4 m. N. of Southwold ; pop. 944. Map 63.

Wrexham, mun. bor. and par., Denbighshire, 10 m. S.W. of Chester ; pop. 18,567. Map 38.

Wribbenhall, par., Worcestershire, an E. suburb of Bewdley ; pop. 1420. Map 57.

Wrington, par. and vil., Somersetshire, 6½ m. N.E. of Axbridge ; pop. 1369. Map 74.

Wrockwardine, par. and vil., Salop, 2 m. W. of Wellington ; pop. 1051. Map 47.

Wrotham, urb. dist. and town, Kent, 6 m. N.E. of Sevenoaks ; pop. 4510. Map 80.

Wroughton, par. and vil., Wiltshire, 3 m. S. of Swindon ; pop. 2462. Map 69.

Wroxeter, par. and vil., Salop, 6 m. S.E. of Shrewsbury ; pop. 551. Map 47.

Wroxham, par. and vil., Norfolk, 7 m. N.E. of Norwich ; pop. 900. Map 53.

Wybunbury, par. and vil., Cheshire, 3 m. S. of Crewe ; pop. 671. Map 39.

Wycombe, Chepping, mun. bor., Buckinghamshire, 10 m. N. of Maidenhead ; pop. 27,987. Map 70.

Wye, market town and par., Kent, 10 m. S.W. of Canterbury ; pop. 1390. Map 83.

Wyke, ry. sta., W.R. Yorkshire, 4 m. S.W. of Bradford. Map 32.

Wyke Regis, par. and vil., Dorsetshire, 2 m. S.W. of Weymouth ; pop. 2397. Map 87.

Wylam, par. and vil., Northumberland, 8¼ m. W. of Newcastle ; pop. 1487. Map 22.

Wylye, par. and vil., Wiltshire, 10 m. N.W. of Salisbury ; pop. 356. Map 75.

Wymeswold, par. and vil., Leicestershire, 4½ m. N.E. of Loughborough ; pop. 777. Map 49.

Wymington, par. and vil., Bedfordshire, 3 m. S. of Higham Ferrers ; pop. 516. Map 60.

Wymondham, par. and town, Norfolk, 10 m. S.W. of Norwich ; pop. 4814. Map 53.

Wymondham, par. and vil., Leicestershire, 6 m. E. of Melton Mowbray ; pop. 610. Map 50.

YALDING, par. and vil., Kent, 6½ m. S.W. of Maidstone ; pop. 2555. Map 82.

Yapton, par. and vil., W. Sussex, 3½ m. S.W. of Arundel ; pop. 712. Map 79.

Yarcombe, par. and vil., Devonshire, 7 m. N.E. of Honiton ; pop. 536. Map 86.

Yardley Gobion, par. and vil., Northamptonshire, 3½ m. N.W. of Stony Stratford ; pop. 416. Map 59.

Yarm, market town and par., N.R. Yorkshire, 4 m. S.S.W. of Stockton ; pop. 171. Map 28.

Yarmouth, seaport and par., Isle of Wight, 10 m. W. of Newport ; pop. 893. Map 77.

Yarmouth, Great, parl. and co. bor., Norfolk, 19 m. E. of Norwich ; pop. 56,769. Map 53.

Yarnton, par. and vil., in co. and 4 m. N.W. of Oxford ; pop. 309. Map 70.

Yarpole, par. and vil., Herefordshire, 5 m. N.W. of Leominster ; pop. 463. Map 56.

Yatton, par. and vil., Somersetshire, 12 m. S.W. of Bristol ; pop. 2176. Map 74.

Yeadon, urb. dist. and par., W.R. Yorkshire, 3 m. S. of Otley ; pop. 7671. Map 32.

Yealmbridge, ham., Devonshire, 1 m. N.E. of Yealmpton. Map 88.

Yealmpton, par. and vil., Devonshire, 7 m. E.S.E. of Plymouth ; pop. 878. Map 88.

Yeardsley cum Whaley, urb. dist., Cheshire, 7½ m. N.E. of Macclesfield ; pop. 1745. Map 40.

Yeldham, Great, par. and vil., Essex, 6½ m. N.W. of Halstead ; pop. 581. Map 62.

Yelverton, residential dist., Devonshire, 5 m. S.E. of Tavistock. Map 88.

Yelverton, par., Norfolk, 6 m. S.E. of Norwich ; pop. 567. Map 53.

Yeovil, mun. bor. and par., Somersetshire, 50¼ m. S. of Bristol ; pop. 19,078. Map 86.

Yerbleston, par., Pembrokeshire, 4½ m. S.W. of Narberth ; pop. 79. Map 64.

Yester, par., East Lothian, 4 m. S.S.E. of Haddington ; pop. 778. Map 10.

Yetholm, par. and vil., Roxburghshire, 7¼ m. S.E. of Kelso ; pop. 772. Map 16.

Yetminster, par. and vil., Dorsetshire, 4¼ m. S.E. of Yeovil ; pop. 522. Map 87.

Yiewsley, par. and urb. dist., Middlesex, 2½ m. S. of Uxbridge ; pop. 13,057. Map 71.

York, parl. and co. bor., co. tn. of Yorks, and co. in itself, 188 m. N.W. of London ; pop. 84,810. Map 33.

York Town, eccl. par. and vil., Surrey, 3 m. S.W. of Bagshot ; pop. 5415. Map 78.

Youghal, seaport town, urb. dist. and par., Cork, 26¾ m. E. of Cork ; pop. 5340. Map 95.

Youlgreave, par. and mining vil., Derbyshire, 3½ m. S.W. of Bakewell ; pop. 1214. Map 40.

Yoxall, par. and vil., Staffordshire, 8 m. S.W. of Burton-on-Trent ; pop. 1025. Map 48.

Yoxford, par. and vil., E. Suffolk, 4 m. N. of Saxmundham ; pop. 978. Map 63.

Yspitty Ystwyth, par. and ham., Cardiganshire, 8 m. N.N.E. of Tregaron ; pop. 476. Map 55.

Ystalyfera, locality, Glamorganshire, 11 m. N.E. of Swansea. Map 66.

Ystradvellte, par. and ham., Breconshire, 10 m. N.W. of Merthyr Tydfil ; pop. 613. Map 66.

Ystradyfodwg, locality, Glamorganshire, in Rhondda urb. dist., 7¼ m. N.W. of Pontypridd. Map 66.

ZEALS, par. and vil., Wiltshire, 1½ m. W. of Mere ; pop. 379. Map 75.

Zennor, par., Cornwall, 4¾ m. S.W. o f St Ives ; pop. 298. Map 90.

THE POCKET SERIES

OF

TOURING MAPS

By J. G. BARTHOLOMEW, F.R.G.S.

LIST OF SPECIAL DISTRICT MAPS & TOWN PLANS.

Those marked with an asterisk are price 1/- Net each, mounted on Cloth and in Case. The other larger Maps are 1/- Net, Paper; and 2/- Net, Cloth.

DISTRICT MAPS.

Aldershot Dist. Scale, 2 m. to in.
British Isles, Railway Map.
*Cambridgeshire. Scale, 4 m. to in.
*Edinburgh, Env. of. Sc. 2 m. to in.
*Glasgow, Envs. of. Do.
*Hampshire. Sc., 4 m. to in.
Isle of Wight, with Guide. 1 in. to m.
*Kent, County of. 4 m. to inch.
Keswick, Ullswater, &c. 1 inch to m.
*Lake District and Windermere. 3 miles to inch.
*Liverpool & Environs. 4 m. to inch.

London & Envs. 50 Mile Radius Map. 4 miles to inch.
London & Envs. Sc. 1 in. to m.
*Manchester & Envs. Sc. 4 m. to in.
Melrose Pocket Guide. 1/-.
*Northumberland Co. Sc. 4 m. to in.
Salisbury Plain Dist. Sc. 2 m. to in.
*Somersetshire. Do.
*Surrey & Sussex. Do.
Thames, The River. Sc. 2 m. to in.
Windermere & Morecambe Bay. Sc. 1 m. to in.
Yorkshire. Sc. 4 m. to in.

SPECIAL CYCLISTS' MAPS.

Scale, Half-an-inch to Mile. Coloured to show Cycling Roads.
Price 1/6 Net each, mounted on cloth.

London: Northern District. | London: Southern District.
Leeds and Sheffield Districts.

TOWN PLANS.

*Birmingham, with Index.
*Dublin, with Index, Guide and Environs.
*Durham, with Environs.
*Eastbourne, with Index and Guide.
*Edinburgh, with Index.
Glasgow, with Index.
*Hastings & St. Leonards, with Index and Guide.
*Harrogate, with Environs.
*Hull, with Index and Guide.

Liverpool, with Index.
London, with Index & Guide.
London, City. Scale, 12 in. to m.
London, East.
London, South.
London, North.
London, West.
Manchester, with Index.
*Oxford, with Environs.
Plymouth and Devonport.
*York, with Environs.

SPECIAL MAPS on Scale of 10 Miles to Inch.

ENGLAND & WALES, GEOLOGICAL, by Sir ARCHIBALD GEIKIE. Cloth, 12/6
SCOTLAND, Do. Do. Cloth, 7/6
Do. Coloured to show Height of Land. Paper, 1/-: Cloth, 2/-
Do. Naturalist's Map, showing Faunal Areas, &c. Do.

THIS SERIES is now to be had at all the leading Booksellers and Railway Bookstalls.

The Geographical Institute

JOHN BARTHOLOMEW & C°
Geographers, Map Draughtsmen, Engravers, and Printers
Under Direction of J. G. Bartholomew, F.R.G.S., F.R.S.E.

GENERAL MAPS FOR TOURISTS AND CYCLISTS.

Scale, 10 Miles to Inch ; showing Main Driving and Cycling Roads.

ENGLAND and WALES in Two Sections.

Northern Section.   Paper, 1s. ; Cl., 2s.
Southern Section.   Paper, 1s. ; Cl., 2s.
Complete in one Sheet.   Cloth, 3s.

SCOTLAND.   Paper, 1s. ; Cloth, 2s.
IRELAND.   Paper, 1s. ; Cloth, 2s.

Contoured Touring Map of England & Wales, for Cyclists.
Scale, 13 Miles to inch.   Paper, 1s. ; Cloth, 2s.

THE SURVEY GAZETTEER OF THE BRITISH ISLES.

Topographical, Statistical, and Commercial.   With appendices and Special Maps.
Reduced Price—Half-Morocco, 12s. 6d, net.

Pall Mall Gazette.—"One of the most comprehensive and accurate works of its kind."

Complete Prospectus on application.

WORLD SERIES OF TOURING MAPS.

General Railway Map of British Isles.   Scale, 19 m. to in.   Paper, 1s. ; Cl., 2s.
Railway Map of Europe.   Scale, 86 m. to in.   Paper, 1s. ; Cloth, 2s.
Route Chart of World.   Mercator's Projection.   Paper, 1s. ; Cloth, 1s. 6d.
Map of South America.   Scale, 1 : 10,000,000.   Paper, 2s. ; Cloth, 3s.
Route Chart to India and the East.   Paper, 1s. ; Cloth, 1s. 6d.
China, Japan, and Korea.   Scale, 1 : 6,060,000.   Paper, 1s. ; Cloth, 2s.
General Map of Africa.   Scale, 1 : 12,000,000.   Paper, 1s. ; Cloth, 2s.
Tourist's Map of Egypt.   Scale, 1 : 1,000,000.   Paper, 2s. ; Cloth, 3s.
Central and South Africa.   Scale, 1 : 5,600,000.   Paper, 2s. ; Cloth, 3s.
Tourist's Map of South Africa.   Scale, 1 : 2,500.000.   Paper, 2s. ; Cloth, 3s.
Chart of Oceania and the Pacific.   Mercator's Projection.   Paper, 2s. ; Cl., 3s.
Commercial Map of Australia.   Scale, 1 : 6,000,000.   Paper, 2s. ; Cloth, 3s.
United States & Part of Canada.   Scale, 1 : 5,000,000.   Paper, 2s. ; Cloth, 3s.

THE ABOVE PRICES ARE NET.

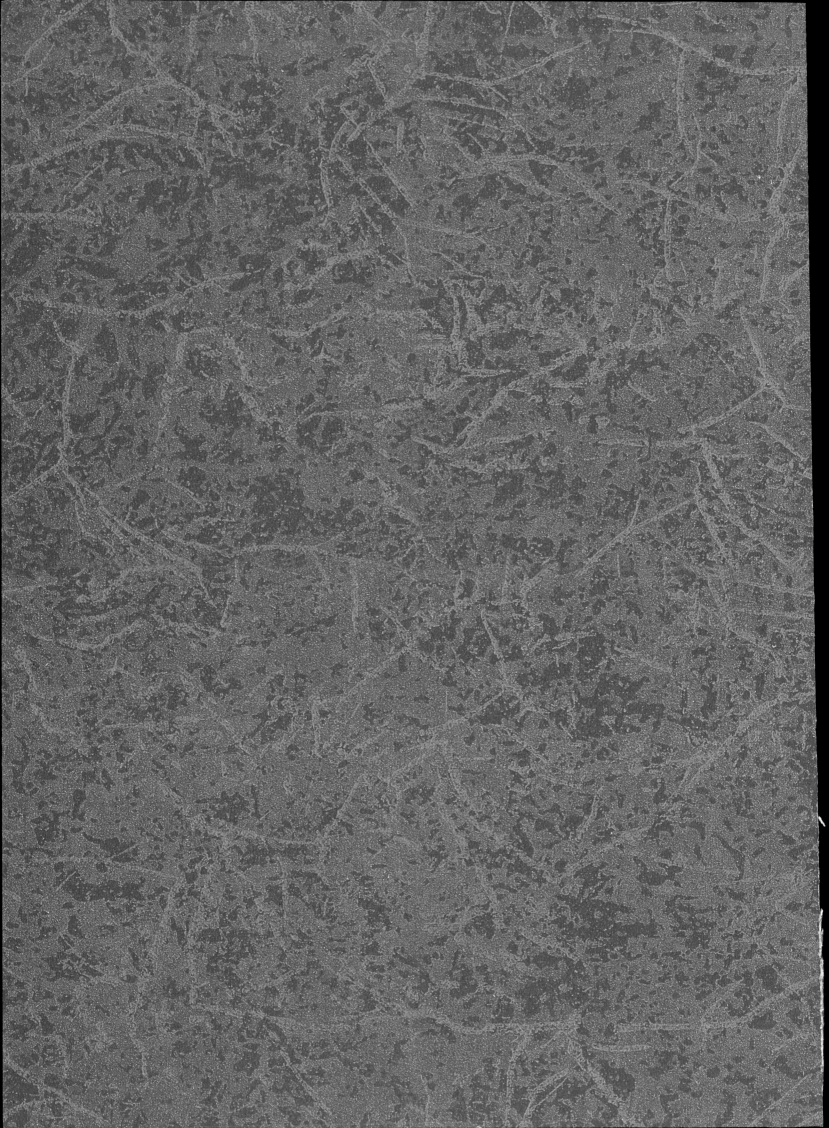